# DISCOVERING

# AUTOCAD®

# RELEASE 10

D1547895

## Mark Dix and Paul Riley

*CAD Support Associates*

PRENTICE HALL, Englewood Cliffs, New Jersey 07632

*Library of Congress Cataloging-in-Publication Data*

DIX, MARK (date)
Discovering AutoCAD release 10 / Mark Dix and Paul Riley.

p.    cm.
ISBN  0-13-215146-4
1. AutoCAD (Computer program)   I. Riley, Paul (date)
II. Title.   III. Title: Discovering AutoCAD release ten.
T385.D6   1991
620'.00425'02855369—dc20                                90-6858
                                                         CIP

Cover design: Lundgren Graphics, Ltd.
Prepress buyer: Linda Behrens
Manufacturing buyer: David Dickey

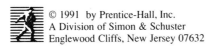 © 1991  by Prentice-Hall, Inc.
A Division of Simon & Schuster
Englewood Cliffs, New Jersey 07632

Printed in the United States of America

10   9   8   7   6   5   4   3

ISBN 0-13-215146-4

Prentice-Hall International (UK) Limited, *London*
Prentice-Hall of Australia Pty. Limited, *Sydney*
Prentice-Hall Canada Inc., *Toronto*
Prentice-Hall Hispanoamericana, S.A., *Mexico*
Prentice-Hall of India Private Limited, *New Delhi*
Prentice-Hall of Japan, Inc., *Tokyo*
Simon & Schuster Asia Pte. Ltd., *Singapore*
Editora Prentice-Hall do Brasil, Ltda., *Rio de Janeiro*

*For Sylvia and Peggy*

# contents

# chapter 3                                                                     *46*

# chapter 4                                                                     *72*

# chapter 5                                                                     *96*

# chapter 6

**Commands: APERTURE, BREAK, EXTEND, OSNAP, STRETCH, TRIM**

# chapter 7

**Commands: CHANGE, DTEXT, SCALE, STYLE, TEXT**

# chapter 8

**Commands: DIM, DIM1, EXPLODE, HATCH**

# chapter 9

# chapter 10

# chapter 11

# chapter 12                                                                                          *286*

**Commands: PLAN, RULESURF, UCS, UCSICON, VPOINT**

# chapter 13                                                                                          *322*

**Commands: BOX, DOME, DVIEW, EDGESURF, HIDE, PYRAMID, REDRAWALL, REGENALL, REVSURF, RULESURF, Surftab 1, Surftab 2, TABSURF, 3DMESH, VPORTS**

# chapter 14                                                                                          *360*

**Commands: CHPROP, HIDE, PEDIT, SPLFRAME, SPLINETYPE, Surftype, 3DFACE**

# preface

Drawing on a CAD system is a skill that can be learned only through many hours of practice. Like driving a car or playing a musical instrument, it cannot be learned by reading about it or watching someone else do it.

Accordingly, this book takes a very active approach to teaching AutoCAD. It is designed as a teaching tool and a self-study guide and assumes that readers will have access to a microcomputer CAD workstation: It is entirely organized around drawing exercises or tasks which offer the reader a demonstration of the commands and techniques being taught at every point, with illustrations that show exactly what to expect on the computer screen when steps are correctly completed.

Topics are carefully grouped and sequenced so that readers will progress logically through the AutoCAD command set. Most important, drawing exercises are included at the end of every chapter so that newly learned techniques are applied to practical drawing situations immediately. The level of difficulty increases steadily as skills are acquired through experience and practice.

All working drawings have been prepared using AutoCAD and are reproduced in a large, clearly dimensioned format on each right-hand page, with accompanying tips and suggestions on the left-hand page. Readers should therefore be able to leave the book propped open to the drawing they are working on. Drawing suggestions offer time-saving tips and explanations on how to use new techniques in actual drawing applications. The book is not a drafting manual, yet the drawings include a wide range of applications and anyone completing all of them will be well equipped to move on to more advanced and specialized applications. While the emphasis is on Release 10, especially in the 3D chapters (12–14), the major portion of the book can be used with other versions of AutoCAD as well.

We would like to thank the many people who have helped us in the preparation of this book. To begin with, thanks to Doug Humphrey, our editor at Prentice Hall, for his encouragement and support; to Judy Winthrop for her expert production editing; and to Russ Ryden, our friend and colleague at CAD Support Associates, for his enthusiasm and technical expertise.

We are grateful to a number of people at Autodesk, Inc., including Gloria Basti-
das for her help; Joe Oakley for the use of software; and Grace Avila for her help in
establishing an authorized AutoCAD Teacher Training Center.

Thanks to Wendel Watson and Kevin Higginbotham at Houston Instruments for
the use of DMP-62 plotters and the supply of pens and plotter paper used in preparing
illustrations. Also thanks to Tom Cox of N.E.C. Information Systems, Inc., for the use
of MultiSync Plus and MultiSync XL monitors. Thanks also to Susan Burns at Summagraphics for the use of Microgrid digitizers.

We are grateful to Mike Pillarella for technical advice and support; and to Clifton
Boyle and Louis D'Abrosca at Johnson and Wales University Graduate School, for their
interest in this project and commitment to CAD education.

Finally, thanks to Stanley Hopkins, Maria Hull, and Donald Wendt, for their
thoughtful reviews and suggestions, and to Dave Sumner and Jim Marshall for
classroom-testing the manuscript.

*Mark Dix and Paul Riley*

# introduction to Release 10

With Release 10, AutoCAD has become a full 3D drafting package. At the same time, there has been little change between Release 9 and Release 10 in the 2D world. If you like, you can even draw in 2D with Release 10 and remain unaware of the 3D interface. On the other hand, Release 10 3D is practical, effective, and worth exploring once you have learned basic AutoCAD drawing and editing conventions.

In this book we follow the most natural learning sequence by introducing 2D drafting commands and techniques first, and saving 3D for separate treatment. The first 11 chapters cover all basic 2D processes, while chapters 12, 13, and 14 deal specifically with Release 10 3D features. Everything you learn in the 2D chapters will be useful when you get to 3D, and nothing will need to be relearned.

## Using this book with earlier versions of AutoCAD

The first 11 chapters of this book can be used effectively with any version of AutoCAD. You will notice some differences, but they can be easily overcome. One very noticeable difference will be the presence or absence of the pull down menu system (see Chapter 1). Release 9 and later versions include the pull down system, while earlier versions do not. Another important difference is that the 3D chapters (12–14) can be used with Release 10 or later versions only.

## Varieties of CAD

AutoCAD has become the industry standard software for two-dimensional computer-aided drafting and design. It is widely used for the preparation of all types of drawings that would previously have been created on a drafting board. Its "open architecture" allows companies and third-party developers to customize it for specific applications so that productivity is further enhanced.

Now that AutoCAD has become a full 3D package, there are additional connections with other forms of CAD that require some explanation. It will be useful to begin to think in terms of a hierarchy of complexity in the use of CAD.

On the first step of the ladder is 2D drafting. This is the world for which Auto-CAD was originally developed. It is the area in which Release 10 shows the least obvious change from previous versions of AutoCAD and is the subject of chapters 1 through 11 of this book. Two-dimensional drawings in AutoCAD can be stored, edited, and plotted to any scale or paper size. The windowing and layering capacities of CAD allow a single drawing to produce a variety of different plots, depending on the type of information required. Through the process of attribute extraction, 2D drawings can also be used in conjunction with database programs to produce numerical data for cost estimates and bills of materials (see Chapter 10).

On a second step in the hierarchy would be 3D wire frame modeling. This is the subject of Chapter 12. Wire frame models share with 2D drawings an emphasis on precise dimensioning that can be used in communicating design specifications for manufacturing, as well as for cost estimates and bills of materials. There is no attempt in either 2D drafting or wire frame modeling to represent the physical qualities of the object being drawn. Rather, the emphasis is on a precise mathematical description of outlines, boundaries, and edges. In Release 10, a wire frame model may be viewed from any angle and may be used to produce 2D orthographic projections.

Surface modeling would occupy the third rung of the ladder. A surface model not only shows the outline of objects, but it also attempts to fill in between the lines. Surface models are discussed in chapters 13 and 14. One of the primary uses of surface modeling is to produce realistic shaded renderings that simulate the effect of light and shadow on real surfaces. This is accomplished by linking AutoCAD surface models with rendering software such as AutoSHADE.

Finally, there is a fourth level of CAD, not addressed in this text, called solid modeling, in which the goal is to represent the shapes and interior characteristics of solid objects. Solid modeling is used by engineering firms to perform finite element analysis (FEA). FEA allows designers and engineers to simulate and predict the behavior of 3D objects based on mathematical representations of their interior physical properties. AutoSOLID is Autodesk's solid modeling software. If you have Release 11, you can purchase AutoSOLID as an add-on package.

# road map

You will notice that all the chapters in this book follow the same layout. This will make it easy for you to find your way around and to know what to expect. Following is a description of each of the major subdivisions of the chapter format along with sample entries.

**COMMANDS**

(sample)

| UTILITY | EDIT |
|---------|-------|
| HELP | ERASE |
| | MOVE |
| | COPY |

The COMMANDS section lists the commands and topics that are introduced in the chapter. Headings are taken from the AutoCAD standard screen menu. For example, you will see LINE and CIRCLE under DRAW; and ERASE, MOVE, and COPY under EDIT, just as they are located in the standard screen menu. See the "primary menu hierarchy" in Appendix B for more information on where to find commands in the screen menu system.

**OVERVIEW**

Each chapter begins with a brief overview that gives you an idea of what you will be able to do with the new commands in that chapter.

**TASKS**

(sample)

1. Read about introductory tasks.
2. Read about drawing projects.
3. Begin Chapter 1.

All the tasks that make up a chapter are listed at the beginning of the chapter. This tells you at a glance exactly what you will be required to do to complete the chapter.

Tasks are divided into two types: step-by-step exercises in which new commands are introduced, and drawing projects that require the use of these commands.

**TASK 1: Introductory tasks**

*Procedure.*   (sample)

**1.**   Type or select "HELP".
**2.**   Press enter for a list or type a command name.

A procedure outline is placed at the beginning of most of the introductory tasks. It is intended as a reference and a quick overview of the command sequence you will be learning. The instructions in the list are general and are not sufficient to give the specific results that are required to complete the task. *The procedure list is not the exercise itself, and we do not recommend that you try to learn the command by following the list.* The bulleted instructions in the "Discussion" section are much more specific.

*Discussion.*   The Discussion section includes specific instructions along with explanations, illustrations, and feedback about what will happen on your monitor when you carry out the instructions. Typically, there will be an instruction followed by AutoCAD's response and any notes or explanation we feel are necessary or helpful.

The following sample instructions show how to use AutoCAD's HELP command. It is included here for reference and as an example. It is not intended for actual execution at this time, though it is useful and you are encouraged to try it out as you go through Chapter 1.

(sample)

> Type or select "help".
AutoCAD will prompt for the name of a command you want help with:

Command name (RETURN for list):

Pressing the "enter" or "return" key in response to this prompt will give you a list of commands on the screen. Typing the name of a command will give you a screen of text describing the command and the keyboard sequence for using it.

NOTE: We have chosen to use the term "enter" to refer to what AutoCAD calls the RETURN key. This is because "enter" is more common on new keyboards.

> Type "LINE" and press enter.
AutoCAD will switch to the text screen and display information on the LINE command.
> Press F1 to return to the graphics screen.

(end of sample)

Notice that all instructions are highlighted with a bullet (>). This will make it easy for you to know exactly what you are expected to do. The comments that accompany instructions are important for your understanding of what is happening and will help you to avoid confusion.

NOTE: You will find the *AutoCAD Reference Manual* cited in numerous places along the way. When you need additional information on a command or topic, this is the best place to go. The reference manual is an indispensable tool, and any experienced AutoCAD user consults it frequently. We encourage you to become familiar with it.

## TASK 2: Drawing projects

There are three to six drawing projects at the end of each chapter. These are progressive and make use of previously learned commands as well as new ones. You will find the drawing itself on the right-hand page and drawing suggestions on the left-hand page.

Remember that any drawing may be executed in a number of ways. Our suggestions are not written in stone. Unlike the instructions in the introductory exercises, drawing suggestions will not take you step by step through the complete project.

Besides the suggestions themselves, there is information on the drawing page that may assist you. This includes a list of commands you will need to use, a list of function keys and their functions, and, of course, the dimensions of the drawing itself.

## TASK 3: Chapter 1

You are now ready to begin Chapter 1.

# chapter

## COMMANDS

| F-KEYS | DRAW | EDIT | UTILITIES |
|---|---|---|---|
| SCREEN (F1) | LINE | UNDO ("U") | END |
| COORD (F6) | | REDO | QUIT |
| GRID (F7) | | | SAVE |
| SNAP (F9) | DISPLAY | | |
| ORTHO (F8) | REDRAW | | |
| | UCSICON | | |

## OVERVIEW

This chapter will introduce you to some of the tools you will use whenever you draw in AutoCAD. You will learn to control basic elements of the drawing editor using five function keys. You will produce drawings involving straight lines and learn to undo your last command with the "U" command. Your drawings will be saved, if you wish, using the END command.

Look over the following tasks to get an idea of where we are going, and then begin Task 1.

## TASKS

1. Begin a new drawing.
2. Explore the drawing editor and the F-keys.
3. Draw a line. Undo it.
4. Review.
5. Draw a square. Use REDRAW to remove "blips".
6. Do Drawing 1-1 ("GRATE").
7. Do Drawing 1-2 ("DESIGN").
8. Do Drawing 1-3 ("SHIM").

1

### TASK 1: Beginning a new drawing

*Procedure.*

1.  Load AutoCAD.
2.  At the Main Menu type "1" and press enter.
3.  Type the name of the drawing and press enter.

*Discussion.*    When you enter the drawing editor for the first time, it will make sense to begin with the name of your first drawing, "1-1" or "Grate". You will be doing some exploration of the AutoCAD drawing editor and trying out the LINE command to draw a line and a square. Then you will be ready to do the first of the three drawings at the end of this chapter.

> Load AutoCAD.

Go to the directory or subdirectory where ACAD.EXE resides and type "ACAD" <enter>. (Your system may have a simpler method, utilizing a batch file to automate the loading process.)

> Begin a new drawing.

Type "1" <enter> at the AutoCAD main menu. Read the note following, then type in a name and press enter. This will be the name of your first drawing.

NOTE: If you are working on a system that is used by others, it is likely that many default settings have been changed. You can avoid the confusion this will cause by typing an equal sign following the drawing name. For example: "1-1=". This technique is explained at the end of Task 4 in Chapter 4. Also, in many CAD courses it is customary for students to save their work on a floppy disk. If this is the case, you should include a drive designation in your drawing name. If you are to save your work on the "A:" drive, for example, type a name like "A:1-1" or "A:1-1=". See your instructor for specific information on how it is to be done in your class.

> Wait....

When you see the word "Command:" at the bottom of the screen, you are ready to proceed.

> Study the screen and *Figure 1-1*. Then try out the F-keys as discussed following.

### TASK 2: Exploring the drawing editor

*Discussion.*    You are looking at the AutoCAD drawing editor. There are many ways that you can alter it to suit a particular drawing application. To begin with, there are a number of features that can be turned on and off using the F-keys or a combination of the control (Ctrl) key with a letter key. Try the F-keys or Ctrl-letter key combinations as suggested. The F-keys are more efficient since a single key does not require you to take your drawing hand off the pointing device. The Ctrl key alternatives are presented in this chapter for reference and are not used elsewhere in this book. Note that the F-keys and their functions are listed at the bottom of every drawing through Chapter 8 of this book, so it is not necessary to memorize them now. You will learn them best through repeated use. Also note that if you are using something other than an IBM-style keyboard, these important functions may be assigned to different keys. If you need more information, refer to the *AutoCAD Installation and Performance Guide*, Section 1.3.

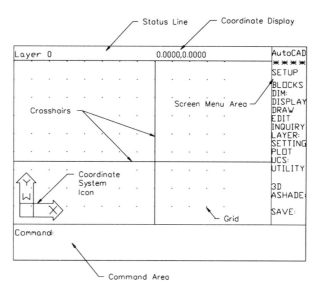

**Figure 1-1**

### The Screen

When you have entered the drawing editor, your screen should appear much like *Figure 1-1*. One major difference is that there will be no grid (dots) on your screen initially. One of the first things you will do is turn the grid on.

On the left side of the status line (at the top of the screen) you will see this: "Layer 0". You don't have to worry about layers until Chapter 3. For now, simply be aware that you are drawing on a layer called "0", and that it uses white, continuous lines.

On the right of the screen, in the "Screen Menu Area", you will see some form of screen menu. Possibly, but not necessarily, it will be the AutoCAD standard screen menu shown here. The AutoCAD standard menu is discussed in Appendix B. If you have some other menu, we assume that there is someone around who can get you started on it. Also, the general discussion of menus in Appendix B will help. In any case, you can do everything in this book without ever using the screen menu or a tablet menu if you wish.

### Switching Screens

> Press F1 (there is no Ctrl key equivalent for F1).

Oops! What happened to the screen?

What you see now is a text screen. You can switch back and forth between text and graphics using F1, the "flip screen" key.

> Press F1 again.

This brings back the graphics screen. Any text which does not fit in the command area is not visible.

NOTE: Sometimes AutoCAD switches to the text screen automatically when there is not enough room in the command area for prompts or messages. If this happens, use F1 when you are ready to return to the graphics screen.

### Cross Hairs

You should see two lines at right angles horizontally and vertically, intersecting somewhere in the display area of your screen. These are the cross hairs, or screen cursor, that tell you where your pointing device (puck, mouse, cursor, stylus, whatever) is located on your digitizer or drawing pad. (If there are no cross hairs on your screen, make sure your pointing device is placed within the digitizing area.)

Move the pointer and see how the cross hairs move in coordination with your hand movements.

### Status Line and Pull Down Menus

If your version of AutoCAD is Release 9 or higher, then you should have another form of screen display available to you. (If you are working with 2.6 or lower, you can skip this section and ignore all references to pull down menus and dialogue boxes from here on.)

> Move the pointer so that the cross hairs move to the top of the screen, into the status line.

Your screen should now resemble *Figure 1-2*.

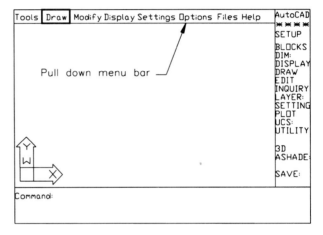

**Figure 1-2**

This is the pull down bar from which you can open up pull down menus that contain a set of the most often used commands. Pull downs are discussed at the beginning of Task 2.

NOTE: Here and throughout this book we show the Release 10 versions of Auto-CAD screens in our illustrations. If you are working with another version, your screen will show slight variations.

> Move the cursor back into the display area and the pull down bar will disappear.

### The Coordinate Display

> Press F6 (or Ctrl-D) to turn on the coordinate display.

The coordinate display on the upper right side of the screen keeps track of the X,Y coordinates as you move the pointer. Move the cursor around slowly and keep your eye on the line of numbers and text at the top of the screen. If nothing is happening, press F6 again.

Watch the coordinate display. It is probably moving very rapidly through four-place decimal numbers. When you stop moving, the numbers will be showing coordinates for the location of the pointer. These coordinates are standard ordered pairs. The first value is the "X" value, showing how far over the cross hairs are, measuring left to right. The second value is "Y", or the vertical position of the cross hairs, measured from bottom to top.

The units AutoCAD uses for coordinates, dimensions, and for measuring distances and angles can be changed at any time. For now we will accept the AutoCAD default values, including the four-place decimals. In the next chapter we will be switching to two-place decimals.

NOTE: The F-keys are toggle switches only; they cannot be used to change settings.

### The Grid

> Press F7 (or Ctrl-G) to turn the grid on.

The grid is simply a matrix of dots that helps you find your way around on the screen. It will not appear on your drawing when it is plotted, and it may be turned on and off at will using F7. You may also change the spacing between dots, using the "GRID" command, as we will be doing in Chapter 2.

You will notice that the grid does not completely cover the screen. There is a blank space on the right next to the screen menu area. This is because the grid is presently set up to emulate the shape of an "A" size piece of paper. There are 10 grid points, numbered 0 to 9, from bottom to top, and 13 points, numbered 0 to 12, across the bottom. This corresponds to a standard 9 × 12 or 8 1/2 × 11 inch drawing sheet.

The AutoCAD command which controls the outer size and shape of the grid is "LIMITS", which will be discussed in Chapter 4. Until then we will continue to use the present format.

### SNAP

> Press F9 (or Ctrl-B) and then move the cursor slowly around the drawing area.

Notice how the cross hairs jump from point to point. If your grid is on, you will see that it is impossible to make the cross hairs touch a point that is not on the grid. Try it.

You will also see that the coordinate display shows only integer values and that the word "SNAP" is displayed on the status line next to "Layer 0".

> Press F9 again.

Snap should now be off and the word no longer displayed on the status line.

If you move the cursor in a circle now, you will see that the cross hairs move smoothly, without jumping. You will also observe that the coordinate display moves rapidly through a series of four-place decimal values.

F9 turns snap on and off. With snap off you can, theoretically, touch every point on the screen. With snap on you can move in predetermined increments only. By default the snap is set to a value of 1.0000. In the next chapter you will learn how to change this setting using the SNAP command. For now we will leave it alone. A snap setting of 1 will be convenient for the drawings at the end of this chapter.

Using an appropriate snap increment is a tremendous timesaver. It allows for a degree of accuracy that is not possible otherwise. If all the dimensions in a drawing fall into one-inch increments, for example, there is no reason to deal with points that are not on a one-inch grid. You can find the points you want much more quickly if all those in between are temporarily eliminated. F9 and the snap setting allow you to do that.

**Ortho**

F8 (or Ctrl-O) turns ortho mode on and off. You cannot observe the ortho mode in action until you have entered the LINE command, however. We suggest that you try it out at the end of Task 3.

**The User Coordinate System Icon**

At the lower left of the Release 10 screen you will see the User Coordinate System (UCS) icon. These two arrows clearly indicate the directions of the X and Y axes, which are currently aligned with the sides of your screen. When you begin to do 3D drawings, in Chapter 12, you will be defining your own coordinate systems that can be turned at any angle and originate at any point in space. At that time you will find that the icon is a very useful visual aid. However, it is hardly necessary in two-dimensional drawing and may be distracting. For this reason you may want to turn the icon off now and keep it turned off until you actually need it.

> Type "ucsicon" and press enter.
    AutoCAD will show the following prompt in the command area:

ON/OFF/All/Noorigin/ORigin <ON>:

As you explore AutoCAD commands you will become familiar with many prompts like this one. It is simply a series of options separated by slashes (/). For now we need only to know about "ON" and "OFF".
> Type "off" and press enter.
    The UCS icon will disappear from your screen. Anytime you want to see it again, type in "ucsicon" again and then type "on".
    By the way, you have just executed your first AutoCAD command.

**TASK 3: Drawing a line**

*Procedure.*

1. Type or select "LINE".
2. Pick a starting point.
3. Pick an end point.
4. Pick another end point to continue in the LINE command, or press enter to stop.

*Discussion.*    You can communicate drawing instructions to AutoCAD in one of four ways: by typing, or by selecting items from a screen menu, a pull down menu, or a tablet menu. Each has its advantages and disadvantages depending on the situation. Often a combination of two or more is the most efficient way to carry out a complete command sequence. The instructions in this book are not specific about which to use, except when necessary. This is because we have no way of knowing what kind of system you may be working with, and because all operators develop their own preferences anyway. Consider the phrase "type or select" to include all four possibilities.
    Each method is described briefly following. You do not have to try them all out at this time; simply read them over to get a feel for the possibilities, and then proceed to the LINE command using whichever method you prefer to start with. As a general rule we suggest learning the keyboard procedure first, but do not stop there. As soon as you know the basic keyboard sequence, try out the other methods to see how they vary and

how you can use them to save time. Ultimately, you will want to type as little as possible and use the differences between the menu systems to your advantage.

*Keyboard:*    The keyboard is the most primitive and fundamental method of interacting with AutoCAD. Screen menus, pull down menus, and tablet menus all function by automating basic command sequences as they would be typed on the keyboard. It is therefore useful to be familiar with the keyboard procedures even if the other methods are sometimes faster.

As you type commands and responses to prompts, the characters you are typing will appear in the command area after the colon (see *Figure 1-3*). Remember that you must press enter to complete your commands and responses.

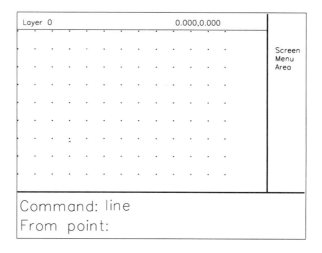

**Figure 1-3**

*Screen Menus:*    All of the menu systems have the advantage that instead of typing a complete command, you çan simply select an item. The screen menu and pull down menus also have the advantage of proximity to your drawing area. You can make selections without taking your eyes off the screen. The major disadvantage of the screen menu is that you will often need to search through two or more submenus before locating the command you want. If you are using the AutoCAD standard menu, see the "Primary Screen Menu Hierarchy" in Appendix B. This chart will show you where all basic commands are located in the standard menu system. It may be useful to make a copy of the chart and keep it handy, so that you do not have to turn to the back of the book to find a command.

To select an item from a screen menu, move the cross hairs to the right side of the screen until a highlight appears in the screen menu area. Then move the highlight up or down until the item you want is highlighted. Press the pick button on your pointing device to select the item. You may have to move through one or more submenus to get to the item you want (see *Figure 1-4*).

*Pull Down Menus:*    The pull down menus contain only a subset of the AutoCAD commands, but it is a useful subset and it is usually quicker to find what you want on a pull down than on a screen menu. The key is to become familiar with what is there and what is not there.

To use a pull down menu, move the cross hairs up into the status line area until the pull down bar appears. Then move left or right to highlight the menu heading you want. Select it with the pick button. Run down the list of items until the one you want is highlighted (see *Figure 1-5*). Press the pick button again to select the item.

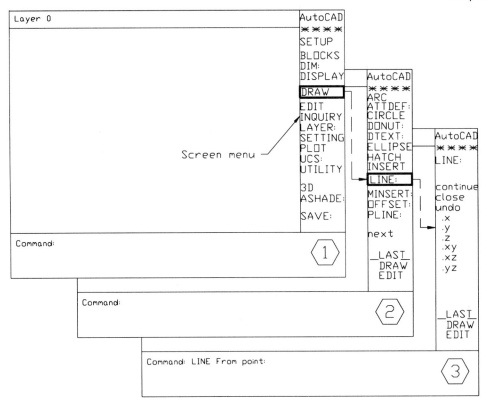

**Figure 1-4**

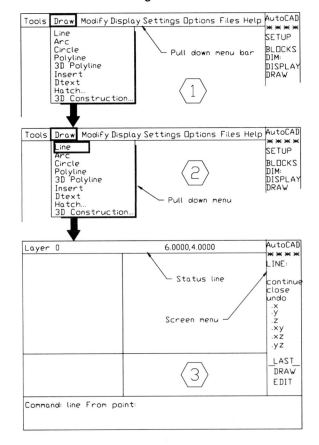

**Figure 1-5**

Some items on pull down menus also make use of dialogue boxes (see Chapter 2) and icon menus (see Chapter 7).

*Tablet Menus:*    In some ways, locating a command on a tablet menu is the quickest method of all. With any good menu system there should be a large number of commands and subcommands available on the tablet, and you will not have to search through submenus to find them. The one disadvantage of the tablet is that in order to use it you must take your eyes off the screen.

On a digitizing tablet simply move the pointing device over the item you want and press the pick button (see *Figure 1-6*).

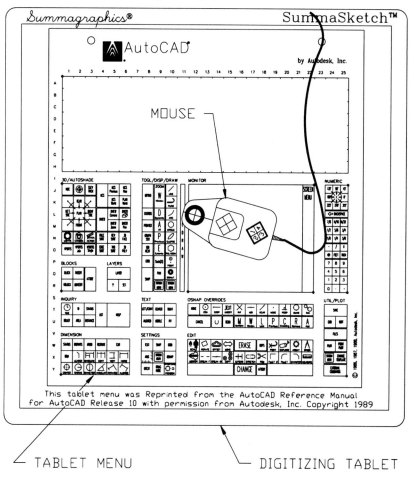

**Figure 1-6**

Finally, you will notice that there is a degree of coordination between the three menu systems. Items picked from both the tablet and the pull downs should bring up appropriate submenus on the screen menu. For example, if you pick the LINE command from the pull down, you should see the LINE command submenu in the screen menu area. Also, you will notice that all of the menu systems call up prompts in the command area, just as if you were typing. The subject of menus and how they work is treated in more depth in Appendix C.

Now let's get started.

> Type or select "LINE" (remember to press enter if you are typing).
        Look at the command area. You should see this:


From point:

This is AutoCAD's way of asking for a starting point.

> Type or select (1.0000,1.0000) as a starting point.

If you are typing coordinates, do it like this:

1,1 <enter> (comma included).

If you are pointing, you need to pay attention to the grid and the coordinate display. If snap is off, switch it on (F9 or Ctrl-B). Move the cursor until the display reads 1.0000,1.0000. Then press the pick button.

Now AutoCAD will ask for a second point. You should be seeing this in the command area:

To point:

There are two new things to be aware of. One is the **"rubber band"** that extends from the starting point to the cross hairs on the screen. If you move the cursor, you will see that this visual aid stretches, shrinks, or rotates like a tether, keeping you connected to the starting point. You will also notice that when the rubber band and the cross hairs overlap (i.e., when the rubber band is at 0, 90, 180, or 270 degrees) they both disappear in the area between the cross hairs and the start point, as illustrated in *Figure 1-7*. This may seem odd at first, but it is actually a great convenience. You will find many instances where you will need to know that the two are exactly lined up.

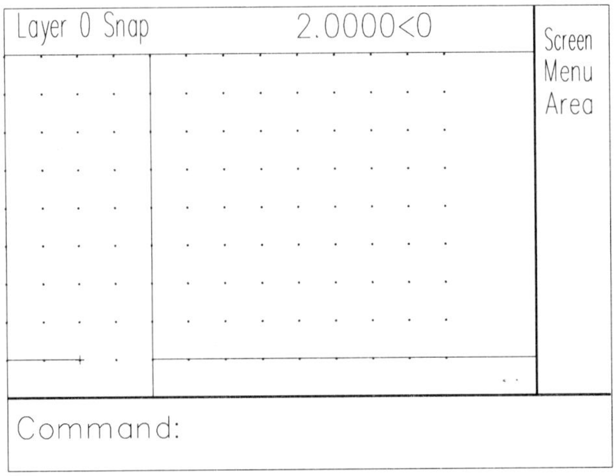

**Figure 1-7**

The other thing to watch is the coordinate display. It has switched from absolute coordinates to polar coordinates. **Polar coordinates** are given relative to the starting point of your line. You are given a distance and an angle. It should look something like this: 4.0000<0 or 5.6569<45. The first number is the distance from the starting point and the second is an angle of rotation, with zero degrees being straight out to the right. Both the distance and the angle can be indispensable tools, so remember to look for them when you need them.

> Select the point (8,8).

The coordinate display will show polar coordinates 9.8995<45.

AutoCAD draws a line between (1,1) and (8,8) and asks for another point. Your screen should now resemble *Figure 1-8*.

To point:

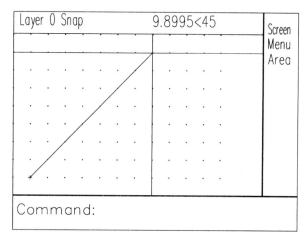

**Figure 1-8**

This will allow you to stay in the LINE command to draw a whole series of connected lines if you wish. You can draw a single line from point to point, or a series of lines from point to point to point to point. In either case, you must tell AutoCAD when you are finished with a set of lines by pressing enter or the enter equivalent button on the cursor, if you have one, or the space bar.

NOTE: When you are drawing a continuous series of lines, the polar coordinates on the display are given relative to the most recent point, not the original starting point.

### Relative Coordinates and "@"

AutoCAD also allows you to enter points using coordinates relative to the last point selected. To do this, use the "@" symbol. For example, after picking the point (1,1) in the last exercise, you could specify the point (8,8) by typing "@7,7", since the second point is over 7 and up 7 from the first point. Or, using polar coordinates relative to (1,1), you could type "@9.8995<45". Both of these methods would give the same results.

### Space Bar and Enter Key

In most cases, AutoCAD allows you to use the space bar as a substitute for the enter or return key. This is a major convenience, since the space bar is easy to locate with one hand while the other hand is on the pointing device. The major exception to this usage is when you are entering text in the TEXT command (see Chapter 7). Since a space may be part of a text string, the space bar must have its usual significance there.

> Press enter or the space bar.

If you entered the LINE command by any method other than the pull down menu, you will now be back to the "Command:" prompt.

If you are using the AutoCAD standard menu and entered the LINE command through the pull downs, you will find that AutoCAD has automatically repeated the command so that you can proceed to another set of lines without having to reenter the command. In order to get back to the command prompt, you will have to cancel the LINE command, as described following, under "CANCEL" (press Ctrl-C).

### Undoing a Line Using "U"

> Type "U" <enter> to undo the line you just drew.

U undoes the last command, so if you have done anything else since drawing the line you will need to type "U" <enter> more than once. In this way you can walk backwards through your drawing session, undoing your commands one by one.

> Type "REDO" <enter> immediately to bring the line back.

*REDO only works immediately after U, and it only works once!* That is, you can only REDO the last UNDO and only if it was the last command executed.

### Ortho

Before completing this section, we suggest that you try the ortho mode.

> Type or select "LINE" <enter> to enter the LINE command.

> Type coordinates or point to a starting point. Any point near the center of the screen will do.

> Press F8 (or Ctrl-O) and move the cursor in slow circles.

Notice how the "rubber band" jumps between horizontal and vertical without sweeping through any of the angles between. Ortho forces the pointing device to pick up points only along the horizontal and vertical quadrant lines from a given starting point. With ortho on, you can select points at 0, 90, 180, and 270 degrees of rotation from your starting point only (see *Figure 1-9*).

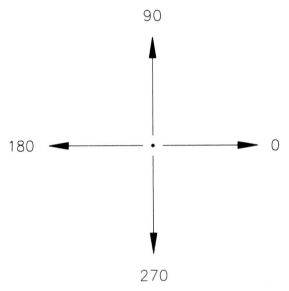

**Figure 1-9**

The advantages of ortho are similar to the advantages of snap mode, except that it limits angular rather than linear increments. It insures that you will get precise and true right angles and perpendiculars easily when that is your intent. Ortho will become more important as drawings grow more complex. In this chapter it is hardly necessary, though it will be convenient in drawings 1 and 3.

### CANCEL

> Hold down the <control> button (Ctrl) and press "c". This will abort the LINE command and bring back the "Command:" prompt.

Ctrl-C is used to cancel a command that has been entered. You may also have a CANCEL button on your cursor and a CANCEL box on your tablet menu. They will perform the same function.

### Arrow Keys

Finally, there is one other way to control the position of the cross hairs and the selection of points that you should be aware of. Using the arrow keys in lieu of the cursor can be useful when you are working with very small increments, when you want to move an exact number of snap points, or when you want to "lock" the cross hairs onto a point so that movements of the pointer will not affect them. An important limitation of the arrow keys is that you cannot use them to move diagonally.

> Press any of the arrow keys to initiate arrow key control of the cross hairs.

Try it. By pressing any of the arrow keys once, you lock in the arrow key system and lock out the cursor.

> Now try moving the cross hairs up, down, left, and right with the appropriate arrow keys.

One press will move the cross hairs one snap point if snap is on and one pixel (the smallest unit your monitor can display) if snap is off. Try it both ways to see what happens.

Holding down an arrow key will give you fast, continuous motion, much as it would on a word processor.

You can also change the size of a single jump by using the page up and page down keys, but it is usually faster to get the cursor near the point you want using the pointing device in the usual manner, and then using the arrow keys close up where you need them.

When the cross hairs have reached the desired point, you can select that point by pressing enter. This will also end arrow key control and reactivate the cursor.

If you want to reactivate the cursor without selecting a point, simply press the "end" key.

### TASK 4: Review

Before going on to the drawings, quickly review the following items. If it all seems familiar, you should be ready for the next drawing task.

- F1 switches between text and graphics screens.
- F6 (or Ctrl-D) turns the coordinate display on and off.
- F7 (or Ctrl-G) turns the grid on and off.
- F8 (or Ctrl-D) turns ortho on and off.
- F9 (or Ctrl-B) turns snap on and off.
- Commands may be entered by typing or selecting from a screen menu, pull down menu, or tablet menu.
- Points may be selected by pointing or by typing coordinates.

- Once inside the LINE command, you can draw a single line or a whole series of connected lines.
- Press enter or the space bar to end working in the LINE command.
- After the first point is selected in the LINE command, coordinates are given in polar form relative to the most recent point.
- U will undo your most recent command.
- REDO will redo an undo.
- Ctrl-C will cancel a command.
- The arrow keys may be used as an alternative way to control the cross hairs.

### TASK 5: Drawing and REDRAWing a square

To practice what you have learned so far, reproduce the square in *Figure 1-10* on your screen. Then erase it using the "U" command as many times as necessary. The coordinates of the four corner points are (2,2), (7,2), (7,7), and (2,7).

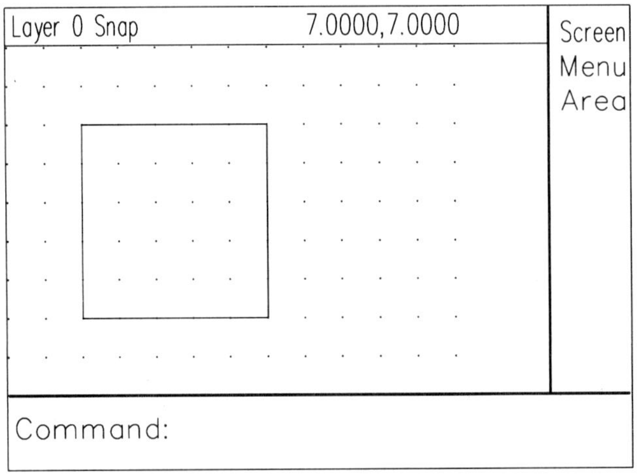

**Figure 1-10**

### CLOSEing a set of lines

For drawing an enclosed figure like this one using the LINE command, AutoCAD provides a convenient CLOSE option. CLOSE will connect the last in a continuous series of lines back to the starting point of the series. In drawing this square, for instance, you would simply type "c" <enter> or select "close" in lieu of drawing the last of the four lines. In order for this to work, the whole square must be drawn without leaving the LINE command.

### REDRAW—Cleaning up your act

You have probably noticed by now that every time you select a point, AutoCAD puts a "blip" on the screen in the form of a small cross. These are only temporary; they are not part of your drawing file database and will not appear on your drawing when it is plotted or printed. However, you will want to get rid of them from time to time to clean up the screen and avoid confusion.

> Type "REDRAW" <enter> or select "REDRAW".
   The display will be redrawn without the blips.

## TASKS 6, 7, and 8: Three simple drawings

You are now ready to complete this chapter by doing drawings 1-1, 1-2, and 1-3. If you wish to save your drawings, see the notes on END, SAVE, and QUIT in the drawing suggestions for Drawing 1-2.

## D R A W I N G   1 - 1 :   G R A T E

The first two drawings in this chapter are given without dimensions. Instead, we have drawn them as you will see them on the screen, against the background of a one-unit grid. Remember that all of these drawings were done using a one-unit snap, and that all points will be found on one-unit increments.

### *DRAWING SUGGESTIONS*

> Remember to watch the coordinate display when searching for a point.
> Be sure that grid, snap, and the coordinate display are all turned on.
> Draw the outer rectangle first. It is 6 units wide and 7 units high, and its lower left-hand corner is at the point (3.0000,1.0000). The three smaller rectangles inside are 4 × 1.

### *IF YOU MAKE A MISTAKE—UNDO*

The "U" command works nicely within the LINE command to undo the last line you drew, or the last two or three if you have drawn a series.

> Type "U" <enter>. The last line you drew will be gone or replaced by the "rubber band" awaiting a new end point. If you want to go back more than one line, type "U" <enter> again, as many times as you need.
> If you have already left the LINE command, "U" will still work, but watch out! Instead of undoing the last line, it will undo the last continuous series of lines. In "GRATE" this could be the whole outside rectangle, for instance.
> Remember, if you have mistakenly undone something, you can get it back by typing "REDO" <enter>. You cannot do other commands between U and REDO.

"U" is quick, easy to use, and efficient as long as you always spot your mistakes immediately after making them. Most of us, however, are more spontaneous in our blundering. We may make mistakes at any time and not notice them until the middle of next week. For us, AutoCAD provides more flexible editing tools, like ERASE, which is introduced in the next chapter.

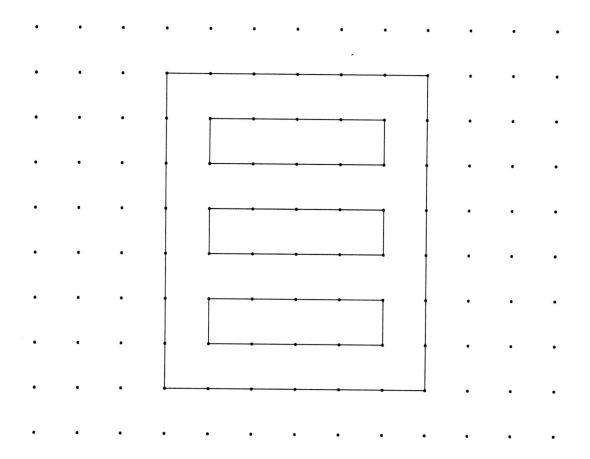

# GRATE
## Drawing 1–1

| | | | |
|---|---|---|---|
| LAYER | 0 | (DRAW) | LINE |
| UNITS | 4 PLACE DECIMAL | (EDIT) | U |
| GRID | 1.0000 | (EDIT) | REDO |
| SNAP | 1.0000 | (DISPLAY) | REDRAW |

| F1 | F6 | F7 | F8 | F9 |
|---|---|---|---|---|
| ON/OFF | ON/OFF | ON/OFF | ON/OFF | ON/OFF |
| SCREEN | COORDS | GRID | ORTHO | SNAP |

# DRAWING 1-2: DESIGN

This design will give you further practice with the LINE command.

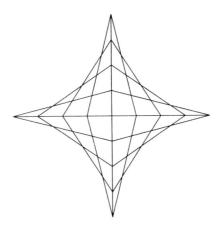

## *DRAWING SUGGESTIONS*

> You can repeat a command by pressing enter or the space bar at the "Command:" prompt. This will be useful here, since you have several sets of lines to draw.

> Draw the horizontal and vertical lines first. Each is eight units long.

> Notice how the rest of the lines work—outside point on horizontal to inside point on vertical then working in, or vice versa.

## *SAVING YOUR WORK—END, SAVE, AND QUIT*

To save your drawing and leave the drawing editor, type END <enter>. Your drawing data will be written to a file with the name you typed when you entered the editor, plus a **.dwg** extension. The .dwg extension is given to all AutoCAD drawing files.

To save your drawing without leaving the editor, type SAVE <enter>. Then answer the "File Name:" prompt with the name of your drawing. Be sure to include a drive designation (e.g., "A:1-2") if you are saving your work on a floppy disk.

To leave the drawing editor without saving your drawing, type QUIT <enter>. Then answer the question "Really want to discard all changes?" with a "y" <enter>.

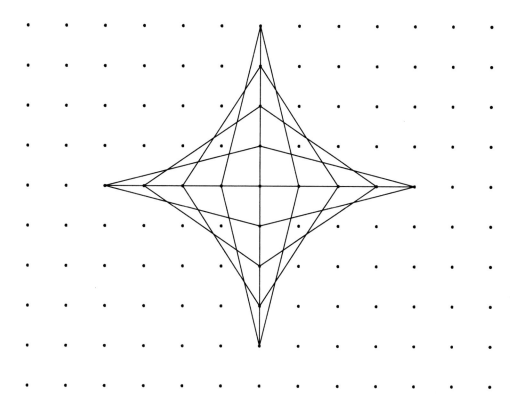

DESIGN # 1

Drawing 1-2

| LAYER | 0 | (DRAW) | LINE |
|---|---|---|---|
| UNITS | 4 PLACE DECIMAL | (EDIT) | U |
| GRID | 1.0000 | (EDIT) | REDO |
| SNAP | 1.0000 | (DISPLAY) | REDRAW |

| F1 | F6 | F7 | F8 | F9 |
|---|---|---|---|---|
| ON/OFF | ON/OFF | ON/OFF | ON/OFF | ON/OFF |
| SCREEN | COORDS | GRID | ORTHO | SNAP |

## DRAWING 1-3: SHIM

This drawing will give you further practice in using the LINE command. In addition, it will give you practice in translating dimensions into distances on the screen. Note that the dimensions are included for your information only; they are not part of the drawing at this point. Your drawing will appear like the reference drawing which follows. Dimensioning is discussed in Chapter 8.

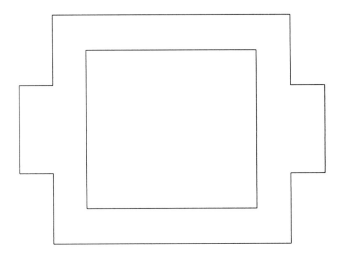

## *DRAWING SUGGESTIONS*

> It is most important that you choose a starting point that will position the drawing so that it fits on your screen. If you begin with the bottom left-hand corner of the outside figure at the point (3,2) you should have no trouble.

> Read the dimensions carefully to see how the geometry of the drawing works. It is good practice to look over the dimensions before you begin drawing. Often the dimension for a particular line may be located on another side of the figure or may have to be extrapolated from other dimensions. It is not uncommon to misread, misinterpret, or miscalculate a dimension, so take your time.

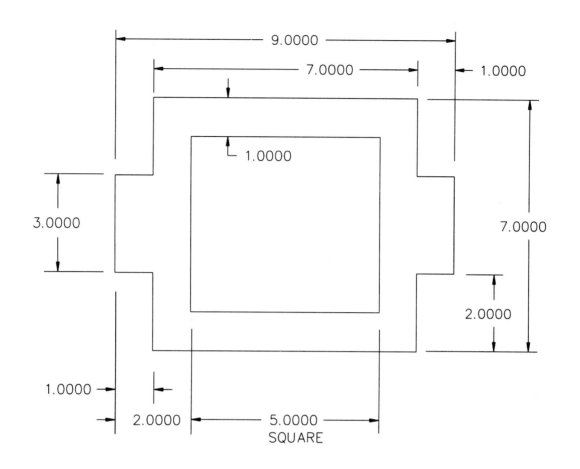

SHIM

Drawing 1—3

| LAYER | 0 | | (DRAW) | LINE |
|-------|---|---|--------|------|
| UNITS | 4 PLACES | | (EDIT) | U |
| GRID | 1.0000 | | (EDIT) | REDO |
| SNAP | 1.0000 | | (DISPLAY) | REDRAW |

| F1 | F6 | F7 | F8 | F9 |
|----|----|----|----|----|
| ON/OFF | ON/OFF | ON/OFF | ON/OFF | ON/OFF |
| SCREEN | COORDS | GRID | ORTHO | SNAP |

# chapter

**COMMANDS**

| SETTINGS | DRAW | EDIT | UTILITIES | INQUIRY |
|----------|------|------|-----------|---------|
| GRID | CIRCLE | ERASE | UNITS | DIST |
| SNAP | | OOPS | | |
| AXIS | | | | |

**OVERVIEW**

In this chapter you will learn to change the spacing of the GRID and the SNAP, and an additional drawing aid called "AXIS". You will also change the UNITS in which coordinates are displayed. You will produce drawings involving straight lines and circles and learn to delete them selectively using several variations of the ERASE command.

**TASKS**

1. Change the SNAP spacing.
2. Change the GRID spacing.
3. Change the AXIS spacing.
4. Change UNITS.
5. Draw three concentric circles using the center point, radius method.
6. Draw three more concentric circles using the center point, diameter method.
7. ERASE the circles, using four selection methods.
8. Mark distances with DIST.
9. Do Drawing 2-1 ("Aperture Wheel").
10. Do Drawing 2-2 ("Roller").
11. Do Drawing 2-3 ("Fan Bezel").
12. Do Drawing 2-4 ("Switch Plate").

### TASK 1: Changing the snap

*Procedure.*

1. Type or select "SNAP".
2. Enter a value.

*Discussion.*   When you begin a new drawing using the AutoCAD prototype (prototypes are discussed in Chapter 4), the grid and snap are set with a spacing of 1. Moreover, they are linked so that changing the snap will also change the grid to the same value. In Task 2 we will set the grid independently.  For now we will leave them linked.

In Chapter 1 all drawings were done without altering the grid and snap spacings from the prototype value of 1. Frequently you will want to·change this, depending on your application. You may want a 10-foot snap for a building layout, or a 0.010 inch snap for a printed circuit diagram.

> Begin a new drawing called "2-1". Remember to include a drive designation if you are saving your work on floppy disks (i.e., "A:2-1"). We will assume from here on that if you are using a floppy disk to save your work, it is in a drive called "A:".,

> Using F7 and F9 be sure that grid and snap are both on.

> Type or select "SNAP" (we will no longer remind you to press enter after typing a command or response to a prompt).

The prompt will appear like this, with options separated by slashes (/):

Snap spacing or ON/OFF/Aspect/Rotate/Style <1.0000>:

You can ignore most of these options for now. The number <1.0000> shows the present setting. AutoCAD uses this format (<default>) in many command sequences to show you a present value or default setting. It usually comes at the end of a series of options. Pressing the enter key or space bar at this point will give you the default setting.

> In answer to the prompt, type ".5" and watch what happens (of course you remembered to press enter).

Because the grid is set to change with the snap, you will see the grid redrawn to a .5 increment.

> Move the cursor around to observe the effects of the new snap setting.

> Try other snap settings. Try 2, .25, and .125.

How small a snap will AutoCAD accept? Notice that when you get smaller than .125, the grid becomes too dense to display, but the snap can still be set smaller.

You can also change SNAP and GRID settings using the pull down menu. The procedure is somewhat different, but the result is the same. If you like, select "Settings" from the pull down bar and then "Drawing Aids" from the pull down menu. This will bring up a "dialogue box" on the screen.  Dialogue boxes appear in numerous software packages and require a combination of pointing and typing that is fairly intuitive. Look at *Figure 2-1* and the following procedural outline.

NOTE: You will see that the dialogue box has places to set both X and Y spacing. It is rare that you would want to have a grid or snap matrix with different horizontal and vertical increments, but the capacity is there if you do.

#### USING A DIALOGUE BOX

1. Move the cross hairs up into the status line until the pull down bar appears.
2. Select a menu heading ("Settings" in this case).

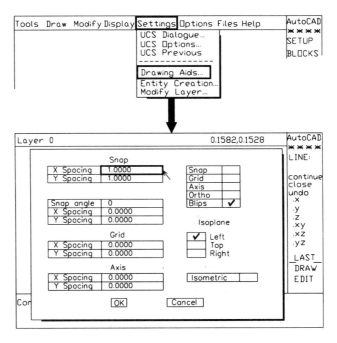

**Figure 2-1**

3. Select an item from the menu ("Drawing Aids").

4. Look at the dialogue box and find the item you want to change.

5. Using the arrow-shaped indicator, highlight the box in the table where the change is to be made (box to the right of "Snap—X Spacing").

6. Type a value and press enter, or select the "OK" box to the right.

7. Make any other desired changes in the same manner.

8. Select the "OK" box at the bottom to confirm changes, or "CANCEL" to cancel changes.

### TASK 2: Changing the grid

*Procedure.*

1. Type or select "GRID".

2. Enter a value.

*Discussion.*    Whether you are typing or using one of your menus, the process for changing the grid setting is the same as changing the snap. In fact the two are similar enough to cause confusion. The grid is only a visual reference. It has no effect on selection of points. Snap is invisible, but it dramatically affects point selection. *Grid and snap may or may not have the same setting.*

> Using F7 be sure the grid is turned on.
> Type or select "GRID".
     The prompt will appear like this, with options separated by slashes (/):

Grid spacing(X) or ON/OFF/Snap/Aspect <1.0000>:

> Type ".5".
> Try other grid settings. Try 2, .25, and .125. What happens when you try .0625?
> Now try setting snap to 1 and the grid spacing to .25. Notice how you cannot touch many of the dots. This is because the visible grid matrix is set to a smaller spacing than the invisible snap matrix.

In practice you are more likely to have this relationship reversed. Since the grid is merely a visual aid, it will often be set "coarser" than the snap.
> Try setting the grid to .5 and the snap to .25.

With this type of arrangement you can still pick exact points easily, but the grid is not so dense as to be distracting.

If you wish to keep snap and grid the same, you can respond with an "s" or a "0" when you set the grid (or select "grid=snap" from the screen menu). The grid will then change to match the snap and will continue to change any time you reset the snap. To free the grid, just give it its own value again using the GRID command.

### TASK 3: Using an axis

*Procedure.*

1.  Type or select "AXIS".
2.  Enter a value.

*Discussion.*    A third drawing aid that works in conjunction with grid and snap is the AXIS command. AXIS puts a line of tick marks across the bottom and the right side of the drawing display as a visual aid. Imagine your grid is set to 1.00 and snap to .25. You will then have four snap increments to every grid increment. In order to avoid having to count snap points or visually gauge where you are, you could add a horizontal and vertical axis with "ticks" at .25 increments to coincide with the snap.

The axis can be easily activated and set from any of the menus or the keyboard in a manner similar to the GRID and SNAP procedures.

> Type or select "axis".
AutoCAD will issue the following prompt:

Tick spacing(X) or ON/OFF/Snap/Aspect <0.0000>:

Responding with a value at this point will set the axis to that value. This is the "Tick spacing" option. The "ON" and "OFF" options are self-explanatory. "Snap" sets the axis to change with the snap setting automatically. The "Aspect" option will allow you to set different values for the horizontal and vertical axis increment.
> Type "s" or select "snap".
Your screen should now resemble *Figure 2-2*.

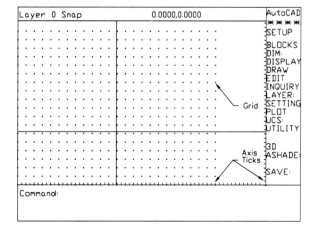

**Figure 2-2**

If you use the pull down menu system, you will find AXIS in the "Drawing aids" dialogue box along with GRID and SNAP.

A final note on the use of AXIS. In the next chapter you will learn to display enlarged portions of your drawing using the ZOOM command so that you can work on small details. When you zoom in far enough, you will find that your grid points spread out too far to be useful. One common usage of the AXIS command is to set up an axis system that is much smaller than the grid. You might, for example, set your grid to 1.00 increments and axis to .01. The axis would then be too dense to display when you are looking at the complete drawing, but it would appear when you zoom in on a small portion.

### TASK 4: Changing units

*Procedure.*

1. Type or select "UNITS".
2. Answer the prompts.
3. Press F1.

*Discussion.*

> Type or select "UNITS".

Presto! No more graphics. We told you this would happen. The command area is too small to display the complete UNITS sequence, so it has disappeared temporarily. What function key will bring it back?

If you don't recall, read on; we will get to it shortly.

What you now see looks like this:

| System of units: | (Examples) |
|---|---|
| 1. Scientific | 1.55E+01 |
| 2. Decimal | 15.50 |
| 3. Engineering | 1'-3.50" |
| 4. Architectural | 1'-3 1/2" |
| 5. Fractional | 15 1/2 |

Enter choice, 1 to 5 <2>:

> Type "2" or simply press enter, since decimal units are the default system, and the one we will use.

Now, and through most of this book, we will stick to decimal units. Obviously, if you are designing a house you will want architectural units. Or if you are building a bridge you may want engineering-style units. Or you might want scientific units if you are doing research.

Whatever your application, once you know how to change units, you can do so easily and at any time. However, as a drawing practice you will want to choose appropriate units when you first begin work on a new drawing. Not only will coordinates be displayed in the units you select, but later, when you use AutoCAD's semiautomatic dimensioning feature (see Chapter 8), your drawing will be dimensioned in these units.

AutoCAD should now be showing the following prompt:

Number of digits to right of decimal point, 1 to 8 <4>:

We will use two-place decimals because they are quite practical and more common than any other choice.

> Type "2" in answer to the prompt for the number of decimal places you wish to use.

AutoCAD now gives you the opportunity to change the units in which angles are measured. In this book we will use all of the default settings for angle measure, since they are by far the most common. If your application requires something different, the UNITS command is the place to change it.

The default system is standard degrees without decimals, measured counterclockwise, with 0 being straight out to the right (3 o'clock), 90 straight up (12 o'clock), 180 to the left (9 o'clock), and 270 straight down (6 o'clock).

> Press enter four times, or until the "Command:" prompt reappears. Be careful not to press enter again, or the UNITS command sequence will be repeated.
> Press F1 to return to the graphics screen. Did you remember?

Looking at the coordinate display, you should now see values with only two digits to the right of the decimal. This setting will be standard in this book.

We suggest, as always, that you experiment with other choices in order to get a feel for the options that are available to you.

## TASK 5: Drawing circles giving center point and radius

*Procedure.*

1. Type or select "CIRCLE".
2. Pick a center point.
3. Enter or drag a radius value.

*Discussion.*    Circles can be drawn by giving AutoCAD three points on the circle's circumference, two points that determine a diameter, two tangents and a radius, a center point and a radius, or a center point and a diameter.  In this chapter we will use the latter two options.

We will begin by drawing a circle with radius 3 and center at the point (6,5). Then we will draw two smaller circles centered at the same point. Later we will erase them using the ERASE command.

> Using what you have just learned, set grid and snap to .5 and units to two-place decimal.
> Type or select "CIRCLE". The prompt which follows will look like this:

3P/2P/TTR/<Center point>:

NOTE: If you are using the AutoCAD screen menu to select commands, the prompt will appear as a submenu instead of a command prompt. You can continue to select options there instead of typing them. If you are using the pull down menu, you can choose options either by typing or by moving over to the screen menu to select them.

> Type coordinates or point to the center point of the circle you want to draw. In our case it will be the point (6,5). AutoCAD will assume that a radius or diameter will follow and will show the following prompt:

Diameter/<Radius>:

If we type or point to a value now, AutoCAD will take it as a radius, since that is the default.

> Type "3" or show by pointing that the circle has a radius of 3. Notice how the "rubber band" works to drag out your circle as you move the cursor.

You should now have your first circle complete. Next, draw two more circles using the center point-radius method. They will be centered at (6,5) and have radii of 2.50 and 2.00. The results are illustrated in *Figure 2-3*.

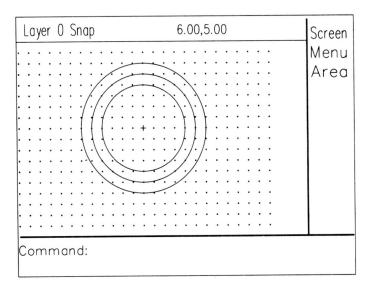

Layer 0 Snap                        6.00,5.00             Screen Menu Area

Command:

**Figure 2-3**

Remember that you can repeat a command, in this case the CIRCLE command, by pressing enter or the space bar. Also, notice that if you have selected the CIRCLE command from the pull down or screen menu, it will be repeated automatically.

### TASK 6: Drawing circles giving center point and diameter

*Procedure.*

1.  Type or select "CIRCLE".
2.  Pick a center point.
3.  Respond to the prompt with a "d".
4.  Type or drag a diameter length.

*Discussion.*  We will draw three more circles centered on (6,5) having <u>diameters</u> of 2, 1.5, and 1. Drawing circles this way is almost the same as in the previous example, except you will not use the default, and you will see that the "rubber band" works differently.

> If necessary, press enter to repeat the CIRCLE command. (Type or select "CIRCLE" if you have done something else, such as a redraw, since drawing the first three circles.)
> Indicate the center point (6,5) by typing coordinates or pointing.
> Answer the prompt with a "d", for diameter. (This step will be done automatically if you have chosen "CEN,DIA" from the AutoCAD screen menu.)

Notice that the cross hairs are now outside the circle you are dragging on the screen (see *Figure 2-4*). This is because AutoCAD is looking for a diameter, but the last point you gave was a center point. So the diameter is being measured from the center point out, twice the radius. Move the cursor around, in and out from the center point, to get a feel for this.

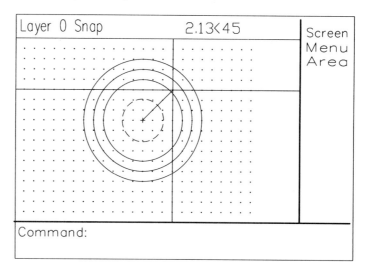

**Figure 2-4**

> Point to a diameter of 2.00, or type "2".

You should now have four circles. Repeat the instructions for using diameter twice more to complete the drawing, giving diameters of 1.5 and 1. Remember that you can use the enter key or the space bar to repeat the CIRCLE command. When you are done, your screen should look like *Figure 2-5*.

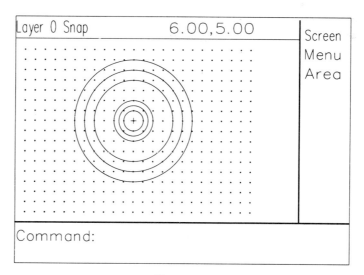

**Figure 2-5**

Sit back and admire your work, because we are about to erase it. In the meantime, studying the following chart will give you a good introduction to the remaining options in the CIRCLE command. None of these is necessary to complete the drawings in this chapter. See the *AutoCAD Reference Manual*, Section 4.3, for additional information.

**TWO-POINT**

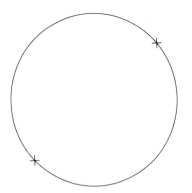

**Figure 2-6**

**THREE-POINT**

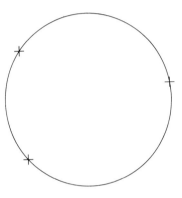

**Figure 2-7**

**TANGENT-TANGENT-RADIUS**

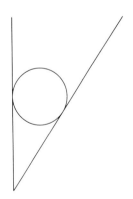

**Figure 2-8**

**NOTES**

Pick two points.
Line between is used as diameter to construct circle.
Rubber band shows diameter.

Pick three points not on straight line.
Arc through all three is completed to form circle.
Circle is visible on screen after second point selection.

Select two objects on the screen ("Tangent Specs").
Type or show radius length.
AutoCAD constructs the circle that has the given radius and is tangent to both objects.

## TASK 7: Using the ERASE command

*Procedure.*

1. Type or select "ERASE".
2. Define a selection set.
3. Press enter.

*Discussion.* The ERASE command works somewhat differently depending on how you enter it and how your menu is programmed. If you are using the AutoCAD standard menu, the keyboard, the screen menu, and the tablet will work one way, while the pull down works another. We will begin with the basic keyboard sequence and then show how the pull down procedure differs.

On the keyboard, ERASE requires a three-step process. First you enter the command, then you define a selection set, and finally you carry out the command by pressing enter.

The second step, selection of objects to be erased, can be done in several ways: by pointing to objects, by "windowing" a group of objects, by indicating "last" or "l", meaning the last entity drawn, or by indicating "previous" or "p" for the previously defined set. There are also options to add or remove objects from the selection set and a "crossing" variation on the "window" option.

The number of selection options available with the ERASE command may seem a bit overwhelming at first, but the time you spend learning them is well worthwhile. Most of these same options will appear in numerous other AutoCAD editing commands (MOVE, COPY, ARRAY, ROTATE, MIRROR).

> Type or select "ERASE." (Do not select from the pull down menu for now).

Notice that the cross hairs have been replaced by a small box. This is the object selection "pickbox." Also notice the command area. It should be showing this:

Select objects:

> Use the box to pick the outer circle.

When you have selected an object, AutoCAD highlights it by changing it to a dotted line (see *Figure 2-9*). It is not yet erased, however. You can go on and add more objects to the selection set and they, too, will become dotted.

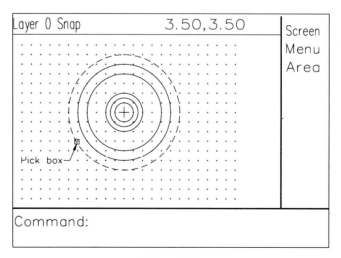

**Figure 2-9**

NOTE: In more complex drawings you may find it convenient or necessary to turn snap off (F9) while selecting objects.

> Use the box to point to the second circle. It too should now be dotted.
> Press enter, the space bar, or the enter equivalent button on your cursor.

The two outer circles should disappear.

## OOPS!

> Type or select "OOPS" and watch the screen.

If you have made a mistake in your erasure, you can get your selection set back by typing (or selecting) "OOPS". OOPS is to ERASE as REDO is to UNDO. *You can use OOPS to undo an ERASE command, as long as you have not done another ERASE in the meantime.* In other words, AutoCAD only saves your most recent ERASE selection set.

You can also use "U" to undo an ERASE, but notice the difference: "U" simply undoes the last command, whatever it might be; "OOPS" works specifically with ERASE to recall the last set of erased objects. If you have drawn other objects in the meantime, you can still use "OOPS" to recall a previously erased set. But if you tried to use "U", you would have to backtrack, undoing any newly drawn objects along the way.

## Selecting the Last Entity

AutoCAD remembers the order in which new objects have been drawn during the course of a single drawing session. As long as you do not leave the drawing editor, you can select the last drawn entity using the "last" option. If you leave the drawing editor and return later, this information will no longer be available.

> Type or select "ERASE".
> Type or select "L" or "last".
> Press enter to carry out the command.
    The inner circle should be erased.

The "p" or "previous" option works with the same procedure, but it selects the previous selection set rather than the last drawn entity. If the difference is not obvious to you now, don't worry, it will become clear as you work more with edit commands and selection sets.

## Selection by "Window"

> Type or select "ERASE" to initiate the ERASE command again.
> Type "w" or select "window" in response to the "Select objects" prompt. You will see a prompt that looks like this:

First corner:

You will now show AutoCAD that you want to erase all of the remaining circles by throwing a temporary selection window around them. The window will be defined by two points that serve as opposite corners of a rectangle. Only entities that lie completely within the window will be selected. See *Figure 2-10*.

> Pick a point at the lower left of the screen. Any point in the neighborhood of (3.5,1) will do.
    AutoCAD will prompt for another corner:

Other corner:

> Pick a point at the upper right of the screen. Any point in the neighborhood of (9.5,8.5) will do. To see the effect of the window, be sure that it crosses the outside circle as in *Figure 2-10*.
> Press enter to indicate that you are through selecting and are ready to carry out the command.
    The circles should now be erased.
> Type or select "OOPS" to retrieve the circles once more. Since ERASE was the last command, "U" will work equally well.

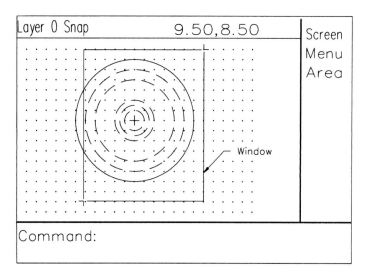

**Figure 2-10**

## Selection by "Crossing"

"Crossing" is an alternative to windowing that is useful in many cases where a standard "window" selection could not be performed. The selection procedure is exactly the same, but all objects that cross the box will be chosen, not just those that lie completely inside the box.

We will use "crossing" to select the inside circles.

> Type or select "ERASE".
> Type "c" or select "Crossing". (Remember, we are not using the pull down menu yet).

AutoCAD will prompt as before:

First corner:

> Pick a point close to (4.5,2.5) as in *Figure 2-11*.

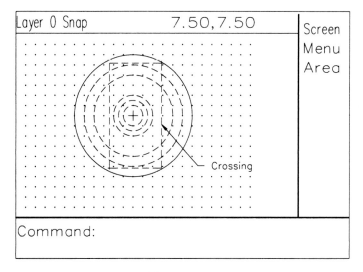

**Figure 2-11**

AutoCAD prompts:

Other corner:

> Pick a point near (7.5,7.5). This point selection must be done carefully in order to demonstrate a "crossing" selection. Notice that the crossing box is shown with dotted lines, whereas the window box was shown with solid lines.

Notice how the circles are selected: those that cross and those that are completely contained within the box, but not those that lie outside.

> Press enter to carry out the command.

> Type or select "OOPS" or "U" to recall the circles.

## Remove and Add

Together, the remove and add options form a toggle switch in the object selection process. Under ordinary circumstances, whatever you select using any of the options above will be added to your selection set. By typing "r" or selecting "remove" you can switch over to a mode in which everything you pick is "de-selected" or removed from the selection set. Then by typing "a" or selecting "add" you can return to the usual mode of adding objects to the set.

## Erase on the Pull Down Menu

The ERASE command works differently in several ways when chosen from the pull down menu. You can make only one selection at a time and the object or objects selected will be erased immediately, without waiting for you to press enter. If you are using Release 9 or higher, try it. Otherwise, skip this section and go on.

> Select ERASE from the pull down menu (under Modify).

If you are using the AutoCAD standard menu, you will see the following in the command area:

Select object: si
Select object: auto
Select object:

The "si" is short for single and "auto" is short for automatic. These are selection options that Autodesk introduced with Release 9. They can be typed directly in response to the "Select objects:" prompt, but they are most useful when programmed into the pull down menu system. See Appendix C for a discussion of how this is done. For now, it is enough to understand the effect that each has on point selection.

Let's try it first to see what happens.

> Select the outer circle.

The circle should be erased immediately without waiting for further object selection. This is the effect of the "single" option.

Because the pull down menu is programmed to repeat commands until you cancel them (remember this from CIRCLE and LINE?), you will be prompted again:

Select object: si
Select object: auto
Select object:

We will now demonstrate the "automatic" option. This option allows you to use three different selection options without telling AutoCAD ahead of time which you will choose.

> Select a point outside and below all the circles, as in *Figure 2-12*.

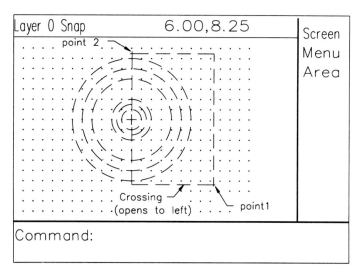

**Figure 2-12**

With the automatic selection option in effect, AutoCAD assumes that you will either point to an object or define a window or crossing box. If your first point is on an object, that object will be selected. If not, it will be taken as the first corner of either a window or crossing selection. Moving to the right for your second point will give you a window. Moving to the left will give you a crossing box.

> Move the cursor to the right and to the left to observe the two-way effect of the "automatic" option, as illustrated in *Figures 2-12* and *2-13*.

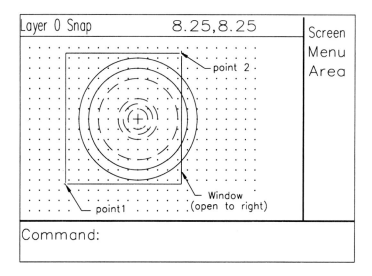

**Figure 2-13**

> Select a point to the left to define a "crossing" selection.
Your circles will be erased immediately.

NOTE: Notice also that many commands on the pull down, including ERASE, are programmed to repeat automatically (see "*^c^c" on the macro characters chart in Appendix C). You can cancel a repeated command by selecting another command from the screen, pull down, or tablet menus. If you want to type your next command, however, you will need to cancel the repeated command using Ctrl-C.

## TASK 8: The DIST command

*Procedure.*

1. Type or select "DIST".
2. Pick first point.
3. Pick second point.
4. Read information in command area or use "blips" as guide points.

*Discussion.* The DIST command is one of AutoCAD's most useful inquiry commands. Inquiry commands give you information about your drawing. DIST works like a simple LINE command procedure, but gives you distances instead of actually drawing a line.

There are two principal uses of the DIST command. The most obvious is that it may be used to measure distances or the lengths of linear objects on the screen. The second use may be less obvious, but is probably more common. Like other commands that ask you to select points, DIST places "blips" on the screen. These can be very handy when used as guide points for drawing lines, circles, or other entities. This "guide" method is introduced in the drawing suggestions for Drawing 2-4, "Switch Plate".

The following exercise will introduce you to the DIST command procedure.

> Type or select "DIST".
  AutoCAD will prompt you to pick a point:

First point:

> Pick a point anywhere near the middle of the screen.
  Notice that AutoCAD gives you a blip at the first point and a rubber band, just as if you were drawing a line. You are also prompted for a second point:

Second point:

> Pick any other point on the screen.
  A blip should be placed at the second point as well, but no line is drawn between the two points. Instead, you should see something like this in the command area:

Distance = 5.00  Angle = 45
Delta X = 3.00  Delta Y = 4.00  Delta Z = 0.00

All of this information can be useful, depending on the situation. "Distance" gives the straight-line distance between the two selected points. "Angle" gives the angle that a line between the two points would make, relative to the polar coordinate system in which 0 degrees is straight out to the right. "Delta X" is the horizontal displacement, which may be either positive or negative. Similarly, "Delta Y" is the vertical displacement. "Delta Z" is the displacement in the plane of elevation. It will always be zero until we begin to explore AutoCAD's 3D drawing capabilities in Chapter 12.

Compare what is on your screen with *Figure 2-14*.

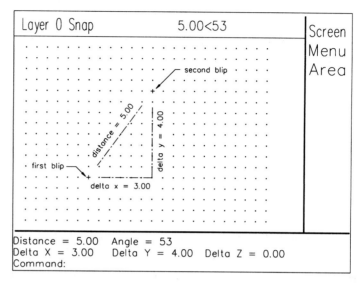

**Figure 2-14**

### TASKS 9, 10, 11, and 12

You are now ready to complete drawings 2-1 through 2-4. Remember to set grid, snap, and units before you begin each drawing. Use either ERASE or U if you make a mistake, depending on the situation. Use whichever form of the CIRCLE command seems most appropriate or efficient to you. Be sure to try out DIST in Drawing 2-4.

Good luck!

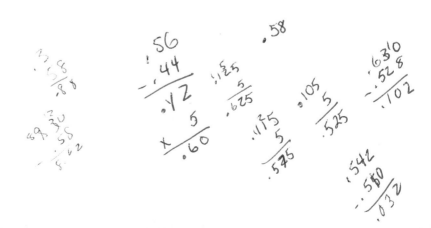

## DRAWING 2-1: APERTURE WHEEL

This drawing will give you practice in drawing circles using the center point, radius method. Refer to the table below the drawing for radius sizes.

 With snap set at .25, some of the circles can be drawn by dragging and pointing. Other circles have radii that are not on a snap point. These circles can be easily drawn by typing in the radius.

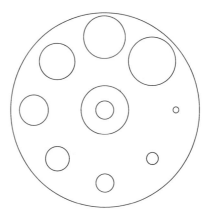

## *DRAWING SUGGESTIONS*

GRID = .50

SNAP = .25

> A good sequence for doing this drawing would be to draw the outer circle first (j), followed by the two inner circles (h and c). These are all centered on the point (6.00,5.00). Then begin at circle "a" and work around clockwise, being sure to center each circle correctly.

> Notice that there are two circle c's and two h's. This simply indicates that the two circles having the same letter are the same size.

> Remember, you may type any value you like and AutoCAD will give you a precise graphic image, but you cannot always show the exact point you want with a pointing device. Often it is more efficient to type a few values than to turn snap off or change its setting for a small number of objects.

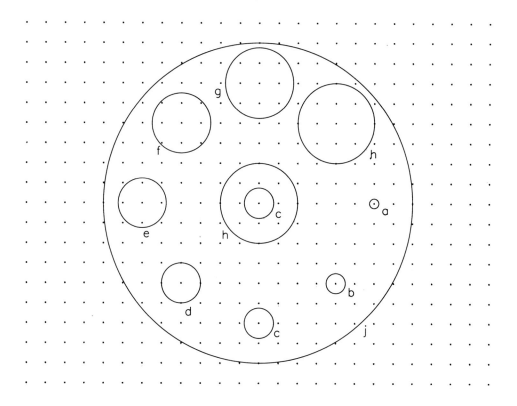

| LETTER | a | b | c | d | e | f | g | h | j |
|--------|------|-----|-----|-----|-----|-----|-----|------|------|
| RADIUS | .12 | .25 | .38 | .50 | .62 | .75 | .88 | 1.00 | 4.00 |

# APERTURE WHEEL

## Drawing 2—1

| | | | |
|---|---|---|---|
| LAYER | 0 | (DRAW) | CIRCLE |
| UNITS | 2 PLACE DECIMAL | (EDIT) | ERASE |
| GRID | .50 | (EDIT) | OOPS |
| SNAP | .25 | (DISPLAY) | REDRAW |

| F1 | F6 | F7 | F8 | F9 |
|---|---|---|---|---|
| ON/OFF | ON/OFF | ON/OFF | ON/OFF | ON/OFF |
| SCREEN | COORDS | GRID | ORTHO | SNAP |

## DRAWING 2-2: ROLLER

This drawing will give you a chance to combine lines and circles and to use the center point, diameter method. It will also give you some experience with smaller objects, a denser grid, and a tighter snap spacing.

> NOTE: Even though units are set to show only two decimal places, it is important to set the snap using three places (.125) so that the grid is on a multiple of the snap (.25 = 2 × .125). AutoCAD will show you rounded coordinate values, like .13, but will keep the graphics on target. Try setting snap to either .13 or .12 instead of .125, and you will see the problem for yourself.

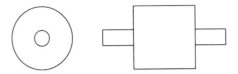

### DRAWING SUGGESTIONS

GRID = .25
SNAP = .125

> The two views of the roller will appear fairly small on your screen, making the snap setting essential. Watch the coordinate display as you work and get used to the smaller range of motion.

> Choosing an efficient sequence will make this drawing much easier to do. Since the two views must line up properly, we suggest that you do the front view first, with circles of diameter .25 and 1.00, and then use these circles to position the lines in the right side view.

> The circles in the front view should be centered in the neighborhood of (2.00,6.00). This will put the upper left-hand corner of the 1 × 1 square at around (5.50,6.50).

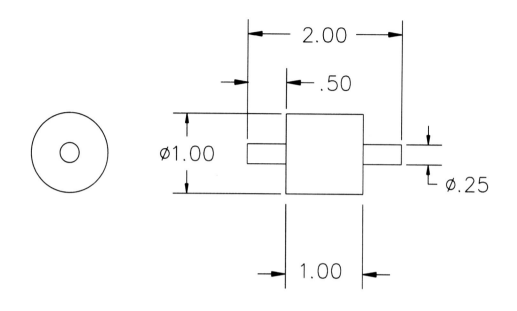

ROLLER

Drawing 2-2

| LAYER | 0 | (DRAW) | LINE |
|---|---|---|---|
| UNITS | 2 PLACE DECIMAL | (DRAW) | CIRCLE |
| GRID | .25 | (EDIT) | ERASE |
| SNAP | .125 | (EDIT) | OOPS |
| | | (DISPLAY) | REDRAW |

| F1 | F6 | F7 | F8 | F9 |
|---|---|---|---|---|
| ON/OFF | ON/OFF | ON/OFF | ON/OFF | ON/OFF |
| SCREEN | COORDS | GRID | ORTHO | SNAP |

# DRAWING 2-3: FAN BEZEL

This drawing should be easy for you at this point. Set grid to .50 and snap to .25 as suggested, and everything will fall into place nicely.

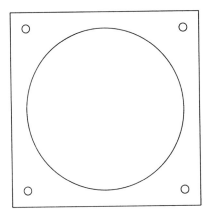

## *DRAWING SUGGESTIONS*

GRID = .50

SNAP = .25

> Notice that the outer figure is a 6 × 6 square and that you are given diameters for the circles.
> You should start with the lower left-hand corner of the square somewhere near the point (3.00,2.00) if you want to keep the drawing centered on your screen.
> Be careful to center the large inner circle at the center of the square.

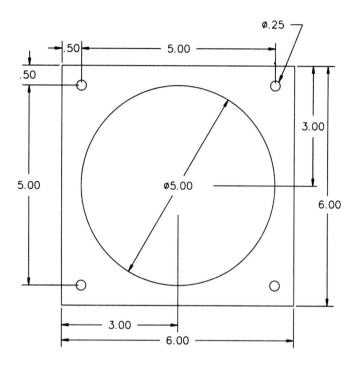

FAN BEZEL

Drawing 2-3

| | | | | |
|---|---|---|---|---|
| LAYER | 0 | | (DRAW) | LINE |
| UNITS | 2 PLACE DECIMAL | | (DRAW) | CIRCLE |
| GRID | .50 | | (EDIT) | ERASE |
| SNAP | .25 | | (EDIT) | OOPS |
| | | | (DISPLAY) | REDRAW |

| F1 | F6 | F7 | F8 | F9 |
|---|---|---|---|---|
| ON/OFF | ON/OFF | ON/OFF | ON/OFF | ON/OFF |
| SCREEN | COORDS | GRID | ORTHO | SNAP |

## DRAWING 2-4: SWITCH PLATE

This drawing is similar to the last one, but the dimensions are more difficult and a number of important points do not fall on the grid. It will give you practice in using grid and snap points and the coordinate display effectively. Refer to the table below the drawing for dimensions of the circles, squares, and rectangles inside the 7 × 10 outer rectangle. The placement of these smaller figures is shown by the dimensions on the drawing itself.

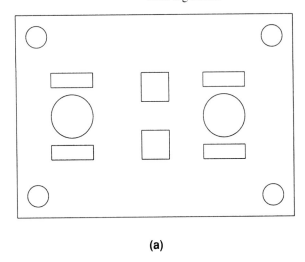

(a)

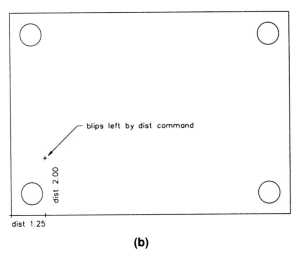

(b)

### *DRAWING SUGGESTIONS*

GRID = .50
SNAP = .25

> Turn ortho on to do this drawing.
> A starting point in the neighborhood of (1,1) will keep you well positioned on the screen.

### *GUIDE POINTS WITH DIST*

The squares, rectangles, and circles in this drawing can be located easily using DIST to set up guide points. For example, set a first point at the lower left corner of the outer rectangle as in *Reference 2-4b*. Then set the second point at 1.25 to the right along the bottom of the rectangle. Now repeat the DIST command and use this second point as the new first point. Set the new second point 2.00 up, and you will have a blip right where you want to begin the "c" rectangle. Look for other places to use this technique in this drawing.

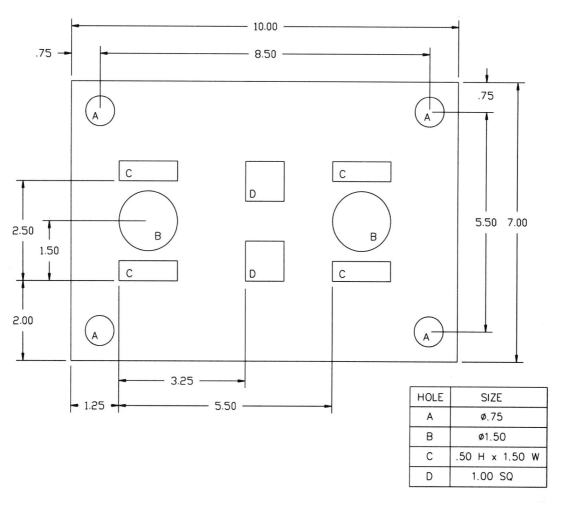

| HOLE | SIZE |
|------|------|
| A | ⌀.75 |
| B | ⌀1.50 |
| C | .50 H x 1.50 W |
| D | 1.00 SQ |

SWITCH PLATE
Drawing 2-4

```
LAYER    0                        (DRAW)      LINE
UNITS    2 PLACE DECIMAL          (DRAW)      CIRCLE
GRID     .50                      (EDIT)      ERASE
SNAP     .25                      (EDIT)      OOPS
                                  (DISPLAY)   REDRAW
```

| F1 | F6 | F7 | F8 | F9 |
|----|----|----|----|----|
| ON/OFF | ON/OFF | ON/OFF | ON/OFF | ON/OFF |
| SCREEN | COORDS | GRID | ORTHO | SNAP |

# chapter

## COMMANDS

| LAYERS | DISPLAY | EDIT | SETTINGS |
|--------|---------|------|----------|
| LAYER | ZOOM | FILLET | LTSCALE |
| | PAN | CHAMFER | |
| | REGEN | | |
| | VPORTS | | |

## OVERVIEW

So far all the drawings you have done have been on a single layer called "0". In this chapter you will create and use three new layers, each with its own associated color and linetype.

You will also learn to FILLET and CHAMFER the corners of previously drawn objects, to magnify portions of a drawing using the ZOOM command, and to move between adjacent portions of a drawing with the PAN command.

## TASKS

1. Create three new layers.
2. Assign colors to layers.
3. Assign linetypes to layers.
4. Change the current layer.
5. Fillet the corners of a square.
6. Chamfer the corners of a square.
7. ZOOM in and out using Window, Previous, and All.
8. PAN to display another area of a drawing.
9. Create multiple view ports (optional).
10. Do Drawing 3-1 ("Mounting Plate").
11. Do Drawing 3-2 ("Stepped Shaft").
12. Do Drawing 3-3 ("Base Plate").
13. Do Drawing 3-4 ("Bushing").
14. Do Drawing 3-5 ("Half Block").

## TASK 1: Creating new layers

*Procedure.*

1. Type or select "LAYER".
2. Type "n" or select "new".
3. Enter the names of new layers.
4. Press enter to leave LAYER command.

*Discussion.*    Layers allow you to treat specialized groups of entities on your drawing separately from other groups. For example, all of the dimensions in this book were drawn on a special dimension layer so that we could turn them on and off at will. We turned off the dimension layer in order to prepare the reference drawings for chapters 1 through 7, which have no dimensions. When a layer is turned off, all the objects on that layer become invisible, though they are still part of the drawing database and can be recalled at any time.

It is common to put dimensions on a separate layer, and there are many other uses of layers as well. Fundamentally, layers are used to separate colors and linetypes, and these in turn take on special significance depending on the drawing application. It is standard drafting practice, for example, to use small, evenly spaced dashes to represent objects or edges that would in reality be hidden from view. On a CAD system with a color monitor, these hidden lines can also be given their own color to make it easy for the operator to remember what layer he or she is working on.

In this book we will use a simple and practical layering system, most of which will be presented in this chapter. You should remember that there are many other systems in use, and many other possibilities. AutoCAD allows as many as 255 different colors and as many layers as you like.

You should also be aware that linetypes and colors are not restricted to being associated with layers. It is possible to mix linetypes and colors on a single layer. But while this may be useful for certain applications, we do not recommend it at this point.

By now you should be used to the idea that different parts of a menu system may be programmed to work in different ways. In the AutoCAD standard menu, the LAYER command is another case where the pull down menu works differently than the keyboard, the screen menu, or the tablet. Try the others first, and we will get to the pull down method later.

> Begin a new drawing called "3-1" or "A:3-1".
> Type or select "LAYER".
    AutoCAD will respond with the following options:

?/Make/Set/New/On/Off/Color/Ltype/Freeze/Thaw:

In this chapter we will be concerned with ?, Make, Set, New, Color, and Ltype.
> Type "n" to select the New option.
    You will now see this prompt:

New layer name(s):

Notice that you can create more than one layer at a time. Many of the options work this way, allowing you to change the characteristics of a number of different layers at the same time.
> Type "1,2,3" <enter>.
    The commas are necessary for this to be read as a list of three names.

Layer names, like file names, may be up to eight characters long. We have chosen single-digit numbers because they are easy to type and because we can match them to AutoCAD's color numbering sequence.

At this point the three layers have been created. To exit from the LAYER command now, we would simply press the enter key again. Instead, we will ask AutoCAD to show us a list of defined layers and see if the new ones are there.
> Type or select "?".

This option asks AutoCAD to list layers presently defined in a drawing. It is followed by a prompt that allows you to specify the layer or group of layers you want listed:

Layer name(s) for listing <*>:

The <*> default tells you that you can use wild card characters to specify layers. The wild card characters * and ? are used as they are in MS-DOS.

If you accept the default, all defined layers will be listed.
> Press enter to list all layers.

You can see by the list that the three new layers "1","2", and "3" are now defined.

| Layer name | State | Color | Linetype |
|---|---|---|---|
| 0 | On | 7 (white) | CONTINUOUS |
| 1 | On | 7 (white) | CONTINUOUS |
| 2 | On | 7 (white) | CONTINUOUS |
| 3 | On | 7 (white) | CONTINUOUS |

> Remember to press F1 when you want to return to the graphics screen. By the way, there is no need to do so until all your layers are defined and you are ready to draw again.

## TASK 2: Assigning colors to layers

*Procedure.*

1. Type or select "LAYER" if not already in the LAYER command.
2. Type or select "c" or "color".
3. Type or select a color name or number.
4. Type the name of a layer or layers.

*Discussion.* We now have four layers, but they are all pretty much the same. Obviously we have more changes to make before our new layers will have useful identities.

Layer "0" has some special features which will be discussed in Chapter 10. Because of these, it is common practice to leave it defined the way it is. We will begin our changes on layer 1.

> (If for any reason you have left the LAYER command, you will need to reenter it by typing or selecting "LAYER", or by pressing enter to repeat the command).
> Type "c" or select "color".
You will see this prompt:

Color:

> Type "1" or select "red". (Typing "red" will also work.)

AutoCAD has assigned numbers to seven colors (1-7). These are standard for all color monitors. Numbers from 8 to 255 specify colors and shades that will vary from one machine to another. The seven standard colors are:

1 - Red      5 - Blue
2 - Yellow    6 - Magenta
3 - Green     7 - White
4 - Cyan

Since the color red is number 1 on AutoCAD's color list, a response of either "red" or "1" will have the same effect.
AutoCAD will now want to know which layer(s) are to be red:

Layer name(s) for color 1 (red) <0>:

Layer 0 is the default because it is the currently active layer, the one you have been drawing on. In Task 4 you will see how to make a different layer current.
> Type "1" and press enter.
If you look at the layer list now (type "?"), you will see that layer 1 is assigned the color red.
> Type "c" again and assign the color yellow (color 2) to layer 2.
> Type "c" again and assign the color green (color 3) to layer 3.
Look at the layer list ("?"). It should look like this:

| Layer name | State | Color | Linetype |
|---|---|---|---|
| 0 | On | 7 (white) | CONTINUOUS |
| 1 | On | 1 (red) | CONTINUOUS |
| 2 | On | 2 (yellow) | CONTINUOUS |
| 3 | On | 3 (green) | CONTINUOUS |

## TASK 3: Assigning linetypes

*Procedure.*

1. Type or select "LAYER".
2. Type "L" or select "Ltype".
3. Type the name of a linetype.
4. Type the name of a layer or layer(s).
5. Press enter to exit the LAYER command.

*Discussion.* AutoCAD has a standard library of linetypes that can be easily assigned to layers. There are eight standard types in addition to continuous lines. If you do not assign a linetype, AutoCAD will assume you want continuous. *Figure 3-1* shows the eight other types. Of these, we will be using primarily hidden and center lines. We will put hidden lines in yellow on layer 2 and center lines in green on layer 3.

> (If for any reason you have left the LAYER command, you will need to reenter it by typing or selecting "LAYER", or by pressing enter to repeat the command.)
> Type "L" or select "Ltype".
You will see the following prompt:

Linetype (or ?) <CONTINUOUS>:

If you respond with a ?, AutoCAD will show you a list of linetypes in use in the present drawing.

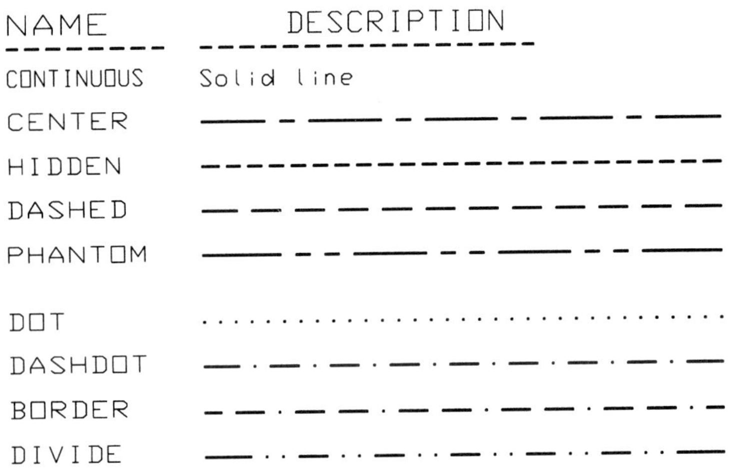

```
NAME                    DESCRIPTION
-------                 -------------------
CONTINUOUS     Solid line

CENTER         —— - —— - —— - —— - ——

HIDDEN         — — — — — — — — — — — —

DASHED         — — — — — — — — — — —

PHANTOM        —— - - —— - - —— - - ——

DOT            · · · · · · · · · · · · · · · · · · · ·

DASHDOT        — · — · — · — · — · — · — ·

BORDER         — — · — — · — — · — — · —

DIVIDE         —— · · —— · · —— · · —— · · ——
```

**Figure 3-1**

If you press enter you will get the default, which is continuous.
> Type or select "hidden".

As in the color sequence, AutoCAD will now ask which layer(s) are to use hidden lines:

> Layer name(s) for linetype hidden <0>:

Layer 0 is the default because it is the current layer.
> Type "2".

Anything drawn on layer 2 will now be drawn with the hidden linetype.
> Type "L" or select "Ltype" again and assign the center linetype to layer 3.
> Now, type "?" once more and examine your layer list. It should look like the one following. If not, use the LAYER command to fix it.

| Layer name | State | Color | Linetype |
|---|---|---|---|
| 0 | On | 7 (white) | CONTINUOUS |
| 1 | On | 1 (red) | CONTINUOUS |
| 2 | On | 2 (yellow) | HIDDEN |
| 3 | On | 3 (green) | CENTER |

## TASK 4: Changing the current layer

*Procedure.*

1. Type or select "LAYER".
2. Type "s" or select "set".
3. Enter a new current layer.
4. Press enter to exit the LAYER command.

*Discussion.* In order to draw new entities on a layer, you must make it the currently active layer. Previously drawn objects on other layers will also be visible and will be plotted if that layer is turned on, but new objects will go on the current layer.

> (If for any reason you have left the LAYER command, you will need to reenter it by typing or selecting "LAYER", or by pressing enter to repeat the command.)
> Type "s" or select "set".

You will be prompted for a layer name:

> New current layer <0>:

Layer 0 has been current up until now, so it is the default.

> Type "1" and press enter.

At this point you should still be in the LAYER command, with the usual options showing:

?/Make/Set/New/On/Off/Color/Ltype/Freeze/Thaw:

Though you have completed the set option sequence, the current layer will not actually be changed until you have left the LAYER command and returned to the "Command:" prompt. To do this, simply press enter again.
> Press enter to exit the layer command.

You have now made layer 1 current. If you go over to the graphics screen (press F1) you will see "Layer 1" in the upper left-hand corner.

NOTE: The "make" option works like the "new" option, except that it makes the newly defined layer current. Of course, this means you can only define one layer at a time with "make".

At this point we suggest that you try drawing some lines to see that you are, in fact, on layer 1 and drawing in red, continuous lines. If you have a monochrome monitor this effect will not be visible. You will see the effect soon, however, when we switch to layer 2 and draw hidden lines. Even if you are working in monochrome it is good practice to use color settings, because they can be used when you plot your drawings if you use colored pens on your plotter.

When you are satisfied with the red lines you have drawn, go into the LAYER command again and set the current layer to 2. Now draw more lines and see that they are hidden yellow lines. (Remember to press enter to exit the LAYER command before entering the LINE command).

Finally, set layer 3 as the current layer and draw some green center lines.

### Layers on the Pull Down Menu

You will find "Modify Layer," the pull down version of the LAYER command, under "Settings." It makes use of the dialogue box illustrated in *Figure 3-2*. The main advantage of this system is that the table of layers is displayed in front of you as you make

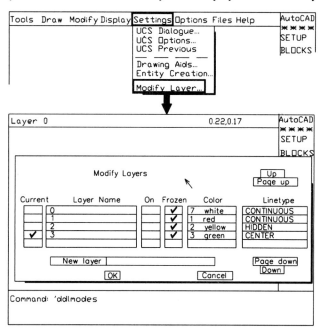

**Figure 3-2**

changes. The major disadvantage is that you cannot load new linetypes through the dialogue box. That is, if you want to define a new layer with a linetype other than those already in use, you will have to leave the box and go back to the basic LAYER command "Ltype" option, as discussed in Task 3.

Before leaving this section, use the dialogue box to set the current layer to layer 1.

> Select "Settings" from the pull down bar.
> Select "Modify Layer" from the "Settings" menu.
> Select the "Current" square next to layer 1.
> Select "OK" to close the box and execute the change.

## TASK 5: Editing corners using FILLET

*Procedure.*

1. Type or select "FILLET".
2. Type or select "r" or "radius".
3. Enter a radius value.
4. Press enter to reselect the FILLET command.
5. Select two lines that meet at a corner.

*Discussion.* Now that you have a variety of linetypes to use, you can begin to do some more realistic mechanical drawings. All you will need is the ability to create filleted (rounded) and chamfered (cut) corners. The two work similarly, and AutoCAD makes them easy.

> Erase any lines left on the screen from the last exercise.
> If you have not already done so, set layer 1 as the current layer.
> Draw a 5 × 5 square on your screen, as in *Figure 3-3*. We will use this figure to practice fillets and chamfers. Exact coordinates and lengths are not important.

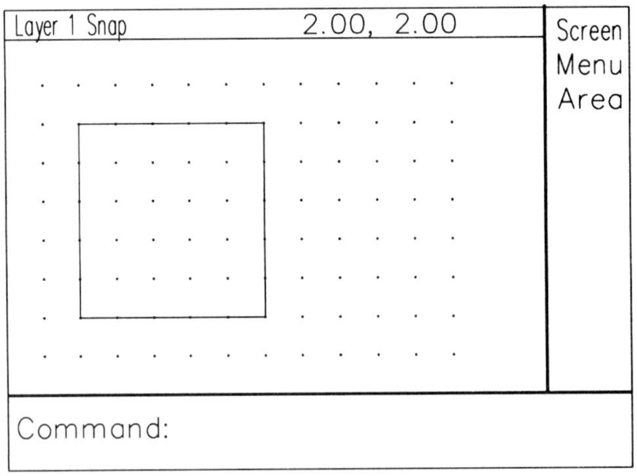

**Figure 3-3**

> Type or select "FILLET".
The following prompt will appear:

Polyline/Radius/<select two points>:

Polylines are discussed in Chapter 8.

The first thing you must do is determine the degree of rounding you want. Since fillets are really arcs, they must be defined by a radius.
> Type "r" or select "radius".
AutoCAD prompts:

Enter fillet radius <0.00>:

The default is 0 because no fillet radius has been defined for this drawing yet.
You can define a fillet radius by typing a value or showing two points that define the radius length.
> Type ".5" or show two points .5 units apart.
You have now set .5 as the standard fillet radius for this drawing. You can change it at any time, but it will not affect previously drawn fillets.
AutoCAD does not assume that you necessarily want to create fillets at this point, so it gives you back the "Command:" prompt. We do wish to draw fillets, however, so we will repeat the FILLET command.
> Press enter to repeat FILLET.
The prompt is the same as before:

Polyline/Radius/<Select two points>:

You will notice that you now have the selection aperture (small box) on the screen. Use it to select two lines that meet at any corner of your square.
Behold! A fillet! You did not even have to press enter. AutoCAD knows that you are done after selecting two lines.
> Press enter to repeat FILLET. Then fillet another corner.

We suggest that you proceed to fillet all four corners of the square. When you are done your screen should resemble *Figure 3-4*.

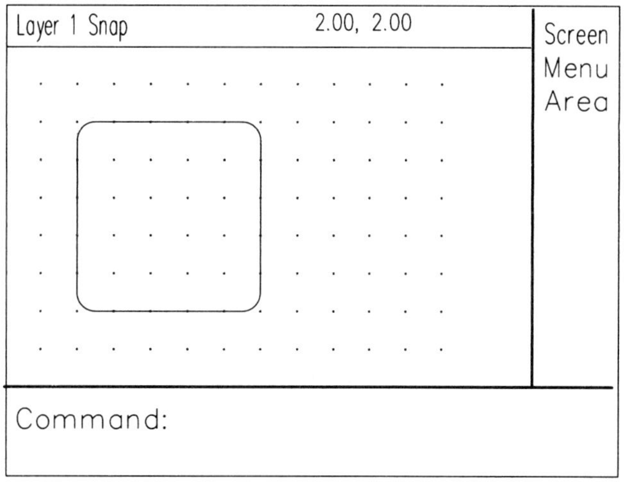

**Figure 3-4**

## TASK 6: Editing corners with CHAMFER

*Procedure.*

1. Type or select "CHAMFER".
2. Type "d" or select "distances".

3. Enter a chamfer distance.
4. Press enter to reselect the CHAMFER command.
5. Select two lines that meet at a corner.

*Discussion.* The CHAMFER command sequence is almost identical to the FILLET command, with the exception that chamfers may be uneven. That is, you may cut back farther on one side of a corner than the other. To do this you must give Auto-CAD two distances instead of one.

> Prepare for this exercise by undoing all your fillets with the "U" command.
> Type or select "CHAMFER".
AutoCAD prompts:

Polyline/Distances/<Select first line>:

> Type "d" or select "distances".
The next prompt will be:

Enter first chamfer distance<0>:

The present default is 0 because we have yet to define a chamfer distance for this drawing.
> Type ".25".
AutoCAD asks for another distance with a prompt like this:

Enter second chamfer distance <0.25>:

The first distance has become the default and most of the time it will be used. If you want an asymmetric chamfer, enter a different value for the second distance.
> Press enter to accept the default, making the chamfer distances symmetrical.
AutoCAD will return the command prompt at this point.
> Press enter to reenter the CHAMFER command.
> Answer the prompt by pointing to a line this time.
> Point to a second line, perpendicular to the first.
You should now have a neat chamfer on your square.

### The "MULTIPLE" Command Modifier

FILLET and CHAMFER are not on the pull down menu and have not been programmed to repeat on the screen or tablet menu (assuming you are using AutoCAD's standard menu system). In Release 9 and higher versions, however, there is an easy way to get the same kind of automatic repetition without reprogramming the menu. At the "Command:" prompt simply type the command modifier "MULTIPLE" before the command itself, with a space between, like this: "multiple chamfer". Then you can proceed to chamfer one corner after another without having to reenter the command. MULTIPLE can be used with other drawing and editing commands as well. When you are ready to move on to another command, press Ctrl-C or Cancel to return to the "Command:" prompt.

We suggest that you continue this exercise by chamfering the other three corners of your square, using "multiple chamfer" if you wish. When you are done, your screen should resemble *Figure 3-5.*

### TASK 7: ZOOMing window, previous, and all

*Procedure.*

1. Type or select "ZOOM".

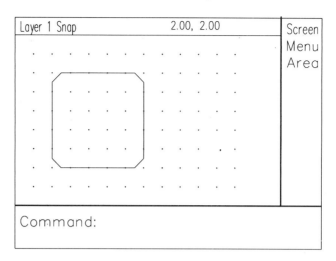

**Figure 3-5**

**2.** Enter a ZOOM method or magnification value.

**3.** Enter values or points if necessary, depending on choice of method.

*Discussion.*    The capacity to zoom in and out of a drawing is one of the more impressive benefits of working on a CAD system. When drawings get complex it often becomes necessary to work in detail on small portions of the drawing space. Especially with a small monitor, the only way to do this is by making the detailed area larger on the screen. This is easily done with the "ZOOM" command.

You should have a square with chamfered corners on your screen from the previous exercise. If not, a simple square will do just as well and you should draw one now.

> Type or select "ZOOM". (From the pull down menu, select "Display").
    The prompt that follows looks like this:

All/Center/Dynamic/Extents/Left/Previous/Window/&lt;Scale(X)&gt;:

We are interested, for now, in All, Previous, and Window, which we will explore in reverse order. See the *AutoCAD Reference Manual*, Section 6.1, for further information.

If you are using the pull down menu, notice that the word "Zoom" is not there, but "Window" and "Previous" under "Display" actually mean "zoom window" and "zoom previous". Otherwise they work the same as the keyboard, with one additional capability (discussed following under "TRANSPARENT COMMANDS").

> Type "w" or select "window".
    This is where you specify the type of zoom you want to perform. As noted, this step may be automated for you depending on how your menu system is programmed and where you selected the command.
    In any case, the prompt that follows will look like this:

First Corner:

You are being asked to define a window, just as in the ERASE command. This window will be the basis for what AutoCAD displays next. Since you are not going to make a window that exactly conforms to the screen size and shape, AutoCAD will interpret the window this way: Everything in the window will be shown, plus whatever additional area is needed to fill the screen. The center of the window will become the center of the new display.

> Pick a point just below and to the left of the lower left-hand corner of your square (like point 1 in *Figure 3-6*).

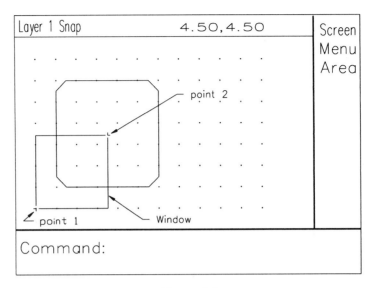

**Figure 3-6**

AutoCAD asks for another point:

Other corner:

> Pick a second point near the center of your square.

The square should now appear enlarged on your screen, as shown in *Figure 3-7*.

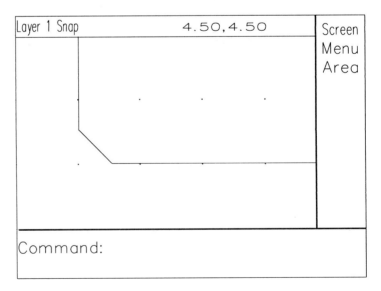

**Figure 3-7**

> Using the same method, try zooming up further on the chamfered corner of the square.

Remember that you can repeat the ZOOM command by pressing enter. When you do this you will have to re-specify the window option, even if the menu did it for you the first time around.

At this point, most people cannot resist seeing how much magnification they can get by zooming repeatedly on the same corner or angle of a chamfer. Go ahead. After a couple of zooms the angle will not appear to change. An angle is the same angle no matter how close you get to it. But what happens to the spacing of the grid and snap as you move in? You may have to turn snap off (F9) in order to continue defining windows. Remember that you can use an axis to replace the grid when you zoom in close. Try setting the axis spacing to .01 and zoom in until it appears. Can you zoom in further so that the axis, too, is no longer usable?

When you are through experimenting with window zooming, try zooming out to the previous display.

> Press enter to repeat the ZOOM command.
> Type "p" or select "previous".
    You should now see your previous display.

    AutoCAD keeps track of your most recent displays. The exact number of displays it stores depends on the version you are using. Release 10 remembers ten previous displays. Experiment to see how many yours can recall.

> ZOOM Previous as many times as you can until you get a message that says:

                        No previous display saved.

One more ZOOM type you should know right now is ZOOM All. ZOOM All zooms out to display the whole drawing. It is useful when you have been working on a number of small areas and are ready to view the whole scene. You do not want to have to wade through previous displays to find your way back. ZOOM All will take you there in one jump.

In order to see it work, you should be zoomed in on a portion of your display before executing ZOOM All.

> Press enter to repeat the ZOOM command.
> Type "a" or select "all".
    There you have it.

### TASK 8: Moving the display area with PAN

*Procedure.*

1.  Type or select "PAN".
2.  Pick a displacement base point.
3.  Pick a second point to show displacement.

*Discussion.*   As soon as you start to use ZOOM you are likely to need PAN as well. While ZOOM allows you to magnify portions of your drawing, PAN allows you to shift the area you are viewing in any direction.

> Type or select "PAN".
    AutoCAD will prompt you to show a displacement:

                        Displacement:

    Imagine that your complete drawing is hidden somewhere behind your monitor, and that the display area is now functioning like a microscope with the lens focused on one portion. If the ZOOM command increases the magnification of the lens, then PAN moves the drawing like a slide under the lens, in any direction you want.

To move the drawing you will indicate a displacement by picking two points on the screen. The line between them will serve as a vector, showing the distance and direction you want to PAN. Notice that the objects on your screen will move in the direction you indicate; if your vector moves to the right, so will the objects.

> Pick a point to begin your displacement vector, as shown in *Figure 3-8*.

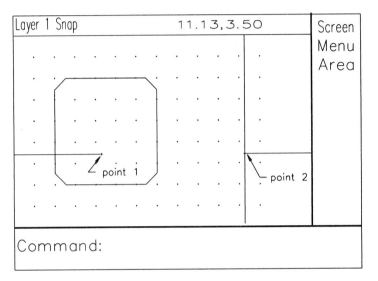

**Figure 3-8**

You will be prompted for another point:

Second point:

> Pick a point to the right of your first point.

As soon as you have shown AutoCAD the second point, objects on the screen will shift to the right, as in *Figure 3-9*.

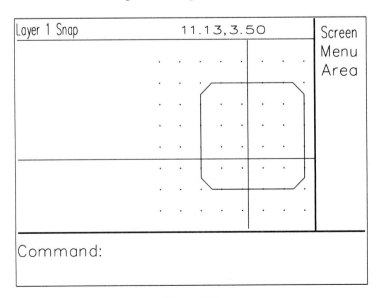

**Figure 3-9**

> Press enter to repeat the PAN command.
> Indicate a displacement to the left, moving objects back near their previous positions.

Experiment with the PAN command, moving objects up, down, left, right, and diagonally. What function key would make it impossible to PAN diagonally? Hint: The name of the function begins and ends with an "o" and the F-key that turns it on and off begins with an F and ends with an 8.

### Transparent Commands

If you have used any of the menus to enter the ZOOM and PAN commands, you may have noticed that they place an apostrophe before the name of the command. If you select PAN from the AutoCAD standard screen menu, for example, you will see the following in the command area:

Command:'pan

The apostrophe is a command modifier introduced in version 2.6 that makes the command "transparent." This means that you can enter it in the middle of another command sequence, and when you are done you will still be in that sequence. For example, you can pan while drawing a line. This is a major convenience if you have already selected the first point and then realize that the second point will be off the screen. A sample procedure using transparent PAN would be as follows:

1. Type or select "LINE".
2. Pick a first point.
3. Type " 'pan" or select "PAN".
4. Show a displacement vector.
5. Pick a second point to complete the line.

The major limitation in the use of transparency is that a command cannot be used transparently if its use would require a regeneration of the drawing (see "REGEN" in Drawing 3-4 drawing suggestions). This would happen, for example, if you tried to pan beyond the limits of a drawing (see LIMITS in Chapter 4). Then AutoCAD would give you this message in the command area:

** Requires a regen, cannot be transparent

and your previous command sequence would be resumed without change.

### TASK 9: Using multiple view ports in 2D (optional)

*Procedure.*

1. Type or select "VPORTS" ("Set Viewports" on the "Display" pull down).
2. Type or select the number of view ports (2, 3, or 4).
3. Specify horizontal and vertical arrangement of windows.

*Discussion .*    If you are working in Release 10 or higher, you have the ability to create multiple view ports, or windows, on your screen. This feature is most useful in 3D drawings and will be discussed in depth in Chapter 13. Multiple view ports may also be used in 2D to allow you to view different parts of a drawing or a complete drawing and a zoomed portion simultaneously. With multiple view ports you have the advantage of switching views less frequently, but this must be weighed against the disadvantage of working in smaller viewing windows.

In this exercise we will create a two view port configuration with a full view in one window and a zoomed view in the other.

> To begin this exercise you should have a full view of the chamferred square, as shown previously in *Figure 3-6*.
> Type or select "vports".

AutoCAD will prompt:

Save/Restore/Delete/Join/SIngle/?/2/<3>/4:

"Save", "Restore", and "Delete" allow you to keep view port configurations in memory once they have been created. "Join" will reduce the number of view ports by joining two adjacent windows. "SIngle" returns you to a single window. "?" will give you a list of view port configurations you have previously saved. The numbers 2, 3, and 4 specify numbers of windows. We will use two windows in this exercise.

> Type or select "2".

AutoCAD wants to know which way to split the screen:

Horizontal/<Vertical>:

We will create a vertical split.

> Type "v" or press enter (since vertical is the default).

Your screen will be redrawn as shown in *Figure 3-10*.

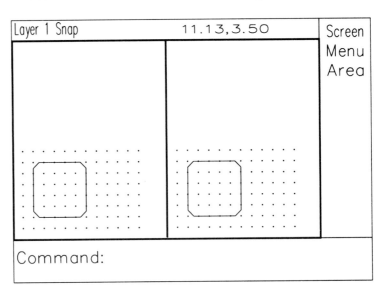

**Figure 3-10**

> Now, move your cursor back and forth between the two windows.

You will see the cross hairs whenever you are in the right view port and a small arrow when you are in the left view port. This indicates that the right view port is currently active. You can perform drawing or editing in the current view port only. However, any changes you make will be immediately reflected in all view ports.

> Move the cursor to the left view port and press the pick button.

The cross hairs will appear on the left. The left view port is now active. If you move back to the right you will see the arrow.

Often you can switch view ports while you are in the middle of a command sequence. With some commands, such as ZOOM and PAN, this will not work.
> With the left view port active, enter the ZOOM command and zoom in on a window around the lower left corner of the square.

Your screen should now resemble *Figure 3-11.*

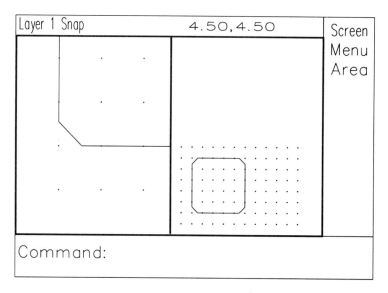

**Figure 3-11**

To complete this exercise, you may want to do some simple drawing and editing in each view port and observe how your changes appear in both view ports.

From here, you will be on your own with multiple view ports until Chapter 13. None of the drawings will require multiple view ports, but you may try them at any time if you wish. If you want more information, see the *AutoCAD Reference Manual,* Section 6.7.

Before going on, return to a single view port by using the "Single" option.

> Type or select "vports".
> Type or select "single".

Notice that the new display is derived from whichever view port was active before you executed the single option.

## TASKS 10, 11, 12, and 13

With layers, colors, linetypes, fillets, chamfers, zooming, and panning you are ready to do the drawings for Chapter 3. Congratulations, you are learning.

Remember to set grid, snap, and units and to define layers before you begin each drawing. Use the ZOOM and PAN commands whenever you think they would help you to draw more efficiently.

## DRAWING 3-1: MOUNTING PLATE

This drawing will give you experience using center lines and chamfers. Since there are no hidden lines, you will have no need for layer 2, but we will continue to use the same numbering system for consistency. Draw the continuous lines in red on layer 1 and the center lines in green on layer 3.

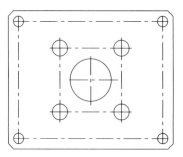

### *DRAWING SUGGESTIONS*

GRID = .5
SNAP = .25
LTSCALE = .5

### *LTSCALE*

The size of the individual dashes and spaces that make up center lines, hidden lines, and other linetypes is determined by a global setting called "LTSCALE". By default it is set to a factor of 1.00. In smaller drawings this setting will be too large and cause some of the shorter lines to appear continuous regardless of what layer they are on.

To remedy this, change LTSCALE as follows:

1. Type or select "LTSCALE".
2. Enter a value.

For the drawings in this chapter use a setting of .5. See *Figure 3-12* for some examples of the effect of changing LTSCALE.

> Draw the chamfered rectangle and the nine circles on layer 1 first. Then set current layer to 3 and draw the center lines.

NOTE: In manual drafting it would be more common to draw the center lines first and use them to position the circles. Either order is fine, but be aware that what is standard practice in pencil and paper drafting may not be efficient or necessary on a CAD system.

———  —  ———   LTSCALE = 1.00

——  -  ———  -  ——   LTSCALE =   .50

—  -  ——  -  ——  -  ——   LTSCALE =   .25

**Figure 3-12**

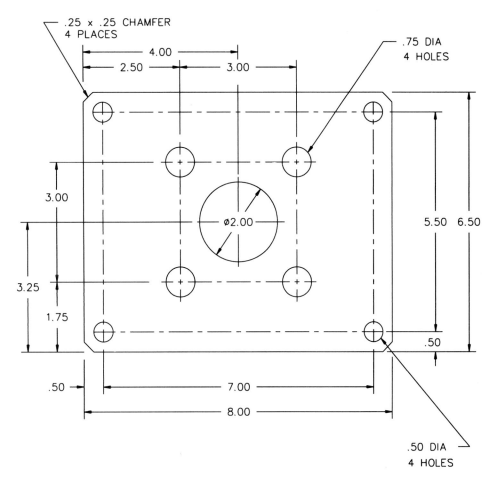

.25 x .25 CHAMFER
4 PLACES

.75 DIA
4 HOLES

Ø2.00

.50 DIA
4 HOLES

# MOUNTING PLATE
## Drawing 3-1

| LAYERS | NAME | COLOR | LINETYPE | | |
|--------|------|-------|----------|---|---|
| | 0 | WHITE | ———— CONTINUOUS | (DRAW) | LINE |
| | 1 | RED | ———— CONTINUOUS | (DRAW) | CIRCLE |
| | | | | (EDIT) | CHAMFER |
| | 3 | GREEN | —·—·— CENTER | (DISPLAY) | ZOOM |

| F1 | F6 | F7 | F8 | F9 |
|----|----|----|----|----|
| ON/OFF | ON/OFF | ON/OFF | ON/OFF | ON/OFF |
| SCREEN | COORDS | GRID | ORTHO | SNAP |

## DRAWING 3-2: STEPPED SHAFT

This two-view drawing uses continuous lines, center lines, chamfers, and fillets. You may want to zoom in to enlarge the drawing space you are actually working in, and pan right and left to work on the two views.

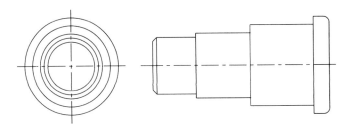

### *DRAWING SUGGESTIONS*

GRID = .25

SNAP = .125

LTSCALE = .5

> Center the front view in the neighborhood of (2,5). The right side view will then have a starting point at about (5,4.12), before the chamfer cuts this corner off.

> Draw the circles in the front view first, using the vertical dimensions from the side view for diameters. Save the inner circle until after you have drawn and chamfered the right side view.

> Draw a series of rectangles for the side view, lining them up with the circles of the front view. Then chamfer two corners of the leftmost rectangle and fillet two corners of the rightmost rectangle.

> Use the chamfer on the side view to line up the radius of the inner circle.

> Remember to set current layer to 3 before drawing the center line through the side view.

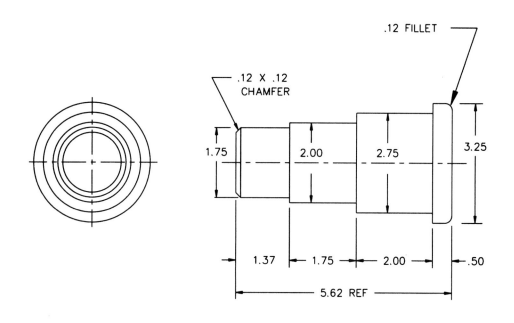

STEPPED SHAFT

Drawing 3-2

| LAYERS | NAME | COLOR | LINETYPE | | | |
|---|---|---|---|---|---|---|
| | 0 | WHITE | ———————— CONTINUOUS | | (DRAW) | LINE |
| | 1 | RED | ———————— CONTINUOUS | | (DRAW) | CIRCLE |
| | | | | | (EDIT) | CHAMFER |
| | 3 | GREEN | — - — CENTER | | (EDIT) | FILLET |
| | | | | | (DISPLAY) | ZOOM |

| F1 | F6 | F7 | F8 | F9 |
|---|---|---|---|---|
| ON/OFF | ON/OFF | ON/OFF | ON/OFF | ON/OFF |
| SCREEN | COORDS | GRID | ORTHO | SNAP |

## DRAWING 3-3: BASE PLATE

This drawing uses continuous lines, hidden lines, center lines, and fillets. The side view should be quite easy once the front view is drawn. Remember to change layers when you want to change linetypes.

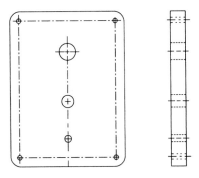

### *DRAWING SUGGESTIONS*

GRID = .25

SNAP = .125

LTSCALE = .5

> Study the dimensions carefully and remember that every grid increment is .25, while snap points not on the grid are exactly halfway between grid points. The four circles at the corners are .38 (actually .375 rounded off) over and in from the corner points. This is three snap spaces (.375 = 3 × .125).

> Position the three circles along the center line of the rectangle carefully. Notice that dimensions are given from the center of the screw holes at top and bottom.

> Use the circle perimeters to line up the hidden lines on the side view, and the centers to line up the center lines.

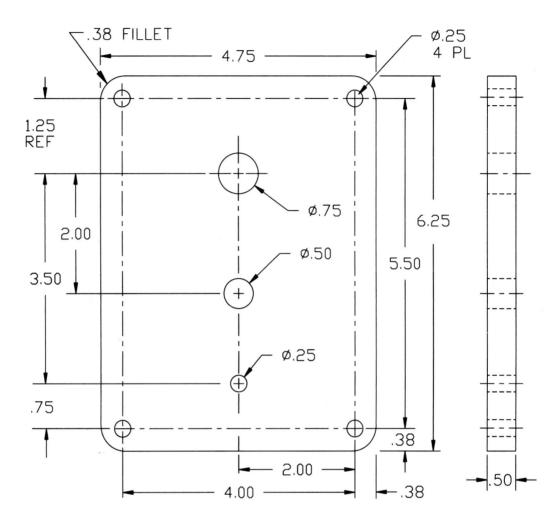

.38 FILLET

Ø.25
4 PL

4.75

1.25
REF

2.00

3.50

6.25

5.50

Ø.75

Ø.50

Ø.25

.75

.38

2.00

.38

4.00

.50

BASE PLATE

Drawing 3-3

| LAYERS | NAME | COLOR | LINETYPE | | | |
|--------|------|-------|----------|---|---|---|
| | 0 | WHITE | ———— | CONTINUOUS | (DRAW) | LINE |
| | 1 | RED | ———— | CONTINUOUS | (DRAW) | CIRCLE |
| | 2 | YELLOW | -------- | HIDDEN | (EDIT) | FILLET |
| | 3 | GREEN | —·—·— | CENTER | (DISPLAY) | ZOOM |

| F1 | F6 | F7 | F8 | F9 |
|----|----|----|----|----|
| ON/OFF SCREEN | ON/OFF COORDS | ON/OFF GRID | ON/OFF ORTHO | ON/OFF SNAP |

## DRAWING 3-4: BUSHING

This drawing will give you practice in chamfers, layers, and zooming. Notice that because of the smaller dimensions here, we have recommended a smaller LTSCALE setting.

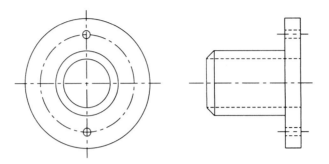

### *DRAWING SUGGESTIONS*

GRID = .25
SNAP = .125
LTSCALE = .25

> Since this drawing will appear quite small on your screen, it would be a good idea to ZOOM in on the actual drawing space you are using, and use PAN if necessary.
> Notice that the two .25 diameter screw holes are 1.50 apart. This puts them squarely on grid points that you will have no trouble finding.

### *REGEN*

When you zoom you may find that your circles turn into polygons. AutoCAD does this to save time. These time savings are not noticeable now, but when you get into larger drawings they become very significant. If you want to see a proper circle, type or select "REGEN". This command will cause your drawing to be regenerated more precisely from the data you have given.

You may also notice that REGENs happen automatically when certain operations are performed, such as adding new layers, or changing the LTSCALE setting after objects are already on the screen.

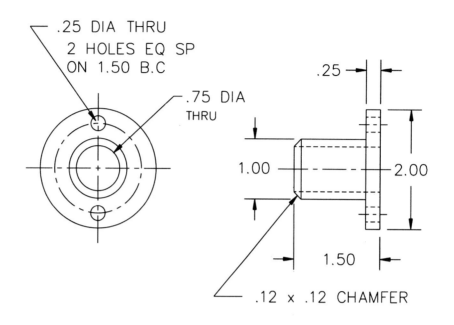

.25 DIA THRU
2 HOLES EQ SP
ON 1.50 B.C

.75 DIA
THRU

.25

1.00

2.00

1.50

.12 x .12 CHAMFER

## BUSHING
## Drawing 3—4

| LAYERS | NAME | COLOR | LINETYPE | | (DRAW) | LINE |
|--------|------|-------|----------|-------------|----------|--------|
| | 0 | WHITE | ———— | CONTINUOUS | (DRAW) | CIRCLE |
| | 1 | RED | ———— | CONTINUOUS | (EDIT) | CHAMFER |
| | 2 | YELLOW | - - - - - | HIDDEN | (DISPLAY) | ZOOM |
| | 3 | GREEN | — - — | CENTER | | |

| F1 | F6 | F7 | F8 | F9 |
|----|----|----|----|----|
| ON/OFF | ON/OFF | ON/OFF | ON/OFF | ON/OFF |
| SCREEN | COORDS | GRID | ORTHO | SNAP |

# DRAWING 3-5: HALF BLOCK

This cinder block is the first project using architectural units in this book. Set units, grid, and snap as indicated, and everything will fall into place nicely.

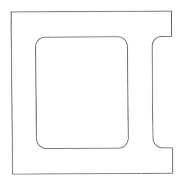

## *DRAWING SUGGESTIONS*

UNITS = Architectural

           smallest fraction = 4   (1/4″ )

GRID = 1/4″

SNAP = 1/4″

> Start with the lower left corner of the block at the point (0′-1″,0′-1″) to keep the drawing well placed on the display.
> After drawing the outside of the block with the 5 1/2″ indentation on the right, use the DIST command to locate the inner rectangle 1 1/4″ in from each side.
> Set the FILLET radius to 1/2″ or .5. Notice that you can use decimal versions of fractions. The advantage is that they are easier to type.
> Use MULTIPLE FILLET to fillet the six corners.

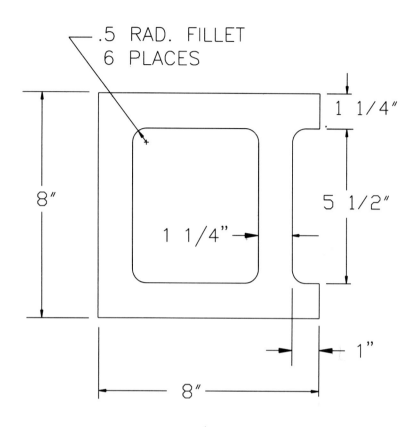

.5 RAD. FILLET
6 PLACES

1 1/4"

8"

5 1/2"

1 1/4"

1"

8"

HALF BLOCK

Drawing 3—5

| LAYERS | NAME | COLOR | LINETYPE | | | (DRAW) | LINE |
|--------|------|-------|----------|---|---|---------|-------|
| | 0 | WHITE | ——————— | CONTINUOUS | | (EDIT) | FILLET |
| | | | | | | (EDIT) | ERASE |
| | 1 | RED | ——————— | CONTINUOUS | | (DISPLAY) | ZOOM |

| F1 | F6 | F7 | F8 | F9 |
|----|----|----|----|----|
| ON/OFF | ON/OFF | ON/OFF | ON/OFF | ON/OFF |
| SCREEN | COORDS | GRID | ORTHO | SNAP |

# chapter

**COMMANDS**

| EDIT | SETTINGS | INQUIRY |
|------|----------|---------|
| COPY | LIMITS | STATUS |
| MOVE | | DIST |
| ARRAY | | |

SPECIAL TOPIC: PROTOTYPE DRAWINGS

**OVERVIEW**

In this chapter you will learn some real timesavers. If you have grown tired of defining the same three layers, along with units, grid, snap, and ltscale for each new drawing, read on. You are about to learn how to define a prototype drawing so that every time you begin a new drawing you will begin with whatever setup you want.

In addition, you will learn to reshape the grid using the LIMITS command and to COPY, MOVE, and ARRAY objects on the screen so that you do not have to draw the same thing twice.

We will begin with LIMITS, since we will want to change the limits as part of defining your prototype.

**TASKS**

1. Change the shape of the grid using the LIMITS command.
2. Create a prototype drawing.
3. Configure AutoCAD to use your prototype.
4. Draw an object and make copies of it.
5. Move an object on the screen.
6. Create multiple copies of an object using ARRAY.
7. Do Drawing 4-1 ("Pattern").
8. Do Drawing 4-2 ("Grill").
9. Do Drawing 4-3 ("Weave").
10. Do Drawing 4-4 ("Test Bracket").
11. Do Drawing 4-5 ("Floor Framing").

### TASK 1: Setting LIMITS

*Procedure.*

1. Type or select "LIMITS".
2. Enter lower left-hand coordinates.
3. Enter upper right-hand coordinates.
4. ZOOM All.

*Discussion.* By now you have changed the density of the screen grid many times, but that empty space on the right, next to the screen menu area, is still there. In Chapter 1 we explained that this is because the grid is presently shaped to represent an "A" size (12 × 9) piece of paper. Now you will learn how to change the shape, first to cover the whole screen, and then to emulate other sheet sizes, or any other space you want to represent.

> Begin a new drawing named "B" or "A:B". After we are finished exploring the LIMITS command, we will use this drawing as your B size prototype.
> Use F7 to turn the grid on.
> Type or select "LIMITS".
AutoCAD will prompt you as follows:

ON/OFF/<lower left corner> <0.0000,0.0000>:

The ON and OFF options determine what happens when you attempt to draw outside the limits of the grid. With LIMITS off, nothing will happen. With LIMITS on, you will get a message that says "Attempt to draw outside of limits". Also, with LIMITS on, AutoCAD will not accept any attempt to begin an entity outside of limits, but will allow you to extend objects beyond the limits as long as they were started within them. By default, LIMITS is off, and we will leave it that way.
> Press enter.
This will enter the default values for the lower left corner (0,0). Another common practice is to move the point (0,0) in slightly from the corner of the screen by using something like (−1,−1) as your lower left limit. This will put the (0,0) point over 1 and up 1. If you do this, remember that you will also have to change the upper right corner if you want to retain sheet sizes and shapes.
For now we will leave the lower left corner at (0,0).
AutoCAD will give you a second prompt:

Upper right corner <12.0000,9.0000>:

Notice the default coordinates. These determine the shape of the grid you have been working with. We will change them so that the grid fills the screen.
> Type "14,9".
When you have entered these new coordinates, the grid will be redrawn with its new shape, which covers the display area.

Next let's set the limits to emulate a "B" size sheet of paper.

> Type or select "LIMITS". (Or press enter if you have not used other commands).
> Press enter to keep the lower left corner at (0,0).
> Type (18,12).
The grid will be regenerated, but you will not see any change. Under the new limits, the complete grid has become larger than the present display, but you are only seeing part of it.

Whenever you set limits larger or smaller than the current display, you will have to do a ZOOM All to see the display defined according to the new limits.

> Type or select "ZOOM".

> Type "A" or select "All".

You should now have an 18 × 12 grid on your screen. Place the cursor on the upper right-hand grid point to check its coordinates. This is the grid you will use for a "B" size prototype.

We suggest that you continue to experiment with setting limits, and that you try some of the possibilities listed in *Figure 4-1*, which is a table of sheet sizes.

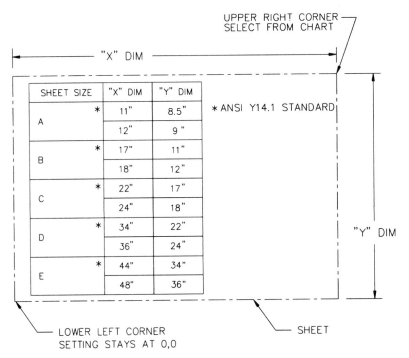

| SHEET SIZE | | "X" DIM | "Y" DIM |
|---|---|---|---|
| A | * | 11" | 8.5" |
| | | 12" | 9 " |
| B | * | 17" | 11" |
| | | 18" | 12" |
| C | * | 22" | 17" |
| | | 24" | 18" |
| D | * | 34" | 22" |
| | | 36" | 24" |
| E | * | 44" | 34" |
| | | 48" | 36" |

**Figure 4-1**

Notice that there are two sets of standards commonly in use. Sometimes the standard you use will be determined by your plotter. This is particularly true for the larger sheet sizes. Some plotters that plot on C size paper, for example, will take a 24″ × 18″ sheet but not a 22″ × 17″.

Also, be aware that using limits to emulate sheet sizes is by no means a necessary practice. There are other factors which may be more important in determining limits, depending on the application. It is not uncommon to go by sheet size as we are doing here; you should realize, however, that with AutoCAD you will be able to scale your drawing to fit any sheet size when it comes time to plot it. Some people, especially those experienced in manual drafting, prefer to think in terms of the sheet of paper they will be plotting on from the very beginning of the drawing process. Others prefer to draw with only full scale dimensions in mind and not be concerned with paper size and scale until they are actually plotting.

## AutoCAD's Setup Utility

If you are using the AutoCAD standard menu, there is a "setup" utility on the screen menu, which can also be used to set limits according to sheet sizes. Simply select "SETUP" from the main menu and then select the style of units, the scale, and the sheet size you want (you will notice that AutoCAD has included some nonstandard sheet sizes). The Setup utility, which is actually an AutoLISP program, will set limits accordingly and put a border on the screen. The border can be easily erased if you don't want it there. Try it if you like, using the following procedure:

1. Select "SETUP" from the screen menu.
2. Select a unit style.
3. Select a scale.
4. Select a sheet size.
5. Erase the border.

> Finally, in preparation for creating a "B" size prototype, return LIMITS to (0,0) and (18,12), using the LIMITS command, and then ZOOM All.

You are now in the drawing that we will use for your prototype, so it is not necessary to begin a new one for the next section.

## TASK 2: Creating a prototype

*Procedure.*

1. Begin a new drawing with a name appropriate for the prototype.
2. Define layers and change settings (grid, snap, units, limits, ltscale, etc.) as desired.
3. Type END to save the prototype.

*Discussion.*    You have been using a prototype drawing all along without knowing it. It is the AutoCAD default prototype, called ACAD.dwg. It is this file which has determined the default settings that you are now accustomed to seeing whenever you begin a new drawing. GRID and SNAP are set to 1, UNITS to 4-place decimal, LIMITS to 12 × 9, and LTSCALE to 1, among other things.

To make your own prototype, so that new drawings will begin with the settings you want, all you have to do is create a drawing that has those settings and then tell AutoCAD that this is the drawing you want to use to define your initial drawing setup.

The first part should be easy for you now, since you have been doing your own drawing setup for each new drawing in this book.

> Make changes to the present drawing ("B.dwg") as follows:

| GRID | 1.00 ON (F7) | COORD | ON (F6) |
|------|--------------|-------|---------|
| SNAP | 0.25 ON (F9) | LTSCALE | 0.5 |
| UNITS | 2-Place Decimal | LIMITS | (0,0) - (18,12) |

## STATUS

At this point, we suggest that you try out the STATUS command. Status gives you information on the current settings in your drawing, including limits, drawing uses (coordinates of actual area in use), display area, snap, grid, and current layer. There is additional information that we have not covered yet, but we will by the end of the book.

> To see the STATUS display, simply type or select "status".
>      AutoCAD will automatically flip over to the text screen.
> When you are ready to move on, press F1 to return to the graphics screen, or continue working on the text screen.

> Create the following layers and associated colors and linetypes.

Remember that you can make changes to your prototype at any time. The layers called "text," "hatch," and "dim" will not be used until Chapters 7 and 8, in which we introduce text, hatch patterns, and dimensions to your drawings. Creating them now will save time and avoid confusion later on.

Layer 0 is already defined.

| Layer name | State | Color | Linetype |
|---|---|---|---|
| 0 | On | 7 (white) | CONTINUOUS |
| 1 | On | 1 (red) | CONTINUOUS |
| 2 | On | 2 (yellow) | HIDDEN |
| 3 | On | 3 (green) | CENTER |
| TEXT | On | 4 (cyan) | CONTINUOUS |
| HATCH | On | 5 (blue) | CONTINUOUS |
| DIM | On | 6 (magenta) | CONTINUOUS |

> When all changes are made, type or select "END" to save your drawing and exit the drawing editor.

NOTE: Do not leave anything drawn on your screen or it will come up as part of the prototype each time you open a new drawing. For some applications this may be useful. For now we want a blank prototype.

If you have followed instructions up to this point, you should now be at the Auto-CAD Main Menu, and B.dwg should be on file. We will now make it your prototype.

## TASK 3: Configuring AutoCAD to use your prototype

*See your instructor before proceeding with this section. Because other people probably use the workstation you are working at, your instructor will want to manage your use of a prototype carefully.*

NOTE TO INSTRUCTORS: If your workstations are used for many classes, you may not want students reconfiguring the prototype. An efficient alternative is to use the equal sign. Students can save their own prototype on a disk and load it whenever they begin a new drawing by typing <new drawing name>=A:<prototype name>.

*Procedure.*

1. Type "5" at the Main Menu.
2. Press enter to move beyond the configuration information screen.
3. Type "8" at the Configuring AutoCAD menu.
4. Type "2" at the Operating parameters menu.
5. Type the name of the new prototype.
6. Type "0" to exit the Operating parameters menu.
7. Type "0" to exit the Configuring AutoCAD menu.
8. Type "Y" or press enter to confirm changes in configuration.

*Discussion.*   Despite the length of this procedure list, configuring AutoCAD to use your drawing as the prototype is really quite simple. You will move through a series of three menus, enter the name of your prototype, and then walk backwards to the Main Menu again. The first thing to remember is this: *Unless you know what you are doing, do not change anything other than the prototype!*

The second thing to remember is that if you do accidentally change the configuration in some unwanted way, you will have a chance to cancel your changes before you are done.

> At the Main Menu, type "5" to select "Configure AutoCAD".

This choice will be followed by a screen that gives you information on your current AutoCAD configuration. You will see information about the video display you are using, your digitizer, your plotter, and your printer. Look over this information and then move on.

> Press enter to move to the next screen.
This will bring you to the Configuring AutoCAD menu, which has eight options.
> Type "8" to select "Operating parameters".
This will bring you to the Operating parameters menu, which has four options.
> Type "2" to select "Initial drawing setup".
Congratulations! You have arrived. You will now see the following prompt:

Enter name of default prototype file for new drawings or . for none <.>:

The current prototype is the ACAD default drawing, which has the same settings as you will get if you respond with a "." for none.
> Type "B".
When you have entered your drawing file name, AutoCAD will return you to the last menu—Operating parameters.
Your B.dwg is now ready to become the prototype, but you still have to exit the configuration menu system before AutoCAD will register this change.
> Type "0" to select "Exit to configuration menu".
This will bring you back to the Configuration menu.
> Type "0" again to select "Exit to Main Menu".
Before letting you go, AutoCAD will give you a chance to change your mind. You will see this prompt:

If you answer N to the following question, all configuration changes
you have just made will be discarded <Y>:

> Type "y" or press enter.

Your configuration change has now been confirmed. You should be back to the Main Menu. If you begin a new drawing now it will be like taking up where you left off; all the changes you made to B.dwg will be there already.

NOTE: There is one other way to control your initial drawing setup. Suppose that you have created three or four different prototypes that you want to use at different times for different projects. You might, for example, have C, D, and E size prototypes as well as a B size. With B as the standard prototype it is still easy to begin a drawing using some other drawing file for the initial setup.

To open a new drawing called GIZMO.dwg and use the setup from C.dwg, for example, you would use the following procedure:

1.  At the Main Menu type 1 to begin a new drawing.
2.  In answer to the prompt for a new drawing name type "GIZMO=C" or "GIZMO=A:C".

The format for this response, then, is:

<new drawing name>=<alternate prototype>

And finally, if you wanted to return to the AutoCAD prototype settings that you have been using up until now, you would simply drop the second name, like this:

<new drawing name>=

Now, in preparation for learning about the MOVE command, begin a new drawing named "4-1" or "A:4-1".

## TASK 4: Using the MOVE command

*Procedure.*

1. Type or select "MOVE".
2. Define a selection set.
3. Press enter when selection is complete.
4. Choose the base point of a displacement vector.
5. Choose a second point.

*Discussion.*   The ability to copy and move objects on the screen is one of the great advantages of working on a CAD system. It can be said that CAD is to drafting as word processing is to typing. Nowhere is this analogy more clear than in the "cut and paste" capacities that the COPY and MOVE commands give you.

> Draw a circle with a radius of 1 somewhere near the center of the screen (9,6), as shown in *Figure 4-2*.

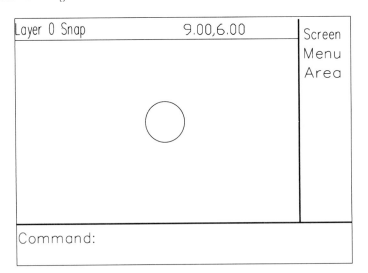

**Figure 4-2**

> Type or select "MOVE".

Just as in ERASE, FILLET, CHAMFER, and many other editing commands, the cross hairs will now be replaced by the selection box. You will use it in the familiar ways to define the set of objects you want to move. In our case this will be the circle you have just drawn. Be aware that the selection set could include as many entities as you like, and that a group of entities could be selected with a window or crossing box.

> Point to the circle.

As in the ERASE command, your circle will become dotted.

> Press enter to indicate that you are through selecting objects.

(If you are using the AutoCAD standard menu and have selected the MOVE command from the pull down system, you can skip this step.)

AutoCAD will now ask where you want to move the objects in the selection set. Most often you will show the movement by defining a vector that gives the distance and direction you want the object to be moved.

The prompt will be this:

Base point or displacement:

We will answer by showing AutoCAD the base point of a vector.

NOTE: In order to define movement with a vector, all AutoCAD needs is a distance and a direction. Therefore, the base point does not have to be on or near the object you are moving. Any point will do, as long as you can use it to show how you want your objects moved. This may seem strange at first, but it will soon become quite natural. Of course, you may choose a point on the object if you wish. With a circle, the center point may be convenient.

> Point to any location not too near the right side of the screen.

AutoCAD will give you a "rubber band" from the point you have indicated and will ask for a second point:

Second point of displacement:

As soon as you begin to move the cursor, you will see that AutoCAD also gives you a circle to drag so that you can immediately see the effect of the movement you are indicating.

Let's say you want to move the circle 3.00 to the right. Watch the coordinate display and stretch the "rubber band" out until the display reads 3.00<0, as in *Figure 4-3*.

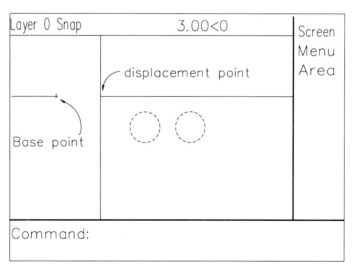

**Figure 4-3**

> Select a point 3.00 to the right of your base point.

The rubber band and your original circle disappear, leaving you a circle in the new location.

Now, if ortho is on, turn it off (F8) and try a diagonal move.

> Type or select "MOVE", or press enter to repeat the command. (If you are working with the pull down system, the command is repeated automatically.)

> Reselect the circle by pointing or by typing "p" for previous.

> If you did not select MOVE from the pull down menu, press enter to end the selection process.

> Select a base point.

> Move the circle diagonally in any direction you like. *Figure 4-4* is an example of how this might look.

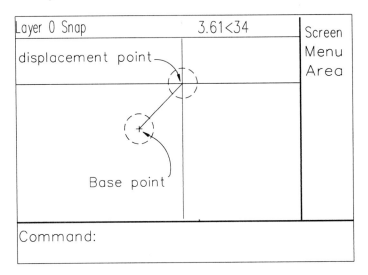

**Figure 4-4**

Try moving the circle back to the center of the screen. It may help to choose the center point of the circle as a base point this time, and choose a point at or near the center of the grid for your second point.

Before you proceed to the COPY command, there is another way to use the MOVE command which is also quite simple and may be convenient in some cases. Instead of showing AutoCAD a distance and direction, you can simply type a horizontal and vertical displacement. Try this:

> Reenter the MOVE command.

> Reselect the circle.

> Type "3,2" in response to the prompt for "base point or displacement".

> Press enter in response to the prompt for a second point.

    The circle will be moved three to the right and up two.

    Finally, move the circle back using negative displacement values.

> Reselect MOVE.

> Reselect the circle.

> Type "-3,-2".

> Press enter.

    The circle will be moved three to the left and two down.

(> If the menu system you are using repeats the MOVE command automatically, remember to cancel the command before going on.)

## TASK 5: Using the COPY command

*Procedure.*

1.  Type or select "COPY".

2. Define a selection set.
3. Press enter to end the selection process.
4. Choose a base point.
5. Choose a second point.

*Discussion.*    The COPY command works so much like the MOVE command that you should find it quite easy to learn at this point. The main difference is that the original object will not disappear when the second point of the displacement vector is given. Also there is an additional option, to make multiple copies of the same object, which we will explore in a moment.

But first, we suggest that you try making several copies of the circle in various positions on the screen. Try making copies both by showing points that define displacement vectors and by typing x and y displacement values. Both of these methods work just as they do in the MOVE command.

When you are satisfied that you know how to use these two versions of the COPY command, move on to the MULTIPLE copy option. What this option does is allow you to show a whole series of vectors starting at the same base point, and AutoCAD will place copies of your selection set accordingly.

> Type or select "COPY".
> Point to one of the circles on your screen.
> If you did not select COPY from the pull down menu, press enter to end the selection process.
> Type "m" or select "multiple".
> Show AutoCAD a base point.
> Show AutoCAD a second point.

You will see a new copy of the circle, and notice also that the prompt for a "Second point of displacement" has returned in the command area. AutoCAD is waiting for another vector, using the same base point as before.

> Show AutoCAD another second point.
> Show AutoCAD another second point.

Repeat as many times as you wish. If you get into this you may begin to feel like a magician pulling ring after ring out of thin air and scattering them across the screen. The results will appear something like *Figure 4-5*.

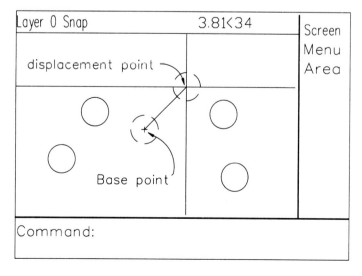

**Figure 4-5**

### TASK 6: Using the ARRAY command—rectangular arrays

*Procedure.*

1. Type or select "ARRAY".
2. Define a selection set.
3. Press enter to end selection.
4. Type "r" or select "rectangular".
5. Enter the number of rows in the array.
6. Enter the number of columns.
7. Enter the distance between rows.
8. Enter the distance between columns.

*Discussion.*    The ARRAY command gives you a powerful alternative to simple copying. It takes an object or group of objects and copies it a specific number of times in mathematically defined, evenly spaced, locations. An array is a repetition in matrix form of the same figure.

There are two types of arrays. Rectangular arrays are linear and defined by rows and columns. Polar arrays are angular and based on the repetition of objects around the circumference of an arc or circle. The dots on the grid are an example of a rectangular array; the lines on any circular dial are an example of a polar array.

Both types are common. We will explore rectangular arrays in this chapter and polar arrays in the next.

> In preparation for this exercise, erase all the circles from your screen. Then draw a single circle, radius .5, centered at the point (2,2).
> Type or select "ARRAY".
> Point to the circle.
> Press enter to end the selection process.
   AutoCAD will now ask which type of array you want:

   Rectangular/Polar array (R/P):

> Type "r" or select "rectangular".
   AutoCAD will prompt you for the number of rows in the array.

   Number of rows (---) <1>:

The (---) is to remind you of what a row looks like, i.e., it is horizontal.

The default is 1. So if you press enter you will get a single row of circles. The number of circles in the row will depend, then, on the number of columns you specify.

We will ask for three rows instead of just one.
> Type "3".
   AutoCAD now asks for the number of columns in the array:

   Number of columns (||||) <1>:

Using the same format, (|||) reminds you that columns are vertical. The default is 1 again. What would an array with three rows and only one column look like?
> Type "5".

   Now AutoCAD needs to know how far apart to place all these circles. There will be 15 of them in this example—three rows with five circles in each row.

AutoCAD prompts:

Unit cell or distance between rows (---):

"Unit cell" means that you can respond by showing two corners of a window. The horizontal side of this window would give the space between columns; the vertical side would give the space between rows. You could do this exercise by showing a 1 × 1 window. We will use the more basic method of typing values for these distances. The distance between rows will be a vertical measure.
> Type "1".

AutoCAD now asks for the horizontal distance between columns:

Distance between columns (||||):

> Type "1" again.

You should have a 3 × 5 array of circles, as shown in *Figure 4-6*.

Notice that AutoCAD builds arrays up and to the right. This is consistent with the coordinate system, which puts positive values to the right on the horizontal (x) axis, and upwards on the vertical (y) axis. Negative values can be used to create arrays in other directions, as we will do soon.

But first let's use the array now on your screen as the selection set to create another array. We will specify an array that has three rows and three columns, with 3.00 between rows and 5.00 between columns. This will keep our circles touching without overlapping.

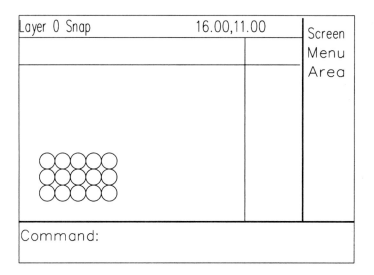

**Figure 4-6**

> Type or select "ARRAY" or press enter to repeat the ARRAY command.
> Using a window, select the whole array of 15 circles.
> Press enter to end the selection process.
> Type "r" or select "rectangular".
> Type "3" for the number of rows.
> Type "3" for the number of columns.
> Type "3" for the distance between rows.
> Type "5" for the distance between columns.

You should now have a screen full of circles, as in *Figure 4-7*.

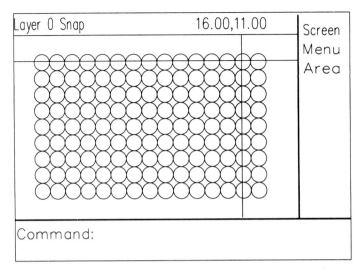

**Figure 4-7**

When you are ready to move on, we will use the "U" command to undo the last two arrays.

> Type "U" to undo the second array.

> Type "U" again to undo the first array.

You should now be back to your original circle centered at (2,2). Notice that the "U" command works nicely to undo an incorrectly drawn array quickly. This is important to know, because it is easy to make mistakes creating arrays. Be aware, however, that for other purposes the objects in an array are treated as separate entities, just as if you had drawn them one by one.

We will now try using some negative distances to create arrays right and down, left and up, and left and down.

> First, use the MOVE command to move your circle to the middle of the screen.

> Type or select "ARRAY".

> Select the circle by pointing or typing "L" for last.

> Press enter to end the selection process.

> Type "r" or select "rectangular".

> Type "3" for the number of rows.

> Type "3" for the number of columns.

> Type "−2" for the distance between rows.

> Type "2" for the distance between columns.

Your array should be built down and over. The −2 distance between rows causes the array to be built going down. The positive 2 distance between columns causes the array to be built across to the right.

Repeat the procedure to create similar arrays from the same circle going left and up, left and down, and right and up. The following table should help.

|            | Dist. between Rows | Dist. between Columns |
|------------|--------------------|------------------------|
| Right,Up   | 2                  | 2                      |
| Left,Up    | 2                  | −2                     |
| Left,Down  | −2                 | −2                     |
| Right,Down | −2                 | 2                      |

NOTE: After an array has been drawn, the "last" drawn entity is the last object in the array to appear on the screen. A "last" selection will select this object. If you want to reselect the selection set used to create the array (in this case the original circle in the center of the screen), use a "previous" selection. "Last," then, refers to the last drawn entity, while "previous" refers to the previous selection set.

## TASKS 7, 8, 9, and 10

All the drawings in this chapter will use your new prototype. Whether you have configured AutoCAD's initial drawing setup or use the equal sign to load your prototype, the settings and layers should be as you have defined them. Do not expect, however, that you will never need to change them. Layers will stay the same throughout this book, but limits will change from time to time, and grid and snap will change frequently.

The main thing you should be focused on in doing these drawings is to become increasingly familiar with the COPY and ARRAY commands.

## DRAWING 4-1: PATTERN

This drawing will give you practice using the COPY command. There are numerous ways in which the drawing could be done. The key is to try to take advantage of the repetition in the pattern by copying in an efficient manner. The following figures suggest one way it could be done.

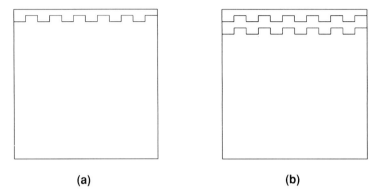

(a)                                           (b)

### DRAWING SUGGESTIONS

GRID = .5

SNAP = .25

> Begin with a 6 × 6 square. Then draw the first set of lines as in *Reference 4-1a*.
> Copy the first set down .5 to produce *Reference 4-1b*.
> Draw the first set of "v" shaped lines. Then use a multiple copy to produce *Reference 4-1c*.
> Finally, make a single copy of all the lines you have so far, using a window for selection. (Be careful not to select the outside lines.) Watch the displacement carefully and you will produce *Reference 4-1d*, the completed drawing.

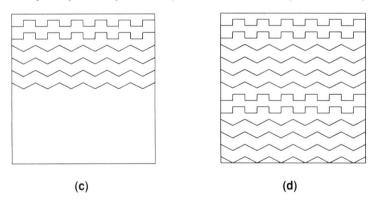

(c)                                           (d)

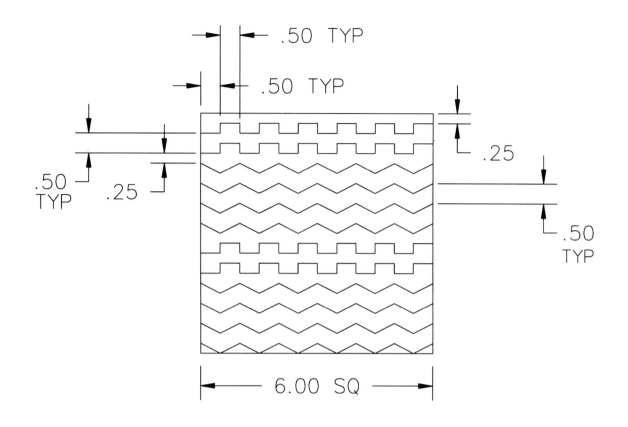

.50 TYP

.50 TYP

.25

.50
TYP

.25

.50
TYP

6.00 SQ

PATTERN

Drawing 4—1

| LAYERS | NAME | COLOR | LINETYPE | | (DRAW) | LINE |
|--------|------|-------|----------|------------|-----------|--------|
| | 0 | WHITE | ———— | CONTINUOUS | (EDIT) | COPY |
| | 1 | RED | ———— | CONTINUOUS | (DISPLAY) | REDRAW |

| F1 | F6 | F7 | F8 | F9 |
|----|----|----|----|----|
| ON/OFF | ON/OFF | ON/OFF | ON/OFF | ON/OFF |
| SCREEN | COORDS | GRID | ORTHO | SNAP |

## DRAWING 4-2: GRILL

This drawing should go very quickly if you use the ARRAY command.

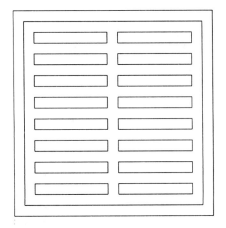

### *DRAWING SUGGESTIONS*

GRID = .5
SNAP = .25

> Begin with a 4.75 × 4.75 square.
> Move in .25 all around to do the inside square.
> Draw the rectangle in the lower left-hand corner first, then use the ARRAY command to create the rest.
> Also remember that you can quickly undo a misplaced array using the "U" command.

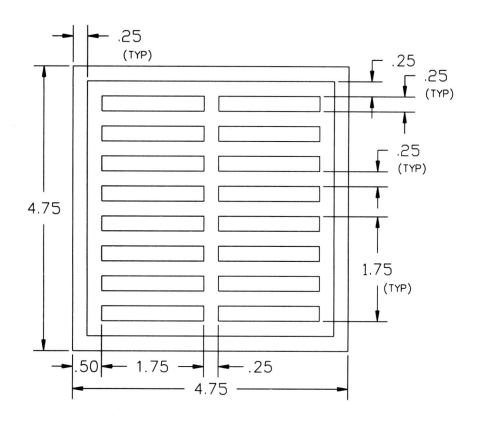

GRILL
Drawing 4-2

| LAYERS | NAME | COLOR | LINETYPE | | | LINE |
|--------|------|-------|----------|--|--|------|
| | 0 | WHITE | ———— CONTINUOUS | (DRAW) | LINE |
| | 1 | RED | ———— CONTINUOUS | (EDIT) | COPY |
| | | | | (EDIT) | ARRAY |
| | | | | (DISPLAY) | REDRAW |

F1          F6          F7          F8          F9

ON/OFF      ON/OFF      ON/OFF      ON/OFF      ON/OFF
SCREEN      COORDS      GRID        ORTHO       SNAP

# DRAWING 4-3: WEAVE

As you do this drawing, watch AutoCAD work for you and think about how long it would take to do by hand! The finished drawing will look like *Reference 4-3*. For clarity, the drawing on the next page shows only one cell of the array and its dimensions.

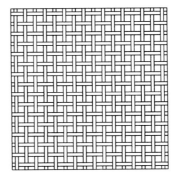

## *DRAWING SUGGESTIONS*

GRID = .25

SNAP = .125

> Draw the 6 × 6 square, then zoom in on the lower left using a window. This will be the area shown in the lower left of the dimensioned drawing.
> Observe the dimensions and draw the line patterns for the lower left corner of the weave. You could use the COPY command in several places if you like, but the time gained will be minimal. Don't worry if you have to fuss with this a little to get it correct; once you've got it right the rest will be easy.
> Use ARRAY to repeat the lower left-hand cell in an 8 × 8 matrix.
> If you get it wrong, use "U" and try again.

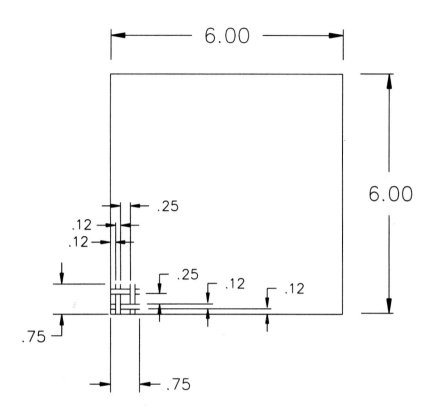

## WEAVE

### Drawing 4-3

| LAYERS | NAME | COLOR | LINETYPE | | (DRAW) | LINE |
|--------|------|-------|----------|---|--------|------|
| | 0 | WHITE | ——— | CONTINUOUS | (EDIT) | ARRAY |
| | 1 | RED | ——— | CONTINUOUS | (DISPLAY) | REDRAW |
| | | | | | (DISPLAY) | ZOOM |

| F1 | F6 | F7 | F8 | F9 |
|----|----|----|----|----|
| ON/OFF | ON/OFF | ON/OFF | ON/OFF | ON/OFF |
| SCREEN | COORDS | GRID | ORTHO | SNAP |

# DRAWING 4-4: TEST BRACKET

This is a great drawing for practicing much of what you have learned up to this point. Notice the suggested snap, grid, ltscale, and limit settings, and use the ARRAY command to draw the 25 circles on the front view.

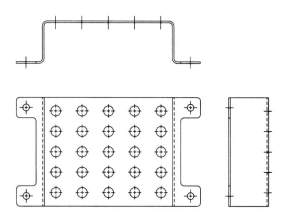

## *DRAWING SUGGESTIONS*

> GRID = .25    LTSCALE = .50
> SNAP = .125    LIMITS  (0,0)  (24,18)

> Be careful to draw all lines on the correct layers, according to their linetypes.
> Draw center lines through circles <u>before</u> copying or arraying them, otherwise you will have to go back and draw them on each individual circle.
> A multiple copy will work nicely for the four .50 diameter holes. A rectangular array is definitely desirable for the twenty-five .75 diameter holes.

## *CREATING CENTER MARKS*
## *WITH THE DIMCEN SYSTEM VARIABLE*

There is a simple way to create the center marks and centerlines shown on all the circles in this drawing. It involves changing the value of a dimension variable called "dimcen" (dimension center). Dimensioning and dimension variables are discussed in Chapter 8, but if you would like to jump ahead, the following procedure will work nicely in this drawing.

> Type "setvar". This command is used to change the value of system variables.
> Type "dimcen" for the name of the variable to change.
> Type "–.09".
> After drawing your first circle, and before arraying it, type "dim". You are now in the dimension command.
> Type "cen", indicating that you want to draw a center mark. This is a very simple dimension feature.
> Point to the circle.

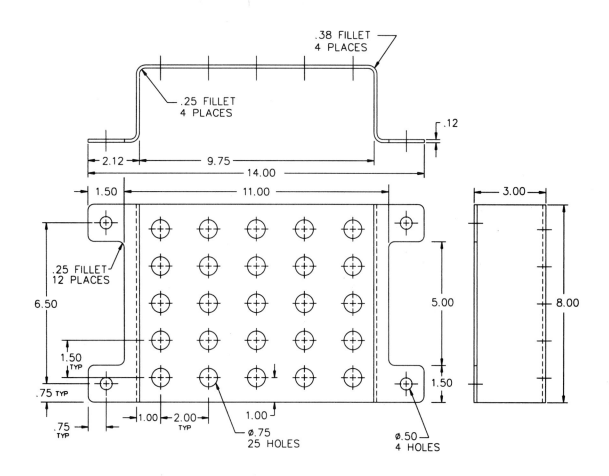

TEST BRACKET

Drawing 4-4

| LAYERS | NAME | COLOR | LINETYPE | | | |
|--------|------|-------|----------|--|--|--|
| | 0 | WHITE | ———— CONTINUOUS | | (DRAW) | LINE |
| | 1 | RED | ———— CONTINUOUS | | (DRAW) | CIRCLE |
| | 2 | YELLOW | - - - - - - HIDDEN | | (EDIT) | FILLET |
| | 3 | GREEN | — - — - CENTER | | (EDIT) | ARRAY |
| | | | | | (DISPLAY) | ZOOM |

| F1 | F6 | F7 | F8 | F9 |
|----|----|----|----|----|
| ON/OFF | ON/OFF | ON/OFF | ON/OFF | ON/OFF |
| SCREEN | COORDS | GRID | ORTHO | SNAP |

# DRAWING 4-5: FLOOR FRAMING

This architectural drawing will require changes in many features of your drawing setup. Pay close attention to the suggested settings.

## DRAWING SUGGESTIONS

UNITS = Architectural,
                 smallest fraction = 1″

LIMITS = 36′, 24′

GRID = 1′

SNAP = 2″

LTSCALE = 12

AXIS = SNAP

> Be sure to use foot (′) and inch (″) symbols when setting limits, grid, and snap (but not ltscale). Also remember that AutoCAD does not accept the dash as part of a coordinate value. A value like 12′-6″ must be entered as 12′6″.

> Begin by drawing the 20′ × 17′-10″ rectangle, with the lower left corner somewhere in the neighborhood of (4′,4′).

> Complete the left and right 2 × 10 joists by copying the vertical 17′-10″ lines 2″ in from each side. You may find it helpful to use the arrow keys when working with such small increments.

> Draw a 19′-8″ horizontal line 2″ up from the bottom and copy it 2″ higher to complete the double joists.

> Array the inner 2 × 10 in a 14 row by 1 column array, with 16″ between rows.

> Set to layer 2 and draw the three 17′-4″ hidden lines down the center.

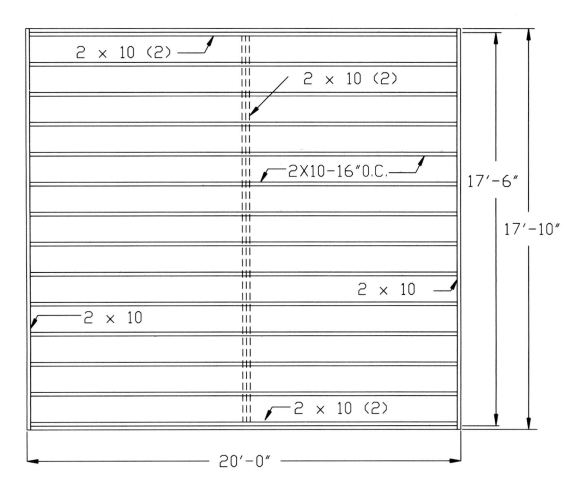

FLOOR FRAMING

Drawing 4—5

| LAYERS | NAME | COLOR | LINETYPE | | | |
|--------|------|-------|----------|--|--|--|
| | 0 | WHITE | ———————— | CONTINUOUS | (DRAW) | LINE |
| | 1 | RED | ———————— | CONTINUOUS | (EDIT) | COPY |
| | 2 | YELLOW | – – – – – | HIDDEN | (EDIT) | ARRAY |
| | | | | | (DISPLAY) | REDRAW |
| | | | | | (DISPLAY) | ZOOM |

| F1 | F6 | F7 | F8 | F9 |
|----|----|----|----|----|
| ON/OFF | ON/OFF | ON/OFF | ON/OFF | ON/OFF |
| SCREEN | COORDS | GRID | ORTHO | SNAP |

# chapter

## COMMANDS

| DRAW | EDIT |
|------|------|
| ARC | ARRAY (polar) |
| | ROTATE |
| | MIRROR |

## OVERVIEW

So far, every drawing you have done has been composed of lines and circles. In this chapter you will learn a third major entity, the ARC. In addition, you will expand your ability to manipulate objects on the screen. You will learn to ROTATE objects and create their MIRROR images. But first, we will pick up where we left off in Chapter 4 by showing you how to create polar arrays.

## TASKS

1. Create three polar arrays.
2. Draw arcs in eight different ways.
3. Rotate a previously drawn object.
4. Create mirror images of previously drawn objects.
5. Do Drawing 5-1 ("Flanged Bushing").
6. Do Drawing 5-2 ("Guide").
7. Do Drawing 5-3 ("Dials").
8. Do Drawing 5-4 ("Alignment Wheel").
9. Do Drawing 5-5 ("Hearth").

### TASK 1: Creating polar arrays

*Procedure.*

1. Type or select "ARRAY".
2. Define a selection set.
3. Press enter to end the selection process.
4. Type "p" or select "polar".
5. Pick a center point.
6. Enter the number of items to be in the array (or press enter).
7. Enter the angle to fill (or 0).
8. Enter the angle between items.
9. Tell whether or not to rotate items.

*Discussion.*    The procedure for creating polar arrays requires some explanation. The first three steps are the same as in rectangular arrays. Step 4 is also the same except that you respond with "polar" or "p" instead of "rectangular" or "r". From here on the steps will be new. First you will pick a center point, and then you will have several options for how you want to define the array.

There are three things that define a polar array, but any two are sufficient. A complete polar array will have: 1) a certain number of items, 2) an angle that these items span, and 3) an angle between each item and the next.

Whichever combination of two of these you use, you will also have to tell Auto-CAD whether or not to rotate the newly created objects as they are copied.

> In preparation for this exercise, begin a new drawing called "5-1" or "A:5-1" and draw a vertical 1.00 line at the bottom center of the screen, near (9.00,2.00), as shown in *Figure 5-1*. We will use a 360 degree polar array to create *Figure 5-2*.

**Figure 5-1**

> Type or select "ARRAY".
> Select the line.
.> Press enter to end selection.
> Type "p" or select "polar".

So far, so good. Nothing new up to this point. Now you have a prompt that looks like this:

Center point of array:

Rectangular arrays are not determined by a center, so we did not encounter this prompt before. Polar arrays, however, are built by copying objects around the circumferences of circles or arcs, so we need a center to define one of these.
> Pick a point directly above the line and somewhat below the center of the screen. Something in the neighborhood of (9.00,4.50) will do.

The next prompt is:

Number of items:

Remember that we have a choice of two out of three among number of items, angle to fill, and angle between items. This time we will give AutoCAD the first two.
> Type "12".

Now that AutoCAD knows that we want 12 items, all it needs is the angle to fill with these, or the angle between each. It will ask first for the angle to fill:

Angle to fill (+=CCW, −=CW) <360>:

The symbols in parentheses tell us that if we give a positive angle the array will be constructed counterclockwise; if we give a negative angle, it will be constructed clockwise. Get used to this; it will come up frequently.

The default is 360 degrees, meaning an array that fills a complete circle.

If we did not give AutoCAD an angle (that is, if we responded with a "0"), we would be prompted for the angle between. This time around we will give 360 as the angle to fill.
> Press enter to accept the default, a complete circle.

AutoCAD now has everything it needs, except that it doesn't know whether we want our lines to retain their vertical orientation or to be rotated along with the angular displacement as they are copied. AutoCAD asks:

Rotate objects as they are copied? <Y>:

Notice the default, which we will accept.
> Press enter or type "y".

Your screen should resemble *Figure 5-2*. Now let's try some of the other options. We will define an array that has 20 items placed 15 degrees apart and not rotated.

> Type "U" to undo the first array.

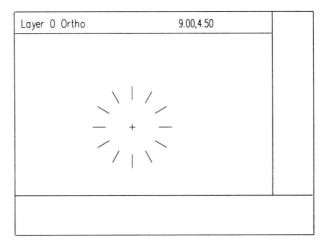

**Figure 5-2**

> Type or select "ARRAY".
> Select the line again.
> Press enter to end selection.
> Type "P" or select "polar".
> Pick the same center point as before.
> Type "20" for the number of items.
> Type "0" for the angle to fill.

As mentioned, this response tells AutoCAD to issue a prompt for the angle between items:

Angle between items (+=CCW, –=CW):

The symbols in parentheses are familiar from the "angle to fill" prompt. Notice that there is no default angle here.
> Type "15" for the angle between items.

All that remains is to tell AutoCAD not to rotate the lines as they are copied.
> Type "n".

Your screen should now resemble *Figure 5-3*.

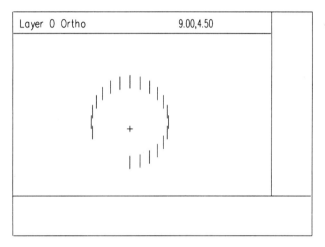

**Figure 5-3**

Try one more and then you will be on your own with polar arrays. For this one, define an array that fills 270 degrees and has −30 degrees between each angle, as in *Figure 5-4*.

> Undo the last array.
> Repeat the first five steps, up to the "number of items" prompt.
> Press enter to skip the "number of items" prompt.

This tells AutoCAD to issue the other two prompts instead.
> Type "270" for the angle to fill.
> Type "−30" for the angle between.

What will the negative angle do?
> Press enter to rotate items as they are copied.

Your screen should resemble *Figure 5-4*.

This ends our discussion of polar arrays. With the options AutoCAD gives you there are many possibilities that you may want to try out. As always, we encourage experimentation. When you are satisfied, erase everything on the screen and do a REDRAW in preparation for learning the ARC command.

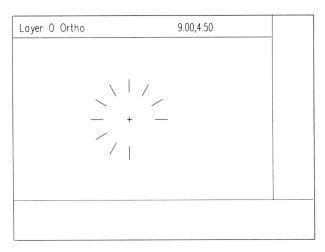

| Layer 0 Ortho | 9.00,4.50 |

**Figure 5-4**

### TASK 2: Drawing ARCs

*Procedure.*

1.  Type or select "ARC".

2.  Type or show where to start the arc, where to end it, and what circle it is a portion of, using any of the 11 available methods.

*Discussion.*    Learning AutoCAD's ARC command is an exercise in geometry. In this section we will give you a firm foundation for understanding and drawing arcs so that you will not be confused by all the options that are available. The information we give you will be more than enough to do the drawings in this chapter and most drawings you will encounter elsewhere. Refer to the *AutoCAD Reference Manual*, Section 4.4, and the chart at the end of this section (*Figure 5-5*) if you need additional information.

AutoCAD gives you 8 distinct ways to draw arcs, and if you count variations in order, 11. With this much to work with, some generalizations will be helpful.

First, notice that every option requires you to specify three pieces of information: where to begin the arc, where to end it, and what circle it is theoretically a part of. To get a handle on the range of options, look at the following standard screen menu abbreviations and meanings.

| Screen Menu | Information needed |
|---|---|
| 1  Three-point: | Three points on arc |
| 2  S,C,E: | Start,Center,End |
| 3  S,C,A: | Start,Center,Angle |
| 4  S,C,L: | Start,Center,Length of chord |
| 5  S,E,A: | Start,End,Angle |
| 6  S,E,R: | Start,End,Radius |
| 7  S,E,D: | Start,End,Starting direction |
| 8  C,S,E: | Center,Start,End |
| 9  C,S,A: | Center,Start,Angle |
| 10  C,S,L: | Center,Start,Length of chord |
| 11  CONTIN: | Start given as endpoint of previous line or arc, circle tangent to previous line or arc, End required |

> Type "a" to indicate that you will specify an angle. If you have selected "S,C,A" from the AutoCAD screen menu, this step will be automated.

You can type an angle specification or show an angle on the screen. Notice that the rubber band now shows an angle only; its length is insignificant. The angle is being measured from the horizontal, but the arc begins at the start point and continues counterclockwise, as illustrated in *Figure 5-5*.

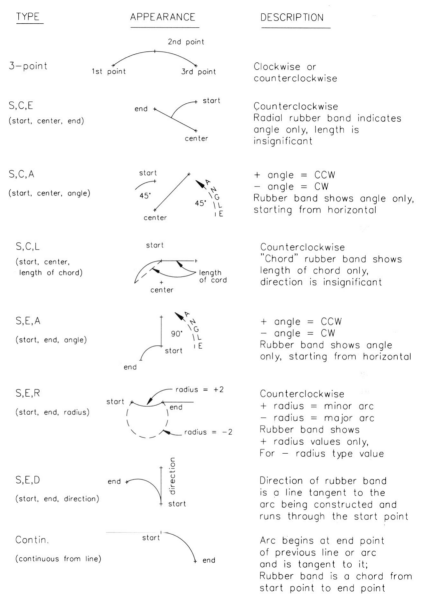

| TYPE | APPEARANCE | DESCRIPTION |
|---|---|---|
| 3-point | 1st point, 2nd point, 3rd point | Clockwise or counterclockwise |
| S,C,E (start, center, end) | end, start, center | Counterclockwise Radial rubber band indicates angle only, length is insignificant |
| S,C,A (start, center, angle) | start, 45°, center, 45° ANGLE | + angle = CCW − angle = CW Rubber band shows angle only, starting from horizontal |
| S,C,L (start, center, length of chord) | start, length of cord, center | Counterclockwise "Chord" rubber band shows length of chord only, direction is insignificant |
| S,E,A (start, end, angle) | 90°, start, end, ANGLE | + angle = CCW − angle = CW Rubber band shows angle only, starting from horizontal |
| S,E,R (start, end, radius) | start, end, radius = +2, radius = −2 | Counterclockwise + radius = minor arc − radius = major arc Rubber band shows + radius values only, For − radius type value |
| S,E,D (start, end, direction) | end, direction, start | Direction of rubber band is a line tangent to the arc being constructed and runs through the start point |
| Contin. (continuous from line) | start, end | Arc begins at end point of previous line or arc and is tangent to it; Rubber band is a chord from start point to end point |

**Figure 5-5**

> Type "45" or show an angle of 45 degrees.

Now that you have tried three of the basic methods for constructing an arc, we strongly suggest that you study the chart and then try out the other options. The notes in the right-hand column will serve as a guide of what to look for.

The differences in the use of the rubber band from one option to the next can be confusing. You should understand, for instance, that in some cases the linear rubber band is only significant as a distance indicator; its angle is of no importance and is ignored by AutoCAD. In other cases it is just the reverse; the length of the rubber band is irrelevant, while its angle of rotation is important.

> NOTE: One additional trick you should try out as you experiment with arcs is as follows: If you press enter or the space bar at the "Center/<Start point>" prompt, AutoCAD will use the end point of the last line or arc you drew as the new starting point and construct an arc tangent to it. This is the same as the "Contin" option on the screen menu.

This completes the present discussion of the ARC command. Constructing arcs, as you may have realized, can be tricky. Another option that is available and often useful is to draw a complete circle and then use the TRIM or BREAK commands to cut out the arc you want. BREAK and TRIM are introduced in the next chapter.

## TASK 3: Using the ROTATE command

*Procedure.*

1. Type or select "ROTATE".
2. Define the selection set.
3. Press enter to end selection.
4. Select a base point.
5. Indicate an angle of rotation.

*Discussion:* ROTATE is a fairly straightforward command, and it has some uses that might not be apparent immediately. For example, it is frequently easier to draw an object in a horizontal or vertical position first and then ROTATE it than it would be to draw it diagonally.

> In preparation for this exercise, clear your screen and draw a horizontally oriented arc near the center of your screen, as in *Figure 5-6*. Exact coordinates and locations are not important.

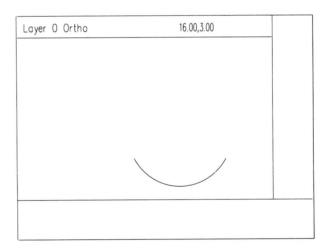

**Figure 5-6**

We will begin by rotating the arc to the position shown in *Figure 5-7*.
> Type or select "ROTATE".
   AutoCAD will prompt:

Select objects:

> Select the arc.
> Press enter to end the selection process.
   You will now be prompted for a base point.

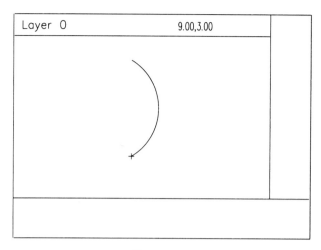

**Figure 5-7**

Base point:

This will be the point around which the object is rotated. The results of the rotation, therefore, are dramatically affected by your choice of base point. We will choose a point at the left tip of the arc.
> Point to the left tip of the arc.
The prompt that follows looks like this:

<Rotation angle>/Reference:

The default method is to indicate a rotation angle directly. The object will be rotated through the angle specified and the original object deleted.

Move the cursor in a circle and you will see that you have a copy of the object to drag into place visually. If ortho is on, turn it off to see the complete range.
> Type "90" or point to a rotation of 90 degrees.
The results should resemble *Figure 5-7.*

Notice that when specifying the rotation angle directly like this, the original orientation of the selected object is taken to be 0 degrees. The rotation is figured counterclockwise from there.

However, there may be times when you want to refer to the coordinate system in specifying rotation. This is the purpose of the "reference" option. To use it, all you need to do is specify the present orientation of the object relative to the coordinate system, and then tell AutoCAD the orientation you want it to have after rotation. Look at *Figure 5-8.* To rotate the arc as shown, you could either indicate a rotation of −45 degrees or tell AutoCAD that it is presently oriented to 90 degrees and you want it rotated to 45 degrees. Try this method for practice.

> Press enter to repeat the ROTATE command.
> Select the arc.
> Press enter to end selection.
> Choose a base point at the lower tip of the arc.
> Type "r" or select "reference".
AutoCAD will now prompt for a reference angle:

Reference angle:

> Type "90".
AutoCAD prompts for an angle of rotation:

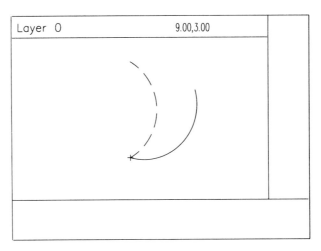

**Figure 5-8**

Rotation angle:

> Type "45".
Your arc should now resemble the solid arc in *Figure 5-8*.

Before leaving the ROTATE command we suggest that you experiment with other base points to see how they affect the rotation. Try base points near the middle of the arc, above and below, to the right and to the left.

When you are done, rotate your arc back into its original horizontal position or erase it and draw a new one. We will use this arc to explore the MIRROR command next.

### TASK 4: Creating MIRROR images of objects on the screen

*Procedure.*

1. Type or select "MIRROR".
2. Define a selection set.
3. Press enter to end selection.
4. Point to two ends of a mirror line.
5. Indicate whether or not to delete original object.

*Discussion.* There are two main differences between the command procedures for MIRROR and ROTATE. First, in order to mirror an object you will have to define a "mirror line," and second you will have an opportunity to indicate whether you want to retain the original object or delete it. In the ROTATE sequence the original is always deleted.

> To begin this exercise you should have a bowl-shaped arc placed left of the center of your screen, as in *Figure 5-9*.
Except as noted, you should have snap and ortho on to do this exercise.
> Type or select "MIRROR".
You will be prompted to select objects:

Select objects:

> Select the arc.
> Press enter to end selection.
Now AutoCAD will be asking you for the first point of a mirror line.

First point of mirror line:

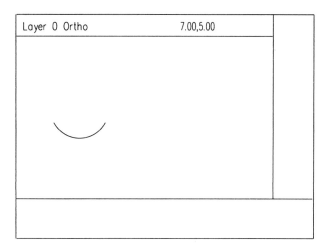

**Figure 5-9**

This line is just what you would expect; all points on your object will be mirrored across the mirror line at a distance equal and opposite to their distance away from it.

We will select a mirror line even with the top of the arc, so that the end points of the mirror images will be touching.

> Select a point even with the left end of the arc, as in *Figure 5-10*.

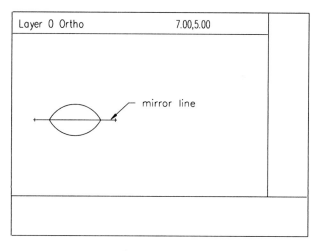

**Figure 5-10**

You are prompted to show the other end of the mirror line:

Second point:

The length of the mirror line is not important. All that matters is its orientation. Move the cursor slowly in a circle and you will see an inverted copy of the arc moving with you to show the different mirror images that are possible, given the first point you have already specified. Turn ortho off to see the whole range of possibilities, then turn it on again to complete the exercise.

We will select a point at 0 degrees from the first point so that the mirror image will be directly above the original arc, and touching at the end points as in *Figure 5-10*.

> Select a point directly to the right (0 degrees) of the first point.

The dragged object will disappear until you answer the next prompt, which asks if you want to delete the original object or not.

Delete old objects? <N>:

This time around we will not delete the original.
> Press enter to retain the old object.

Your screen will look like *Figure 5-10*, without the mirror line in the middle.

Now let's repeat the process, deleting the original this time, and using a different mirror line, to produce *Figure 5-11*.

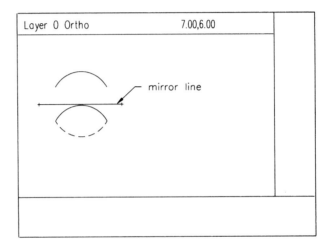

**Figure 5-11**

> Press enter to repeat the MIRROR command.
> Select the original (lower) arc.
> Press enter to end selection.

We will create a mirror image above the last one by choosing a mirror line slightly above the two arcs as in *Figure 5-11*.
> Select a first point of the mirror line slightly above and to the left of the figure.
> Select a second point directly to the right of the first point.
> Type "y" indicating that you want the old object, the lower arc, deleted.

Your screen should now resemble *Figure 5-12*.

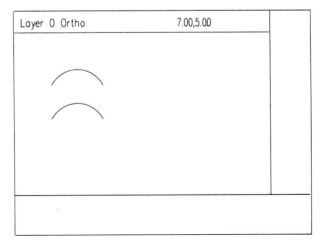

**Figure 5-12**

For further practice with the MIRROR command, do two more mirrors to produce *Figures 5-13* and *5-14*. Use a window to select all four arcs in *Figure 5-13* to produce *Figure 5-14*.

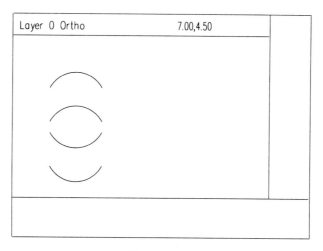

**Figure 5-13**

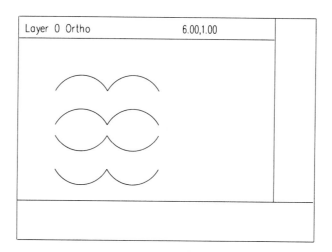

**Figure 5-14**

## TASKS 5, 6, 7, 8, and 9

You have learned some complex sequences in this chapter, especially in the ARC and polar ARRAY commands, so take your time doing the next five drawings and be sure that you understand the commands involved. Your knowledge of AutoCAD and CAD operation is increasing rapidly at this point, and it will be important that you practice what you have learned carefully.

# DRAWING 5-1: FLANGED BUSHING

This drawing makes use of a polar array to draw eight screw holes in a circle. It will also review the use of layers and linetypes.

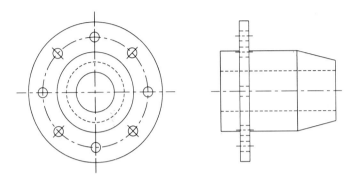

## *DRAWING SUGGESTIONS*

GRID = .25   LTSCALE = .50
SNAP = .25   LIMITS = (0,0) (18,12)

> Draw the concentric circles first, using dimensions from both views.  Remember to change layers as needed.
> Once you have drawn the 2.75 DIA bolt circle, use it to locate one of the bolt holes. Any of the circles at a quadrant point (0, 90, 180, or 270 degrees) will do.
> Draw a center line across the bolt hole and then array the hole and the center line 360 degrees. Be sure to rotate the objects as they are copied, otherwise you will get strange results from your center lines.

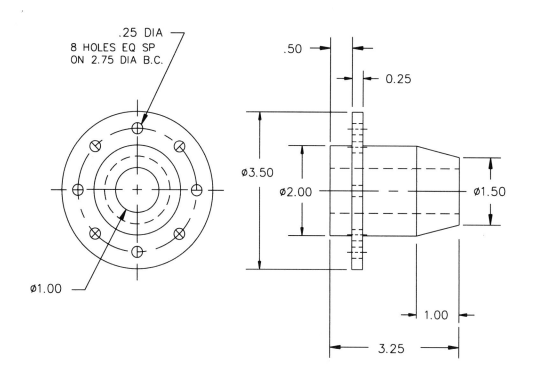

.25 DIA
8 HOLES EQ SP
ON 2.75 DIA B.C.

.50

0.25

ø3.50

ø2.00

ø1.50

ø1.00

1.00

3.25

FLANGED BUSHING

Drawing 5-1

| LAYERS | NAME | COLOR | LINETYPE | | (DRAW) | LINE |
|---|---|---|---|---|---|---|
| | 0 | WHITE | ———— | CONTINUOUS | (DRAW) | CIRCLE |
| | 1 | RED | ———— | CONTINUOUS | (EDIT) | ARRAY |
| | 2 | YELLOW | – – – – | HIDDEN | (EDIT) | MIRROR |
| | 3 | GREEN | — – — – | CENTER | (DISPLAY) | ZOOM |

| F1 | F6 | F7 | F8 | F9 |
|---|---|---|---|---|
| ON/OFF | ON/OFF | ON/OFF | ON/OFF | ON/OFF |
| SCREEN | COORDS | GRID | ORTHO | SNAP |

## DRAWING 5-2: GUIDE

There are six arcs in this drawing, and while some of them could be drawn as fillets, we suggest that you use the ARC command for practice. Furthermore, by drawing arcs you will avoid a common problem with fillets. Since fillets are designed to round intersections at corners, when you create a fillet in the middle of a line it will erase part of that line. This would affect the center line on the left side of the front view, for example.

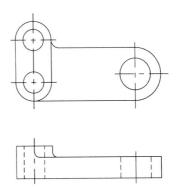

### *DRAWING SUGGESTIONS*

GRID = .25    LTSCALE = .50
SNAP = .125   LIMITS = (0,0) (12,9)

> The three large arcs in the top view can all be drawn easily using start, center, end.

> The smaller .375 arc in the top view could be drawn by filleting the top arc with the horizontal line to its right. However, we suggest you try an arc giving start, center, end or start, center, angle. Note that you can easily locate the center by moving .375 to the right of the end point of the upper arc.

> The same method will work to draw the .25 arc in the front view. Begin by dropping a line down .25 from the horizontal line. Start your arc at the end of this line and move .25 to the right to locate its center. Then the end will simply be .25 down from the center (or you could specify an angle of 90 degrees).

> Similarly, the smallest arc, at the center line, can be drawn from a start point .25 up from the horizontal. It will have a radius of .25 and make an angle of 90 degrees.

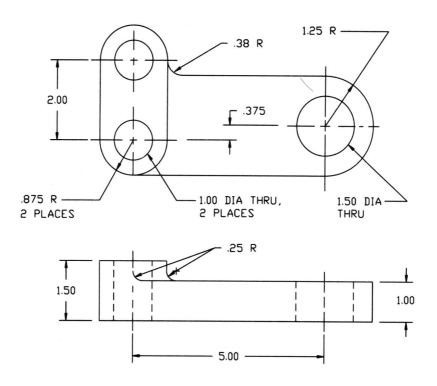

## GUIDE
### Drawing 5-2

| LAYERS | NAME | COLOR | LINETYPE | | | |
|--------|------|-------|----------|---|---|---|
| | 0 | WHITE | ———————— CONTINUOUS | (DRAW) | LINE |
| | 1 | RED | ———————— CONTINUOUS | (DRAW) | CIRCLE |
| | 2 | YELLOW | – – – – – HIDDEN | (DRAW) | ARC |
| | 3 | GREEN | — — — — CENTER | (EDIT) | COPY |
| | | | | (DISPLAY) | ZOOM |

| F1 | F6 | F7 | F8 | F9 |
|----|----|----|----|----|
| ON/OFF | ON/OFF | ON/OFF | ON/OFF | ON/OFF |
| SCREEN | COORDS | GRID | ORTHO | SNAP |

## DRAWING 5-3: DIALS

This is a relatively simple drawing that will give you some good practice with polar arrays and the ROTATE and COPY commands.

Notice that the needle drawn at the top of the next page is only for reference; the actual drawing includes only the plate and the three dials with their needles.

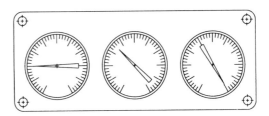

### *DRAWING SUGGESTIONS*

GRID = .50    LIMITS = (0,0) (18,12)

SNAP = .125

> After drawing the outer rectangle and screw holes, draw the leftmost dial, including the needle. Draw a .50 vertical line at the top and array it to the left (counterclockwise—a positive angle) and to the right (negative) to create the 11 larger lines on the dial. Use the same operation to create the 40 small (.25) markings.

> Complete the first dial and then use a multiple copy to produce two more dials at the center and right of your screen. Be sure to use a window to select the entire dial.

> Finally, use the ROTATE command to rotate the needles as indicated on the new dials. Use a window to select the needle and rotate it around the center of the dial.

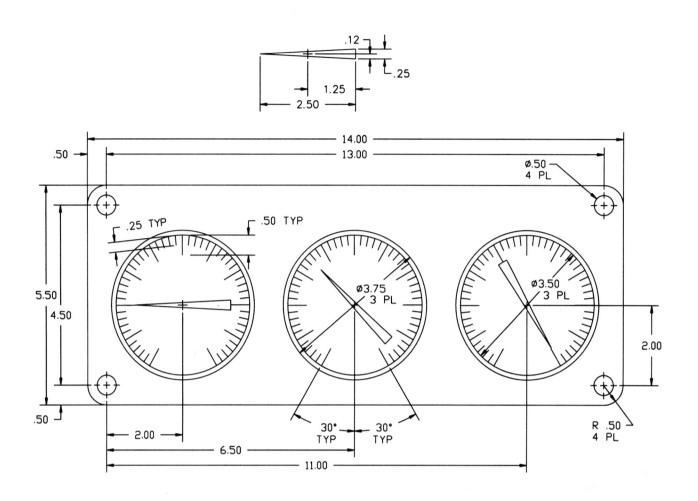

DIALS

Drawing 5-3

| LAYERS | NAME | COLOR | LINETYPE | | | (DRAW) | LINE |
|--------|------|-------|----------|---|---|--------|------|
| | 0 | WHITE | ——————— | CONTINUOUS | | (DRAW) | CIRCLE |
| | 1 | RED | ——————— | CONTINUOUS | | (EDIT) | ARRAY |
| | | | | | | (EDIT) | COPY |
| | | | | | | (EDIT) | FILLET |
| | 3 | GREEN | — — — — | CENTER | | (EDIT) | ROTATE |
| | | | | | | (DISPLAY) | ZOOM |

| F1 | F6 | F7 | F8 | F9 |
|----|----|----|----|----|
| ON/OFF | ON/OFF | ON/OFF | ON/OFF | ON/OFF |
| SCREEN | COORDS | GRID | ORTHO | SNAP |

# DRAWING 5-4: ALIGNMENT WHEEL

This drawing shows a typical use of the MIRROR command. Carefully mirroring sides of the symmetrical front view will save you from duplicating some of your drawing efforts. Notice that you will need a small snap setting to draw the vertical lines at the chamfer.

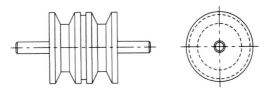

## *DRAWING SUGGESTIONS*

GRID = .25    LTSCALE = .50
SNAP = .0625    LIMITS = (0,0) (12,9)

> There are numerous ways to use MIRROR in drawing the front view. As the reference shows, there is top-bottom symmetry as well as left-right symmetry. The exercise for you is to choose an efficient mirroring sequence.
> Whatever sequence you use, consider the importance of creating the chamfer and the vertical line at the chamfer <u>before</u> this part of the object is mirrored.
> Once the front view is drawn, the right side view will be easy. Remember to change layers for center and hidden lines and to line up the small inner circle with the chamfer.

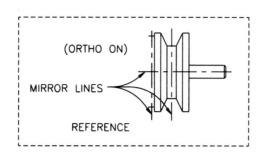

(ORTHO ON)

MIRROR LINES

REFERENCE

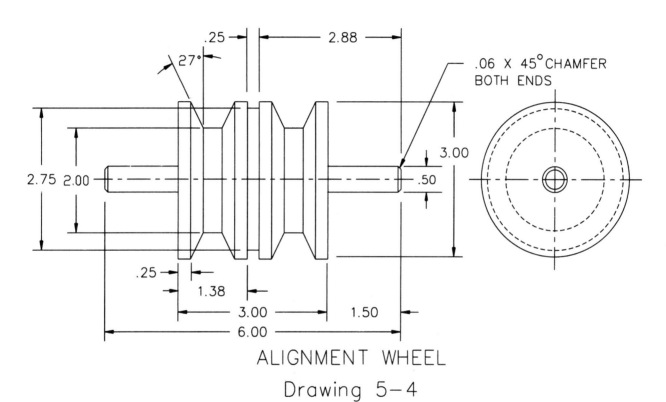

.25

2.88

27°

.06 X 45° CHAMFER
BOTH ENDS

3.00

2.75  2.00

.50

.25

1.38

3.00

1.50

6.00

ALIGNMENT WHEEL
Drawing 5-4

| LAYERS | NAME | COLOR | LINETYPE | | (DRAW) | LINE |
|--------|------|-------|----------|--|--------|------|
| | 0 | WHITE | ——— CONTINUOUS | | (DRAW) | CIRCLE |
| | 1 | RED | ——— CONTINUOUS | | (EDIT) | CHAMFER |
| | 2 | YELLOW | - - - - HIDDEN | | (EDIT) | MIRROR |
| | 3 | GREEN | — — CENTER | | (DISPLAY) | ZOOM |

| F1 | F6 | F7 | F8 | F9 |
|----|----|----|----|----|
| ON/OFF SCREEN | ON/OFF COORDS | ON/OFF GRID | ON/OFF ORTHO | ON/OFF SNAP |

## DRAWING 5-5: HEARTH

Once you have completed this architectural drawing as it is shown, you might want to experiment with filling in a pattern of firebrick in the center of the hearth. The drawing itself is not complicated, but little errors will become very noticeable when you try to make the row of 4″ × 8″ bricks across the bottom fit with the arc of bricks across the top, so work carefully.

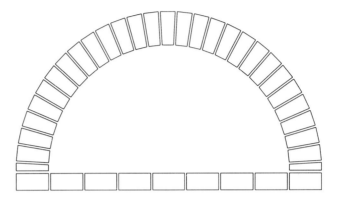

*DRAWING SUGGESTIONS*

UNITS = Architectural
smallest fraction = 8 (1/8″ )
LIMITS = (0,0) (12′,9′ )
GRID = 1′
SNAP = 1/8″    AXIS = 1/8″

> Zoom in to draw the wedge-shaped brick indicated by the arrow on the right of the dimensioned drawing. Draw half of the brick only and mirror it across the centerline as shown. (Notice that the centerline is for reference only.) It is very important that you use MIRROR so that you can erase half of the brick later.
> Array the brick in a 29 item, 180 degree polar array.
> Erase the bottom halves of the end bricks at each end.
> Draw a new horizontal bottom line on each of the two end bricks.
> Draw a 4″ × 8″ brick directly below the half brick at the left end.
> Array the 4″ × 8″ brick in a 1 row, 9 column array, with 8.5″ between columns.

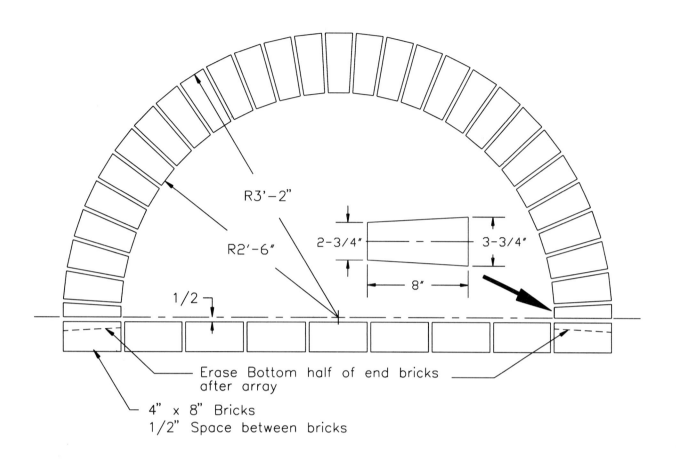

R3'-2"

R2'-6"

2-3/4"          3-3/4"

8"

1/2

Erase Bottom half of end bricks
after array

4" x 8" Bricks
1/2" Space between bricks

# HEARTH

## Drawing 5—5

Courtesy of Thomas Casey

| LAYERS | NAME | COLOR | LINETYPE | | | (DRAW) | LINE |
|--------|------|-------|----------|--|--|--------|------|
| | 0 | WHITE | ———— | CONTINUOUS | | (EDIT) | ERASE |
| | 1 | RED | ———— | CONTINUOUS | | (EDIT) | MIRROR |
| | | | | | | (EDIT) | ARRAY |
| | | | | | | (EDIT) | MOVE |
| | 3 | GREEN | – – – | CENTER | | (DISPLAY) | ZOOM |

| F1 | F6 | F7 | F8 | F9 |
|----|----|----|----|----|
| ON/OFF | ON/OFF | ON/OFF | ON/OFF | ON/OFF |
| SCREEN | COORDS | GRID | ORTHO | SNAP |

# chapter

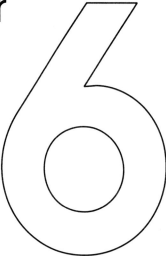

**COMMANDS**

| EDIT | SETTINGS |
|------|----------|
| BREAK | OSNAP |
| TRIM | APERTURE |
| EXTEND | |
| STRETCH | |

SPECIAL TOPIC: Object Snap (OSNAP)

**OVERVIEW**

This chapter will continue to expand your repertoire of editing commands. You will learn to BREAK entities on the screen into pieces so that they may be manipulated separately, or so that you can erase parts. You will also learn to shorten entities using the TRIM command, or to lengthen them with the EXTEND command.

But most important, you will begin to use a very powerful tool called Object Snap that will take you to a new level of accuracy and efficiency as a CAD operator.

**TASKS**

1. Use OSNAP to select specifiable points on an entity using single point overrides.
2. Select points with OSNAP using running modes.
3. Change the APERTURE size.
4. Use BREAK to break a previously drawn entity into two separate entities.
5. Use TRIM to shorten entities.
6. Use EXTEND to lengthen entities.
7. Use STRETCH to move selected objects while retaining their connections to other objects.
8. Do Drawing 6-1 ("Bike Tire").
9. Do Drawing 6-2 ("Archimedes Spiral").
10. Do Drawing 6-3 ("Spiral Designs").
11. Do Drawing 6-4 ("Grooved Hub").
12. Do Drawing 6-5 ("Cap Iron").
13. Do Drawing 6-6 ("Deck Framing").

### TASK 1: Selecting points with OSNAP (single point override)

*Procedure.*

1. Enter a drawing command, such as LINE, CIRCLE, or ARC.
2. Type or select the name of an OSNAP mode.
3. Point to a previously drawn object.

*Discussion.* Some of the drawings in the last two chapters have pushed the limits of what you can accomplish accurately on a CAD system with incremental snap alone. Object snap is a related tool that works in a very different manner. Instead of snapping to points defined by the coordinate system, it snaps to geometrically specifiable points on objects that you have already drawn.

Let's say you want to begin a new line at the end point of one that is already on the screen. If you are lucky it may be on a snap point, but it is just as likely not to be. Turning snap off and using the arrow keys may appear to work, but chances are that when you zoom in you will find that you have actually missed the point. Using object snap is the only precise way, and it is as precise as you could want. Let's try it.

> To prepare for this exercise, enter a new drawing called "6-1" or "A:6-1" and draw a 6 × 6 box with a circle inside, as in *Figure 6-1*. Exact sizes and locations are not important; however, the circle should be centered at the center of the square.

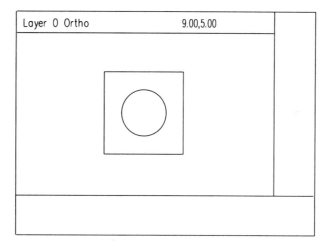

Layer 0 Ortho                9.00,5.00

**Figure 6-1**

> Now enter the LINE command.

We are going to draw a line from the lower left corner of the square to a point on a line tangent to the circle, as shown in *Figure 6-2*. Notice that this task would be extremely difficult without osnap. The corner is easy to locate, since you have probably drawn it on snap, but the tangent may not be.

We will use an "end point" object snap to locate the corner and a "tangent" object snap to locate the tangent point.

> At the "From point:" prompt, type "end" or select "ENDpoint" instead of specifying a point.

On the AutoCAD screen menu, select the row of asterisks at the top (****), then select "ENDpoint". On the pull down, select "Tools", then "ENDpoint". You may also have a "Tools" button on your cursor that will open up this menu directly. If so, it will be quicker to use it.

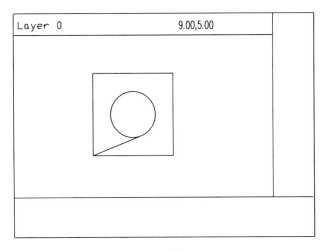

**Figure 6-2**

Entering "END" in any of these methods tells AutoCAD that you are going to select the start point of the line by using an end point object snap rather than direct pointing or entering coordinates.

Now that AutoCAD knows that we want to begin at the end point of a previously drawn entity, it needs only to know which one.

A "target box" has been added to the cross hairs. The size of this box can be changed with the APERTURE command, as discussed later. To be selected, a point must be within the aperture, or an entity containing the point must pass through the target area defined by the box, as in *Figure 6-3*.

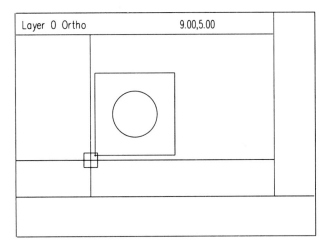

**Figure 6-3**

> Position the cursor so that the lower left corner is within the target box, then press the pick button.

There are, of course, two end points, so it is necessary to point to the half of the line that contains the end point you want. Aside from this, you could point anywhere along the line, just as you do when you select an object for editing.

Now we will draw the tangent.

> At the "Second point:" prompt, type "tan" or select "TANgent".

> Move the cursor to the right and position the aperture so that the circle crosses the target box. Press the pick button.

AutoCAD will locate the tangent point and draw the line.

> Press enter to exit the LINE command as usual.
Your screen should now resemble *Figure 6-2*.

NOTE: In more complex drawings it is quite possible that there will be more than one point that fits the definition of the osnap mode you have selected (two or more distinct end points or objects with end points within the box, as in *Figure 6-4*). In this case AutoCAD will first search for all possible candidates and then select the one nearest the cross hairs. An exception to this can be made using the "quick" mode described on the chart at the end of this discussion of OSNAP (see *Figure 6-7*).

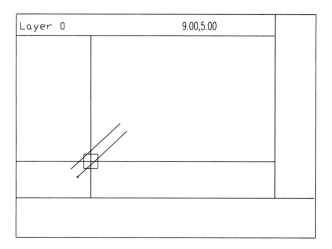

**Figure 6-4**

We will repeat the process now, but go from the midpoint of the lower side of the square instead of its end point.

> Repeat the LINE command (if you are using the pull down menu the command will repeat automatically).
> At the prompt for a point, type "mid" or select "MIDpoint".
> Position the aperture anywhere along the bottom side of the square and press the pick button.
> At the prompt for a second point, type "tan" or select "tangent".
> Position the aperture along the lower right side of the circle and press the pick button.
> Press enter or the space bar to exit the LINE command.

That's all there is to it. Remember the steps: 1) enter a command; 2) when Auto-CAD asks for a point, type or select an OSNAP mode instead; 3) select an object to which the mode can be applied and AutoCAD will find the point.
At this point your screen should resemble *Figure 6-5*.

## TASK 2: Selecting points with OSNAP (running mode)

*Procedure.*

1. Type or select "OSNAP".
2. Type or select one or more OSNAP modes.
3. Enter drawing commands.

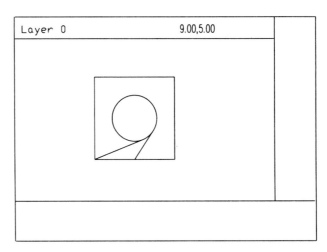

**Figure 6-5**

*Discussion.* So far we have been using object snap one point at a time. Since osnap is not constantly in use for most applications, this single point method is probably most common. But if you find that you are going to be using one or a number of osnap types repeatedly and will not need to select many points without them, there is a way to keep osnap modes on so that they affect all point selection. These are called "running object snap modes." We will use this method to complete the drawing shown in *Figure 6-6*.

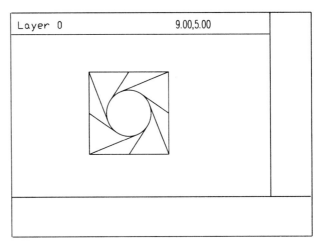

**Figure 6-6**

> Type or select "OSNAP".

You will be asked to specify the running modes that you want to have in effect:

Object snap modes:

You will find a complete list of modes on the chart (*Figure 6-7*) later in this chapter, but for now we will be using three: midpoint, tangent, and intersect. Midpoint and tangent you already know. Intersect snaps to the point where two entities meet or cross. We will use intersect instead of end point to select the remaining three corners of the square.

> Type "mid,tan,int".

If you are selecting osnap modes from the screen menu, be sure to add the comma between types. The pull down menu will only allow you to enter one running OSNAP mode at a time, so do not use it for this step.

AutoCAD returns you to the "Command:" prompt and you are ready to draw with the running osnap modes in effect. We will draw tangent lines from the corners of the square and from the midpoints of their sides to produce *Figure 6-6*.

> Enter the LINE command.

Notice the target box on the cross hairs. This tells you that there are osnap modes in effect. When you select points now, AutoCAD will look for the point nearest the center of the aperture that fulfills the geometric requirements of one of the three running osnap modes you have chosen. If there is more than one point, it will select the one nearest the intersection of the cross hairs.

> Position the aperture so that the lower right corner is within the box and press the pick button.

AutoCAD will select the intersection of the bottom and the right sides and give you the rubber band and the prompt for a second point.

Notice that the target box is still on the cross hairs.

> Move the cross hairs up and along the right side of the circle and press the pick button.

Be sure that the intersection of the previous tangent and the circle is <u>not</u> within the aperture.

AutoCAD will construct a new tangent from the lower right corner to the circle.

> Press enter to complete the command sequence.

> Press enter again to repeat LINE so you can begin with a new start point. (If you are using the pull down menu this will happen automatically.)

We will continue to move counterclockwise around the circle. This should begin to be easy now.

> Position the aperture along the right side of the square and press the pick button. Be sure the corner is <u>not</u> within the aperture.

AutoCAD selects the midpoint of the side.

> Move up along the upper right side of the circle and press the pick button.

> Press enter to exit LINE.

> Press enter again to repeat LINE (if necessary) and continue around the circle drawing tangents like this: upper right corner to top of circle, top side midpoint to top left of circle, upper left corner to left side, left side midpoint to lower left side.

Remember that running osnap modes should give you both speed and accuracy, so push yourself a little to see how quickly you can complete the figure.

Your screen should now resemble *Figure 6-6*.

Now turn off the osnap modes. It is done just as if you were setting up new modes, but choose "none" or simply press enter when you are prompted for modes.

> Type or select "OSNAP".

At this point you could select new modes if you wanted, but we will return to ordinary point selection.

> At the prompt for osnap modes press enter.

AutoCAD will return you to the command prompt, and when you begin drawing again, you will see that the aperture is gone.

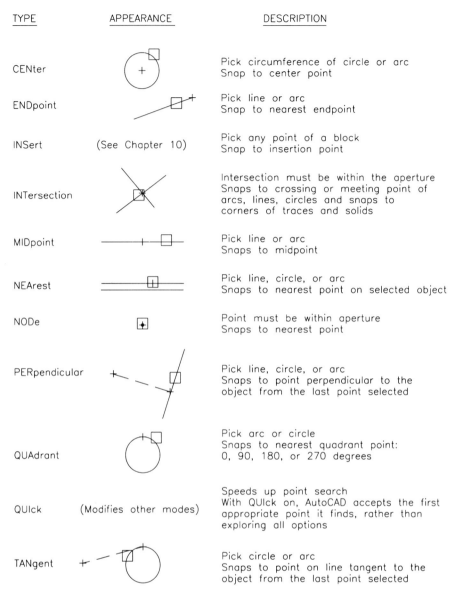

| TYPE | APPEARANCE | DESCRIPTION |
|------|------------|-------------|
| CENter | | Pick circumference of circle or arc<br>Snap to center point |
| ENDpoint | | Pick line or arc<br>Snap to nearest endpoint |
| INSert | (See Chapter 10) | Pick any point of a block<br>Snap to insertion point |
| INTersection | | Intersection must be within the aperture<br>Snaps to crossing or meeting point of arcs, lines, circles and snaps to corners of traces and solids |
| MIDpoint | | Pick line or arc<br>Snaps to midpoint |
| NEArest | | Pick line, circle, or arc<br>Snaps to nearest point on selected object |
| NODe | | Point must be within aperture<br>Snaps to nearest point |
| PERpendicular | | Pick line, circle, or arc<br>Snaps to point perpendicular to the object from the last point selected |
| QUAdrant | | Pick arc or circle<br>Snaps to nearest quadrant point:<br>0, 90, 180, or 270 degrees |
| QUIck | (Modifies other modes) | Speeds up point search<br>With QUIck on, AutoCAD accepts the first appropriate point it finds, rather than exploring all options |
| TANgent | | Pick circle or arc<br>Snaps to point on line tangent to the object from the last point selected |

**Figure 6-7**

## TASK 3: Changing the size of the aperture

*Procedure.*

1. Type or select "APERTURE".
2. Enter a value.

*Discussion.* When you use this command you are actually setting an Auto-CAD system variable. You will have a choice of sizes from 1 to 50 pixels, and the size you pick will stay in effect until you change it again. Other drawings will be affected as well as the one you are in when you make the change.

> Type or select "APERTURE".

AutoCAD will prompt you for a size in pixels, the smallest displayable video screen unit.

Object snap target height (1-50 pixels) <15>:

For practice we will change the aperture to 10 pixels.
> Type or select "10".

Now if you enter a drawing command and select an osnap mode, you will see that the aperture is smaller.

The best size for your aperture depends on your drawing. If you are doing a lot of point selection in tight spaces, and especially if you are using multiple osnap modes, you may want a smaller aperture to avoid confusion. If you have plenty of room to work in, you may want a larger aperture to make the selection process "looser" and faster.

NOTE: By the way, the aperture is distinct from the box you see when you go to select objects in the edit commands. Changing the osnap aperture has no effect on the size of the object selection box. The size of this box is controlled by another system variable called "PICKBOX". There is no PICKBOX command, but it can be changed using the SETVAR command. SETVAR is discussed in Chapter 9 of this book and in the *AutoCAD Reference Manual*, Sections 3.10 and 8.6.5.

We will now move on to four very useful and important new editing commands, BREAK, TRIM, EXTEND, and STRETCH. Before leaving OSNAP, be sure to study the chart, *Figure 6-7.*

### TASK 4: BREAKing previously drawn objects

*Procedure.*

1.  Type or select "BREAK".
2.  Select an object to be broken.
3.  Show the first point of the break.
4.  Show the second point of the break.

*Discussion.*   The BREAK command allows you to break an object on the screen into two entities, or to cut a segment out of the middle or off the end. The command sequence is similar for all options. The action taken will depend on the points you select for breaking. BREAK works on lines, circles, arcs, traces, and polylines (see Chapter 9).

> In preparation for this section, clear your screen of any objects left over from Task 2 and draw a 5.0 horizontal line across the middle of your screen, as in *Figure 6-8*. Exact lengths and coordinates are not important. Also, turn off any running osnap modes that may be on from the last exercise (type or select "OSNAP" and press enter when prompted for osnap modes to turn on).

We begin by breaking the line you have just drawn into two independent lines.

> Type or select "BREAK".
AutoCAD will prompt you to select an object to break:

Select object:

You may select an object in any of the usual ways, but notice that you can only break one object at a time. If you try to select more, with a window, for example, AutoCAD will still give you only one. Because of this you are most likely to show the object you want to break by pointing to it.

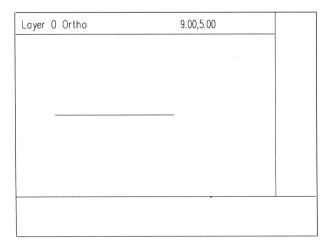

Layer 0 Ortho                                9.00,5.00

**Figure 6-8**

NOTE: Osnap modes do work perfectly well in edit commands like BREAK. If you wished to break a line at its midpoint, for example, you could use the osnap to midpoint mode to select the line and the break point.

> Select the line by picking any point near its middle. (The exact point is not critical; if it were we could use a midpoint osnap.)

The line has now been selected for breaking, and since there can be only one object, you do not have to press enter to end the selection process as you often do in other editing commands.

AutoCAD will prompt as follows:

Enter second point (or F for first point):

When you are selecting an object by pointing, AutoCAD will assume that the point you use for selection is also the first point of the break. It will be most efficient, therefore, if you do select the object with a break point. Then you can proceed by selecting the second point immediately. If not, type F and you will be prompted for the first break point, as the parentheses tell you.

What we want to do now is to select a point that will break the object in two without erasing anything. To do this, simply pick the same point again.

> Point to the same point that you just used to select the line.

The break is complete. In order to demonstrate that the line is really two lines now, we will select the right half of it for our next break.

> Press enter or the space bar to repeat the BREAK command.
> Point to the line on the right side of the last break.

The right side of the line should become dotted, as in *Figure 6-9*. Clearly the line is now being treated as two separate entities.

We will shorten the end of this dotted section of the line. Assume that the point you just used to select the object is the point where you want it to end; now all you need to do is to select a second point anywhere beyond the right end of the line.

> Select a second point beyond the right end of the line.

Your line should now be shortened, as in *Figure 6-10*.

Next we will cut a piece out of the middle of the left side.

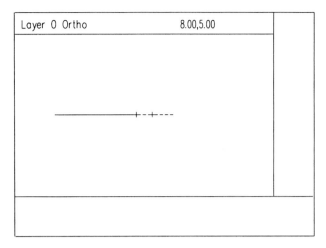

**Figure 6-9**

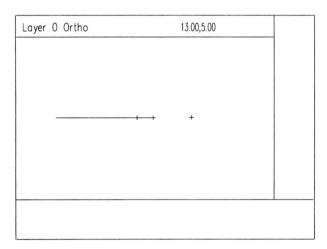

**Figure 6-10**

> Press enter or the space bar to repeat BREAK.
> Select the left side of the original line with a point toward the left end.

We want to cut a piece out of the middle of the left side, so the second point needs to be to the right of the first point, but still toward the middle of the left-hand line.

NOTE: It is actually not necessary that the second point be on the line at all. It could be above or below it, as in *Figure 6-11*. AutoCAD will break the line along a perpendicular between the point we choose and the line we are breaking. The same system would apply if we were breaking a polyline or a trace. An arc or a circle would be broken along a line between the selected point and the center of the arc or circle.

> Select a second point on or off the line, somewhat to the right of the first point.

Your line should now have a piece cut out, as in *Figure 6-11*. Notice that there are now three separate lines on the screen.

BREAK is a very useful command, but there are times when it is cumbersome to shorten objects one at a time. The TRIM command has some limitations that BREAK does not, but it is much more efficient in situations where you want to shorten objects at intersections.

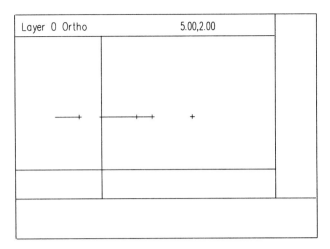

**Figure 6-11**

### TASK 5: Using the TRIM command

*Procedure.*

1. Type or select "TRIM".
2. Select a cutting edge, or edges.
3. Press enter to end the cutting edge selection process.
4. Select object to trim.
5. Select other objects to trim.
6. Press enter to return to command prompt.

*Discussion.*    The TRIM command works wonders in many situations where you want to shorten objects at their intersections with other objects. It will work with lines, circles, arcs, and polylines (see Chapter 9). The only limitation is that you must have at least two objects and they must cross or meet. If you are not trimming to an intersection, use BREAK.

> In preparation for exploring TRIM, clear your screen and then draw two horizontal lines crossing a circle, as in *Figure 6-12*. Exact locations are not important.

We will first use the TRIM command to go from *Figure 6-12* to *Figure 6-13*.

> Type or select "TRIM".

The first thing AutoCAD will want you to specify is at least one cutting edge. A cutting edge is an entity you want to use to trim another entity. That is, you want the trimmed entity to end at its intersection with the cutting edge. The prompt looks like this:

>                     Select cutting edge(s)...
>                     Select objects:

The first line reminds you that you are selecting edges first—the objects you want to trim will be selected later. The option of selecting more than one edge is a useful one, which we will get to shortly.

For now we will select the circle as an edge and use it to trim the upper line.

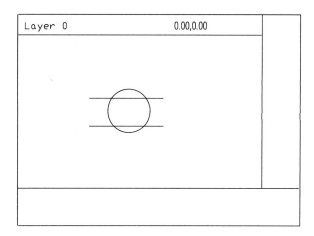

**Figure 6-12**

> Select the circle by pointing.

    The circle becomes dotted and will remain so until you leave the TRIM command.

    AutoCAD will now prompt for more objects until you indicate that you are through selecting edges.

> Press enter or the space bar to end the selection of cutting edges.

    You will be prompted for an object to trim:

Select object to trim:

    We will trim off the segment of the upper line that lies outside the circle on the left. The important thing is to point to the part of the object you want to remove, as shown by the blips in *Figure 6-13*.

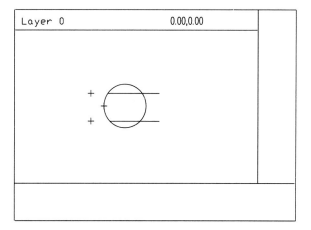

**Figure 6-13**

> Point to the upper line to the left of where it crosses the circle.

    The line is trimmed immediately, but the circle is still dotted, and AutoCAD continues to prompt for more objects to trim. Note how this differs from the BREAK command, in which you could only break one object at a time.

> Point to the lower line to the left of where it crosses the circle.

    You have now trimmed both lines.

> Press enter or the space bar to end the TRIM operation.

    Your screen should now resemble *Figure 6-13*.

This has been a very simple trimming process, but more complex trimming is just as easy. The key is that you can select as many edges as you like and that an entity may be selected as both an edge and an object to trim, as we will demonstrate.

> Repeat the TRIM command (it will repeat automatically if you are using the pull down menu).

> Select both lines and the circle as cutting edges.

This could be done with a window or with a "crossing" box. If you have not used the crossing method for selection yet, now is a good time to try it. Type "c" or select "crossing" where you would usually select "window" or type "w". If you have selected the TRIM command from the pull down menu, simply open a crossing box to the left instead of to the right.

> Press enter to end the selection of edges.

> Point to each of the remaining two line segments that lie outside the circle on the right and to the top and bottom arcs of the circle to produce the "Band-Aid" shaped object in *Figure 6-14*.

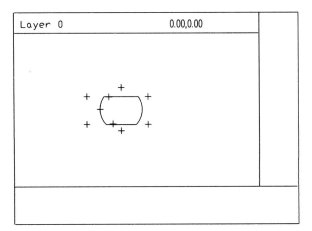

**Figure 6-14**

> Press enter to exit the TRIM command, or cancel it if you are using the pull down system.

### TASK 6: The EXTEND command

*Procedure.*

1. Type or select "EXTEND".
2. Select a boundary, or boundaries.
3. Press enter to end the boundary selection process.
4. Select object to extend.
5. Select other objects to extend.
6. Press enter to return to command prompt.

*Discussion.* If you compare the procedures of the EXTEND command and the TRIM command you will notice a remarkable similarity. Just substitute the word "boundary" for "cutting edge" and the word "extend" for "trim" and you've got it. These two commands are so quick to use that it is sometimes efficient to draw a cutting edge or boundary on your screen and erase it later if it is not really part of your drawing.

> Leave *Figure 6-14*, the "Band-Aid," on your screen and draw a vertical line to the right of it, as in *Figure 6-15*. We will use this line as a boundary to which to extend the two horizontal lines, as in *Figure 6-16*.

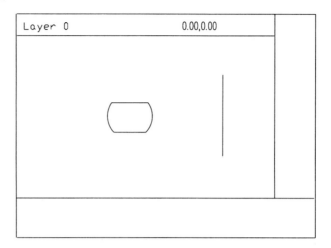

**Figure 6-15**

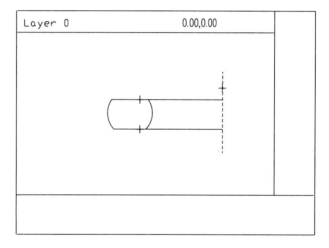

**Figure 6-16**

> Type or select "EXTEND".

You will be prompted for objects to serve as boundaries:

Select boundary edge(s)...
Select objects:

Look familiar? As with the TRIM command, any of the usual selection methods will work. For our purposes, simply point to the vertical line.
> Point to the vertical line on the right.

You will be prompted for more boundary objects until you press enter.
> Press enter or the space bar to end the selection of boundaries.

AutoCAD now asks for objects to extend:

Select objects to extend:

> Point to the right half of one of the two horizontal lines.

Notice that you have to point to the line on the side closest to the selected boundary. Otherwise AutoCAD will look to the left instead of the right and give you the following message:

Entity does not intersect an edge

Note also that you can only select objects to extend by pointing. Windowing, crossing, or last selections will not work.
> Point to the right half of the other horizontal line.

Both lines should now be extended to the vertical line. Your screen should resemble *Figure 6-16*.

> If your menu makes use of "auto" repetition, cancel the EXTEND command before going on.

### TASK 7: The STRETCH command

*Procedure.*

1. Type or select "STRETCH".
2. Select objects to stretch, using at least one window or crossing selection.
3. Press enter to end selection.
4. Show first point of stretch displacement.
5. Show second point of stretch displacement.

*Discussion.* The STRETCH command is a phenomenal timesaver in special circumstances in which you want to move objects without disrupting their connections to other objects. Often STRETCH can take the place of a whole series of moves, trims, breaks, and extends. It is commonly used in such applications as moving doors or windows within walls without having to redraw the walls.

The term "stretch" must be understood to have a special meaning in AutoCAD. When a typical stretch is performed some objects are lengthened, while others are shortened, and others are simply moved.

We will do a simple stretch on the objects you have already drawn on your screen. This will give you a good basic understanding of the STRETCH command. Further experimentation on your own is also recommended.

> Type or select "STRETCH".
AutoCAD will prompt for objects to stretch in the following manner:

Select objects to stretch by window...
Select objects:

The first line of this prompt reminds you of a unique quality of the STRETCH command procedure. You must include at least one window or crossing selection in your selection set. Beyond that you can also include other selection types.

This restriction should not cause any trouble, because if you are using the command correctly you will most often use a crossing selection anyway.

Also notice that if you are using the AutoCAD menu, both the pull down and screen menus are programmed with macros that automate a "crossing" selection, which will make the next step unnecessary.

> If necessary, type "C" or select "crossing".

This tells AutoCAD that you want to select objects using the crossing method. You will be prompted for a corner:

First corner:

> Point to the first corner of a crossing box, as shown in *Figure 6-17*.

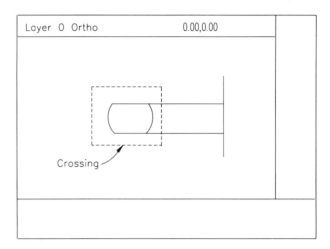

**Figure 6-17**

AutoCAD will prompt for a second corner:

Second corner:

> Point to a second corner, as shown in *Figure 6-17*.

AutoCAD will continue to prompt for objects, so we need to show that we are through selecting.

> Press enter or the space bar to end the selection process.

Now you will need to show the degree of stretch you want. In effect, you will be showing AutoCAD how far to move the objects that are completely within the box. Objects that cross the box will be extended or shrunk so that they remain connected to the objects that move.

The prompt sequence for this action is similar to the sequence for a move:

Base point:

> Pick any point near the middle of the screen, leaving room to indicate a horizontal displacement to the right.

AutoCAD prompts:

New point:

> Pick a second point to the right of the first, as shown in *Figure 6-18*.

The arcs will be moved to the right and the horizontal lines will be shrunk as shown. Notice that nothing here is being literally stretched. The arcs are being moved and the lines are being compressed. This is one of the ways STRETCH can be used.

Try performing another stretch like the one illustrated in *Figures 6-19* and *6-20*. Here the lines are being lengthened, while one arc moves and the other stays put, so that the original "Band-Aid" is indeed stretched.

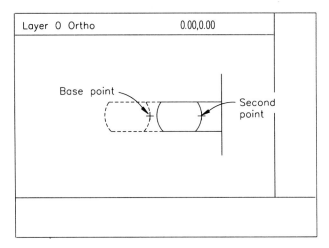

**Figure 6-18**

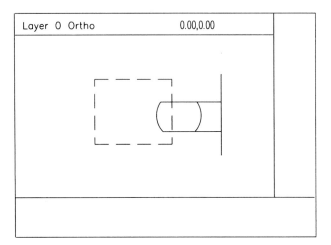

**Figure 6-19**

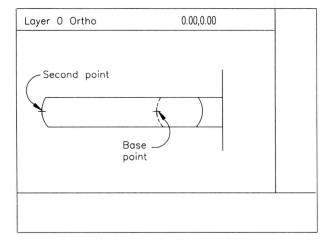

**Figure 6-20**

## TASKS 8, 9, 10, 11, 12, and 13

With OSNAP and the new editing commands you have learned in this chapter, you have reached a significant plateau. Most of the fundamental drawing, editing, and set-ting tools are now in your repertoire of CAD skills. The six drawings that follow will give you the opportunity to practice what you have learned. Notice that BREAK and TRIM are often used deliberately as part of a planned drawing sequence, whereas EXTEND and STRETCH tend to appear more frequently as "quick fixes" when something needs to be moved or changed.

# DRAWING 6-1: BIKE TIRE

This drawing can be done very quickly with the tools you now have. It makes use of one osnap, three trims, and a polar array. Be sure to set the limits large, as suggested.

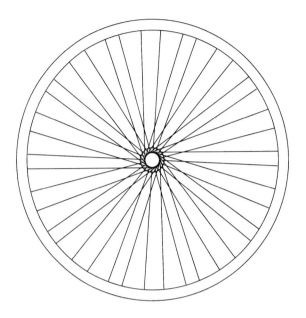

## *DRAWING SUGGESTIONS*

GRID = 1.00     LIMITS = (0,0) (48,36)
SNAP =   .25

> Begin by drawing the 1.25", 2.50", 24.00", and 26.00" diameter circles centered on the same point near the middle of your display.
> Draw line (a) using a QUADrant osnap to find the first point on the inside circle. The second point can be anywhere outside the 24" circle at 0 degrees from the first point. The exact length of the line is insignificant since we will be trimming it back to the circle.
> Draw line (b) from the center of the circles to a second point anywhere outside the 24" circle at an angle of 14 degrees. Remember to use the coordinate display to construct this angle. This line will also be trimmed.
> Trim lines (a) and (b) using the 24" circle as a cutting edge.
> Trim the other end of line (b) using the 1.25" circle as a cutting edge.
> Construct a polar array, selecting lines (a) and (b). There are 20 items in the array, and they are rotated as they are copied.

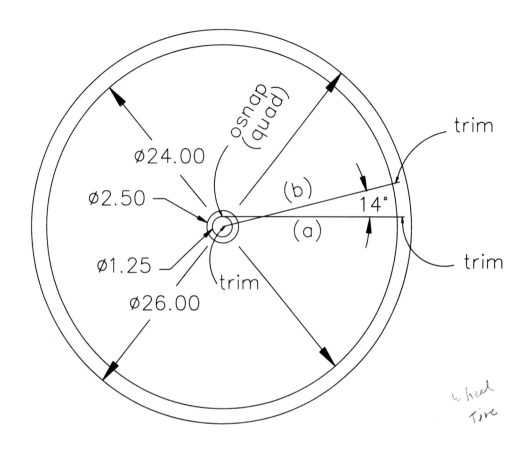

BIKE TIRE

Drawing 6-1

| LAYERS | NAME | COLOR | LINETYPE | | | (DRAW) | LINE |
|---|---|---|---|---|---|---|---|
| | 0 | WHITE | ——— | CONTINUOUS | | (DRAW) | CIRCLE |
| | 1 | RED | ——— | CONTINUOUS | | (EDIT) | ARRAY |
| | | | | | | (EDIT) | TRIM |
| | | | | | | (DISPLAY) | ZOOM |

| F1 | F6 | F7 | F8 | F9 |
|---|---|---|---|---|
| ON/OFF | ON/OFF | ON/OFF | ON/OFF | ON/OFF |
| SCREEN | COORDS | GRID | ORTHO | SNAP |

## DRAWING 6-2: ARCHIMEDES SPIRAL

This drawing and the next go together as an exercise you should find interesting and enjoyable. These are not technical drawings, but they will give you valuable experience with important CAD commands. You will be creating a spiral using a radial grid of circles and lines as a guide. Once the spiral is done, you will use it to create the designs in the next drawing, 6-3, "Spiral Designs."

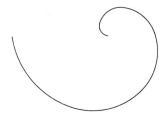

### *DRAWING SUGGESTIONS*

> GRID = .5    LIMITS = (0,0) (18,12)
> SNAP = .25   LTSCALE = .5

> The alternating continuous and hidden lines work as a drawing aid. If you have color they will be even more helpful.
> Begin by drawing all the continuous circles on layer 0, centered near the middle of your display. Use the continuous circle radii as listed.
> Draw the continuous horizontal line across the middle of your six circles and then array it in a three-item polar array.
> Set to layer 2 for the hidden lines. The procedure for the hidden lines and circles will be the same as for the continuous lines, except the radii are different and you will array a vertical line instead of a horizontal one.
> Set to layer 1 for the arc itself.
> Turn on a running osnap to intersection mode and construct a series of three-point arcs. Start points and end points will be on continuous line intersections; second points will always fall on hidden line intersections.
> When the spiral is complete, turn off layers 0 and 2. There should be nothing left on your screen but the spiral itself. Save it or go on to Drawing 6-3.

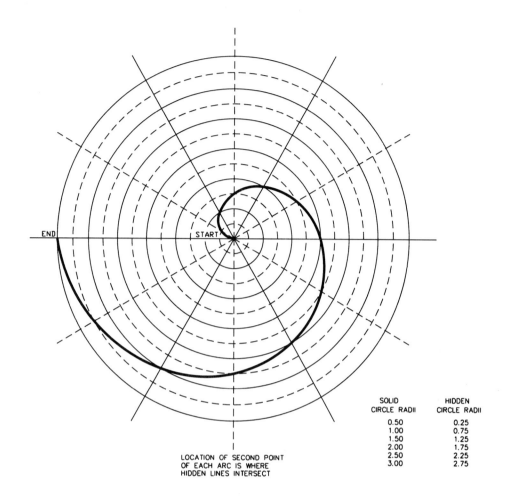

| SOLID CIRCLE RADII | HIDDEN CIRCLE RADII |
|---|---|
| 0.50 | 0.25 |
| 1.00 | 0.75 |
| 1.50 | 1.25 |
| 2.00 | 1.75 |
| 2.50 | 2.25 |
| 3.00 | 2.75 |

LOCATION OF SECOND POINT
OF EACH ARC IS WHERE
HIDDEN LINES INTERSECT

# ARCHIMEDES SPIRAL

## Drawing 6-2

| LAYERS | NAME | COLOR | LINETYPE | | | |
|---|---|---|---|---|---|---|
| | 0 | WHITE | ——— CONTINUOUS | (DRAW) | LINE |
| | 1 | RED | ——— CONTINUOUS | (DRAW) | CIRCLE |
| | 2 | YELLOW | - - - - HIDDEN | (DRAW) | ARC |
| | | | | (EDIT) | ARRAY |
| | | | | (DISPLAY) | PAN |
| | | | | (DISPLAY) | ZOOM |

| F1 | F6 | F7 | F8 | F9 |
|---|---|---|---|---|
| ON/OFF SCREEN | ON/OFF COORDS | ON/OFF GRID | ON/OFF ORTHO | ON/OFF SNAP |

# DRAWING 6-3: SPIRAL DESIGNS

These designs are different from other drawings in this book. There are no dimensions and you will use only edit commands now that the spiral is drawn. Below the designs is a list of the edit commands you will need. Don't be too concerned with precision. Some of your designs may come out slightly different from ours. When this happens, try to analyze the differences.

There is an important new technique described following. It is necessary for two of these designs and will also be used in Drawing 6-4, so be sure that you understand it. Otherwise, you are on your own.

## DRAWING SUGGESTIONS

$$LIMITS = (0,0) (34,24)$$

These large limits will be necessary if you wish to draw all of these designs on the screen at once.

## HOW TO ROTATE AN OBJECT
## AND RETAIN THE ORIGINAL

When you use the MIRROR command, you are given an option to retain the original along with the new mirror image. The ROTATE command has no such option. Here is a simple way to get around this:

> Make a copy of the objects you want to rotate directly on top of their originals. In other words, give the same point for the base point and the second point of displacement. In the designs here you will be copying the spiral and will want to use a window selection, since the spiral is made up of six arcs. When the copy is done your screen will not look any different, but there will actually be two spirals there, one on top of the other.
> Type or select "ROTATE" and give "p" or "previous" in response to the "select objects" prompt. This will select all the original objects from the last COPY sequence, without selecting the newly drawn copies.
> Rotate as usual. In this exercise the base point you choose for rotation will depend on the design you are trying to create.
> After the ROTATE sequence is complete, you will need to do a REDRAW before the objects copied in the original position will be visible.

SPIRAL DESIGNS

(Make from Drawing 6-2)

Drawing 6-3

| LAYERS | NAME | COLOR | LINETYPE | | | |
|--------|------|-------|----------|---|---|---|
| | 0 | WHITE | ———— CONTINUOUS | | (EDIT) | COPY |
| | 1 | RED | ———— CONTINUOUS | | (EDIT) | MOVE |
| | | | | | (EDIT) | ROTATE |
| | | | | | (EDIT) | ARRAY |
| | | | | | (EDIT) | MIRROR |
| | | | | | (DISPLAY) | PAN |
| | | | | | (DISPLAY) | ZOOM |

| F1 | F6 | F7 | F8 | F9 |
|----|----|----|----|----|
| ON/OFF SCREEN | ON/OFF COORDS | ON/OFF GRID | ON/OFF ORTHO | ON/OFF SNAP |

## DRAWING 6-4: GROOVED HUB

This drawing includes a typical application of the rotation technique just discussed. The hidden lines in the front view must be rotated 120 degrees and a copy retained in the original position. There are also good opportunities to use MIRROR, object snap, and TRIM.

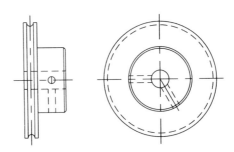

### *DRAWING SUGGESTIONS*

GRID = .5      LIMITS = (0,0) (18,12)

SNAP = .0625   LTSCALE = 1

> Draw the circles in the front view and use these to line up the horizontal lines in the left side view.

> There are several different planes of symmetry in the left side view which suggest the use of mirroring. We leave it up to you to choose an efficient sequence.

> A quick method for drawing the horizontal hidden lines in the left side view is to use a quadrant osnap to begin a line at the top and bottom of the .62 DIA circle in the front view. Draw this line across to the back of the left side view and use TRIM to erase the excess on both sides.

> The same method can be used to draw the two horizontal hidden lines in the front view. Snap to the top and bottom quadrants of the .25 DIA circle in the left side view as a guide and draw lines through the front view. Then trim to the 2.25 DIA circle and the .62 DIA circle.

> Once these hidden lines are drawn, rotate them, retaining a copy in the original position.

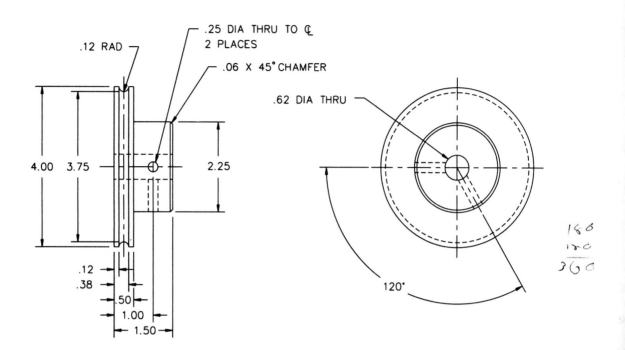

.12 RAD

.25 DIA THRU TO ₵
2 PLACES

.06 X 45° CHAMFER

.62 DIA THRU

4.00  3.75    2.25

.12
.38
.50
1.00
1.50

120°

GROOVED HUB
Drawing 6-4

| LAYERS | NAME | COLOR | LINETYPE | | (DRAW) | LINE |
|--------|------|-------|----------|--|--------|------|
| | 0 | WHITE | ———— CONTINUOUS | | (DRAW) | CIRCLE |
| | | | | | (DRAW) | ARC |
| | 1 | RED | ———— CONTINUOUS | | (EDIT) | CHAMFER |
| | 2 | YELLOW | ------- HIDDEN | | (EDIT) | COPY |
| | | | | | (EDIT) | BREAK |
| | 3 | GREEN | —·—·— CENTER | | (EDIT) | TRIM |
| | | | | | (EDIT) | MIRROR |
| | | | | | (EDIT) | ROTATE |
| | | | | | (DISPLAY) | ZOOM |

| F1 | F6 | F7 | F8 | F9 |
|----|----|----|----|----|
| ON/OFF | ON/OFF | ON/OFF | ON/OFF | ON/OFF |
| SCREEN | COORDS | GRID | ORTHO | SNAP |

# DRAWING 6-5: CAP IRON

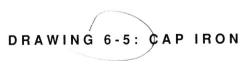

This drawing is of a type of blade used in a wood plane. When wood is planed, the cap iron causes it to curl up out of the plane so that it does not jam. There are several good applications for the TRIM command.

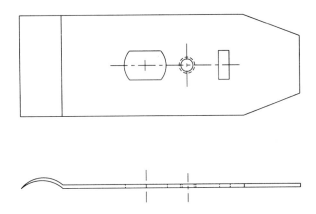

## *DRAWING SUGGESTIONS*

GRID = .5      LIMITS = (0,0) (18,12)
SNAP = .0625   LTSCALE = .25

> The circle with a hidden line outside a continuous line indicates a tapped hole. The dimension is given to the hidden line; the continuous inner line is drawn just inside, with a slightly smaller radius that is not specified.

> You may find it helpful to use the DIST command to position the smaller figures within the top view.

> The figure near the center of the top view that has two arcs with .38 radii can be drawn exactly as the "Band-Aid," *Figure 6-14* in Task 4 of this chapter. Draw a circle and two horizontal lines and then trim it all down.

> The .54 and .58 arcs in the front view can be drawn using start, end, and radius.

> The small vertical hidden lines in the front view can be done using a system introduced in the previous drawing. Draw lines down from the figures in the top view and then trim them. For the tapped hole and the arced opening in the middle you will have to use osnaps to right and left quadrant points to locate the start of these lines.

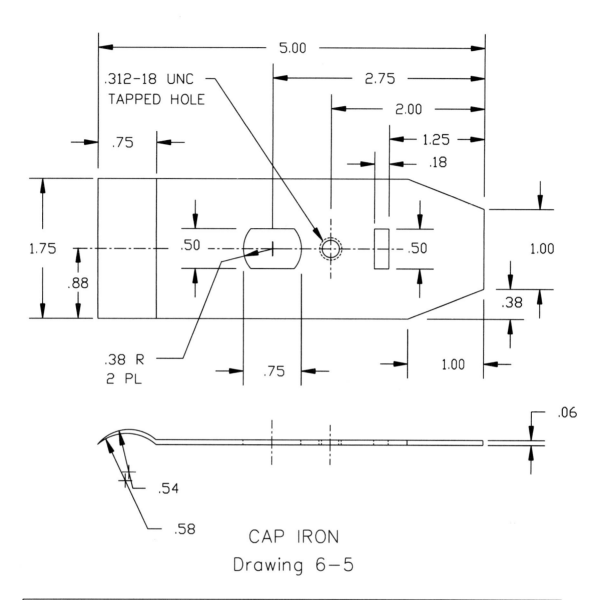

.312-18 UNC
TAPPED HOLE

.38 R
2 PL

CAP IRON
Drawing 6-5

| LAYERS | NAME | COLOR | LINETYPE | | | |
|---|---|---|---|---|---|---|
| | 0 | WHITE | —————— CONTINUOUS | | (DRAW) | LINE |
| | 1 | RED | —————— CONTINUOUS | | (DRAW) | CIRCLE |
| | 2 | YELLOW | ------------ HIDDEN | | (DRAW) | ARC |
| | 3 | GREEN | —-—-— CENTER | | (EDIT) | BREAK |
| | | | | | (EDIT) | TRIM |
| | | | | | (EDIT) | CHAMFER |
| | | | | | (DISPLAY) | ZOOM |

| F1 | F6 | F7 | F8 | F9 |
|---|---|---|---|---|
| ON/OFF | ON/OFF | ON/OFF | ON/OFF | ON/OFF |
| SCREEN | COORDS | GRID | ORTHO | SNAP |

## DRAWING 6-6: DECK FRAMING

This architectural drawing may take some time, although there is nothing in it you have not done before. Notice that the settings are quite different from our standard prototype, so be sure to change them before beginning.

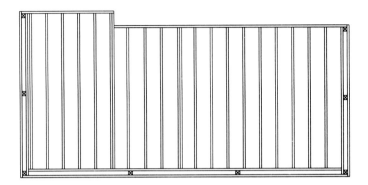

### *DRAWING SUGGESTIONS*

UNITS = Architectural
                    smallest fraction = 1
LIMITS = (0,0) (36′,24′)
GRID = 1′
SNAP = 2″
AXIS = SNAP

> Whatever order you choose for doing this drawing, we suggest that you make ample use of COPY, ARRAY, and TRIM.
> Keep ortho on, except to draw the lines across the middle of the squares.
> With snap set at 2″ it is easy to use the arrow keys to copy lines 2″ apart, as you will be doing frequently to draw the 2″ × 8″ studs.
> You may need to turn snap off when you are selecting lines to copy, but be sure to turn it on again to specify displacements.
> Notice that you can use ARRAY effectively, but that there are three separate arrays. They are all 16″ on center, but the double boards in several places make it inadvisable to do a single array of studs all the way across the deck. What you can do, however, is to draw, copy, and array all the vertical studs first and then go back and trim them to their various lengths using the horizontal boards as cutting edges.

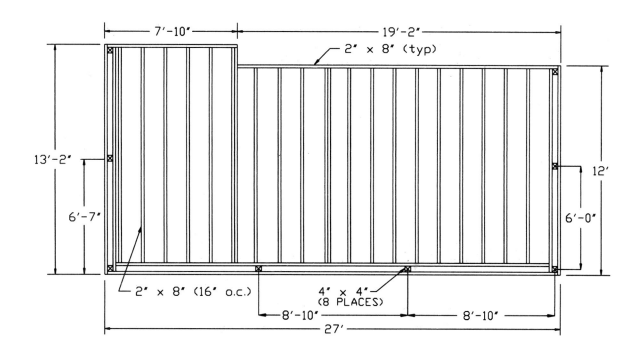

## DECK FRAMING

### Drawing 6-6

| LAYERS | NAME | COLOR | LINETYPE | | | (DRAW) | LINE |
|--------|------|-------|----------|---|---|--------|------|
| | 0 | WHITE | ——— CONTINUOUS | | | (EDIT) | COPY |
| | 1 | RED | ——— CONTINUOUS | | | (EDIT) | TRIM |
| | | | | | | (EDIT) | ARRAY |
| | | | | | | (EDIT) | EXTEND |
| | | | | | | (DISPLAY) | ZOOM |
| | | | | | | (DISPLAY) | PAN |

| F1 | F6 | F7 | F8 | F9 |
|----|----|----|----|----|
| ON/OFF SCREEN | ON/OFF COORDS | ON/OFF GRID | ON/OFF ORTHO | ON/OFF SNAP |

234
- 8
———
6

'27
7
———
34

7'  10"
7    2"
————
14  12"

'25
- 8
———
7

# chapter

**COMMANDS**

| DRAW | EDIT |
|------|------|
| TEXT | CHANGE |
| DTEXT | SCALE |
| STYLE | |

**OVERVIEW**

It's time to add text to your drawings. In this chapter you will learn to find your way around the AutoCAD TEXT commands and subcommands. In addition, you will learn two new editing commands, CHANGE and SCALE, that are often used with text but that are equally important for editing other objects.

**TASKS**

1. Enter standard text using six placement options.
2. Enter multiline text.
3. Enter multiline text using the DTEXT command.
4. Change fonts and styles.
5. Use the CHANGE command to edit previously drawn text.
6. Use the CHANGE command to edit other entities.
7. Use SCALE to change the size of objects on the screen.
8. Do Drawing 7-1 ("Title Block").
9. Do Drawing 7-2 ("Gauges").
10. Do Drawing 7-3 ("Stamping").
11. Do Drawing 7-4 ("Control Panel").

### TASK 1: Enter text in standard style

*Procedure.*

1.  Type or select "TEXT".
2.  Type or select an option.
3.  Pick a location.
4.  Answer prompts regarding height and rotation.
5.  Type text.

*Discussion.*    TEXT is one of the more complex of the AutoCAD commands. There are six options for placing text in a drawing and also a variety of fonts to use and styles that can be created from them. In the first three tasks we will focus on placement and stick to the standard text style. In Task 4 we will explore other styles and fonts.

> To prepare for this exercise, begin a new drawing called "7-1" or "A:7-1". Draw a 4.00 horizontal line beginning at (1,1). Then create a 6 row by 1 column array with 2.00 between rows, as shown in *Figure 7-1*.

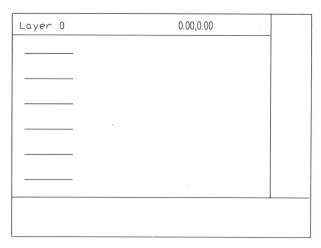

**Figure 7-1**

> Type or select "TEXT".
    You will see a prompt with a number of options:

Start point or Align/Center/Fit/Middle/Right/Style:

    In this task, we will be going through all the options given, except for the "Style" option. For this option, see the note at the end of Task 4.
    The simplest response is to indicate a start point. This point will become the point from which left-justified text is drawn.
> Pick a start point at the left end of the upper line.
    Look at the prompt that follows and be sure that you do not attempt to enter text yet:

Height <0.20>:

    This gives you the opportunity to set the text height. The number you type specifies the height of uppercase letters in the units you have specified for the current drawing. For now we will accept the default height.

> Press enter to accept the default height (0.20).

The prompt that follows allows you to place text in a rotated position.

Rotation angle <0>:

The default of 0 degrees orients text in the usual horizontal manner. Other angles can be specified by typing a degree number relative to the polar coordinate system, or by showing a point. If you show a point, it will be taken as the second point of a baseline along which the text string will be placed. For now, we will stick to horizontal text.

> Press enter to accept the default angle (0).

Now, at last, it is time to enter the text itself. AutoCAD prompts:

Text:

For our text we will type the word "Left" since this is an example of left-justified text.

> Type "Left" and press enter. (Remember that you cannot use the space bar in place of the enter key when entering text.)

*Figure 7-2* shows the left-justified text you have just drawn along with the other options as we will demonstrate them in the rest of this exercise.

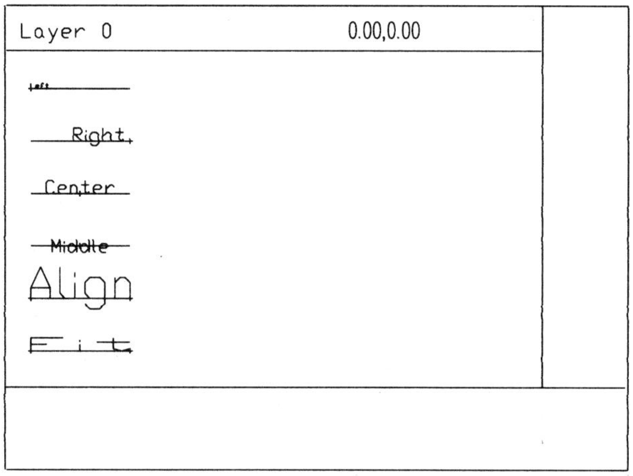

**Figure 7-2**

We will proceed to try out all the other text placement options, beginning with right-justified text, as shown on the second line of *Figure 7-2*. We will also specify a change in height.

*Right-justified text:*

> Reenter the TEXT command.

You will see the same prompt as before.

> Type "r" or select "Right".

Now AutoCAD prompts you for an end point instead of a start point:

End point:

We will choose the end of the second line.

> Point to the right end of the second line.

We will change the height to .50. Notice that AutoCAD gives you a rubber band from the end point. It can be used to specify height and rotation angle by pointing, if you like.

> Type ".5" and press enter or show a height of .50 by pointing.
> Press enter to retain 0 degrees of rotation.

You are now prompted to enter text.

> Type "Right" and press enter.

Your screen should now include the second line of text.

*Centered text:*

> Reenter the TEXT command.
> Type "c" or select "Center".
AutoCAD prompts:

Center:

> Point to the midpoint of the third line.
> Press enter to retain the current height, which is now set to .50.
> Press enter to retain 0 degrees of rotation.
> Type "Center" and press enter.

*Middle text:*

> Reenter the TEXT command.
> Type "m" or select "Middle".
AutoCAD prompts:

Middle point:

> Point to the midpoint of the fourth line.
> Press enter to retain the current height of .50.
> Press enter to retain 0 degrees of rotation.
> Type "Middle" and press enter.

Notice the difference between center and middle. Center refers to the midpoint of the baseline below the text. Middle refers to the actual middle of the text itself, so that the line now runs through the middle of the text.

*Aligned text:*

> Reenter the TEXT command.
> Type "a" or select "aligned".
AutoCAD prompts:

First text line point:

> Point to the left end of the fifth line.
AutoCAD prompts for another point:

Second text line point:

> Point to the right end of the fifth line.

Notice that there is no prompt for height. AutoCAD will calculate a height based on the space between the points you chose.

There is also no prompt for an angle, because the angle between your two points (in this case 0) will be used.
> Type "Align" and press enter.

*Text drawn to fit between two points:*

> Reenter the TEXT command.
> Type "f" or select "Fit".
   You will be prompted for two points as in the "Align" option.
> Point to the left end of the sixth line.
> Point to the right end of the sixth line.
> Press enter to retain the current height.
   As in the align option, there will be no prompt for an angle of rotation.
> Type "Fit" and press enter.
   Even though the text is considerably stretched to make it fit between the given points, the height is .50, as specified. This is the difference between fit and align. In the align option, text height is determined by the width you show. With fit, the specified height is retained and the text is stretched or compressed to fill the given space.

## TASK 2: Entering multiline text

*Procedure.*

1. Enter a line of text using any of the placement options.
2. Press enter to reenter the TEXT command.
3. Press enter at the "Start point or Align..." prompt.
4. Type text and press enter.

*Discussion.*    If you have several lines of text to enter in one place on your drawing, you will want to avoid having to position each line separately. To do this, enter the first line of text in the usual manner, with any of the placement options discussed previously. Then press enter twice to repeat the TEXT command and bring back the "Text:" prompt. New text will be positioned directly beneath the previous line with the same height and rotation angle. Line spacing will be determined by AutoCAD based on text height.

In this exercise we will create three lines of left-justified text, one below the other, all rotated 45 degrees.

> Reenter the TEXT command.
   You will see the familiar prompt:

Start point or Align/Center/Fit/Middle/Right/Style:

> Pick a starting point near (9.50,7.50), as shown by the blip next to the word "These" in *Figure 7-3*.
> Press enter to retain the current height.
> Type "45" or show an angle of 45 degrees.
> Type "These lines" and press enter.
   The text will be drawn on the screen at a 45 degree angle and you will be returned to the "Command:" prompt. The steps that follow are the new ones for drawing multiline text.
> Press enter to repeat the TEXT command.

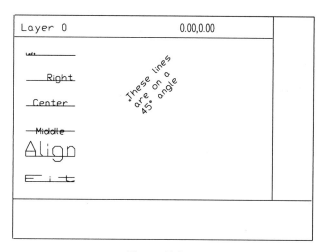

**Figure 7-3**

> Press enter again.

This tells AutoCAD that you want to continue entering text below the previous line. Other prompts will be skipped and you will be prompted for text.

> Type "are on a" and press enter.

> Press enter again to repeat the TEXT command.

> Press enter once more to indicate that you want to add another line of multiline text.

Other prompts will be skipped and you will be prompted for text.

The next line contains a degree symbol. Since you do not have this character on your keyboard, AutoCAD provides a special method for drawing it. Type the text with the %% signs just as shown and then study *Figure 7-4*, which lists other special characters that can be drawn this way.

| CONTROL CODES AND SPECIAL CHARACTERS | |
|---|---|
| Type at TEXT PROMPT | TEXT on Drawing |
| %%O OVERSCORE | OVERSCORE |
| %%U UNDERSCORE | UNDERSCORE |
| 180 %%D | 180 ° |
| 2.00 %%P.01 | 2.00 ±.01 |
| %%C4.00 | ⌀4.00 |
| (%%ASCII CODE #) | (ASCII SYMBOL) |
| %%125 | } |
| %%126 | ~ |
| %%128 | ± |

**Figure 7-4**

> Type "45%%d angle." and press enter.

Your screen should now resemble *Figure 7-3*.

**TASK 3: Writing text directly to the screen with DTEXT**

*Procedure.*

1. Type or select "DTEXT".
2. Type or select an option.
3. Pick a location.
4. Answer prompts regarding height and rotation.
5. Type a line of text and press enter.
6. Type a line of text and press enter.
7. Type a line of text and press enter...
8. Press enter to exit the command.

*Discussion.*    The DTEXT command ("dynamic text") is a variation of the TEXT command that allows you to see how your text will appear on the screen as you enter it. It also creates multiline text automatically, without having to repeat the command, and allows you to edit by backspacing through these multiple lines.

> At the "Command:" prompt, type or select "DTEXT".
You will be prompted as if you were in the TEXT command:

Start point or Align/Center/Fit/Middle/Right/Style:

Notice that the command sequence is identical for TEXT and DTEXT. Any of the options could be selected, but left-justified text works best. With other options you will not see the text as it will actually appear until after you have completed the command sequence.
> Pick a start point near (9.50,5.00), as shown by the blip next to the word "Dynamic" in *Figure 7-5.*

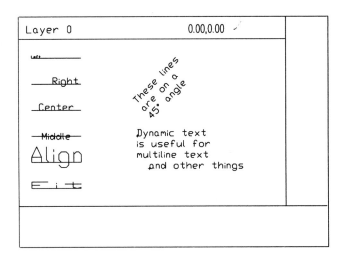

**Figure 7-5**

> Press enter twice to retain the height (0.5).
You will be prompted for rotation angle next. Notice that the current angle is now 45:

Rotation angle <45>:

> Type "0" to return to horizontal orientation.

You should now see the prompt for text.

You will also see that a text location box has been placed next to your start point. This box is the height and width of your text. As you type, watch the screen to see how DTEXT works.

> Type "Dynamic text" and press enter.

Instead of exiting the command after drawing the text, DTEXT returns you to the text prompt for another line of text.

> Type "is useful for" and press enter.

> Type "multiline text" and press enter.

You should be at the "Text:" prompt again to try out one more convenient feature of the DTEXT command. Move your cursor and notice that you still have control of the cross hairs. If you select a new start point now, your next line of text will be placed there. Try it.

> At the "Text:" prompt, pick a new starting point near (10.50,2.00), as shown by the blip near the word "and" in *Figure 7-5*.

> Type "and other things".

DTEXT will continue to return the "Text:" prompt until it receives a null response.

> Press enter to exit DTEXT.

### TASK 4: Changing styles

*Procedure.*

1.  Type or select "STYLE".
2.  Type a new style name.
3.  Type a font file name.
4.  Answer prompts for height, width, angle, and orientation.

Or, from the pull down menu bar:

1.  Select "Options".
2.  Select "Fonts".
3.  Select a font from the icon menu.
4.  Answer prompts for height, width, angle, and orientation.

*Discussion.*    By default, the current text style in any AutoCAD drawing is one called "standard." It is a specific form of a font called "txt" that comes with the software. All the text you have entered so far has been drawn with the standard style of the "txt" font. With Release 9, AutoCAD introduced 20 new fonts, including ones for mapping, musical, astronomical, and meteorological symbols.

Changing fonts is a simple matter. However, there is a lot of room for confusion in the use of the words "style" and "font". You can avoid this confusion if you remember that fonts are the basic patterns of character and symbol shapes that can be used with the TEXT and DTEXT commands, while styles are variations in the size, orientation, and spacing of the characters in those fonts. It is possible to create your own fonts, but for most of us this is an esoteric activity. In contrast, creating your own styles is easy and practical.

We will begin by creating a variation of the STANDARD style you have been using. If you are using Release 9 or higher versions of AutoCAD, there is a convenient icon menu that we will get to shortly. However, the whole system will make more sense if you do not use the pull down menu yet.

> Type or select "STYLE".

You will be prompted as follows:

Text style name (or ?) <STANDARD>:

By now you should be familiar with the elements of this prompt. We will use the "?" first to see a list of available styles.

> Type "?".

AutoCAD will switch over to the text screen and give you the following information:

Text styles:

Style name: STANDARD      Font files: txt
Height: 0.00   Width factor: 1.00   Obliquing angle: 0
Generation: Normal

Current text style: STANDARD

If anyone has used text commands in your prototype drawing, it is possible that there will be other styles listed. However, STANDARD is the only one that is certain to be there, because it is created automatically.

We will create our own variation of the STANDARD style and call it "VERTICAL." It will use the same "txt" character font, but will be drawn down the display instead of across.

> Press enter to repeat the STYLE command.

You will see this prompt again:

Text style name (or ?) <STANDARD>:

> Type "vertical".

AutoCAD will respond:

New style.
Font file <txt>:

We will continue to use the "txt" font.

> Press enter to retain the current font.

AutoCAD prompts:

Height <0.00>:

It is important to understand what 0 height means in the STYLE command. It does not mean that your characters will be drawn 0.00 units high. It means that there will be no fixed height, so you will be able to set it whenever you use this style. Notice that STANDARD currently has no fixed height. That is why you are prompted for a height whenever you use it. In general, it is best to leave height variable unless you know that you will be drawing a large amount of text with one height.

For practice, try giving "VERTICAL" a fixed height.

> Type ".5".

AutoCAD prompts:

Width factor <1.00>:

This prompt allows you to stretch or shrink characters in the font based on a factor of one. Let's double the width to see how it looks.

> Type "2".

AutoCAD prompts:

Obliquing angle:

This allows you to put any font on a slant, right or left, creating an italic effect. We will leave this one alone for the moment; italics look better in horizontal text.

> Press enter to retain 0 degrees of slant.

AutoCAD follows with a series of three prompts regarding the orientation of characters. The first one is:

Backwards? <N>:

Obviously this is for special effects. You can try this one in a moment.

> Press enter to retain "frontwards" text.

The second orientation prompt is even more peculiar:

Upside down? <N>:

> Press enter if you want your text to be drawn right-side up.

Finally, the one we've been waiting for:

Vertical? <N>:

This is what allows us to create a vertical style text.

> Type "y".

Before returning the "Command:" prompt, AutoCAD will tell you that your new style is now current:

VERTICAL is now the current text style.

To see your new style in action you will need to enter some text.

> Type or select "TEXT".

> Pick a start point, as shown by the blip near the letter "V" in *Figure 7-6*.

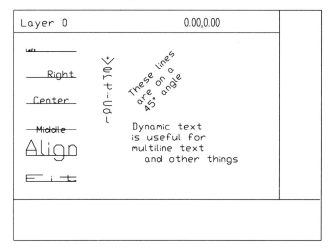

**Figure 7-6**

Notice that you are not prompted for a height because the current style has height fixed at .50.

> Press enter to retain 270 degrees of rotation.
> Type "Vertical".
Your screen should resemble *Figure 7-6*.

*Icon Menus:*    Now that you are familiar with the STYLE command try creating a new style from the pull down icon menu. (If your version of AutoCAD is 2.6 or earlier, enter the Style command again and try creating new styles using the "Simplex," "Complex," and "Italic" fonts.)

> Select "Options" from the pull down menu bar.
> Select "Fonts" from the menu.

What you see next will be the font icon menu, as illustrated in *Figure 7-7*. Icon menus are similar to dialogue boxes but offer an illustrated set of options from which to choose. You will look through the images presented and then pick the item you want by selecting the small box beside it. Try it.

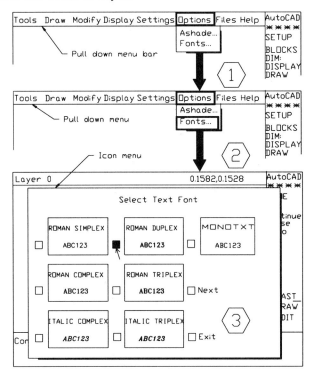

**Figure 7-7**

> Select "Roman Duplex".
The icon menu will disappear, leaving you in the middle of the STYLE command sequence as follows:

        Text style name (or ?) <VERTICAL>: romand
        New style.
        Font file <txt>: romand  Height <0.0000>:

Reading this series of prompts and responses will show what the icon menu has done for you. It has entered the STYLE command and initiated a new style called "romand" (Roman Duplex). The font file to be used in the creation of this style has the same name as the style itself, "romand". Now AutoCAD is asking you to complete the style definition, beginning with a height.

> Press enter to retain variable height (0.00).

The rest of the command sequence will be familiar from the STYLE command. We will retain all the defaults except for the obliquing angle.

> Press enter to retain a width factor of 1.

> Type "−45" and press enter.

This will cause your text to be slanted 45 degrees to the left. For a right slant, of course, you would type a positive number.

> Press enter three more times to retain the defaults for backwards, upside-down, and vertical.

AutoCAD will now tell you:

ROMAND is now the current text style.

Now enter some text to see how this slanted Roman Duplex style looks.

> Type or select "TEXT" or "DTEXT" and answer the prompts to draw the words "Roman Duplex" with a .50 height, as shown in *Figure 7-8.*

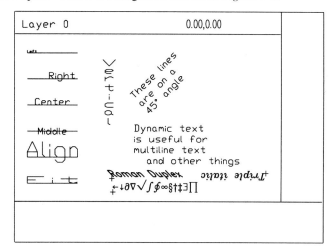

**Figure 7-8**

After you have completed the Roman Duplex text, use the icon menu to create two more lines of text, as shown in *Figure 7-8.* The last line is in mathematical symbols, the characters that are called out by typing "abcdefghijklm" when the "symath" font file has been chosen and styled with all the defaults and a .50 height. For a complete chart of alphabet to symbol correspondence in all the symbolic fonts, see the *AutoCAD Reference Manual,* Appendix A.6.

NOTE: Once you have a number of styles defined in a drawing, you can switch from one to another with the "Style" option of the TEXT and DTEXT commands. This option is only for switching previously defined styles; it will not allow you to define new ones.

### TASK 5: Changing previously drawn text with CHANGE

*Procedure.*

1. Type or select "CHANGE".
2. Select objects (text).
3. Pick a new location or press enter for no change.
4. Type or select a new text style or press enter for no change.

5. Type or show a new height or press enter for no change.
6. Type or show a new rotation angle or press enter for no change.
7. Type new text or press enter for no change.

*Discussion.* The CHANGE command is a very useful tool that allows you to change a number of different entities, text being only one of them. The qualities of previously drawn text that can be changed are location, style, height, rotation angle, and the text itself. You can change all the properties at once if need be, but more often you will be changing only one or two. Properties you do not wish to change are retained by pressing enter.

In this exercise we will use the CHANGE command twice to edit some of the text you have already drawn.

> Type or select "CHANGE".

You will be prompted to select objects:

Select objects:

> Point to the word "Left", the first line of text you entered in Task 1.
> Press enter to end selection.

AutoCAD will now issue the first of a series of prompts that ask you to specify what you would like to change:

Properties/<Change point>:

"Properties" refers to a list of options, including color, layer, and linetype, which we will discuss in Task 6. "Change point" has different meanings with different types of entities. In the case of text, it allows you to relocate the text (this could also be done with the MOVE command).

> Pick a point slightly above the line that the text is written on.

The text will be moved and another prompt issued. This prompt will allow you to change styles:

Text style: Standard
New style or RETURN for no change:

Let's change to Roman Duplex.

> Type "romand".

You are now prompted for a change in height:

New height <0.00>:

We will change to .50 so that this line of text matches the ones below it.

> Type ".5".

The next prompt is for a change in rotation angle:

New rotation angle <0>:

We will retain this angle.

> Press enter to retain horizontal orientation.

Finally, AutoCAD prompts for a change in the characters themselves:

New Text <left>:

Two common applications for this option are rewording and respelling. A less obvious but very useful application is shown in Drawing 7-2, "Gauges."

We will change the wording to "Left justified".
> Type "Left justified".
Your screen should now resemble *Figure 7-9*.

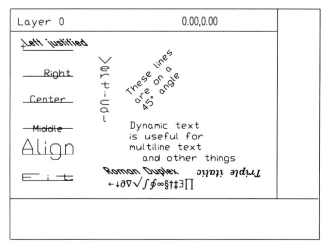

**Figure 7-9**

## TASK 6: CHANGEing other entities

*Procedure.*

1. Type or select "CHANGE".
2. Define a selection set.
3. Press enter to end selection.
4. Type or select properties or show a change point.

*Discussion.* You can change the properties, including layer, color, linetype, elevation (3D), and thickness (3D), of any entity. In addition, you can use a change point to alter the size of lines and circles. With lines, CHANGE will perform a function similar to the EXTEND command, but without the necessity of a boundary to extend them to. With circles, CHANGE will cause them to be redrawn so that they pass through the change point.

> Reenter the CHANGE command.
You will be prompted to:

Select objects:

> Select the first two lines, under the words "Left justified" and "Right".
> Press enter to end selection.
AutoCAD prompts:

Properties/<Change point>:

We will use a change point first to alter the selected lines, as shown in *Figure 7-10*.
> If ortho is on turn it off (F8).
> Pick a point between the two lines and to the right, in the neighborhood of (6.50,10.00).
The lines will be redrawn so that the change point becomes the new end point of both lines.

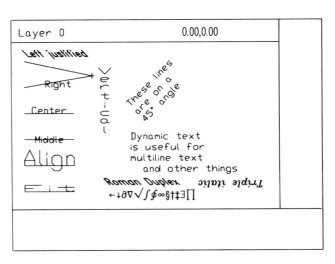

**Figure 7-10**

To maintain horizontal or vertical orientation of lines while using the change point option of the CHANGE command, turn ortho on. Try it.

> Turn ortho on.
> Reenter the CHANGE command.
> Select the third, fourth, fifth, and sixth lines where the words "center," "middle," "align," and "fit" are drawn.
> Press enter to end selection.
> Pick a change point to the right of the lines, as shown by the blip in *Figure 7-11*.

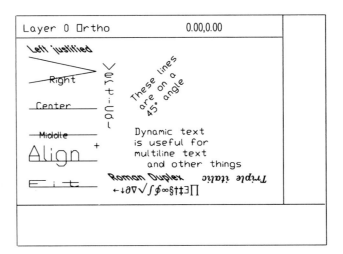

**Figure 7-11**

Be careful not to pick this point too low or too high. This could cause Auto-CAD to redraw one or more of the lines vertically.

All four lines will be "extended" horizontally, as in *Figure 7-11*.

NOTE: If you use the change point option to edit a circle, the circle will be redrawn so that it passes through the change point. See *Figure 7-12*.

Now we will use CHANGE to move an object to a different layer.

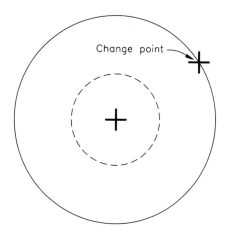

Change point

**Figure 7-12**

> Reenter the CHANGE command.
> Select any of the lines on your screen.
> Press enter to end selection.
> Type "p" or select "properties".

You will see a prompt with a list of options:

Change what property (Color/Elev/LAyer/LType/Thickness)?

Remember that in this book we are adhering to a system of associating colors and linetypes with layers, and that elevation and thickness are elements of a 3D drawing. The only property change option we will make use of at this time is the layer option. This is an important editing capability for correcting the common mistake of drawing an object on the wrong layer and for those instances where it is convenient to draw objects on one layer and then move them to other layers after they are drawn.

> Type "la" or select "layer".

Notice that you must type two letters to avoid confusion between "layer" and "ltype".

AutoCAD will now prompt for a layer change:

New layer:

We will move this line to layer 2, so that it will appear as a yellow, hidden line.

> Type "2" and press enter.

The line will be redrawn on the new layer.

## TASK 7: SCALEing previously drawn entities

*Procedure.*

1. Type or select "SCALE".
2. Select objects.
3. Press enter to end selection.
4. Pick a base point.
5. Enter a scale factor.

*Discussion.*    Any object or group of objects can be scaled up or down using the SCALE command. In this exercise we will practice the SCALE command on some of the text and lines that you have drawn on your screen. Remember, however, that there is no special relationship between SCALE and TEXT and that other types of entities can be scaled just as easily.

> Type or select "SCALE".
AutoCAD will prompt you to define a selection set:

Select objects:

> Select the set of six lines and text drawn in Task 1. Remember to type "w" or "c" to use either a window or crossing.
> Press enter to end selection.
You will now be prompted to pick a base point:

Base point:

Imagine for a moment that you are looking at a square and you want to shrink it using a scale-down procedure. All the sides will, of course, be shrunk the same amount, but how do you want this to happen? Should the lower left corner stay in place and the whole square shrink toward it? Or should everything shrink toward the center? Or toward some other point on or off the square (see *Figure 7-13*)?

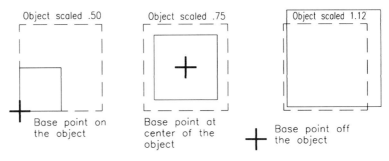

**Figure 7-13**

This is what you will tell AutoCAD when you pick a base point. In most applications you will choose a point somewhere on the object.
> Pick a base point at the left end of the bottom line of the selected set (the blip in *Figure 7-14*).
AutoCAD now needs to know how much to shrink or enlarge the objects you have selected:

<Scale factor>/Reference:

We will get to the reference method in a moment. When you enter a scale factor, all lengths, heights, and diameters in your set will be multiplied by that factor and redrawn accordingly. Scale factors are based on a unit of 1. If you enter .5, objects will be reduced to half their original size. If you enter 2, objects will become twice as large.
> Type ".5" and press enter.
Your screen should now resemble *Figure 7-14*.

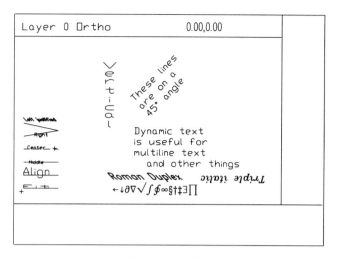

**Figure 7-14**

## SCALEing by Reference

This option can save you from doing the arithmetic to figure out scale factors. It is useful when you have a given length and you know how large you want that length to become after the scaling is done. For example, we know that the lines we just scaled are now 2.00 long. Let's say that we want to scale them again to become 2.33 long (a scale factor of 1.165, but who wants to stop and figure that out?). This could be done using the following procedure:

1. Type or select "SCALE".
2. Select the "previous" set.
3. Pick a base point.
4. Type "r" or select "reference".
5. Type "2" for the reference length.
6. Type "2.33" for the new length.

   NOTE: You can also perform reference scaling by pointing. In the example we have just been through, you could have pointed to the ends of the 2.00 line for the reference length and then shown a 2.33 line for the new length.

## TASKS 8, 9, 10, and 11

The drawings that follow contain typical applications of TEXT, DTEXT, STYLE, CHANGE, and SCALE. Pay particular attention to the suggestions on the use of DTEXT in the first drawing, and CHANGE in the second, third, and fourth drawings. These will save you time and help you to become a more efficient CAD operator.

# DRAWING 7-1: TITLE BLOCK

This title block will give you practice in using a variety of text styles and sizes. You may want to save it and use it as a title block for future drawings. In Chapter 10 we will show you how to insert one drawing into another, so you will be able to incorporate this title block into any drawing.

| QTY REQ'D | DESCRIPTION | | | PART NO. | ITEM NO. |
|---|---|---|---|---|---|
| | BILL OF MATERIAL | | | | |
| UNLESS OTHERWISE SPECIFIED DIMENSIONS ARE IN INCHES | DRAWN BY: B. A. Cad Designer | DATE | **YOUR CAD CO.** | | |
| REMOVE ALL BURRS & BREAK SHARP EDGES | APPROVED BY: | | | | |
| TOLERANCES FRACTIONS ± 1/64  DECIMALS ANGLES   ± 0°-15'  XX ± .01  XXX ± .005 | ISSUED: | | DRAWING TITLE: | | |
| MATERIAL: | FINISH: | | SIZE | CODE IDENT NO. | DRAWING NO. | REV. |
| | | | C | 38178 | | |
| | | | SCALE: | DATE: | SHEET | OF |

## *DRAWING SUGGESTIONS*

GRID = 1

SNAP = .0625

> Make ample use of DIST and TRIM as you draw the line patterns of the title block. Take your time and make sure that at least the major divisions are in place before you start entering text into the boxes.

> Set to the "text" layer before entering text.

> Use DTEXT with all the STANDARD, .09, left-justified text. This will allow you to do all of these in one command sequence, moving the cursor from one box to the next and entering the text as you go.

> Remember that once you have defined a style you can make it current using the TEXT or DTEXT commands. This will save you from having to restyle more than necessary.

> Use "%%D" for the degree symbol and "%%P" for the plus or minus symbol.

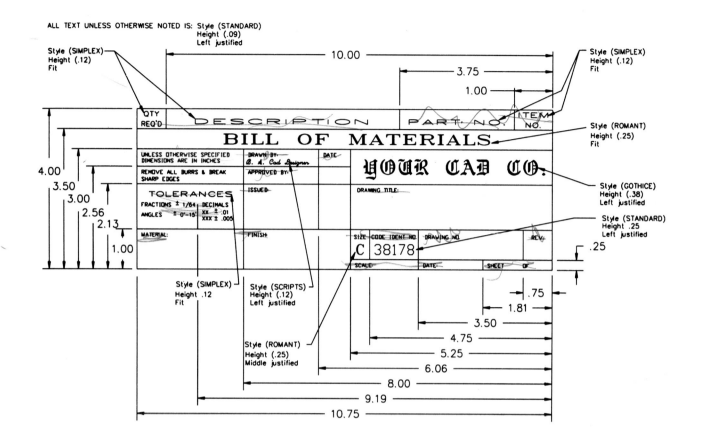

## TITLE BLOCK

### Drawing 7-1

| LAYERS | NAME | COLOR | LINETYPE | | | |
|--------|------|-------|----------|--|--|--|
| | 0 | WHITE | ——— CONTINUOUS | (DRAW) | LINE |
| | 1 | RED | ——— CONTINUOUS | (DRAW) | TEXT |
| | | | | (EDIT) | CHANGE |
| | | | | (DISPLAY) | PAN |
| | TEXT | CYAN | ——— CONTINUOUS | (DISPLAY) | ZOOM |

| F1 | F6 | F7 | F8 | F9 |
|----|----|----|----|----|
| ON/OFF | ON/OFF | ON/OFF | ON/OFF | ON/OFF |
| SCREEN | COORDS | GRID | ORTHO | SNAP |

*P, 2*

## DRAWING 7-2: GAUGES

This drawing will teach you some typical uses of the SCALE and CHANGE commands. Some of the techniques used will not be obvious, so read the suggestions carefully.

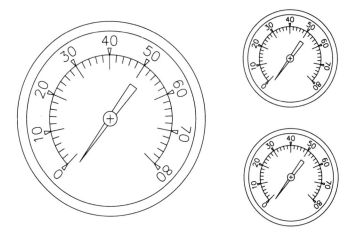

## *DRAWING SUGGESTIONS*

GRID = .5

SNAP = .125

> Draw three concentric circles of 5, 4.5, and 3 diameters. The bottom of the 3.0 circle can be trimmed later.

> Zoom in to draw the arrow-shaped tick at the top of the 3.0 circle. Then draw the .50 vertical line directly below it and the number "0" (middle-justified text) above it.

> These three objects can be arrayed to the left and right around the perimeter of the 3.0 circle using angles of +135 and −135 as shown.

> Use the CHANGE command to change the arrayed zeros into 10, 20, 30, etc.

> Draw the .25 vertical tick directly on top of the .50 mark at top center and array it left and right. There will be 20 marks each way.

> Draw the needle horizontally across the middle of the dial.

> Make two copies of the dial; use SCALE to scale them down as shown. Then move them into their correct positions.

> Rotate all three needles as shown.

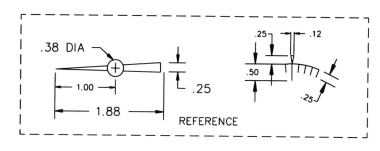

.38 DIA
1.00
1.88
.25
REFERENCE
.25
.12
.50
.25

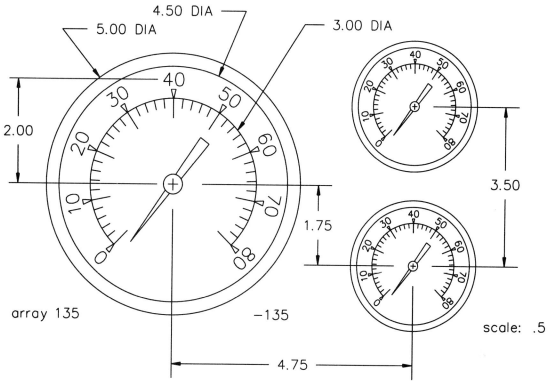

5.00 DIA
4.50 DIA
3.00 DIA
2.00
array 135
−135
1.75
4.75
3.50
scale: .5

GAUGES
Drawing 7−2

| LAYERS | NAME | COLOR | LINETYPE | | | |
|--------|------|-------|----------|---|---|---|
| | 0 | WHITE | ———— CONTINUOUS | | (DRAW) | LINE |
| | 1 | RED | ———— CONTINUOUS | | (DRAW) | CIRCLE |
| | | | | | (DRAW) | TEXT |
| | | | | | (EDIT) | SCALE |
| | | | | | (EDIT) | ROTATE |
| | 3 | GREEN | – – – CENTER | | (EDIT) | COPY |
| | TEXT | CYAN | ———— CONTINUOUS | | (EDIT) | ARRAY |
| | | | | | (EDIT) | CHANGE |
| | | | | | (DISPLAY) | ZOOM |

| F1 | F6 | F7 | F8 | F9 |
|----|----|----|----|----|
| ON/OFF SCREEN | ON/OFF COORDS | ON/OFF GRID | ON/OFF ORTHO | ON/OFF SNAP |

# DRAWING 7-3: STAMPING

This is a drawing that is trickier than it appears. There are many ways that it could be done. The way we have chosen not only works well but makes use of a number of the commands and techniques you have learned in the last two chapters. Notice that a change in limits is needed to take advantage of some of the suggestions.

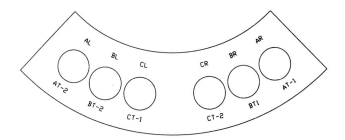

## *DRAWING SUGGESTIONS*

GRID = .50    LIMITS = (0,0) (24,18)

SNAP = .25

> Draw two circles, radius 10.25 and 6.50, centered at about (13,15). These will be trimmed later.

> Draw a vertical line down from the center point to the outer circle. We will copy and rotate this line to form the ends of the stamping.

> Copy the line on itself, then rotate "previous" 45 degrees and rotate the remaining line −45 degrees.

> Trim the lines and the circles to form the outline of the stamping.

> Draw a 1.50 diameter circle in the center of the stamping, 8.50 down from (13,15). Draw "middle" text, "AR", 7.25 down, and "AT-1" down 9.75 from (13,15).

> Copy text and circle on themselves and rotate "last" 33 degrees with (13,15) as base point of rotation. Then repeat this step 5 times, rotating circles and text into the positions shown (+11 degrees, −11 degrees, +22 etc.)

> Change all text to agree with the drawing.

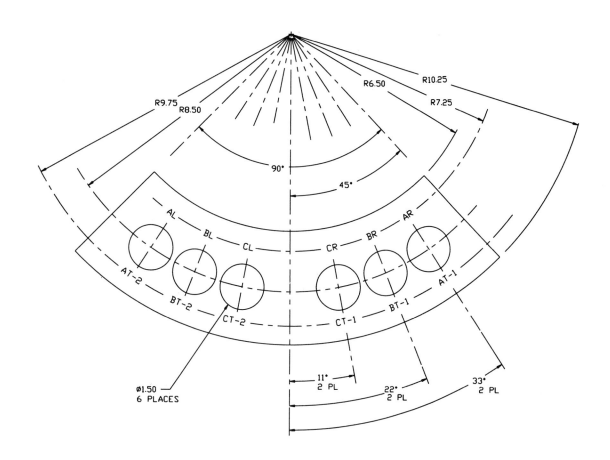

## STAMPING
## Drawing 7-3

| LAYERS | NAME | COLOR | LINETYPE | | (DRAW) | LINE |
|--------|------|-------|----------|---|--------|------|
| | | | | | (DRAW) | CIRCLE |
| | 0 | WHITE | ———— CONTINUOUS | | (DRAW) | TEXT |
| | 1 | RED | ———— CONTINUOUS | | (EDIT) | COPY |
| | | | | | (EDIT) | TRIM |
| | | | | | (EDIT) | ROTATE |
| | 3 | GREEN | – – – CENTER | | (EDIT) | BREAK |
| | TEXT | CYAN | ———— CONTINUOUS | | (EDIT) | CHANGE |
| | | | | | (DISPLAY) | ZOOM |

| F1 | F6 | F7 | F8 | F9 |
|----|----|----|----|----|
| ON/OFF SCREEN | ON/OFF COORDS | ON/OFF GRID | ON/OFF ORTHO | ON/OFF SNAP |

# DRAWING 7-4: CONTROL PANEL

Done correctly, this drawing will give you a good feel for the power of the commands you now have available to you. Be sure to take advantage of combinations of ARRAY and CHANGE described following.

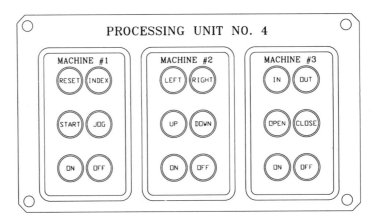

## DRAWING SUGGESTIONS

GRID = .50

SNAP = .0625

> After drawing the outer rectangles, draw the double outline of the left button box, and fillet the corners. Notice the different fillet radii.

> Draw the "on" button with its text at the bottom left of the box. Then array it 2 × 3 for the other buttons in the box.

> CHANGE the lower right button text to "off" and draw the "MACHINE #" text at the top of the box.

> ARRAY the box 1 × 3 to create the other boxes.

> CHANGE text for buttons and machine numbers as shown.

> Complete the drawing.

## MOVING THE ORIGIN
## WITH RELEASE 10'S UCS COMMAND

The dimensions of this drawing are shown in "datum line" form, measured from a single point of origin in the lower left-hand corner. In effect this establishes a new coordinate origin. If we move our origin to match this point, then we will be able to read dimension values directly from the coordinate display. This may be done by setting the lower left-hand limits to (–1,–1). But in Release 10 it may also be done using the UCS command to establish a "User Coordinate System" with the origin at a point you specify. User Coordinate Systems are discussed in depth in Chapter 12. For now, here is a simple procedure:

> Type "ucs".
> Type "o" for the "Origin" option.
> Point to the new origin.

That's all there is to it. Move your cursor to the new origin and watch the coordinate display. It should show 0.00,0.00, and all values will be measured from there.

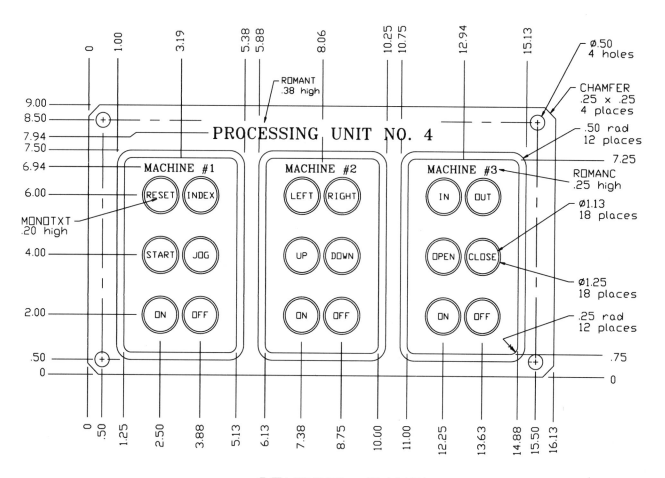

CONTROL PANEL

Drawing 7-4

| LAYERS | NAME | COLOR | LINETYPE | | (DRAW) | LINE |
|---|---|---|---|---|---|---|
| | 0 | WHITE | ———————— | CONTINUOUS | (DRAW) | CIRCLE |
| | 1 | RED | ———————— | CONTINUOUS | (DRAW) | TEXT |
| | | | | | (EDIT) | COPY |
| | | | | | (EDIT) | ARRAY |
| | 3 | GREEN | — — — | CENTER | (EDIT) | FILLET |
| | TEXT | CYAN | ———————— | CONTINUOUS | (EDIT) | CHAMFER |
| | | | | | (DISPLAY) | ZOOM |

| F1 | F6 | F7 | F8 | F9 |
|---|---|---|---|---|
| ON/OFF | ON/OFF | ON/OFF | ON/OFF | ON/OFF |
| SCREEN | COORDS | GRID | ORTHO | SNAP |

# chapter

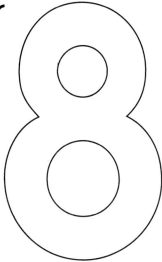

## COMMANDS

| DIM: | DRAW | EDIT |
|------|------|------|
| DIM | HATCH | EXPLODE |
| DIM1 | | |

## OVERVIEW

The ability to dimension your drawings and add crosshatch patterns will greatly enhance the professional appearance and utility of your work.

AutoCAD's semiautomatic dimensioning feature is a complex subsystem of commands, subcommands, and variables. We encourage you to learn by experimentation, to study the charts and examples given here, and to use the *AutoCAD Reference Manual*, Section 10.1, when you need further information.

The HATCH command is simple by comparison, but it does not always perform the way you expect. Both DIM and HATCH frequently require some manipulation using editing techniques we will introduce in the drawing suggestions at the end of this chapter.

## TASKS

1. Draw linear dimensions (horizontal, vertical, and aligned).
2. Draw baseline and continued linear dimensions.
3. Draw angular dimensions.
4. Draw center marks and diameter and radius dimensions.
5. Draw leaders to dimension objects.
6. Set new values for dimension variables.
7. Use the EXPLODE command so that elements of dimensions can be edited separately.
8. Add cross hatching to previously drawn objects.
9. Do Drawing 8-1 ("Tool Block").
10. Do Drawing 8-2 ("Flanged Wheel").
11. Do Drawing 8-3 ("Shower Head").
12. Do Drawing 8-4 ("Nose Adaptor").
13. Do Drawing 8-5 ("Plot Plan").

### TASK 1: Drawing linear dimensions

*Procedure.*

1. Type or select "DIM" or "DIM1".
2. Type or select an orientation (horizontal, vertical, etc.).
3. Select an object or show two extension line origins..
4. Type text or press enter to accept AutoCAD's measurement.

*Discussion.* The DIM command has more options than any other AutoCAD command. In addition to the options, there are numerous system variables that determine how dimensions will appear in your drawing. This exercise will not teach you everything there is to know about dimensioning in AutoCAD, but it will get you off to a good start.

One way in which the DIM command differs from most other commands is that you stay within it until you cancel it. This is not a matter of menu macros that reenter the command when you finish one sequence. It is actually built into the command so that it will repeat until you decide to exit. This is a convenience, because you will be doing most of your dimensioning at one time. Typically you will finish the objects in a drawing and then go on to dimension them.

The DIM1 command allows you to enter a single dimension and then return to the command prompt. Otherwise, there is no difference between DIM and DIM1. That said, we will use DIM throughout this discussion.

> To prepare for this exercise, begin a new drawing called "8-1" or "A:8-1". Draw a triangle (ours is 3.00, 4.00, 5.00) and a line (6.00) above the middle of the display, as shown in *Figure 8-1*. Exact sizes and locations are not critical.

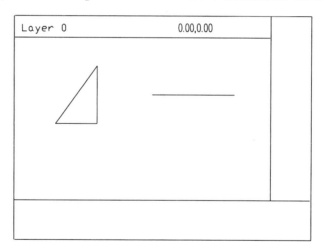

**Figure 8-1**

We will begin by adding dimensions to the triangle.
> Type "dim" or select "DIM".

AutoCAD simply acknowledges that you are now in the DIM command system and waits for your choice of an option.

Dim:

If you are using the AutoCAD standard screen menu, you will have to take the additional step of selecting "LINEAR" in order to arrive at the linear dimensions submenu before you can take the next step.

The options available for linear dimensions are horizontal, vertical, aligned, rotated, baseline, and continue. We will use the first three to dimension the triangle.

> Type "hor" or select "horizontal".

You will be prompted to show what you want to dimension and where you want the dimension to go:

First extension line origin or RETURN to select:

There are two ways to proceed at this point. One is to show where the extension lines should begin, and the other is to select the line itself and let Auto-CAD position the extension lines. In most simple applications the latter is faster.

> Press enter (RETURN) to indicate that you will select an object.

AutoCAD will replace the cross hairs with a pickbox and prompt for your selection:

Select line, arc, or circle:

> Select the horizontal line at the bottom of the triangle.

Now you will need to indicate the area in which the dimension is to be placed. AutoCAD will put the dimension line and text as far away from the selected line as you indicate, but will center the text between the extension lines. The prompt is as follows:

Dimension line location:

> Pick a location about .50 below the triangle, as shown by the blip in *Figure 8-2*.

Notice that this figure and others in this chapter are shown "zoomed in" on the relevant object for the sake of clarity. You may zoom or not as you like.

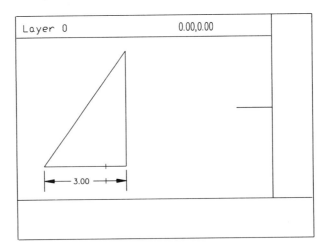

**Figure 8-2**

Now AutoCAD shows you the dimension text from its own measurement and gives you the opportunity to change it. In our drawing the line is 3.00 long, as you can see:

Dimension text <3.00>:

> Press enter to accept the dimension text.

Bravo! You have completed your first dimension.

At this point, take a good look at the dimension you have just drawn to see what it consists of.

As in *Figure 8-2*, you should see the following components: two extension lines, two "arrows," a dimension line on each side of the text, and the text itself. Notice also that AutoCAD has automatically placed the extension line origins a short distance away from the triangle base. This distance is controlled by a dimension variable called "dimexo". Variables are discussed in Task 6.

> You should be at the "Dim:" prompt before continuing.
> Type "ver" or select "vertical".

You will be prompted for extension line origins as before:

First extension line origin or RETURN to select:

This time we will show the extension line origins manually.
> Pick the right angle corner at the lower right of the triangle.

AutoCAD will prompt for a second point:

Second extension line origin:

Even though you are manually specifying extension line origins, it is not necessary to show the exact point where you want the line to start. AutoCAD will automatically set the dimension lines slightly away from the line as before.
> Pick the top intersection of the triangle, the other end point of the vertical line.

From here on, the prompts will be the same as before:

Dimension line location:

> Pick a point about .50 to the right of the triangle.

AutoCAD prompts:

Dimension text <4.00>:

> Press enter.

Your screen should now include the vertical dimension, as shown in *Figure 8-3*.

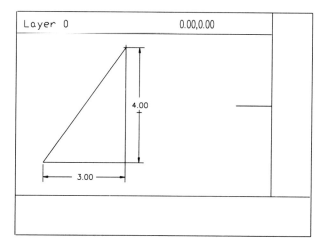

**Figure 8-3**

NOTE: You can use "U" within the DIM command just as in the LINE command. If you type "U" at the "Dim:" prompt, your last dimension will be undone. If you have drawn a series of dimensions without leaving DIM, you can "walk backwards" through them, undoing them one by one. But be careful, there is no "REDO" within the DIM subsystem.

Now let's place a dimension on the diagonal side of the triangle. For this we will need the "align" option. You should be at the "Dim:" prompt before continuing.

> Type "ali" or select "aligned".
> Press enter (RETURN), indicating that you will select an object.
    AutoCAD will give you the pickbox and position the extension lines automatically, according to your selection.
> Select the hypotenuse of the triangle.
> Pick a point approximately .50 above and to the left of the line.
> Press enter to accept the dimension text.
    Your screen should now resemble *Figure 8-4*.

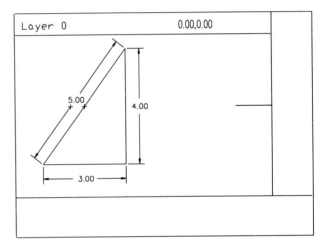

**Figure 8-4**

NOTE: The last option for an individual linear dimension is "rotated". Try it if you like. It works much like "aligned" except that you will be prompted for a rotation angle first and the dimension line will be oriented according to this angle. The difficulty with "rotated" is that AutoCAD will measure the distance between its own extension lines instead of the length of the line you are dimensioning. Because of this we recommend that you use "aligned" unless your application requires a specific rotation that is different from the line itself. In these cases you may need to use a "rotated" dimension, but do not depend on AutoCAD's measurement.

### TASK 2: Multiple linear dimensions—baseline and continue

*Procedure.*

1. Draw an initial linear dimension.
2. Type "bas" or "con" or select "baseline" or "continue".
3. Pick a second extension line origin.
4. Press enter or type text.

*Discussion.* Baseline and continue allow you to draw multiple linear dimensions more efficiently. In baseline format you will have a series of dimensions all measured from the same initial origin. In continue there will be a string of dimensions in which the second extension line for one dimension becomes the first extension for the next.

> To prepare for this exercise, be sure that you have a 6.00 horizontal line as shown in *Figure 8-1* at the beginning of Task 1. Although the figures in this exercise will show only the line, leave the triangle on your screen, because we will come back to it in the next task.

In this exercise we will be placing a set of baseline dimensions on top of the line and a continued series on the bottom.

> To begin, you should be at the "Dim:" prompt. (If necessary, type or select "DIM".)

In order to use either baseline or continue, you must have one linear dimension already drawn on the line you wish to dimension. So we will begin with this.

> Type "hor" or select "horizontal".
> Pick the right end point of the line for the origin of the first extension line.
> Pick a second extension origin 2.00 to the left of the first.
> Pick a point .50 above the line for dimension text.
> Press enter to accept AutoCAD's text.

You should now have the initial "2.00" dimension shown in *Figure 8-5*. We will use "baseline" to add the other dimensions above it.

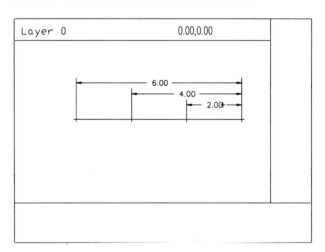

**Figure 8-5**

> At the "Dim:" prompt, type "bas" or select "baseline".

AutoCAD uses the first extension line origin you picked again and prompts for a second:

Second extension line origin:

> Pick a point 4.00 to the left of the first extension line.

AutoCAD prompts for text and shows its own measure of the distance from the right end of the line to the point you selected. Ours looks like this:

Dimension text <4.00>:

> Press enter to accept the dimension text.

    The second baseline dimension shown in *Figure 8-5* should be added to your drawing. We will add one more.

NOTE: Within the DIM command you can press enter or the space bar to repeat an option.

> Type "bas" or select "baseline", or press enter to repeat the option.
> Pick the left end point of the line.
> Press enter to accept AutoCAD's text.
    Your screen should now resemble *Figure 8-5*.

    We will now place three continued dimensions along the bottom of the line, as shown in *Figure 8-6*. You should need little help to do this at this point.

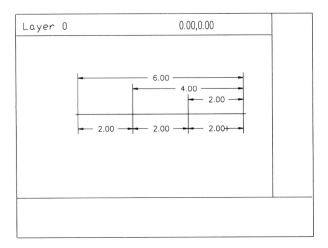

**Figure 8-6**

> Begin by placing an initial horizontal dimension below the line, from the left end in 2.00, as shown in *Figure 8-6*.
> Type "con" or select "continue".
> Pick a second extension line origin 2.00 to the right of the last extension line.
> Press enter to accept AutoCAD's dimension text.

    You should now have a set of two continued dimensions below the line. We leave it to you to complete the exercise by drawing the third continued dimension shown in *Figure 8-6*.

### TASK 3: Angular dimensions

*Procedure.*

1. Type or select "DIM".
2. Type "ang" or select "angular".
3. Select two lines that form an angle.
4. Pick an arc location.
5. Type text or press enter.
6. Pick a text location or press enter.

**183**

*Discussion.* Angular dimensioning works much like linear dimensioning except that you will be prompted for an arc location as well as a text location. If you press enter in response to the prompt for location, AutoCAD will split the arc and place the text between the two halves.

For this exercise we will return to the triangle and add angular dimensions as shown in *Figures 8-7* and *8-8*.

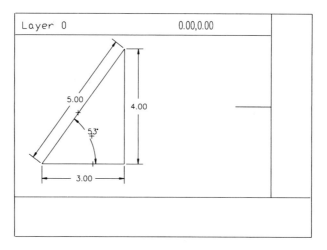

**Figure 8-7**

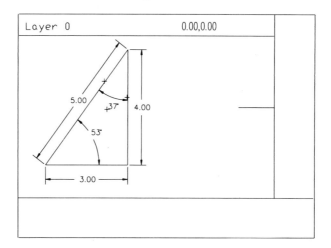

**Figure 8-8**

> At the "Dim:" prompt type "ang" or select "angular".

AutoCAD will prompt for two lines and will measure the angle between. The first prompt will be:

Select first line:

> Select the base of the triangle.
You will be prompted for another line:

Second line:

> Select the hypotenuse.
The next prompt is for an arc location. You will choose a point between the two lines that shows how far away from the corner you want the arc placed.

Enter dimension line arc location:

> Pick a point between the two selected lines, as shown by the blip in *Figure 8-7*.

AutoCAD will prompt you for text and give you its own measure of the angle between the lines you have chosen:

Dimension text <53>:

> Press enter to accept the given angle measure.

Now you will be prompted for a text location:

Enter text location:

You can select any point, or press enter to place the text in the middle of the arc.

> Press enter to place the text in the middle of the arc.

The lower left angle of your triangle should now be dimensioned, as in *Figure 8-7*. Notice that the degree symbol is automatic in angular dimension text.

We will dimension the upper angle and place the text outside the arc, as shown in *Figure 8-8*.

> At the "Dim:" prompt, type "ang" or select "angular" (or press enter to repeat the option).

> Select the vertical line at the right and the hypotenuse in response to the prompts for first line and second line.

> Pick a point within the angle for arc placement.

> Press enter to accept the default text.

> Pick a point outside the arc, as shown by the blip near the text in *Figure 8-8*.

## TASK 4: Dimensioning arcs and circles

*Procedure.*

1. Type or select "DIM".
2. Type "rad", "dia", or "cen" or select "radius", "diameter", or "center".
3. Pick the arc or circle at the point where you want the dimension line to run.
4. Type text or press enter.

*Discussion.*    The basic process for dimensioning circles and arcs is simpler than those we have already covered. There are only three options, one for a diameter dimension, one for a radius, and one to draw a center mark. It can get tricky, however, when AutoCAD does not place the dimension where you want it. We will be discussing solutions to these problems in the drawing suggestions at the end of this chapter.

> To prepare for this exercise, draw three circles across the bottom of your screen, as shown in *Figure 8-9*. The circles we have used have radii of 2.00, 1.50, and .50. It is most important that the last circle be small.

Although the remaining figures in this section will show the circles only, keep the triangle on your screen, because it will be used again in Task 6.

> Type or select "DIM".

Center marks resemble blips, but they are actual lines and will appear on a plotted drawing. They are the simplest of all dimension features to create and are created automatically as part of some radius and diameter dimensions.

> At the "Dim:" prompt, type "cen" or select "center".

AutoCAD prompts:

Select arc or circle:

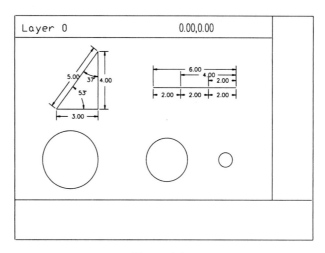

**Figure 8-9**

> Select the middle circle.

A center mark will be drawn, as shown in *Figure 8-10*. You may want to REDRAW your display to see the difference between blips and center marks.

Now we will add the diameter dimension shown on the largest circle in *Figure 8-10*.

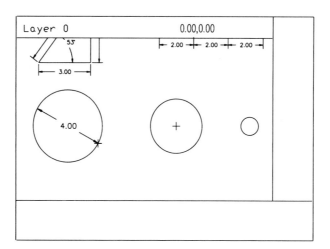

**Figure 8-10**

> At the "Dim:" prompt, type "dia" or select "diameter".

AutoCAD will prompt:

Select arc or circle:

> Select the largest circle.

The important thing about this selection is that the point you choose will be taken as one end point of the dimension line.

As usual, AutoCAD will show you its default text and give you the opportunity to change it:

Dimension text <4.00>:

> Press enter to accept the text.

AutoCAD will draw the text at the center of the circle with dimension lines on each side, as shown in *Figure 8-10*. Notice that the diameter symbol is added automatically. This placement of the dimension text is frequently a problem. In drawings where you have concentric circles, for example, you would have one circle's text placed on top of another. Solutions for this involve moving the text and are discussed in the drawing suggestions at the end of this chapter.

The procedure for radius dimensioning is exactly the same.

> At the "Dim:" prompt, type "rad" or select "radius".
> Select the 1.50 (middle) circle.
> Press enter to accept the given text.

Your screen should now resemble *Figure 8-11*. The "R" for radius is added automatically.

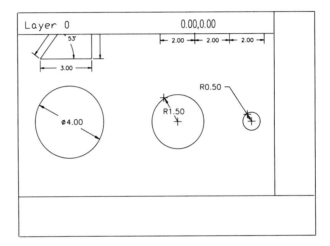

**Figure 8-11**

Finally, try adding a radius dimension to the third circle to see how AutoCAD deals with situations in which the text will not fit within the circle.

> Type "rad" or select "radius" (or press enter to repeat the option).
> Select the .50 (right) circle.
> Press enter to accept the text.
      AutoCAD gives you the following message:

Text does not fit.
Enter leader length for text:

Notice that there is now a rubber band extending from the last selection point to the cross hairs. When you pick an end point, AutoCAD will draw a leader from the last point, add a short horizontal extension line at the end, and place the text next to it.
      Try it.
> Pick an end point for the leader, as shown in *Figure 8-11*.

Leaders are very useful and can also be drawn independently of specific arc and circle dimension processes, as we will do in the next task.

**TASK 5: Dimensioning with leaders**

*Procedure.*

1. Type or select "DIM".
2. Type "lea" or select "leader".

**3.** Select a start point.

**4.** Select an end point.

**5.** Type dimension text.

*Discussion.*    Leaders are used in dimensioning objects in crowded areas of a drawing. Unlike other dimension formats in which you select an object or show a length, a leader is simply a line or series of lines with an arrow at the end to connect an object with its dimension text. Because you do not select an object when drawing a leader, you will need to know the dimension text you want to use <u>before</u> you begin.

If you look at the small circle we just dimensioned, you will see a radius line inside and a leader outside. This would be undesirable if there were other dimensions, hatch patterns, or other objects inside the circle. In such a case we would dimension with a leader only.

Let's try it.

> At the "Dim:" prompt type "lea" or select "leader".

AutoCAD will prompt you for a start point:

Leader start:

Usually you will want the leader arrow to start on the object, not offset like an extension line would be. This suggests that an object snap may be in order.

> Type "nea", or select "NEArest" from an OSNAP menu ("Tools" on the Auto-CAD pull down menu and "* * * *" on the screen menu).

This specifies that you want to snap to the nearest point on the circle. You will see that the aperture has been added to the cross hairs.

> Position the cross hairs so that the middle circle crosses the aperture and press the pick button.

The leader will be snapped to the circle and a rubber band shown extending to the cross hairs. AutoCAD will prompt for a second point just as in the LINE command:

To point:

> Pick a point, as shown in *Figure 8-12*.

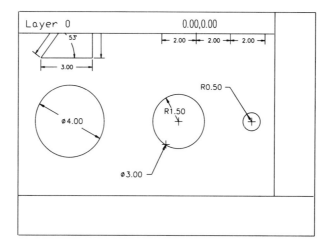

**Figure 8-12**

AutoCAD will continue to prompt for points so that you can draw a broken leader. This is sometimes necessary in order to "get around" other objects. More often, however, you will need only a single line.

> Press enter to end the leader at the second point.

AutoCAD will now give you the familiar text prompt:

Dimension text <0.50>:

Notice that the text is not taken from a measurement of the present circle. Instead it is "left over" from the last dimension you entered and is of no use at this point.

> Type "%%c3.00".

The leader and text are drawn, as in *Figure 8-12*.

Notice that the short horizontal "jog" at the text end of the leader is added automatically.

### TASK 6: Dimension variables

*Procedure.*

1. Type or select "DIM".
2. Type a variable name.
3. Type a new value.

*Discussion.*    Setting dimension variables is easy, but the sheer number of them can be overwhelming. The chart included in this chapter (*Figure 8-16*) will give you a summary of the information you need. By studying it carefully you will gain a good sense of the possibilities. In the following discussion and exercises we will give a brief example of one variable, "dimscale", and some new commands and features that were introduced with AutoCAD 2.6.

NOTE: To see a list of dimension variables and their current values, type "sta" or select "status" at the "Dim:" prompt.

### Associative Dimensioning

This exercise assumes that you are working in AutoCAD 2.6 or higher and that no one has changed the "dimaso" variable in your prototype drawing. By default, dimaso is "on" and all dimensions you draw are "associative". This means, for one thing, that they are treated as single entities. All the lines, arrowheads, and text of an associative dimension can be selected for editing with one pick. If dimensions are drawn with dimaso "off" (or if your version of AutoCAD is earlier than 2.6), their components will be treated separately.

In this exercise we will change the value of "dimscale" and then UPDATE some of your dimensions to reflect this change. Then we will use the regular SCALE command to change the size of an object and show how associative dimensioning works.

> At the "Dim:" prompt, type "dimscale".

If you want to select "dimscale" from the screen menu, you will have to first select "dim vars".

AutoCAD will show you the current value of the variable so that you can either retain it or type a new value:

Current value <1.0000>:

> Type "2".

You will be returned to the "Dim:" prompt.

Nothing has changed on your screen, but you would find that if you drew new dimensions now, the size of the text and the arrows would be doubled. Instead, we will use the UPDATE command to change some of your previously drawn dimensions according to the new scale.

> Type "upd" or select "UPDATE" from the screen menu.

To reach UPDATE on the AutoCAD standard screen menu you will have to first select "next".

You are prompted to select objects:

Select objects:

> Select the triangle and all of its dimensions using a window or crossing.
> Press enter to end selection.

Your dimensions will be redrawn as shown in *Figure 8-13*. (If nothing has changed, check to be sure that the variable dimaso is on. If it is off, you will have to turn it on and draw some new dimensions to achieve the results shown in this exercise.)

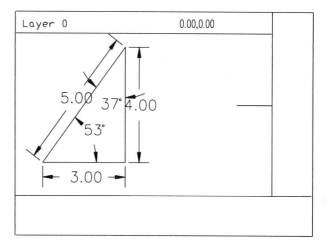

**Figure 8-13**

Now let's see what happens when you use SCALE to scale up the object itself along with its associated dimensions.

> Cancel or exit the DIM command.
> Enter the SCALE command.
> Select the triangle and all its dimensions using a window or crossing.
> Pick a base point near the center of the triangle.
> Type a scale factor of "1.25".

As the triangle is scaled up, AutoCAD also changes the associated dimension text and repositions all of the dimension entities. Sometimes this will cause problems, such as dimensions being placed on top of each other. The solution to this is to use the EXPLODE command, as described in Drawing 8-2.

Your screen should now resemble *Figure 8-14*.

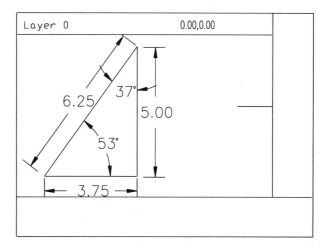

**Figure 8-14**

Finally, there is one more useful DIM subcommand, NEWTEXT.

> Type or select "DIM".

> Type "new" or select "NEWTEXT" from the screen menu.

> Enter a new value, such as "5.0000" or "5.00mm".

> Select the vertical text ("5.00") on the right of the triangle.

The text will be redrawn, as shown in *Figure 8-15*. This command is very convenient when all you want to do is change the text of a dimension.

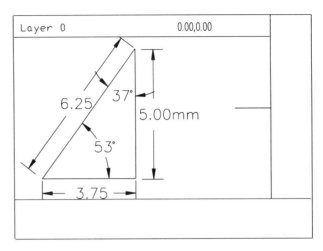

**Figure 8-15**

You are now on your own with AutoCAD's dimensioning commands. Once again, we highly recommend that you take a good look at *Figure 8-16* before moving on to the EXPLODE and HATCH commands.

### TASK 7: Using the EXPLODE command

*Procedure.*

1.  Type or select "EXPLODE".
2.  Select objects.
3.  Press enter to carry out the command.

*Discussion.* The EXPLODE command becomes very important when you have to edit dimensions or hatch patterns. This is because both of these entities are ordinarily treated as "blocks" (assuming that "dimaso" is "on"). Blocks are fully discussed in Chapter 10. For now, simply notice that if you select a dimension or a hatch pattern in, say, the MOVE command, the whole complex of dimension elements or the whole hatch pattern is selected. This is a problem when you want to edit an individual element. For example, you will frequently need to move the text in a dimension. One solution is to turn dimaso off so that dimensions are not created as "associated." Another solution is to EXPLODE dimensions that need editing. EXPLODE takes "blocks," groups of entities that are being treated as a single entity, and recreates them as independent objects.

> To see why you need this command, try moving the text of the vertical dimension on the triangle <u>without</u> moving the lines and arrows. You will find that all of the elements of the dimension are selected as one.

> Cancel the MOVE command.

> Now, type or select "EXPLODE".

> Select the vertical dimension.

| COMMONLY USED DIMENSION VARIABLES | | | | | |
|---|---|---|---|---|---|
| VARIABLE | DEFAULT VALUE | APPEARANCE | DESCRIPTION | NEW VALUE | APPEARANCE |
| dimaso | on | All parts of dim are one entity | Associative dimensioning | off | All parts of dim are separate entities |
| dimscale | 1.00 | ⊢—2.00—⊣ | Changes size of text & arrows, not value | 2.00 | ◄—2.00—► |
| dimasz | .18 | ► | Sets arrow size | .38 | ► |
| dimcen | .09 | ⊕ | Center mark size and appearance | −.09 | ⊕ |
| dimdli | .38 | | Spacing between continued dimension lines | .50 | |
| dimexe | .18 | | Extension above dimension line | .25 | |
| dimexo | 0.06 | | Extension line origin offset | .12 | |
| dimtp | 0.00 | 1.50 | Sets plus tolerance | .01 | $1.50^{+0.01}_{-0.00}$ |
| dimtm | 0.00 | 1.50 | Sets minus tolerance | .02 | $1.50^{+0.00}_{-0.02}$ |
| dimtol | off | 1.50 | Generate dimension tolerances (dimtp & dimtm must be set) (dimtol & dimlim cannot both be on) | on | $1.50^{+0.01}_{-0.02}$ |
| dimlim | off | 1.50 | Generate dimension limits (dimtp & dimtm must be set) (dimtol & dimlim cannot both be on) | on | 1.51 1.48 |
| dimtad | off | ⊢— 1.50 —⊣ | Places text above the dimension line | on | 1.50 |
| dimtxt | .18 | 1.50 | Sets height of text | .38 | 1.50 |
| dimtsz | .18 | ⊢— 1.50 —⊣ | Sets tick marks & tick height | .25 | 1.50 |
| dimtih | on | 1.50 | Sets angle of text When off rotates text to the angle of the dimension | off | 1.50 |

**Figure 8-16**

> Press enter to carry out the command.
> Now try moving the text again.

The arrows, lines, and text of the exploded dimension can now be edited separately. If you are working in color, you should see a change in their color as well (to black if you are working on a gray background or white if you are on a black background). This is because EXPLODE automatically moves exploded objects to layer 0. We will discuss the relationship between blocks and layer 0 in Chapter 10.

The exploded dimension is no longer "associative". It will not be recalculated or repositioned if the triangle is scaled or stretched. Also, the NEWTEXT command will no longer work on it. You can still edit the text, however, using the CHANGE command.

### TASK 8: Using the HATCH command

*Procedure.*

1. Type or select "hatch".
2. Select a pattern.
3. Define style parameters.
4. Define boundaries of object to be hatched.

*Discussion.*    Automated hatching is an immense timesaver. However, the HATCH command is also one of the most imprecise of the AutoCAD commands and is very likely to perform in odd, unpredictable ways. If you follow the directions for the following exercises, you should have no trouble understanding how the system is designed to work in the best of circumstances. At the end of the chapter, when you encounter more realistic drawing problems, we will show you techniques for dealing with those common situations in which HATCH does not do what you expect.

> To prepare for this exercise, clear your screen of all previously drawn objects and then draw three rectangles, one inside the other, as shown in *Figure 8-17.*

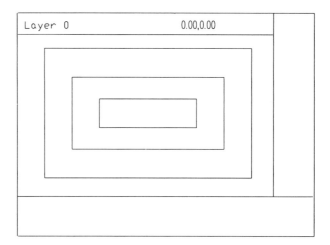

**Figure 8-17**

First we will use a standard HATCH procedure to create the hatching shown in *Figure 8-18.*

Although the AutoCAD standard pull down menu includes a very handy icon menu for hatching patterns, you will understand the command sequence better if you do not use it yet.

> Type "hatch" or select it from the screen menu.
    The first prompt you will see looks like this:

Pattern (? or name/U,style):

With this peculiar prompt you are given three choices. You can choose a predefined pattern by typing its name, or see a list of pattern names by typing a "?", or create a simple (user-defined) pattern of hatch lines. We will begin with the last option.
> Type "u".

In order to define a user pattern, AutoCAD will prompt for a number of parameters. The first is this:

Angle for crosshatch lines <0>:

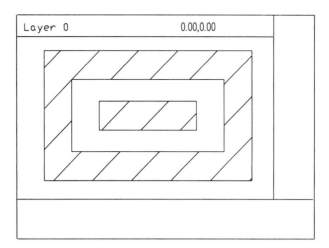

**Figure 8-18**

> Type "45".
> > AutoCAD prompts:

Spacing between lines <1.0000>:

> Press enter to accept the default spacing.
> > AutoCAD prompts:

Double hatch area? <N>

If you choose to double hatch, you will get two sets of lines perpendicular to each other. We will try this next time around.
> Press enter to retain single hatching.

Now you are prompted to select objects for hatching. The way you define the boundaries you want will be extremely important and often difficult in a complex drawing. In this example we will keep it simple.
> Use a window or crossing to select all three rectangles.

Your screen should resemble *Figure 8-18*.

This style of hatching, in which alternate areas are hatched, is the default style and is called "normal". There are two other styles called "outermost" and "ignore." "Outermost" will only hatch the area between the outer figure and the next boundaried figure inside. "Ignore" will ignore all boundaries and hatch everything. Of course, the three styles are indistinguishable if you do not have areas within areas to hatch.

We will do the next example using "outermost."

> Type "u" to undo the last HATCH command. Then REDRAW the display. Do not confuse this "u" with the "u" for a user-defined hatch pattern.
> Type or select "hatch". Avoid the pull down icon menu again; we will use it in the next example.

Notice that our user-defined pattern has now been added to the prompt as the current hatch style:

Pattern (? or name/U, style) <U>:

> Type or select "u,o".

The "o" is essential to select the "outermost" style.
> Type "45" again for the hatch angle.

This time we will change the line spacing.
> Type ".5".

We will use a double crosshatch this time.
> Type "y" to double hatch the area.
> Select all three rectangles as before.
    Your screen should resemble *Figure 8-19.*

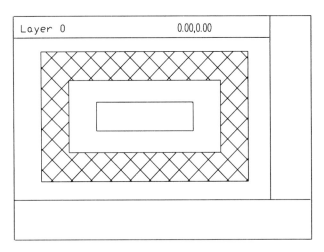

**Figure 8-19**

Beyond these simple line patterns, the AutoCAD package also includes a library of over 40 predefined hatch patterns. You can see a list of these by typing "?" at the "Pattern..." prompt. However, the pull down icon menu which shows you examples of some of the patterns is much more convenient, because you do not have to know the names in order to retrieve the pattern you want. Two shortcomings of the icon menu are that not all the patterns are represented, and it does not allow you to specify the "outermost" or "ignore" styles. "Normal" style is assumed.

In this final hatching exercise, we will use the pull down menu to hatch the rectangles one more time. If you do not have Release 9 or higher, you can achieve the same results by typing a pattern name.

> Type "u" to undo the last HATCH command. Then REDRAW the display before continuing.
> Select "Draw" from the pull down menu bar.
> Select "Hatch" from the menu.
    AutoCAD will display an icon menu showing hatch patterns, as in *Figure 8-20.* When you select one, its name will be written as the response to the "Pattern..." prompt.
    There are two "pages" to this icon menu. The pattern we have used is on the second page.
> Select "next" to move to the second icon menu page.
> Select the "escher" pattern, as shown in *Figure 8-20.*
    The icon menu disappears and you will see the following in the command area:

```
Command: hatch
Pattern (? or name/U,style) <U>: escher
Scale for pattern <.50>:
```

For this pattern we used a larger scale.
> Type "1.5".
> Type "0" to return the angle from 45 to standard orientation.
> Select all three rectangles as before.
    Your screen should now resemble *Figure 8-21.*

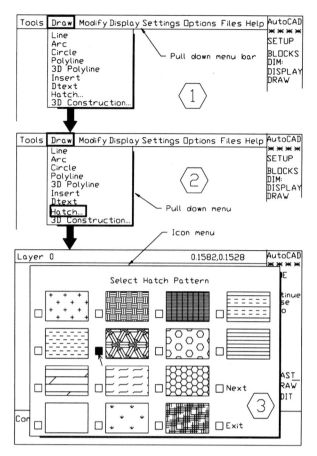

Figure 8-20

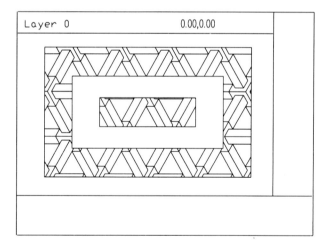

Figure 8-21

### TASKS 9, 10, 11, and 12

The drawing suggestions in this chapter are particularly important. Specifically, pay close attention to the suggestions for defining hatch boundaries in Drawing 8-1, for editing dimensions in Drawings 8-2 and 8-3, and for editing in hatched areas in Drawing 8-5.

You will find that hatching and dimensioning can be both time consuming and frustrating. But remember, in most applications your drawings will be of little use until the dimensions are clearly and correctly placed.

# DRAWING 8-1: TOOL BLOCK

In this drawing the dimensions should work well without editing. The following procedure for defining HATCH boundaries is used frequently, and you will need it in all the drawings in this chapter.

## DRAWING SUGGESTIONS

GRID = 1.0

SNAP = .125

> As a general rule, complete the drawing first, including all cross-hatching, then add dimensions and text.

> Place all hatching on the "hatch" layer. When hatching is complete, set to the "dim" layer and turn the "hatch" layer off so that hatch lines will not interfere with dimensioning.

## BOUNDARIES FOR THE HATCH COMMAND

HATCH works on boundaried areas and will not perform properly if the boundaries of the area you want to hatch are not clear. This means you will need to BREAK lines at their intersections with the areas to be hatched, as shown in the reference. One efficient way to do this is as follows:

1. Turn on a running OSNAP to intersection.
2. Enter the BREAK command and select the line you want to break, staying away from intersections.
3. Type "F" to use the first point option.
4. Pick the intersection where you want to break a line as the first point of the break.
5. Pick the same point again as the second break point.

> Zooming in on the area being hatched is advisable to see that the whole boundary is defined clearly. Remember that inner boundaries, such as the circle in the bottom view, must be selected in the HATCH command as well or they will be ignored.

> The section lines in this drawing can be easily drawn as "leaders" in the DIM command. Set the "dimasz" variable to .38 first. Check to see that ortho is on, then begin the leader at the tip of the arrow, and make a right angle as shown. After picking the other end point of the leader, press the space bar to bring up the "Dimension text" prompt. Then press the space bar again so that you will have no text, and finally, press enter to complete the sequence.

> Extra lines of text in a dimension must be drawn using the TEXT or DTEXT commands (stay on "dim" layer). Text height should match dimension text height (.18), and the style should be the same.

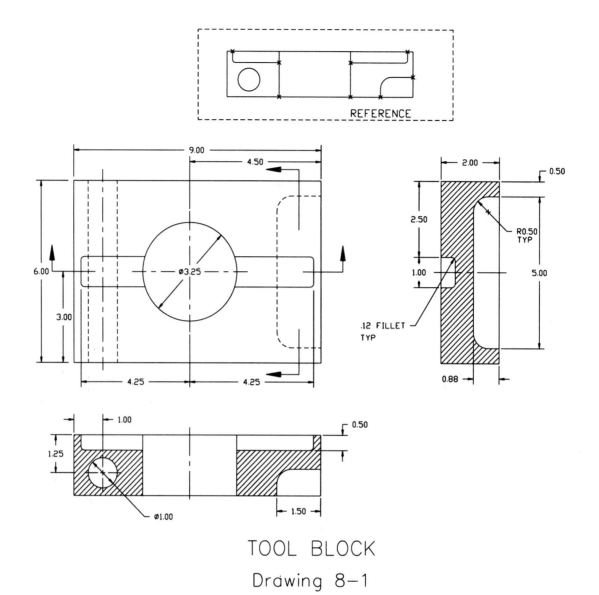

REFERENCE

9.00
4.50
6.00
3.00
Ø3.25
4.25
4.25

2.00
0.50
2.50
1.00
R0.50 TYP
5.00
.12 FILLET TYP
0.88

1.00
0.50
1.25
1.50
Ø1.00

# TOOL BLOCK

## Drawing 8-1

| LAYERS | NAME | COLOR | LINETYPE | | | |
|--------|------|-------|----------|--|--|--|
| | 0 | WHITE | ——————— | CONTINUOUS | (DRAW) | LINE |
| | 1 | RED | ——————— | CONTINUOUS | (DRAW) | CIRCLE |
| | 2 | YELLOW | - - - - - | HIDDEN | (DRAW) | HATCH |
| | 3 | GREEN | — - — - | CENTER | (EDIT) | BREAK |
| | TEXT | CYAN | ——————— | CONTINUOUS | (EDIT) | FILLET |
| | HATCH | BLUE | ——————— | CONTINUOUS | (DISPLAY) | ZOOM |
| | DIM | MAGENTA | ——————— | CONTINUOUS | | |

| F1 | F6 | F7 | F8 | F9 |
|----|----|----|----|----|
| ON/OFF SCREEN | ON/OFF COORDS | ON/OFF GRID | ON/OFF ORTHO | ON/OFF SNAP |

## DRAWING 8-2: FLANGED WHEEL

Most of the objects in this drawing are straight-forward. The keyway is easily done using the TRIM command. The procedure for editing diameter dimensions is common and will be used in the next three drawings.

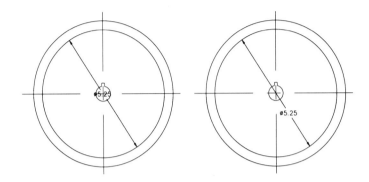

### DRAWING SUGGESTIONS

GRID = .25

SNAP = .0625

HATCH line spacing = .50

> You will need a .0625 snap to draw the keyway. Draw a .125 × .125 square at the top of the .63 diameter circle. Drop the vertical lines down into the circle so that they may be used to TRIM the circle. TRIM the circle and the vertical lines, using a window to select both as cutting edges.
> Remember to set to layer "hatch" before hatching, layer "text" before adding text, and layer "dim" before dimensioning.

### EDITING DIAMETER DIMENSIONS

To create the diameter dimensions with text moved from the center as shown in the front view, follow this procedure (*Reference 8-2*):

1.  Draw the dimension, letting AutoCAD place the text in the center.
2.  EXPLODE the dimension.
3.  MOVE the text to its final position as shown.
4.  Use CHANGE (change point), with an end point OSNAP to connect the dimension line on the left side of the center with the dimension line on the right.
5.  BREAK the dimension line on both sides of the text.

> Notice that when you use EXPLODE, the exploded objects are recreated on layer 0. You can move them back to the "dim" layer using the CHANGE command, or leave them on 0 to show that they have been exploded. Another solution to this problem is offered in the next drawing (see the "NOTE").

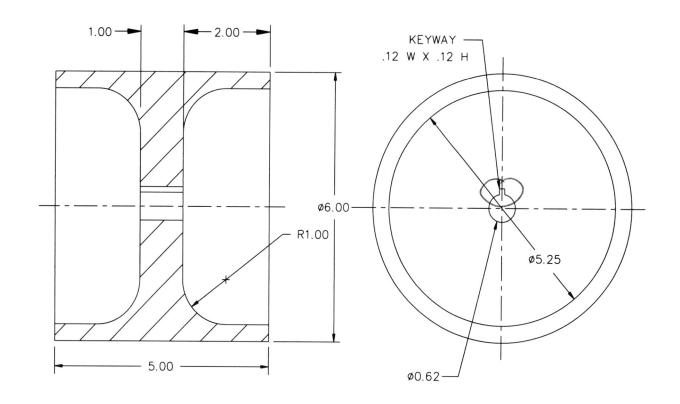

FLANGED WHEEL

Drawing 8-2

| LAYERS | NAME | COLOR | LINETYPE | | | |
|--------|------|-------|----------|---|---|---|
| | 0 | WHITE | ——————— CONTINUOUS | | ⟨DRAW⟩ | LINE |
| | 1 | RED | ——————— CONTINUOUS | | ⟨DRAW⟩ | CIRCLE |
| | | | | | ⟨EDIT⟩ | MOVE |
| | | | | | ⟨EDIT⟩ | BREAK |
| | 3 | GREEN | — · — CENTER | | ⟨EDIT⟩ | HATCH |
| | TEXT | CYAN | ——————— CONTINUOUS | | ⟨EDIT⟩ | FILLET |
| | HATCH | BLUE | ——————— CONTINUOUS | | ⟨EDIT⟩ | EXPLODE |
| | DIM | MAGENTA | ——————— CONTINUOUS | | ⟨DISPLAY⟩ | ZOOM |

| F1 | F6 | F7 | F8 | F9 |
|----|----|----|----|----|
| ON/OFF SCREEN | ON/OFF COORDS | ON/OFF GRID | ON/OFF ORTHO | ON/OFF SNAP |

## DRAWING 8-3: SHOWER HEAD

This drawing makes use of the procedures for hatching and dimensioning you learned in the last two drawings. In addition, it uses an angular dimension, leaders, and "%%c" for the diameter symbol.

### *DRAWING SUGGESTIONS*

GRID = .50

SNAP = .125

HATCH line spacing = .25

> You can save some time on this drawing by using MIRROR to create half of the left side view. You will save additional time if you break out the boundaries to be hatched before you mirror. Notice, however, that you cannot hatch before mirroring, because the mirror command will reverse the angle of the hatch lines.

> The series of baseline dimensions in the left side view are drawn from right to left. AutoCAD will place the "1.25" text to the right of the dimensioned area. To achieve the placement shown here, EXPLODE this dimension and MOVE the text.

> AutoCAD needs two lines for an angular dimension, so you need to draw the vertical line coming down on the left. Select this line and the angular line at the left end of the shower head and the angular extension will be drawn automatically. Add the text "2 PL" using the TEXT command.

> Notice that the diameter symbols in the vertical dimensions at each end of the left side view are not automatic. Use %%c to add the diameter symbol to the text.

> Use leaders and the %%c diameter symbol for the 2.25 and 1.00 DIA circles in the front view.

NOTE: When you know ahead of time that you will need to edit a dimension or a number of dimensions it may be best to create them as nonassociative dimensions in the first place, rather than drawing them and then exploding them. The advantage to this method is that you will not have to worry about dimensions being moved to layer 0 by the EXPLODE command. To turn associated dimensioning off, type or select "dimaso" at the "Dim:" prompt and then type "off".

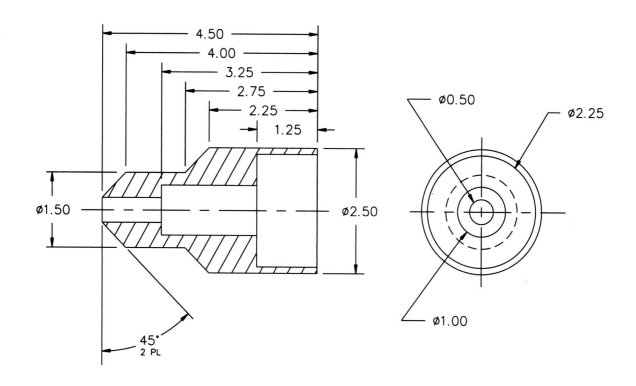

SHOWER HEAD

Drawing 8-3

| LAYERS | NAME | COLOR | LINETYPE | | | |
|---|---|---|---|---|---|---|
| | 0 | WHITE | ——————— CONTINUOUS | | (DRAW) | LINE |
| | 1 | RED | ——————— CONTINUOUS | | (DRAW) | CIRCLE |
| | 2 | YELLOW | – – – – HIDDEN | | (EDIT) | BREAK |
| | 3 | GREEN | — — — CENTER | | (EDIT) | MIRROR |
| | TEXT | CYAN | ——————— CONTINUOUS | | (EDIT) | HATCH |
| | HATCH | BLUE | ——————— CONTINUOUS | | (EDIT) | EXPLODE |
| | DIM | MAGENTA | ——————— CONTINUOUS | | (EDIT) | MOVE |
| | | | | | (DISPLAY) | ZOOM |

| F1 | F6 | F7 | F8 | F9 |
|---|---|---|---|---|
| ON/OFF | ON/OFF | ON/OFF | ON/OFF | ON/OFF |
| SCREEN | COORDS | GRID | ORTHO | SNAP |

# DRAWING 8-4: NOSE ADAPTOR

Make ample use of ZOOM to work on the details of this drawing. Notice that the limits are set larger than usual, and the snap is rather fine by comparison.

## DRAWING SUGGESTIONS

LIMITS = (0,0) (36,24)

GRID = .50    SNAP = .125

HATCH line spacing = .25

> You will need a .125 snap to draw the thread representation shown in the reference. Understand that this is nothing more than a standard representation for screw threads; it does not show actual dimensions. Zoom in close to draw it and you should have no trouble.

> Zoom in on the areas to be hatched and BREAK the lines around them carefully. Notice that there are actually two areas, one to the left of the .50 diameter hole and a smaller one to the right.

> There are three places where the dimension text is on more than one line. Remember, there is no way to do this in the DIM command itself. Draw the first line as usual in the DIM command. Then exit DIM and draw the rest using TEXT or DTEXT.

> This drawing includes two examples of "simplified drafting" practice. The thread representation is one, and the other is the way in which the counter bores are drawn in the front view. A precise rendering of these holes would show an ellipse, since the slant of the object dictates that they break through on an angle. However, to show these ellipses in the front view would make the drawing more confusing and less useful. Simplified representation is preferable in such cases.

120
210
220

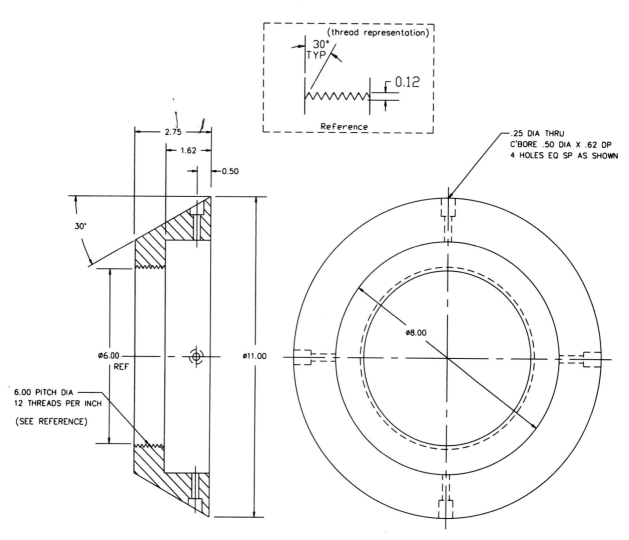

NOSE ADAPTOR
Drawing 8-4

| LAYERS | NAME | COLOR | LINETYPE | | | (DRAW) | LINE, CIRCLE |
|--------|------|-------|----------|---|---|--------|--------------|
| | 0 | WHITE | ———— | CONTINUOUS | | (DRAW) | HATCH |
| | 1 | RED | ———— | CONTINUOUS | | (EDIT) | BREAK |
| | 2 | YELLOW | - - - - | HIDDEN | | (EDIT) | TRIM |
| | 3 | GREEN | — — — | CENTER | | (EDIT) | MOVE |
| | TEXT | CYAN | ———— | CONTINUOUS | | (EDIT) | ARRAY |
| | HATCH | BLUE | ———— | CONTINUOUS | | (EDIT) | MIRROR |
| | DIM | MAGENTA | ———— | CONTINUOUS | | (EDIT) | EXPLODE |
| | | | | | | (DISPLAY) | ZOOM |

| F1 | F6 | F7 | F8 | F9 |
|----|----|----|----|----|
| ON/OFF SCREEN | ON/OFF COORDS | ON/OFF GRID | ON/OFF ORTHO | ON/OFF SNAP |

# DRAWING 8-5: PLOT PLAN

This architectural drawing makes use of three hatch patterns and several dimension variable changes. Be sure to make these settings as shown.

Notice that we have simplified the format of the drawing page for this drawing. This is because the drawings are becoming more involved and because you should need less information to complete them at this point. We will continue to show drawings this way for the remainder of the book.

## *DRAWING SUGGESTIONS*

$$GRID = 10' \quad LIMITS = 180', 120'$$
$$SNAP = 1' \quad LTSCALE = 2'$$

> The "trees" shown here are symbols for oaks, willows, and evergreens.
> Use the DIST command to find starting points for the inner rectangular objects (the garage, the dwelling, etc.).
> Opening up a space in a hatch pattern around text, as we have done here, can be done in several ways:

1. You might draw a box around the text area before hatching and then erase it later.

2. With the simple user-defined line pattern on the "garage" and the "dwelling," you could EXPLODE the hatch, draw a temporary rectangle around the text area, use its sides as cutting edges to TRIM the crosshatch lines out of the inside of the box, and then ERASE the box.

3. With broken patterns like those on the patio and the pool, you could EXPLODE the hatch, enter the ERASE command, and window the area that you want to clear for text.

*Scale for pattern (1.0007 /0   or /00*

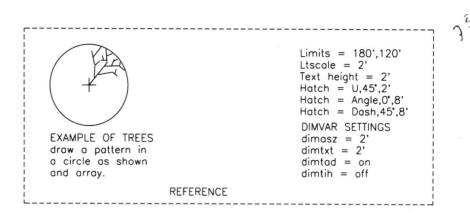

EXAMPLE OF TREES
draw a pattern in
a circle as shown
and array.

Limits = 180',120'
Ltscale = 2'
Text height = 2'
Hatch = U,45°,2'
Hatch = Angle,0°,8'
Hatch = Dash,45°,8'
DIMVAR SETTINGS
dimasz = 2'
dimtxt = 2'
dimtad = on
dimtih = off

REFERENCE

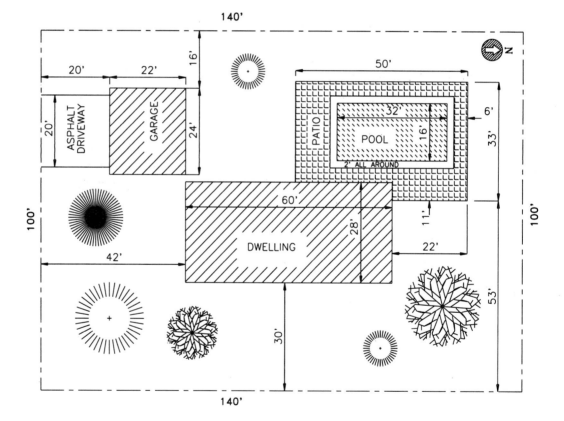

PLOT PLAN

Drawing 8-5

# chapter

## COMMANDS

| DRAW | DISPLAY | EDIT | SETTINGS |
|------|---------|------|----------|
| POINT | FILL | PEDIT | SETVAR |
| POLYGON | | OFFSET | |
| DONUT | UTILITY | | |
| SOLID | VSLIDE | | |
| TRACE | MSLIDE | | |
| PLINE | | | |
| SKETCH | | | |

## OVERVIEW

This chapter should be fun. As you can see by the preceding list, you will be learning a large number of new commands. You will see new things happening on your screen with each command. The commands in this chapter are used to create special entities, some of which could not be drawn any other way. Some of them, like polygons and points, are familiar geometric figures, while others, like "polylines" and "traces," are peculiar to CAD.

## TASKS

1. Draw POINTs in various styles.
2. Draw POLYGONs.
3. Draw DONUTs.
4. Use the FILL command.
5. Draw SOLIDs.
6. Draw TRACEs.
7. Draw straight polyline segments.
8. Draw arc polyline segments.
9. Edit polylines with PEDIT.
10. Use the OFFSET command to create parallels.
11. Draw freehand lines using SKETCH (optional).
12. Do Drawing 9-1 ("Backgammon Board").
13. Do Drawing 9-2 ("Dart Board").
14. Do Drawing 9-3 ("Printed Circuit Board").
15. Do Drawing 9-4 ("Carbide Tip Saw Blade").
16. Do Drawing 9-5 ("Gazebo").

### TASK 1: Drawing "points"

*Procedure.*

**1.**  Type or select "POINT".
**2.**  Pick a point.

*Discussion.*   On the surface this is the simplest DRAW command in AutoCAD. However, if you look at *Figure 9-1*, you will see figures which were drawn with the POINT command that do not look like ordinary points. This capability adds a bit of complexity to this otherwise simple command.

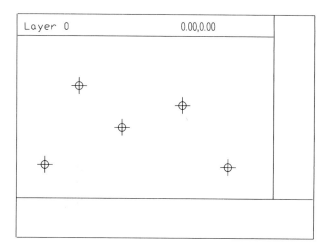

**Figure 9-1**

In this exercise we will try out the POINT command and also take the opportunity to introduce you to AutoCAD's "slide" feature along the way.

> Begin a new drawing called "9-1" or "A:9-1".
> Turn off the grid (F7).
> Type or select "POINT".
> Pick a point anywhere on the screen.

AutoCAD will place a blip at the point and return you to the "Command:" prompt. In order to see what has really happened, you will need to perform a REDRAW to clear away the blip.

> Type or select "REDRAW".

Look closely and you will see the point you have drawn. Besides those odd instances in which you may need to draw tiny dots like this, points can also serve as object snap "nodes." See the OSNAP chart, *Figure 6-7* in Chapter 6.

But what about those circles and crosses in *Figure 9-1*? AutoCAD has about 20 other simple forms that can be drawn as "points".

Before we change the point form, we need to see our options. To do this we call out a "slide" named "points". Slides are simply "snapshots" of AutoCAD drawings that are saved in a reduced format so they can be loaded very quickly. They are often used in developing business presentations.

> Type "VSLIDE" or select "Complex Points example:" from the POINT command screen menu.

VSLIDE stands for "view slide." As you would expect, it loads a slide onto your screen. There is an associated command called "MSLIDE" for "make slide."

It is as simple as VSLIDE to use, and we have included an optional MSLIDE exercise procedure at the end of this section.

(If you have used the screen menu you will already have the slide showing, so skip the next step.)
> Type "points".

AutoCAD loads and displays a slide called "points" shown in *Figure 9-2*. This is like a primitive icon menu. It shows you a graphic image of your choices, but it does not allow you to pick them directly. Instead, you look for the number of the form you want and use that number in setting a system variable called "pdmode".

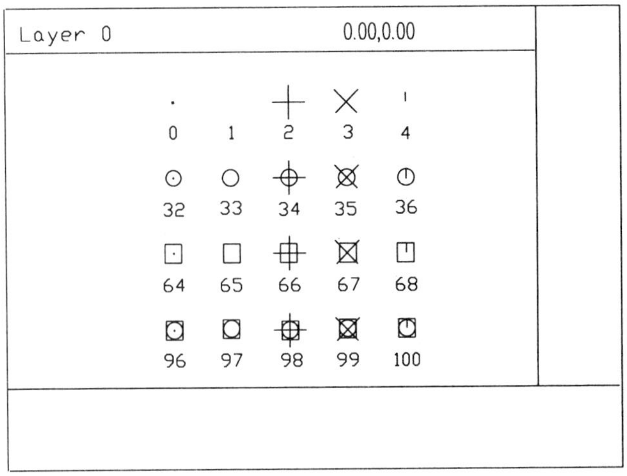

**Figure 9-2**

"Pdmode" is set using the SETVAR command. SETVAR is an important command that allows you to change a large number of variables that affect basic drawing properties. It is often used in menu writing, and it includes variables for settings such as SNAP and LTSCALE, which you already know how to change in a more direct way. For more information on variables and SETVAR, see the *AutoCAD Reference Manual*, Section 3.10 and Appendix A.6.
> Type "setvar" (or select "Pdmode" from the screen menu and skip the next step).

AutoCAD prompts:

Variable name or ?:

What would the "?" give you?

Right, it gives you a list of variables. Try it if you like, then return to this procedure by reentering SETVAR.
> Type "pdmode" (if not using the screen menu).

AutoCAD prompts for a new value:

New value for PDMODE <0>:

Of course "0" is the number for the standard point form that you have already drawn. Try any of the other forms. We chose number 34.
> Type "34" or one of the other numbers from the slide.

Now REDRAW the screen to remove the slide, enter the POINT command again, and draw some new points. This is how we created *Figure 9-1*.

If you are using the screen menu, you will also notice that there is a second variable called "pdsize". PDSIZE changes the size of "points" just as PDMODE changes their form. *Also notice that when you do a "regen", all "points" you have drawn are updated to the new form and size.*

NOTE: In effect this means that you can use only one of the forms from the slide at a time. In other words, you cannot have two different types of "points" in one drawing.

Before continuing, it would be wise to set pdmode back to 0.

> Type "setvar".
> Type "pdmode" or press enter if pdmode is the default.
> Type "0".

### Making Slides with MSLIDE

Slides are very easily created. Once created they can be displayed using the VSLIDE command any time you are in the drawing editor. Since slides resemble drawings, it is important that you understand the primary difference: Slides cannot be edited, added to, or changed in any way. To change a slide you must overwrite the slide file with a new one of the same name.

To create a slide of your present display, follow this procedure:

1. Type or select "mslide".

2. Type a name for the file.

It's that simple. Your display will be saved as a file with a **.sld** extension. To see that it is really there, you must first alter your screen in some way. Clear away all the points, for example. Then follow this procedure:

1. Type or select "vslide".

2. Type the name of the slide you just created.

Your slide will appear. Redraw the screen to erase it.

Most slide applications use a series of slides, exactly as you would in a photographic slide show. This process can be automated and timed using a special kind of file called a Script file. There are a number of special commands used in the making of a script file, including SCRIPT, DELAY, RESUME, and RSCRIPT, in addition to MSLIDE and VSLIDE. See the *AutoCAD Reference Manual*, Section 11.2, if your goals include the use of slide presentations.

### TASK 2: Drawing polygons

*Procedure.*

1. Type or select "POLYGON".

2. Type number of sides.

3. Pick center point.

4. Indicate "Inscribed" or "Circumscribed".

5. Show radius of circle.

*Discussion.*   Polygons with any number of sides can be drawn using the POLYGON command. In the default sequence, AutoCAD will construct a polygon based on the number of sides, the center point, and a radius. Optionally, the "edge" method allows you to specify the number of sides and the length and position of one side (see *Figure 9-3*).

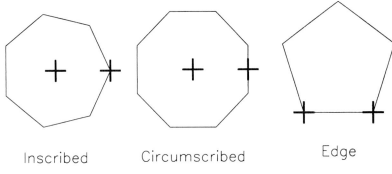

Inscribed          Circumscribed          Edge

**Figure 9-3**

As usual, we begin with the default system.

> If you have not already done so, clear your display of points before continuing.
> Type or select "polygon".

AutoCAD's first prompt will be for the number of sides:

Number of sides:

> Type "8".

You are now prompted to show either a center point or the first point of one edge:

Edge/<Center of polygon>:

> Pick a center point as shown by the blip in *Figure 9-4*.

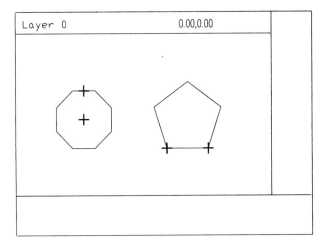

**Figure 9-4**

From here the size of the polygon can be specified in one of two ways, as shown in *Figure 9-3*. The radius of a circle will be given and the polygon drawn either inside or outside the imaginary circle. Notice that in the case of the "inscribed" polygon, the radius is measured from the center to a vertex, while in the "circumscribed" polygon it is measured from the center to the midpoint of a side.

You will have to tell AutoCAD which you want by typing "i" or "c" or selecting from the screen.

Inscribed in circle/Circumscribed about circle (I/C):

> Type "c" or select "circumscribed".
Now you will be prompted to show a radius of this imaginary circle (that is, a line from the center to a midpoint of a side).

Radius of circle:

> Show a radius similar to the one in *Figure 9-4*.

We leave it to you to try out the "inscribed" option.

We will draw one more polygon, using the "edge" method.

> Reenter the POLYGON command.
> Type "5" for the number of sides.
> Type "e" or select "edge".
AutoCAD will issue a different series of prompts:

First endpoint of edge:

> Pick a point as shown in *Figure 9-4*.
AutoCAD prompts:

Second endpoint of edge:

> Pick a second point as shown.
Your screen should now resemble *Figure 9-4*.

## TASK 3: Drawing "donuts"

*Procedure.*

1. Type or select "donut".
2. Type or show an inside diameter.
3. Type or show an outside diameter.
4. Pick a center point.
5. Pick another center point...
6. Press enter to exit the command.

*Discussion.* The DONUT command is logical and easy to use. You show inside and outside diameters and then draw as many donut-shaped objects of the specified size as you like.

> Clear your display of polygons before continuing.
> Type or select "donut".
AutoCAD prompts:

Inside diameter <0.50>:

We will change the inside diameter to 1.00.
> Type "1".

AutoCAD prompts:

Outside diameter <1.00>:

We will change the outside diameter to 2.00.
> Type "2".
    AutoCAD prompts:

Center of doughnut:

> Pick any point.
    A "donut" will be drawn around the point you chose, as shown in *Figure 9-5*. (If your donut is not "filled," see Task 4.)

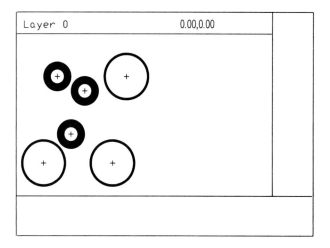

**Figure 9-5**

    AutoCAD stays in the DONUT command, allowing you to continue drawing donuts.
> Pick a second center point.
> Pick a third center point.
    You should now have three "donuts" on your screen as shown.
> Press enter to exit the donut command.

Now reenter the donut command, change the inside diameter to 3.00 and the outer diameter to 3.25, and draw three more donuts as shown in *Figure 9-5*.
    When you are done, leave the donuts on the screen so that you can see how they are affected by the FILL command.

### TASK 4: Using the FILL command

*Procedure.*

1. Type or select "FILL".
2. Type "on" or "off".
3. Type or select "regen".

*Discussion.*    Donuts, solids (Task 5), traces (Task 6), and polylines (Tasks 7 and 8), are all affected by FILL. With FILL "on," these entities are displayed and plotted as solid filled objects. With FILL "off," only the outer boundaries are displayed (donuts are shown with radial lines between the inner and outer circles). The most common use for this feature is to speed up regeneration time. Filled objects are much slower to regenerate than outlined ones. Frequently you will want to set FILL off as you are working on a drawing and turn it on when you are ready to print or plot.

> For this exercise you should have at least one donut on your screen from Task 3.
> Type or select "fill".
   AutoCAD prompts:

ON/OFF &lt;ON&gt;:

> Type or select "off".
   You will not see any change in your display when you do this. In order to see the effect, you will have to regenerate your drawing.
> Type or select "regen".

Your screen will be regenerated with FILL off and will resemble *Figure 9-6*. All of the special entities that we will be discussing in the remainder of this chapter can be filled, so we encourage you to continue to experiment with FILL as you go along.

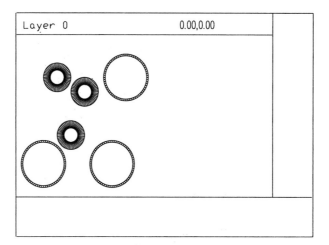

**Figure 9-6**

## TASK 5: Drawing "solids"

*Procedure.*

1. Type or select "solid".
2. Pick a first point.
3. Pick a second point.
4. Pick a third point.
5. Pick a fourth point or press enter to draw a triangular section.
6. Pick another third point or press enter to exit the command.

*Discussion.*    SOLID allows you to draw rectangluar and triangular solid filled shapes by specifying points that become corners or vertices. There is a trick to using SOLID for rectangular sections involving the order in which you enter points. If you enter them in the wrong order you will get the "hourglass" effect shown in *Figure 9-7*.

It is natural to enter points in a rectangle by moving around the perimeter. However, solids are drawn with edges between point 1 and point 3, and between point 2 and point 4.

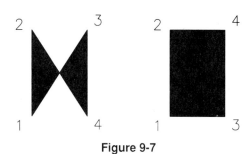

**Figure 9-7**

> FILL and ORTHO should be on for this exercise.
>> We will begin with a rectangular solid.
> Type or select "solid".
>> AutoCAD will prompt for a series of points, beginning with:

First point:

> Pick a point similar to "P1" in *Figure 9-8*.

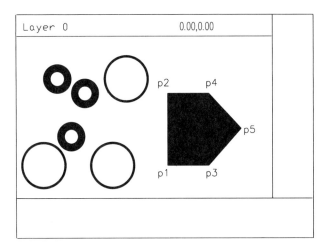

**Figure 9-8**

AutoCAD prompts:

Second point:

> Pick a point similar to "P2".
>> These first two points will become the end points of one side of a rectangular solid.
>> AutoCAD prompts:

Third point:

> Pick a point similar to "P3".
>> Remember that a side will be drawn between point 1 and point 3.
>> AutoCAD prompts:

Fourth point:

> Pick a point similar to "P4" in *Figure 9-8*.
AutoCAD prompts for more points.

Third point:

If you continue entering points, the previous points 3 and 4 will become points 1 and 2 of the new section.

You can draw a triangular section by picking a third point and then pressing enter in response to the prompt for a fourth point. This also means that you will need to press enter twice when you want to exit SOLID.

We will draw a triangular solid before exiting.
> Turn ortho off and pick a point similar to "P5" in *Figure 9-8*.
> Press enter in response to the "Fourth point:" prompt.
Your screen should now resemble *Figure 9-8*.

## TASK 6: Drawing "traces"

*Procedure.*

1. Type or select "TRACE".
2. Type or show a width.
3. Pick a first point.
4. Pick an end point.
5. Pick another end point...
6. Press enter to exit the command.

*Discussion.* A "trace" in AutoCAD is a line with a specified width. Once the width has been given, you can draw a whole series of traces just as if you were drawing lines. Typically, traces are used to draw straight line entities that have thickness, such as walls in an architectural drawing. There are some problems with traces, however, especially when you need to edit them. Because of this limitation, it is usually more efficient to use polylines in place of traces. Polylines are introduced in the next task so that you can compare the two forms.

> Clear your screen to prepare for this exercise.
We will draw a rectangular border using traces.
> Type or select "trace".
AutoCAD prompts first for a width:

Trace width <0.00>:

In both traces and polylines, a 0 width gives you an ordinary line. There are some good reasons for constructing a 0 width polyline, but a 0 width trace is useless.
> Type ".25".
Now that AutoCAD has the width specification, you are ready to start entering points. Notice that traces are drawn on center, so that the points you select will be on the centerline of the trace rather than at edges and corners.
AutoCAD prompts just as if you were in the LINE command:

From point:

> Pick a starting point.

Continue picking points to construct the rectangle shown.

> Pick a second point.

> Pick a third point.

Notice how AutoCAD waits to display a trace segment until the segment that follows has been specified. This is so that it can determine the angle of the vertex. You will see that this problem is handled differently in PLINE.

> Pick a fourth point.

> Finally, complete the rectangle with a trace drawn back to the starting point.

Notice that AutoCAD draws traces on center, so connecting the last trace to the original starting point creates a "step" at the corner. This is usually not desirable and can be avoided by drawing the last trace to the edge, rather than the start point.

Your screen should now resemble *Figure 9-9*.

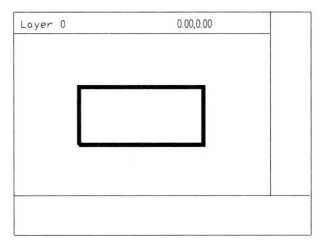

**Figure 9-9**

## TASK 7: Drawing straight "polyline" segments

*Procedure.*

1.  Type or select "PLINE".
2.  Pick a starting point.
3.  Type or select widths, halfwidth, or other options.
4.  Pick other points.

*Discussion.*    In AutoCAD there are several ways in which collections of entities can be treated as one unit. In the last chapter you saw how dimensions and hatch patterns work as "blocks." In the next chapter you will see how to create blocks. Here you will see another kind of conglomerate, the "polyline."

You have already drawn several polylines without knowing it. Donuts and Polygons are both drawn as polylines and can therefore be edited using the same edit commands that work on other polylines. You can, for instance, fillet all the corners of a polygon at once.

Using the PLINE command itself, you can draw anything from a simple line to a series of lines and arcs with varying widths. Most important, polylines can be edited using many of the ordinary edit commands as well as a whole set of specialized editing procedures found in the PEDIT command.

We will begin by creating another rectangle like the one we just drew with traces. The process is similar, but the command sequence is more complex.

> Type or select "pline".

AutoCAD begins with a prompt for a starting point:

From point:

> Pick a starting point.

From here the PLINE prompt sequence becomes more complicated:

Current line-width is 0.00<br>
Arc/Close/Halfwidth/Length/Undo/Width/&lt;Endpoint of line&gt;:

The first line gives you the current line width, left from any previous use of the PLINE command (a width of 0 will draw a simple line).

The second line gives you options in the usual format. Choosing "Arc" will lead you into another set of options that deal with drawing polyline arcs. We will save polyline arcs for Task 8.

To continue drawing our polyline rectangle, we need to specify the width of our lines. This could be done with either the "width" or "halfwidth" option.

> Type "w" or select "width".

AutoCAD will respond with:

Starting width &lt;0.00&gt;:

You will be prompted for two widths, a starting width and an ending width. This makes it possible to draw tapered lines. For this exercise, our lines will have the same starting and ending width.

NOTE: The "halfwidth" option differs from "width" only in that the width of the line to be drawn is measured from the center out, rather than the complete width. With either option you can specify by showing rather than typing a value.

> Type ".25".

AutoCAD prompts:

Ending width &lt;0.25&gt;

Notice that the starting width has become the default for the ending width. To draw a polyline of uniform width, we accept this default.

> Press enter to keep starting width and ending width the same.

AutoCAD now returns to the previous prompt:

Arc/Close/Halfwidth/Length/Undo/Width/&lt;Endpoint of line&gt;:

> Pick an end point as shown in *Figure 9-10*.

NOTE: You will save yourself some trouble later if you draw this polyline rectangle moving in a counterclockwise direction.

AutoCAD continues to prompt in the same manner, allowing you to enter more polyline segments of the same width or to switch to one of the other options:

Arc/Close/Halfwidth/Length/Undo/Width/&lt;Endpoint of line&gt;:

> Continue picking points to draw a second rectangle as shown in the figure.

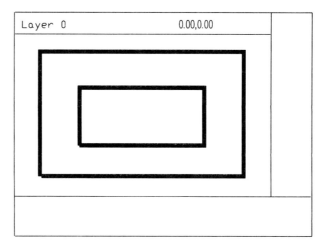

**Figure 9-10**

When you get to the last point, you could pick a point at the edge of the initial polyline segment so that a box corner is formed. PLINE does have a "close" option. Using it in this case would connect you back to the starting point and create a stepped corner. In Task 9 we will deliberately create this kind of corner and show you how to fix it with PEDIT.

The remaining options for drawing straight line segments of polylines are easily understood. "Close" completes a figure by drawing a segment back to the original starting point, just as it does in the LINE command. "Length" allows you to type or show a value and then draws a segment of that length starting from the end point of the previous segment and continuing in the same direction (tangent if the last segment was an arc). "Undo" undoes the last segment, just as in LINE or DIM.

### TASK 8: Drawing arc polyline segments

*Procedure.*

1.  Type or select "PLINE".
2.  Pick a start point.
3.  Type "a" or select "arc".
4.  Type or select options or pick an end point.

*Discussion.*    A word of caution: Because of the flexibility and power of the PLINE command, it is tempting to think of polylines as always having weird shapes, tapered lines, and strange sequences of lines and arcs. Most books, including the *Auto-CAD Reference Manual*, perpetuate this by consistently giving peculiar examples to show the range of what is possible with polylines. This is useful but misleading. Remember, polylines are practical entities even for relatively simple applications like the rectangle in Task 7.

Having said that, we will proceed to add our own bit of strangeness to the lore of the polyline. We will draw a polyline with three arc segments and two straight line segments, as shown in *Figure 9-11*. We call this thing a "goosenecked funnel." You may have seen something like it at your local garage.

> Type or select "PLINE".
> Pick a new start point as shown in *Figure 9-11*.
> Type "w" or select "width" to set new widths.
> Type "0" for the starting width.
> Type ".5" for the ending width.

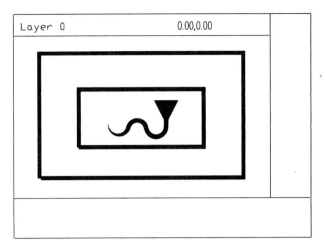

**Figure 9-11**

> Type "a" or select "arc".

This will bring up the arc prompt, which looks like this:

Angle/CEnter/CLose/Direction/Halfwidth/Line/Radius/Second pt/Undo/Width/<Endpoint of arc>:

Let's look at this prompt for a moment. To begin with there are four options that are familiar from the previous prompt. "CLose", "Halfwidth", "Undo", and "Width" all function exactly as they would in drawing straight polyline segments. The "Line" option returns you to the previous prompt so that you can continue drawing straight line segments after drawing arc segments.

The other options, "Angle", "CEnter", "Direction", "Radius", "Second pt", and "Endpoint of arc", allow you to specify arcs in ways similar to the ARC command. One thing that is different is that AutoCAD assumes that the arc you want will be tangent to the last polyline segment entered. This is often not the case. The "center" and "direction" options let you override this assumption where necessary, or you can begin with a short line segment to establish direction before entering the arc prompt.

> Pick an end point to the right to complete the first arc segment, as shown in *Figure 9-11*.

NOTE: If you did not follow our previous suggestion about drawing the rectangle counterclockwise, or if you have drawn other polylines, you will now find that the arc does not curve downward as shown in *Figure 9-11*. You can fix this by using the "Direction" option. Type "d" and then point straight down. Now you can pick an end point to the right.

AutoCAD prompts again:

Angle/CEnter/CLose/Direction/Halfwidth/Line/Radius/Second pt/Undo/Width/<Endpoint of arc>:

For the remaining two arc segments, use a uniform width of .50.

> Type "w" or select "width".
> Press enter to retain the current width as the starting width.
> Press enter to retain the current width as the ending width.
> Enter points to draw the remaining two arc segments as shown.

To draw the two straight line segments that complete the polyline, follow this procedure:

1. Type "L" or select "line" (this takes you back to the original prompt).

2. Pick a point straight up about 1.00 as shown.

3. Type "w" or select "width".

4. Press enter to retain ".5" as the starting width.

5. Type "3" for the ending width.

6. Pick an end point up about 2.00 as shown.

Your screen should now resemble *Figure 9-11*.

### TASK 9: Editing polylines with PEDIT

*Procedure.*

1. Type or select "PEDIT".

2. Select a polyline.

3. Type or select a PEDIT option.

4. Follow the prompts.

*Discussion.* The PEDIT command provides a whole subsystem of special editing capabilities that work only on polylines. We will not attempt to have you use all of them, because most are rarely needed. Most important is that you be aware of the possibilities so that when you find yourself in a situation calling for a PEDIT procedure you will know what is available. After executing the following task and reviewing *Figure 9-14*, the PEDIT chart, we recommend that you study the *AutoCAD Reference Manual*, Section 5.4, for additional information.

We will perform two edits on the polylines already drawn.

> Type or select "PEDIT".

You will be prompted to select a polyline:

Select polyline:

> Select the polyline rectangle drawn in Task 7.

Notice that PEDIT works on only one object at a time and that selected polylines <u>do not</u> become dotted.

You are now prompted as follows:

Close/Join/Width/Edit vertex/Fit curve/Decurve/Undo/eXit/<X>

"Edit vertex" brings up a subset of options that we will discuss shortly. "Undo" and "eXit" are self-explanatory. We will demonstrate "Width" and then move on to vertex editing. Refer to the chart at the end of this task for samples of the other options.

> Type "w" or select "width".

This option allows you to set a new uniform width for an entire polyline. All tapering and variation is removed when this edit is performed.

AutoCAD prompts:

Enter new width for all segments:

> Type ".5".

Your screen will be redrawn to resemble *Figure 9-12*.

You should be at the "Close/Join/Width/Edit vertex..." prompt before continuing. The last polyline is still selected so that you can continue shaping it with other PEDIT options.

Notice that the width adjustment we just made created a stepped corner at the lower left. We can fix this easily using the "Move" option of the "Edit vertex" prompt.

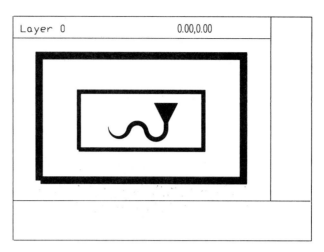

**Figure 9-12**

> Type "e" or select "Ed vrtx".

This brings up the "Edit vertex" prompt:

Next/Previous/Break/Insert/Move/Regen/Straighten/Tangent/Width/eXit <N>:

AutoCAD places an "X" on the starting point of the rectangle. This is the first vertex and will be the one that is edited according to the option we choose. "Next" will move the "X" to the next vertex, and "Previous" would move it back. We will use "Move" in this exercise; see the chart for the other options.

> Type "m" or select "move".

AutoCAD prompts:

Enter new location.

You will also see a rubber band from the vertex to the cross hairs.

> Pick a point .25 to the left of the "X".

Nothing will happen until you exit the "Edit vertex" prompt.

> Type "x" or select "exit".

Your screen will be redrawn to resemble *Figure 9-13*.

> Exit or cancel the PEDIT command.

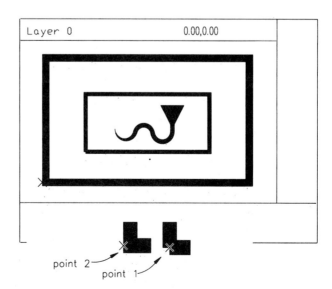

**Figure 9-13**

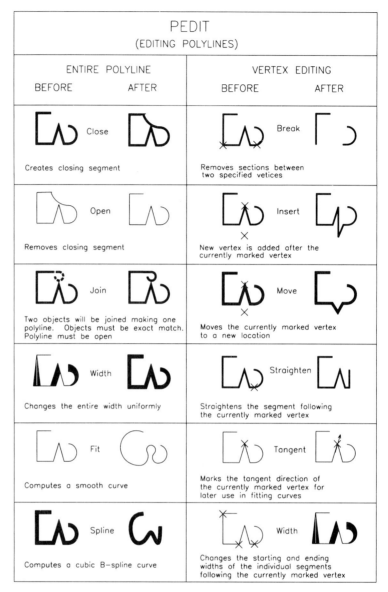

**Figure 9-14**

## TASK 10: Creating parallel copies with OFFSET

*Procedure.*

1. Type or select "OFFSET".
2. Type or show an offset distance.
3. Select object to offset.
4. Show which side to offset.

*Discussion.* Offset creates parallel copies of lines, circles, arcs, or polylines. You will find a number of typical applications in the drawings at the end of this chapter. In this brief exercise we will perform an offset operation to add a third border, as shown in *Figure 9-15*.

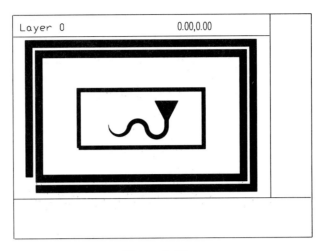

**Figure 9-15**

> Type or select "offset".
 AutoCAD prompts:

Offset distance or Through <Through>:

There are two methods. You can type or show a distance or you can show a point that you want the new copy to run through. We will use the distance method. Then if you like you can undo the command and try it again using the "through point" system.
> Type ".75".
 AutoCAD prompts for an object:

Select object to offset:

> Point to the rectangle.
 AutoCAD now needs to know whether to create the offset image to the inside or outside of the rectangle:

Side to offset:

> Pick a point anywhere outside the rectangle.
 Your screen should now resemble *Figure 9-15*.

To create the same border using the "through point" method, follow this procedure.

1. Type or select "offset".
2. Type "t" or select "through".
3. Select the rectangle.
4. Pick a "through point" 0.75 out from any of the sides of the rectangle.

Notice how the OFFSET operation on this polyline rectangle creates a gap at the corner. A good exercise at this point would be to use PEDIT to move vertices and close the gap.

### TASK 11: The SKETCH command (optional)

*Procedure.*

1. Type or select "SKETCH".
2. Type an increment.
3. Pick a start point (pen down).
4. Move cursor to sketch lines.
5. Pick an end point (pen up).
6. Record, exit, quit, or erase.

*Discussion.*    The SKETCH command allows you to draw freehand lines. We include it here as an optional task so that you will know that it is available. It is not used in any of the drawings that follow.

The key to SKETCH is becoming familiar with its "pen up, pen down" action. Also, get used to the idea that SKETCHed lines are not part of your drawing until you "record" them or "exit" the SKETCH command.

> Type or select "sketch".
    AutoCAD prompts:

SKETCH record increment <0.10>:

This will allow you to decide how fine or coarse you want your lines to be. Remember also that AutoCAD will continue to observe your snap. If you want a small record increment, turn snap off.
> Press enter to accept .10 as the record increment, or change it if you like.
    You will see the following prompt:

Sketch. Pen eXit Quit Record Erase Connect .

We will discuss these options in a moment. They will make more sense after you have done some sketching.
> In order to begin sketching, choose any point on your screen and press the pick button.
    This puts your imaginary sketching pen down.
> Move the cursor and watch the lines that appear on the screen.
> Press the pick button again.
    This picks your imaginary pen up again. If you move the cursor again, no new lines will be drawn.
> Press the pick button once again and move the cursor.
    The pen is down and you can continue sketching from a new start point.
    Now look at the other options:

Sketch. Pen eXit Quit Record Erase Connect .

"P" picks the imaginary pen up and down, but the pick button is more convenient. "X" records the lines you have drawn and exits the command. "Q" exits without recording. "R" records without exiting. "E" allows you to erase some of the lines you have sketched in the last sequence. The action of this erase option is interesting and you should try it out. "C" connects you to the point where you last picked up your pen. "." draws a straight line from the point where you left off to the current position of the cross hairs.

NOTE: Since SKETCHed objects are made up of large numbers of very small lines, they take up a great deal of memory.

## TASKS 12, 13, 14, 15, and 16

You now know how to draw nearly all of AutoCAD's 2-dimensional entities.  In the next chapter we will explore ways to create and manipulate blocks made up of multiple entities, all of which will be drawn and edited using the commands you already know.

The drawings you are about to do are intended to be fun and interesting as well as to give you experience with the new entities you have learned in this chapter.

## DRAWING 9-1: BACKGAMMON BOARD

This drawing should go very quickly. It is a good warm-up and will give you practice with SOLID and TRACE. Remember that the dimensions are always part of your drawing now, unless otherwise indicated.

### *DRAWING SUGGESTIONS*

GRID = 1.00
SNAP = .125

> Draw the 15 × 13 rectangle first and add the trace around the outside later.
> You will need the .125 snap to draw the trace around the outside of the board. The trace itself is .25 wide; since it is drawn on center, you will need to find points .125 away from the outside of the 15 × 13 rectangle.
> Draw the four triangles at the left of the board and then array them across. The filled triangles are drawn with the SOLID command; the others are just outlines drawn with LINE.
> The dimensions in this drawing are quite straightforward and should give you no trouble. Remember to set to layer "dim" before dimensioning.

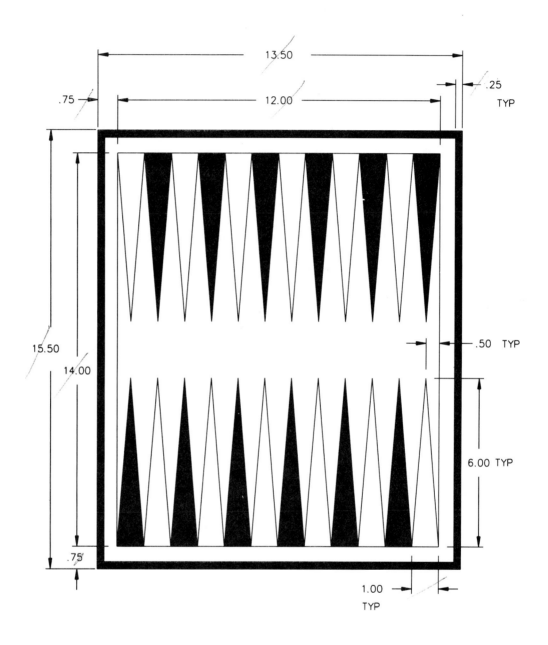

BACKGAMMON BOARD
Drawing 9−1

## DRAWING 9-2: DART BOARD

Although this drawing may seem to resemble the previous one, it is quite a bit more complex and is drawn in an entirely different way. Using SOLID to create the filled areas here would be impractical, to say the least. Instead, we use DONUTs and TRIM them to the radial lines.

### *DRAWING SUGGESTIONS*

LIMITS = (0,0) (24,18)
GRID = 1.00
SNAP = .125

> The filled inner circle is a donut with 0 inner and .62 outer diameters.

> The second circle is a simple 1.50 diameter circle. From here, draw a series of donuts. The outside diameter of one will become the inside diameter of the next. The 13.00 and 17.00 diameter circles must be drawn as circles rather than donuts so they will not be filled.

> Draw a radius line at one of the quadrants and array it around the circle.

> You may find it easier and quicker to turn fill off before trimming the donuts. Also, use layers to keep the donuts separated visually by color.

> To TRIM the donuts, select the radial lines as cutting edges. This is easily done using a very small crossing box around the center point of the board. Otherwise you will have to pick each line individually in the area between the 13.00 and 17.00 circle.

> Draw the number 5 at the top of the board using a "middle" text position and a rotation of 2 degrees. Array it around the circle and then use the CHANGE command to change the copied fives to the other numbers shown. You can select all the fives at once with a window and then make all the changes without leaving the CHANGE command.

CIRCLE DIAMETERS

⌀.62
⌀1.50
⌀7.50
⌀8.25
⌀13.00
⌀17.00

DART BOARD

Drawing 9-2

## DRAWING 9-3: PRINTED CIRCUIT BOARD

This drawing uses donuts, solids, and polylines. Notice that the "datum line" dimensions are done in the TEXT command; there is nothing in the DIM command that will create this format.

### *DRAWING SUGGESTIONS*

> UNITS = 4-place decimal
> LIMITS = (−1,−1) (17,11) or change
>           origin with UCS
> GRID = 0.5000
> SNAP = 0.1250

> Moving the 0 point of the grid by changing the limits as suggested or using UCS to change the origin point will make the placement of figures in this drawing very easy. If you use the 0 point of your grid as the 0 point shown in the dimensions, then you will be able to read distances directly from the coordinate display as you draw.

> The 26 rectangular tabs at the bottom can be drawn as polylines, traces, or solids. We drew solids and used DIST to lay out corners before entering the SOLID command.

> After placing the donuts according to the dimensions, draw the connections to them using polyline arcs and line segments. These will be simple polylines of uniform .03125 halfwidth. The triangular tabs will be added later.

> Remember, AutoCAD begins all polyline arcs tangent to the last segment drawn. Often this is not what you want. One way to correct this is to begin with a line segment that establishes the direction for the arc. The line segment can be extremely short and still accomplish your purpose. Thus many of these polylines will consist of a line segement, followed by an arc, followed by another line segment.

> Most of the dimensions in this drawing are done without the use of DIM. Draw the extension lines out of the circuit board, draw a temporary box to trim them evenly, and then draw the text at the end of the extension lines. Notice that text on the right will be left-justified, while that on the left will be right-justified.

> There are two sizes of the triangular tabs, one on top of the rectangular tabs and one at each donut. Draw one of each size in place and then use multiple COPY, MOVE, and ROTATE commands to create all the others.

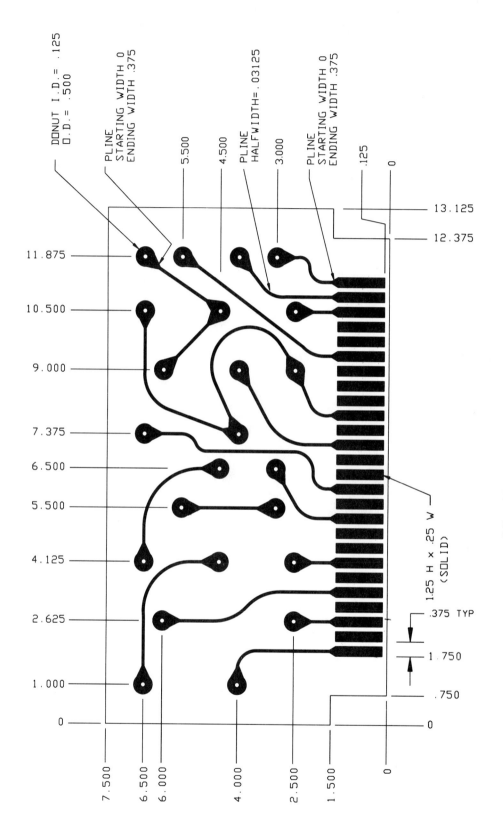

PRINTED CIRCUIT BOARD
DRAWING 9-3

# DRAWING 9-4: CARBIDE TIP SAW BLADE

This is a nice drawing that will give you some good experience with the OFFSET command. How would you draw the sides of the carbide tip if you could not use OFFSET?

## *DRAWING SUGGESTIONS*

GRID = 1.00
SNAP = .125

> After drawing the 7.25 diameter circle, draw a vertical line 1.50 over from the center line. This line will become the left side of the detailed "cut."

> Use DIST with an osnap to the intersection of the circle and the vertical line to locate the .58 vertical distance.

> Draw the horizontal center line through the .58 point and the vertical center line .16 to the right.

> Use the center lines in drawing the .16 radius arc.

> From the right end point of the arc, draw a line extending out of the circle at 80 degrees. The dimension is given as 10 degrees from the vertical, but the coordinate display will show 80 degrees from the horizontal instead.

> OFFSET this line .06 to the right and left to create the lines for the left and right sides of the carbide tip.

> Draw a horizontal line .12 up from the center line. TRIM it with the sides of the carbide tip and create .06 radius fillets right and left.

> Draw the 3.68 radius circle to locate the outside of the tip.

> BREAK and TRIM the three 80 degree lines, leaving three "extension" lines for use in dimensioning. Then copy the whole area out to the right for the detail. When you start working on the detail, SCALE it up 2.00.

> In the original view, erase the extension lines and then array the cut and carbide tip around the circle. TRIM the circle out of the new cuts and tips.

> You can use a "Rotated" dimension at −10 degrees to create the .12 and .06 dimensions in the detail.

> Be sure to type in your own values as you dimension the detail, since it has been scaled.

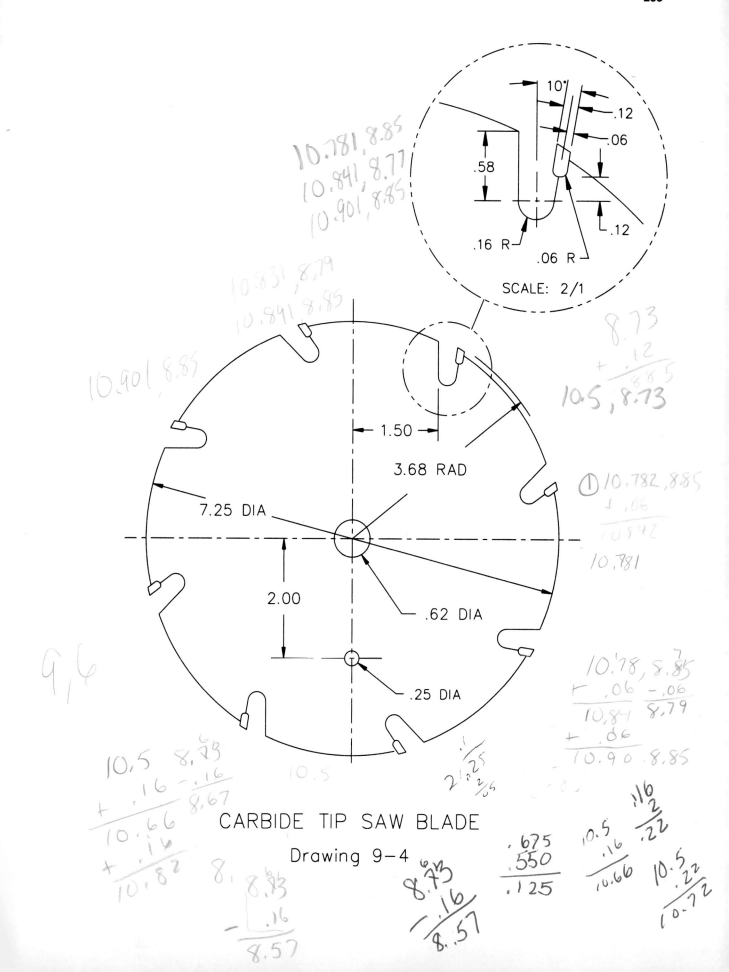

SCALE: 2/1

10°
.12
.06
.58
.16 R
.06 R
.12

CARBIDE TIP SAW BLADE

Drawing 9–4

1.50

3.68 RAD

7.25 DIA

2.00

.62 DIA

.25 DIA

*Handwritten annotations:*

10.781, 8.85
10.841, 8.77
10.901, 8.85

10.831, 8.79
10.891, 8.85

10.901, 8.85

8.73
+ .12
10.5, 8.73
.885

①10.782, 8.85
+ .06
10.842
10.781

10.78, 8.85
+ .06  − .06
10.84   8.79
+ .06
10.90   8.85

9, 6

10.5  8.73
+ .16  − .16
10.66  8.67
+ .16
10.82

8.
8.73
− .16
8.57

10.5

2.25
.05

8.73
.16
8.57

.675
.550
.125

8.73
.16
8.57

10.5  .16
2
.16  .22
10.66

10.5
.22
10.72

8.57

# DRAWING 9-5: GAZEBO

This architectural drawing makes extensive use of both the POLYGON command and the OFFSET command.

## *DRAWING SUGGESTIONS*

UNITS = Architectural

GRID = 1′

SNAP = 2″

LIMITS = (0′,0′) (48′,36′)

> All radii except the 6″ polygon are given from the center point to the midpoint of a side. In other words, the 6″ polygon will be "inscribed," while all the others will be "circumscribed."

> Notice that all polygon radii dimensions are given to the outside of the 2″ × 4″. OFFSET to the inside to create the parallel polygon for the inside of the board.

> Create radial studs by drawing a line from the midpoint of one side of a polygon to the midpoint of the side of another, or the midpoint of one to the vertex of another as shown, then offset 1″ each side and erase the original. Array around the center point.

> TRIM lines and polygons at vertices.

> You can make effective use of MIRROR in the elevation.

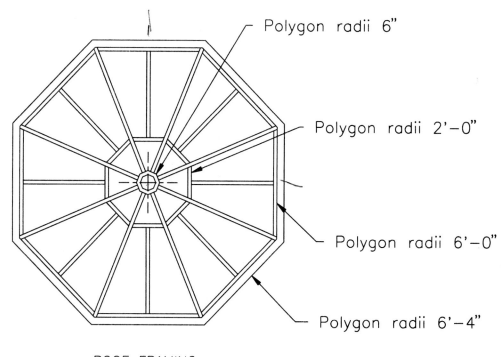

Polygon radii 6"

Polygon radii 2'–0"

Polygon radii 6'–0"

Polygon radii 6'–4"

ROOF FRAMING

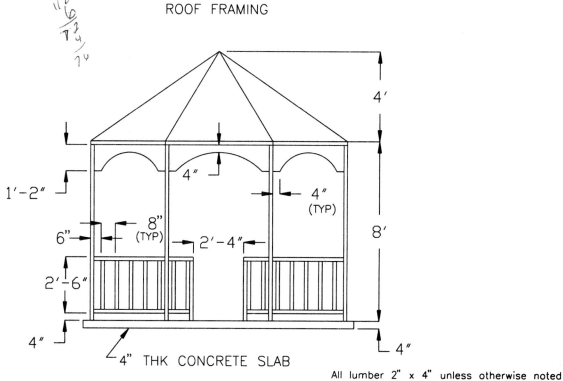

4'

1'–2"

4"

4"
(TYP)

8"
(TYP)

6"

2'–4"

8'

2'–6"

4"

4"

4" THK CONCRETE SLAB

All lumber 2" x 4" unless otherwise noted

FRONT ELEVATION

GAZEBO
Drawing 9–5

1:2,66

# chapter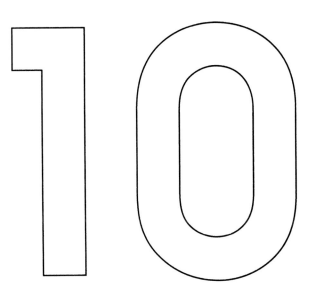

## COMMANDS

| BLOCKS | EDIT | UTILITY |
|--------|------|---------|
| BLOCK | ATTEDIT | ATTEXT |
| INSERT | | |
| ATTDEF | DISPLAY | |
| | ATTDISP | |

## OVERVIEW

You have seen several ways in which AutoCAD can treat a complex object as a single entity. In this chapter you will learn to create "blocks," which can be "inserted" repeatedly in many drawings and which can also be given "attributes." An attribute is an item of information about a block, such as a part number or price, that is stored along with the block definition. All the information stored in attributes can be "extracted" from a drawing and used to produce itemized reports. This is a powerful feature of CAD which has no direct counterpart in manual drafting.

Two added benefits of blocks are that they can be updated when specifications change, and that they take up significantly less memory than the sum of their components.

## TASKS

1.  Create blocks using BLOCK.
2.  INSERT and assemble blocks.
3.  Create attributes using ATTDEF.
4.  Edit attributes using ATTEDIT.
5.  Extract information about attributes in a drawing using ATTEXT—(optional).
6.  Do Drawing 10-1 ("CAD Room").
7.  Do Drawing 10-2 ("Base Assembly").
8.  Do Drawing 10-3 ("Double Bearing Assembly").
9.  Do Drawing 10-4 ("Scooter Assembly").

## TASK 1: Creating blocks

*Procedure.*

1. Type or select "BLOCK".
2. Type a name.
3. Pick an insertion point.
4. Select objects to be included in the block definition.

*Discussion.* Blocks can be stored as part of an individual drawing or as separate drawings. In general, the blocks which are most useful are those which will be used repeatedly and can therefore become part of a "library" of predrawn objects, used by you and others in your work group. In mechanical drawing, for instance, you may want a set of screws drawn to standard sizes that you can call out any time you wish. Or, if you are doing architectural drawing, you might find a library of doors and windows useful.

In this chapter we will create a set of simple symbols for some of the tools we know you will be using no matter what kind of CAD you are doing—namely, computers, monitors, keyboards, digitizers, plotters, and printers. We will draw them, define them as blocks, and then assemble them into a "workstation." Later we will insert workstations into an architectural drawing called "CAD ROOM" and use attributes to produce an inventory of the equipment in the room.

You will need to follow the instructions here carefully. Doing so will greatly enrich your understanding of what a CAD system can do.

> Begin a new drawing called "10-1" or "A:10-1" and make the following changes in the setup:

1. Set to layer 0 (see following note).
2. Change to Architectural units, with smallest fraction = 1.
3. Set GRID = 1'.
4. Set SNAP = 1".
5. Set LIMITS = (0',0') (48',36').

NOTE: There is a special relationship between blocks and layer 0. If you create a block on layer 0 you can insert it later on any other layer and it will take on the linetype and color of that layer. If you create a block on a layer other than 0 it will be fixed in that layer.

> Zoom into an area approximately 12' × 9'.
> Draw the four objects in *Figure 10-1*.

The text and dimensions in the figure are for your reference only; do not draw them on your screen.

We will now define each of these symbols as a block, beginning with the "computer."

> Type or select "block".

The first thing AutoCAD wants is a name for the block:

Block name (or ?):

A "?" will get you a list of blocks defined within the current drawing. Right now there are none.

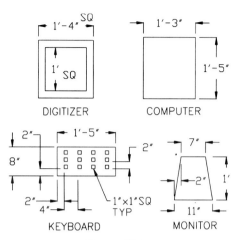

**Figure 10-1**

> Type "computer".
AutoCAD prompts:

Insertion base point:

Insertion points and insertion base points are critical in the whole matter of using blocks. The insertion base point is the point on the block at which the block will always be inserted. Therefore, when defining a block, try to anticipate the point on the block you would be most likely to use to position the block on the screen.
> Use a midpoint osnap to pick the middle of the bottom line of the computer as the insertion point, as shown in *Figure 10-2*.

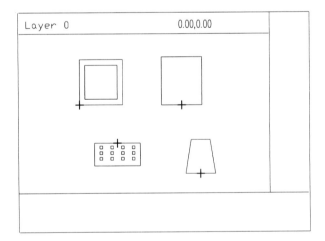

**Figure 10-2**

Finally, AutoCAD needs to know what to include in the block.

Select objects:

> Use a window to select the whole computer box.

When a block is defined, the first thing that happens is that it is erased from the display. The Block definition is now part of the drawing database, and you can insert the block anywhere in the drawing, but the original is gone. This facilitates the practice of creating a number of blocks, one after the other, and then assembling them at the end. If the originals did not disappear you would often have the added step of erasing them or panning to another part of the display to find room for the next block.

> NOTE: If for any reason you want the original back right away, the OOPS command will bring it back, just as it does in the ERASE command. Do not use "U", because this would undo the block definition.

You have now created a "computer" block definition. Now repeat the process to make a "monitor" block.

> Type or select "block".
> Type "monitor".
> Pick the midpoint of the bottom line of the monitor as the insertion base point.
> Select the monitor with a window.

Repeat the blocking process two more times to create "keyboard" and "digitizer" blocks, with insertion base points as shown in *Figure 10-2*. When you are done, your screen should be blank. Look at this description of the WBLOCK command before proceeding to Task 2.

*WBLOCK.* The WBLOCK command is very similar to BLOCK, except that it writes a block out to a separate file so that it may be inserted in other drawings. You can WBLOCK a previously defined block or create a new block definition as you write the block out. You can also WBLOCK an entire drawing. This can be quite useful, since a WBLOCKed drawing takes up less memory than a SAVEd one. We will be using WBLOCK as well as BLOCK extensively in the drawing tasks at the end of this chapter.

### TASK 2: INSERTing previously defined blocks

*Procedure.*

1. Type or select "INSERT".
2. Type a block name.
3. Pick an insertion point.
4. Answer prompts for horizontal and vertical scale and rotation angle.

*Discussion.* The INSERT command is used to call out blocks. The four block definitions you created in Task 1 are now part of the drawing database and can be inserted in this drawing anywhere you like. Among other things, this is a very handy way to do assembly drawings. You will find that assembling blocks can be done efficiently using appropriate OSNAP modes to place objects in precise relation to one another. Assembly drawing will be the focus of the drawing tasks at the end of this chapter.

In this task we will insert the computer, monitor, keyboard, and digitizer back into the drawing to create the "workstation" assembly shown in *Figure 10-3*.

> Type or select "insert".
AutoCAD needs to know which block to insert:

Block name (or ?):

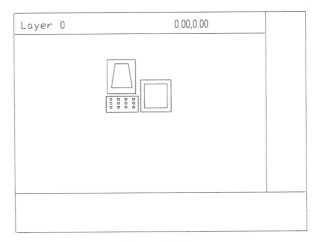

**Figure 10-3**

Now is a good time to see that your block definitions are still in your database, even though there is nothing on the screen.
> Type "?" to see a list of blocks.
You should see a list like this:

```
                    Defined blocks.
                    COMPUTER
                    MONITOR
                    KEYBOARD
                    DIGITIZER
                    4 blocks, 0 unnamed blocks
```

> Repeat the INSERT command.
> At the "Block name (or ?):" prompt, type "computer".
AutoCAD now needs to know where to insert the computer:

Insertion point:

Notice that AutoCAD gives you a block to drag into place and that it is positioned with the block's insertion base point at the intersection of the cross hairs.
> Pick a point near the middle of the screen, as shown in *Figure 10-3*.
What comes next is a set of prompts that allow you to scale and rotate the block as you insert it. This vastly increases the flexibility and power of the blocking system, although in many instances, including this one, you will accept all the defaults.
The first prompt asks for a scale factor:

X scale factor <1> / Corner / XYZ:

Unlike the SCALE command, which automatically scales both horizontally and vertically, blocks can be stretched or shrunk in either direction as you insert them. You can type an X scale factor or specify both an X and a Y factor at once by showing two corners of a window using the "Corner" option. The third option, "XYZ", is reserved for 3D applications.
Pressing enter will retain the block's present length.
> Press enter to retain an X scale factor of 1.
AutoCAD follows with a prompt for vertical scale:

Y scale factor (default = X):

> Press enter to retain a Y factor of 1.
   You now have the opportunity to rotate the object:

Rotation angle <0>:

> Press enter to retain 0 degrees of rotation.

Now let's add a monitor.

> Repeat the INSERT command.
   Notice that the last block inserted becomes the default block name. This facilitates the common procedure in which you insert the same block in several different places in a drawing.
> Type "monitor".
> Pick an insertion point two or three inches above the insertion point of the computer, as shown.
> Press enter three additional times to retain X and Y scale factors of 1, and a rotation of 0.

You should now have the monitor sitting on top of the computer, and be back at the command prompt. We will insert the keyboard, as shown in *Figure 10-3.*

> Repeat the INSERT command.
> Type "keyboard".
> Pick an insertion point one or two inches below the computer, as shown.
> Press enter three additional times to retain X and Y scale factors of 1, and a rotation of 0.

You should now have the keyboard in place. Repeat the INSERT command once more and place the digitizer block to the right of the other blocks as shown.
   Congratulations, you have completed your first assembly. Now that you are familiar with BLOCK, WBLOCK, and INSERT, you have the primary tools needed to create and utilize a symbol library.
   The tasks that follow introduce you to "attributes". First, we will create attributes to hold information about CAD workstations and include them in the definition of a new "ws" block. Then we will insert several workstations into our drawing and edit some of the attribute information. Finally, we will produce an inventory of the equipment included in our workstations.

## TASK 3: Defining attributes with ATTDEF

*Procedure.*

1. Type or select ATTDEF.
2. Specify attribute modes.
3. Press enter to end mode specification.
4. Type an attribute tag.
5. Type an attribute prompt.
6. Type a default attribute value or press enter.
7. Include the attribute in a block definition.

*Discussion.*    Attributes can be confusing and you should not spend too much time worrying over their details unless you are currently involved in an application that requires their use. On the other hand, they are a powerful tool, and if you have a basic understanding of what they can do, you could be the one in your work setting to recognize when to use them.

One of the difficulties of learning about attributes is that you have to define them before you see them in action. It is therefore a little hard to comprehend what your definitions mean the first time around. Bear with us and follow instructions closely; it will be worth your effort.

In this task we will define attributes that will hold information about CAD workstations. The attributes will be defined in a flexible manner so that the workstation block can represent any number of hardware configurations.

When we have defined our attributes, we will create a block called "ws" that includes the whole assembly and its attributes.

> To begin this task you should have the assembled workstation from Task 2 on your screen.

First we will define an attribute that will allow us to specify the type of computer in any individual occurrence of the "ws" block.

> Type or select "attdef".
AutoCAD shows you a prompt for something called "attribute modes":

Attribute modes-Invisible:N  Constant:N  Verify:N Preset:N
Enter (ICVP) to change, RETURN when done:

To change a mode from N (no) to Y (yes) you will type the first letter of the mode, as shown in the parentheses (ICVP). We will be using all the defaults in our first attribute definition. This means that when a workstation is inserted, the computer attribute value will be visible in the drawing, variable with each insertion of the block, verified only once, and not preset to a value.

NOTE: If your version of AutoCAD is earlier than Release 9, there will be no "Preset" mode.

> Press enter to retain default attribute modes.
AutoCAD prompts us for something called an attribute tag. Like a field name in a database file, a tag identifies the kind of information this particular attribute is meant to hold. The prompt is:

Attribute tag:

> Type "Computer".
AutoCAD now asks for an attribute prompt:

Attribute prompt:

The key to understanding the attribute prompt is to be clear about the difference between attribute definitions and actual occurrences of attributes in a drawing. Right now we are defining an attribute. The attribute definition will become part of the definition of the "ws" block and will be used whenever "ws" is inserted.

However, attribute definitions function as containers for information, not necessarily as complete information in themselves. Each time we insert "ws" we can specify some or all of the information that its attributes hold. This is what will allow us to use our "ws" block to represent different hardware configurations. With the definition we are now creating there will be a prompt to tell us to enter information about the computer in a given configuration.

> Type "Enter computer type".

We now have the opportunity to specify a default attribute value if we wish:

Default attribute value:

We will use no default in this attribute definition.
> Press enter for no default.

The prompts that follow are just like those you have used in the TEXT command. When attributes are visible they appear as text on the screen, therefore, the appearance of the text needs to be specified:

Start point or Align/Center/Fit/Middle/Right/Style:

We will place our attributes 8 inches below the keyboard, as shown in *Figure 10-4*.

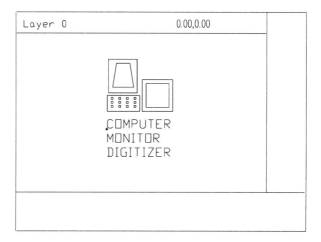

**Figure 10-4**

> Pick a start point 8 inches below the left side of the keyboard, as shown.
AutoCAD prompts:

Height <0′-0″>:

We will set our text height to 4 inches.
> Type " 4″ ".
AutoCAD prompts:

Rotation angle <0>:

> Press enter to retain 0 degrees of rotation.

The word "Computer" should be drawn as shown. Remember, this is an attribute definition, not an occurrence of the attribute. "Computer" is our attribute "tag". After we define the workstation as a block and the block is inserted, you will answer the "Enter computer name" prompt with the name of a computer, and the name itself will be in the drawing rather than this tag.

We will now proceed to define three more attributes, using some different modes.

> Repeat the ATTDEF command.

We will use all the "N" modes again, but we will provide a default monitor in this attribute definition.
> Press enter to accept current attribute modes.

> Type "Monitor" for the attribute tag.
> Type "Enter monitor type" for the attribute prompt.
> Type "NEC MultiSync" for the default attribute value.

As in the text command, you can align a series of attributes by pressing enter in response to the "Start point..." prompt.

> Press enter.

The attribute tag "Monitor" should be added to the workstation below the "Computer" tag.

Next, we will add an "invisible, preset" attribute for the digitizer. Invisible means that the attribute text will not be visible when the block is inserted, although the information will be in the database and can be extracted. Preset means that the attribute has a default value and does not issue a prompt to change it. However, unlike "constant" attributes, you can change preset attributes using the ATTEDIT command, which we will explore in Task 5.

> Repeat the ATTDEF command.
> Type I to change the "invisible" mode to "Y".
> Type P to change the "preset" mode to "Y".

Your attribute modes should now read YNNY.

> Press enter (RETURN) to end mode selection.
> Type "Digitizer" for the attribute tag.
> Type "Digitizer type" for the attribute prompt.

This prompt will not be issued on the command line, but it will appear in a dialogue box if you select INSERT from the pull down menu. The INSERT dialogue box is discussed later.

> Type "Summagraphics 1201" for the default attribute value.
> Press enter to align the "digitizer" attribute tag below the "monitor" tag.

The "Digitizer" attribute tag should be added to your screen, as shown. Once again, remember that this is the attribute definition. When "ws" is inserted, the attribute value "Summagraphics 1201" will be written into the database, but nothing will appear on the screen.

Finally, the most important step of all: We must define the workstation as a block that includes all our attribute definitions.

> Type or select "block".
> Type "ws" for the block name.
> Pick an insertion point at the midpoint of the bottom of the keyboard.
> Window the workstation assembly and all three attribute tags.

As usual, the newly defined block will disappear from the screen.

In the next two tasks we will insert several workstations back into your drawing, use ATTEDIT to change an attribute value, and then extract the information from them into a report using the ATTEXT command and a sample extraction program called ATTEXT.bas.

## TASK 4: Editing attributes with ATTEDIT

*Procedure.*

1. Type or select "ATTEDIT".
2. Specify one by one or global editing.
3. Specify blocks and attributes to include in the editing process.
4. In one by one editing, specify property to be edited and edit it.
5. In global editing, specify string to change and new string.

*Discussion.*   The ATTEDIT command provides the capacity to change values and text properties of attributes in blocks that have been inserted. It does <u>not</u> allow you to edit attribute definitions. *Block definitions and attribute definitions can be changed only by recreating them.*

There are two ways to use ATTEDIT. One by one editing allows you to change individual attribute values, text position, height, angle, style, layer, and color. Global editing allows you to change values only.

> To begin this task, you should be in the Drawing 10-1 begun in Task 1 and you should have a clear screen.

> Insert three workstations, using the following procedure (note the attribute prompts):

1.   Type or select "INSERT".

2.   Type "ws" for the block name.

3.   Pick an insertion point.

4.   Press enter for X and Y scale factors and rotation angle.

5.   Answer the attribute prompts for computers and monitors.

We specified two Zenith and one NEC computers for this exercise and retained all the monitor defaults (NEC MultiSync). Your hardware information may be entirely different, but this exercise will make more sense if you use ours. Notice that you are not prompted for digitizers because that attribute is preset.

NOTE: If you are using AutoCAD Release 9 or higher, there is a dialogue box version of the INSERT command which can be accessed from the "Draw" pull down menu. The box displays attribute prompts and defaults in the usual tabular dialogue form.

When you are done, your screen should resemble *Figure 10-5.*

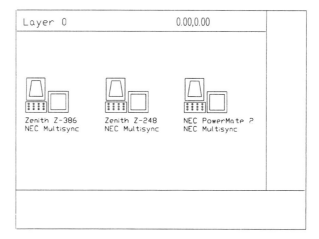

**Figure 10-5**

The first thing we will do is use ATTDISP ("attribute display") to turn invisible attributes on.

> Type or select "attdisp".

The prompt shows you three options:

Normal/On/Off <Normal>:

Normal means that visible attributes are visible and invisible attributes are invisible. On turns all attributes on. Off turns all attributes off.
> Type "on".

Your screen will be regenerated with invisible attributes on, as shown in *Figure 10-6*.

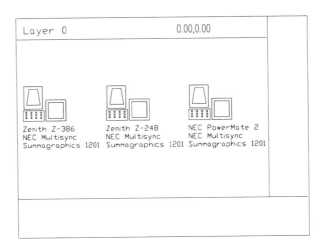

**Figure 10-6**

You can leave ATTDISP on in this exercise or turn it back to "normal".

Now we will do an edit. Imagine that these three workstations represent part of a small work site and that we just purchased a new "MultiSync PLUS" monitor. We could erase one of the workstations and reinsert it with new attribute information, but it will be simpler to edit just the one attribute that needs to change.

> Type or select "attedit".

The first prompt allows you to choose between global and individual editing:

Edit attributes one at a time? <Y>:

> Press enter for one by one editing.

AutoCAD issues a series of three prompts that allow you to narrow down the field of attributes to be edited.

Block specification <*>:

If we had more than one type of block on the screen, we could limit editing to occurrences of whatever block we wished to name. But we have only the "ws" block.
> Press enter.

AutoCAD prompts:

Attribute tag specification <*>:

This allows us to narrow the field to a single tag—all the monitors, for example.
> Type "monitor".

AutoCAD now prompts for an attribute value:

Attribute value specification <*>:

This would allow us to specify only monitors with the value "NEC MultiSync", for example. Since they all have the same value, at this point this would be useless.
> Press enter.

Now AutoCAD asks us to select attributes by pointing or windowing:

Select Attributes:

> Select the text "NEC MultiSync" on the middle workstation.

Now AutoCAD knows which attribute to edit. It needs to know the type of edit you want to perform:

Value/Position/Height/Angle/Style/Layer/Color/Next <N>:

These options are self-explananatory except for "Next". When you have windowed a set of attributes that fit your previous specifications, you can edit them one after another by pressing enter for the default "N" at this prompt.

We will edit the value of our selected attribute.
> Type "v" or select "value".

AutoCAD prompts:

Change or Replace <R>:

The "Change" option would allow you to change a portion of a text string.
> Press enter to replace the text.

AutoCAD prompts:

New attribute value:

> Type "NEC MultiSync PLUS".

AutoCAD returns the editing options prompt that would allow you to further edit the selected attribute, or move on to another, if others were highlighted.
> Press enter to exit the ATTEDIT command.

The monitor attribute will be changed, as shown in *Figure 10-7*. The ATTEDIT command can be quite tricky, and we recommend that you see the *AutoCAD Reference Manual*, Section 9.2, if you need additional information.

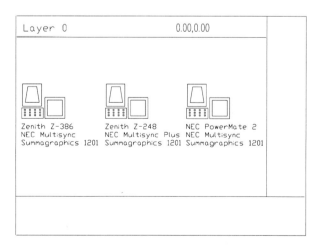

**Figure 10-7**

NOTE: If you are using Release 9 or higher, there is a dialogue box version of the ATTEDIT command. It is activated by typing "DDATTE" and can only be used to change attribute values block by block.

## TASK 5: Extracting information from attributes with ATTEXT

*NOTE: This exercise is optional and should only be attempted if you have used BASIC previously and are familiar with MS-DOS, or if you have your instructor's support. In addition, it will help if you have some familiarity with databases.*

### Procedure.

1. Type or select "ATTEXT".
2. Specify an extract file format.
3. Specify a template file.
4. Specify an extract file name.

*Discussion.*     Although there are many good reasons to use attributes, the most impressive is the ability to create extract files which can be processed by other programs to generate reports, bills of material, inventories, parts lists, and quotations. This means, for example, that with a well-managed CAD system you could do a drawing of a construction project and get a complete price breakdown and supply list directly from the drawing database, all processed by computer.

In order to accomplish this, you need a complete library of parts with carefully defined attributes and a program like dBASE III or LOTUS 1-2-3 that is capable of receiving and formatting the extract information into a useful report. Inherent in the success of this kind of application is a degree of coordination between CAD drafting personnel and programmers that is not common. However, we suspect that as the CAD field grows it will become more common, and that the uses of attribute extraction will grow with it.

For this exercise, you will need to make use of a program in BASIC, called ATTEXT.bas, that Autodesk includes in the AutoCAD software package. Its capabilities are quite limited, but it provides an effective demonstration of attribute extraction. The important thing is to see the ease with which information contained in your drawing attributes can be transferred to programs designed to deal with text and numbers.

If you do not have BASIC and ATTEXT.bas on your system, or if you do not know how to use BASIC, you will get the idea by simply reading this section.

> You should still be in Drawing 10-1 with the three workstations on your screen to begin this task.
> Type or select "attext".

AutoCAD will prompt for a file format:

CDF, SDF or DXF Attribute extract (or Entities)? <C>

The "Entities" option would allow you to choose blocks from a drawing to be included in the extract. In most cases you will want all of them and can disregard this option. The other options specify formats for the extract.

We are now in the arena of interprogram communications. CDF, SDF, and DXF are formats that can be used in extracting attribute information from a drawing so that it may be read by other programs. In any given application, the one you choose will depend on the program you want to communicate with.

For the purposes of this exercise, it is not necessary that you understand the differences between the formats. They are defined in the *AutoCAD Reference Manual*,

Section 9.2. SDF and CDF extracts require a "template file" that must be prepared with a word processor or text editor before the extract can be done. The template gives the attribute information a form that can be read by dBASE III and other programs. DXF does not require a template and is the format used by ATTEXT.bas, which we will use in this exercise. DXF extracts create files with .dxx extensions.

> Type "d" or "dxf".
AutoCAD switches to the text screen and prompts you to name the extract file:

Extract file name <10-1>:

The name of the current drawing is the default and will be fine for our purposes; however, be sure that your default is "A:10-1" if you want to write the file to your floppy disk.
> Press enter to accept the default file name, or type "A:10-1" to write the file to the disk in the A: drive.

When the extraction is complete, you will see a message that looks like this:

15 entities in extract file.

Now we will leave AutoCAD and create a simple report from our extract file.

NOTE: Extracting attributes has no effect on the drawing itself.

> END Drawing "10-1".
> Type "0" at the Main Menu to exit AutoCAD.
> Load BASIC.
Methods for doing this will vary from system to system. See your instructor or your DOS manual if you need information on how to load BASIC on your system.
> Load ATTEXT.bas into your BASIC editor.
If your instructor is preparing your system for this exercise, we would recommend placing ATTEXT.bas in the same directory as BASIC (BASIC.com). In that case you will need to type:

LOAD"ATTEXT

Otherwise, you will need to add a drive and directory. If ATTEXT.bas is in a directory on the C: drive called \ACAD, you would type the following:

LOAD"C:\ACAD\ATTEXT

Or, if you are loading ATTEXT.bas off a floppy disk:

LOAD"A:ATTEXT

If you see the BASIC "ok" prompt after entering your "LOAD... " line, the program has been successfully loaded.
> Type "run".
When the program is run, it will prompt you for an extract file name:

Enter extract file name:

> Use whatever drive and directory names are called for to clearly locate your extract file.

If you have written your extract to a disk, for example, type:

A:10-1.dxx

The .dxx extension is necessary.

If all has gone well, you will see a report on your screen like the one following. If not, don't be too concerned; the attribute creation and extraction process is a long and winding road and there are many places to get lost along the way. Get some help from your instructor and review the steps in the last two tasks to make sure you have done them correctly.

| Computer | Digitizer | Monitor |
|----------|-----------|---------|
| Zenith | Summagraphics 1201 | NEC MultiSync |
| Zenith | Summagraphics 1201 | NEC MultiSync |
| NEC | Summagraphics 1201 | NEC MultiSync PLUS |

This extract is simply an inventory, of course, but with a little imagination you should be able to see the possibilities it represents. With dBASE III, for example, we could match these equipment items to a price list contained in a database file, calculate totals and subtotals, and format a more elaborate report. This is a matter worthy of a whole book of its own, and we have only scratched the surface here. But before going on, we do hope you will take the time to appreciate the power of what you have just accomplished.

When you are ready:

1. Type "system" to leave BASIC and return to the DOS prompt.
2. Reload AutoCAD.
3. Type "2" and enter Drawing 10-1 again.
4. Erase the screen and proceed to the real drawing 10-1, the "CAD ROOM", which makes use of everything you have just learned.

Finally, take a look at the chart at the end of this section ("Other Commands To Use With Blocks"). It is a list and description of other commands that are frequently used in conjunction with blocks. The "ARM" section numbers are from the *AutoCAD Reference Manual*.

## TASKS 6, 7, 8, and 9

The first drawing exercise focuses on the use of attributes, while the other three are purely assembly drawings. We will be making some suggestions on how to manage drawing files and blocks in assembly drawings. These techniques will be useful and necessary in any industrial application, but they may not be required to complete the drawings as classroom exercises. You will need to find out from your instructor what is expected in your class.

Remember to create objects to be BLOCKed on layer 0, unless you have a specific reason for doing otherwise.

OTHER COMMANDS TO USE WITH BLOCKS

| Command | Usage |
| --- | --- |
| BASE | Allows you to specify a base insertion point for an entire drawing. The base point will be used when the drawing is inserted in other drawings. ARM,* Section 9.1. |
| DBLIST | Displays information for all entities in the current drawing database. Information includes type of entity and layer. Additional information depends on the type of entity. For blocks it includes insertion point, x scale, y scale, rotation, and attribute values. Due to length, a database list must usually be printed using printer echo (Ctrl-Q) or viewed with scroll pause (Ctrl-S to pause, any key to resume scrolling). See "LIST", below, and ARM, Section 5.6. |
| DDATTE | Provides a dialogue box for attribute editing. ARM, Section 9.2, Release 9 or higher only. |
| EXPLODE | Creates a copy of a block in which all objects in the block are defined as separate entities. *Do not EXPLODE blocks that contain attribute information. The information will be replaced by attribute tags.* ARM, Section 5.4. |
| LIST | Lists information about a single block or entity. Information listed is the same as that in DBLIST, but for the selected entity only. ARM, Section 5.6. |
| MINSERT | "Multiple Insert". Allows you to insert arrays of blocks. MINSERT arrays take up less memory than ARRAYs of INSERTed blocks. ARM, Section 9.1. |
| PURGE | Deletes unused blocks, layers, linetypes, shapes, or text styles from a drawing. PURGE must be the first command executed when you enter the drawing editor; otherwise it will not work. ARM, Section 3.12. |
| WBLOCK | Saves a block to a separate file so that it can be inserted in other drawings. Does not save unused blocks or layers, and can therefore be used to reduce drawing file size. ARM, Section 9.1. |

* ARM stands for *AutoCAD Reference Manual*.

# DRAWING 10-1: CAD ROOM

This architectural drawing is primarily an exercise in using blocks and attributes. Use your "ws" block and its attributes to fill in the workstations and text after you draw the walls and counter top. New blocks should be created for the plotters and printers, as described following.

## *DRAWING SUGGESTIONS*

> The "plotter" block is a 1' × 3' rectangle, with two visible, variable attributes (NNNN). The first attribute is for a manufacturer and the second for a model. The "printers" are 2' × 2.5' with the same type of attributes. Draw the rectangles, define their attributes 8 inches below them using ATTDEF, create the BLOCK definitions, and then INSERT plotters and printers as shown.

NOTE: Do not include the labels "plotter" or "laser printer" in the block, because text in a block will be rotated with the block. This would give you inverted text on the front counter top. Insert the blocks and add the text afterwards. The attribute text can be handled differently, as described following.

> The "8 pen plotter" was inserted with a Y scale factor of 1.25.
> The two workstations on the front counter could be inserted with a rotation angle of 180 degrees, but then the attribute text would be inverted also and would have to be turned around using ATTEDIT. Instead, we have reset the "mirrtext" system variable so that we could mirror blocks without attribute text being inverted:

1.  Enter the SETVAR command.
2.  Type "mirrtext".
3.  Type "0".

Now you can mirror objects on the back counter to create those on the front. With the "mirrtext" system variable set to "0," text included in a MIRROR procedure is not inverted as it would be with mirrtext set to "1" (the default). This applies to attribute text as well as ordinary text. However, it does not apply to ordinary text included in a block definition.
> If you have completed Task 6 on attribute extracts, we encourage you to create an extract from this drawing using the same procedures outlined there.

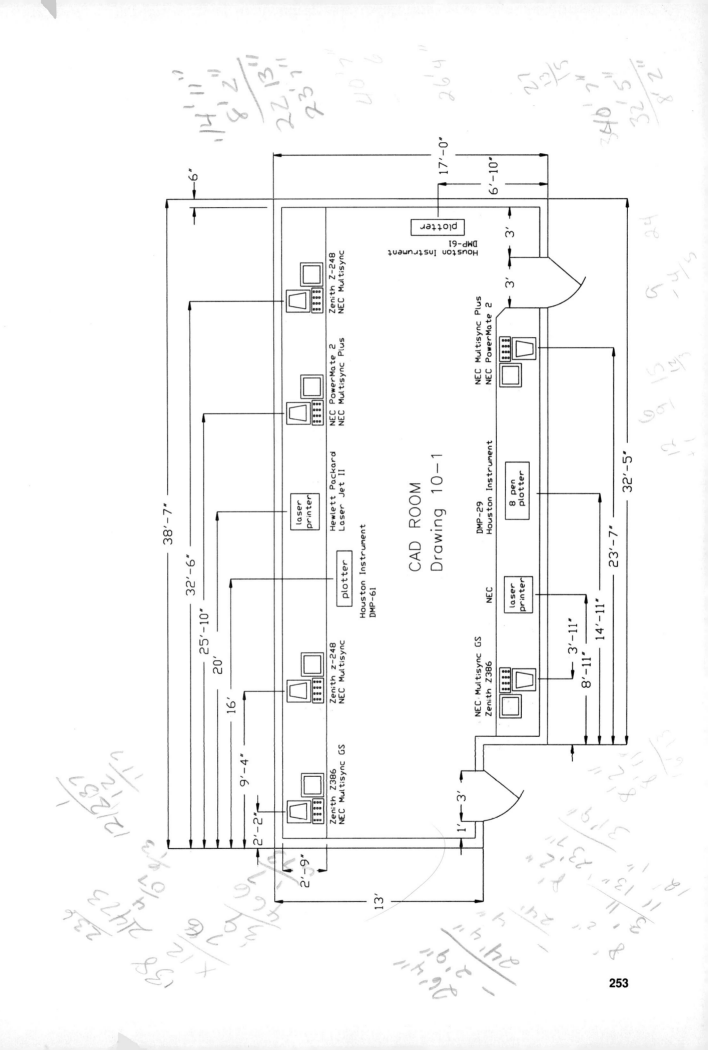

CAD ROOM
Drawing 10-1

253

## DRAWING 10-2: BASE ASSEMBLY

This is a good exercise in assembly drawing procedures. You will be drawing each of the numbered part details and then assembling them into the "Base Assembly."

### *DRAWING SUGGESTIONS*

We will no longer provide you with units, grid, snap, and limit settings. You can determine what you need by looking over the drawing and its dimensions. Remember that you can always change a setting later if it becomes necessary.

> You can create your own title block from scratch or develop one from "Title Block," Drawing 7-1, if you have saved it. Once created and SAVEd or WBLOCKed, it can be inserted and scaled to fit any drawing.
> The parts list should also be defined as a block. Since many drawings include parts lists, you will want to be able to quickly create a table with any given number of lines. Try this:

1. Define a block that represents one line of the parts list.
2. WBLOCK it so it can be used in any drawing.
3. When you insert it, use either ARRAY or MINSERT to create the number of lines in the table (MINSERT creates an array of a block as part of the insertion process).

> You will be drawing each of the numbered parts (B101-1, B101-2, etc.) and then assembling them. In an industrial application the individual part details would be sent to different manufacturers or manufacturing departments, so they must exist as separate, completely dimensioned drawings as well as blocks that can be used in creating the assembly. This suggests that for each part detail you should create three separate blocks: one for dimensions and one for each view in the assembly. The dimensioned part drawings will include both views. The two assembly blocks will be the views of the part with dimensions, hidden lines, and centerlines erased. You may want to adopt some kind of block naming system like this: "B101-1D" for the dimensioned drawing; "B101-1T" for a top view without dimensions; and "B101-1F" for a front view without dimensions. Such a system will make it easy to call out all the top view parts for the top view assembly, for example. A more detailed procedure is outlined for drawings 10-3 and 10-4.
> Notice that the assembly requires you to do a considerable amount of trimming away of lines from the blocks you insert. This can be easily done, but you must remember to EXPLODE the inserted blocks first.

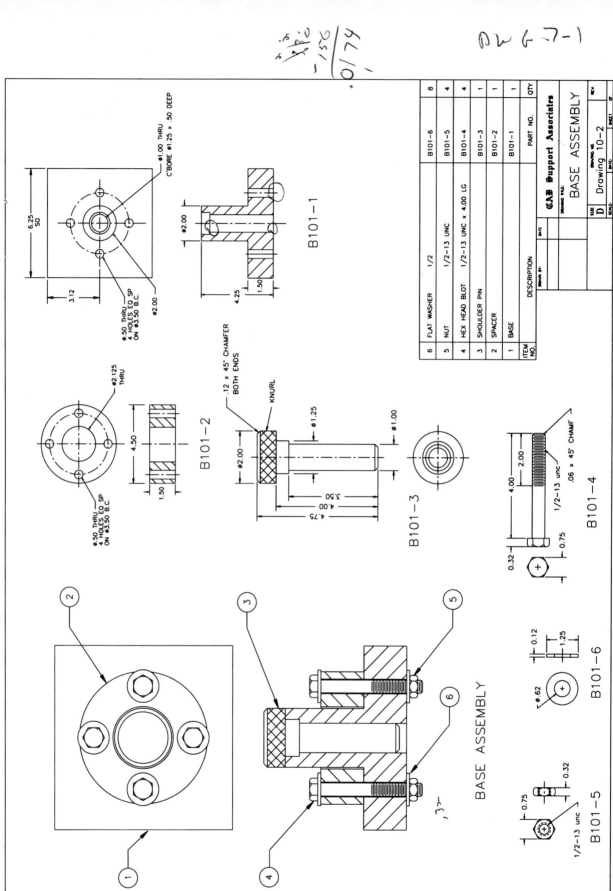

DWG-7-1

## B101-1

6.25 SQ

3.12

Ø2.00

∅1.00 THRU
C'BORE ∅1.25 x .50 DEEP

∅.50 THRU
4 HOLES EQ SP
ON ∅3.50 B.C.

Ø2.00

1.50

4.25

## B101-2

∅2.125 THRU

4.50

1.50

∅.50 THRU
4 HOLES EQ SP
ON ∅3.50 B.C.

## B101-3

.12 x 45° CHAMFER
BOTH ENDS

KNURL

Ø2.00

Ø1.25

Ø1.00

3.50

4.00

4.75

## B101-4

4.00

2.00

.06 x 45° CHAMF

1/2-13 unc

0.32

0.75

## B101-6

0.12

1.25

Ø.62

## B101-5

0.75

0.32

1/2-13 unc

## BASE ASSEMBLY

| ITEM NO. | | DESCRIPTION | | PART NO. | QTY |
|---|---|---|---|---|---|
| 6 | FLAT WASHER | 1/2 | | B101-6 | 8 |
| 5 | NUT | 1/2-13 UNC | | B101-5 | 4 |
| 4 | HEX HEAD BOLT | 1/2-13 UNC x 4.00 LG | | B101-4 | 4 |
| 3 | SHOULDER PIN | | | B101-3 | 1 |
| 2 | SPACER | | | B101-2 | 1 |
| 1 | BASE | | | B101-1 | 1 |

CAB Support Associates

BASE ASSEMBLY

DRAWING NO. Drawing 10-2

SIZE D

REV.

DRAWN BY:

DATE:

SCALE:

# DRAWINGS 10-3 AND 10-4: DOUBLE BEARING ASSEMBLY AND SCOOTER ASSEMBLY

All of the specific drawing techniques required to do the individual part details in these two drawings are ones that you have encountered in previous chapters. What is new is the blocking and assembly process. The procedure outlined is one we consider to be standard, though there is certainly room for variation.

## DRAWING SUGGESTIONS

1. Draw each part detail in whatever two- or three-view form is given. Make the drawing complete with hidden lines, centerlines, and dimensions.

2. WBLOCK the part, giving it a file name that identifies it as a complete, dimensioned drawing. For example: "CAPD".

3. Use OOPS to return the part to the display.

4. ERASE dimensions, hidden lines, and centerlines. If you have kept your layers separated, you can turn off layer 0 and then erase everything left using a window or crossing. Then turn 0 on again.

5. BLOCK the views separately, giving each a name that will identify it with its view. For example: "CAPT", for the top view of the cap, "CAPF" for cap front, and "CAPR" for cap right. It is essential that your naming system keep these BLOCKed views distinct from the WBLOCKed dimensioned drawing of step 2.

6. Insert blocks from step 5 to create the assembly. EXPLODE and TRIM where necessary.

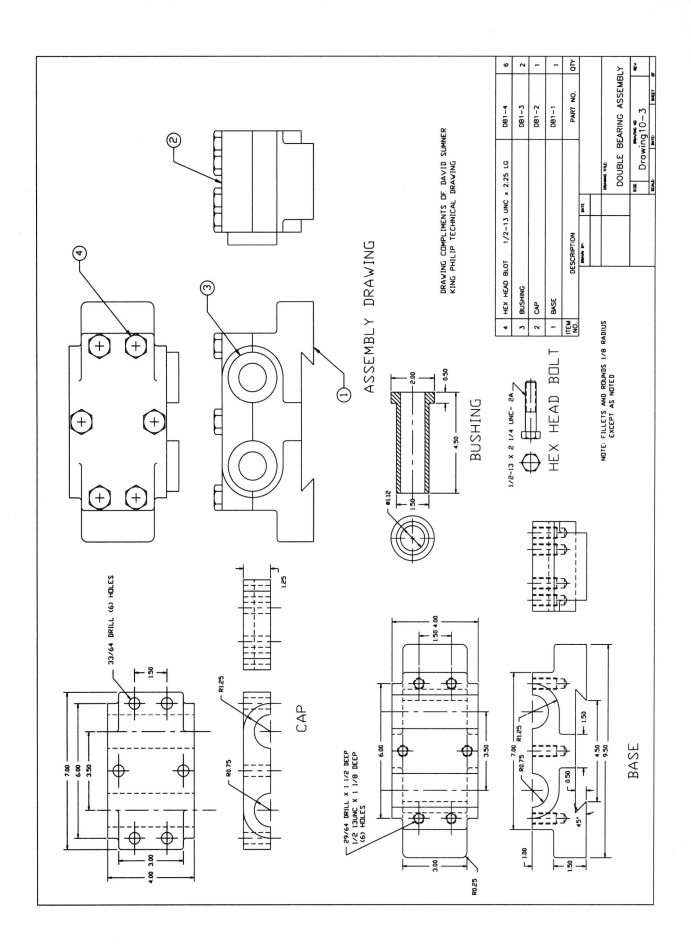

ASSEMBLY DRAWING

DRAWING COMPLIMENTS OF DAVID SUMNER
KING PHILIP TECHNICAL DRAWING

BUSHING

HEX HEAD BOLT

1/2-13 x 2 1/4 UNC- 2A

NOTE: FILLETS AND ROUNDS 1/8 RADIUS
EXCEPT AS NOTED

CAP

33/64 DRILL (6) HOLES

29/64 DRILL x 1 1/2 DEEP
1/2 13UNC x 1 1/8 DEEP
(6) HOLES

BASE

| ITEM NO. | PART NO. | DESCRIPTION | QTY |
|---|---|---|---|
| 4 | DB1-4 | HEX HEAD BLOT   1/2-13 UNC x 2.25 LG | 6 |
| 3 | DB1-3 | BUSHING | 2 |
| 2 | DB1-2 | CAP | 1 |
| 1 | DB1-1 | BASE | 1 |

DRAWING TITLE:
DOUBLE BEARING ASSEMBLY

DRAWING NO.
Drawing10-3

SIZE    SCALE:    DATE:    SHEET:   OF    REV.

DRAWN BY:    DATE:

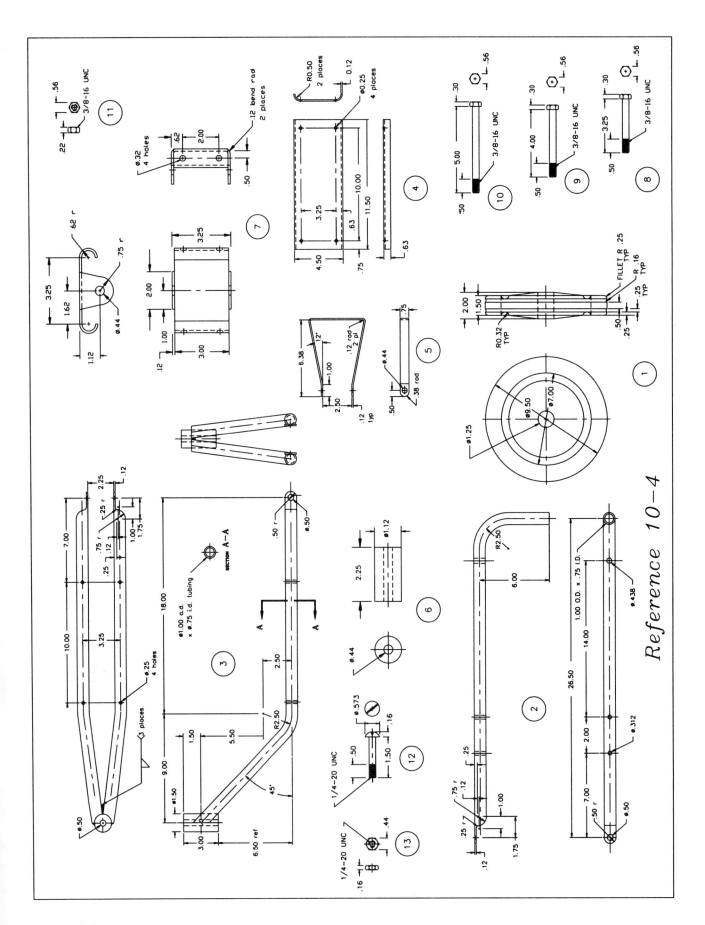

*Reference 10-4*

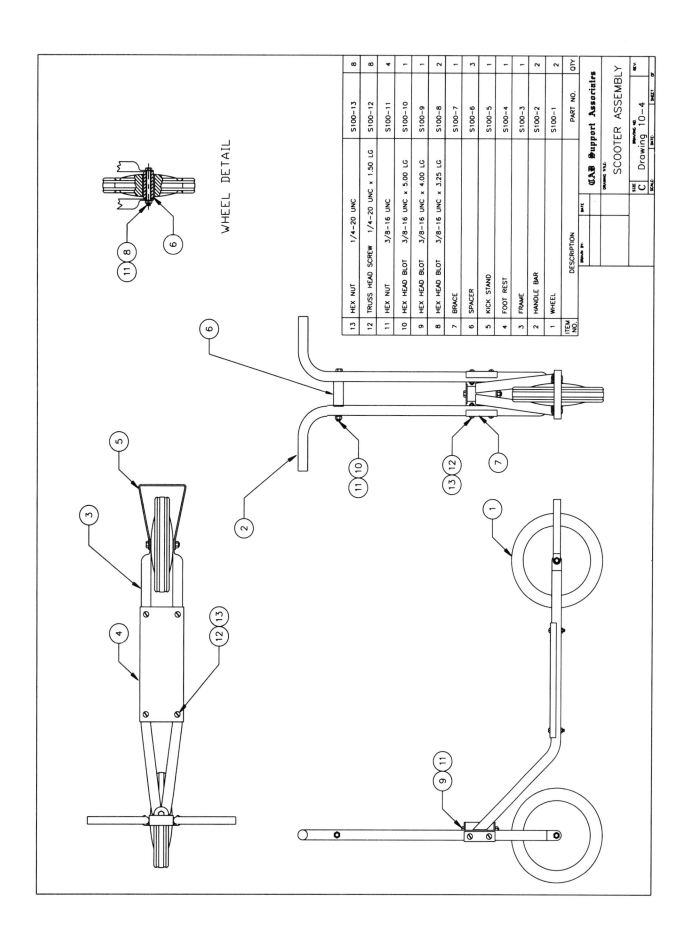

WHEEL DETAIL

| ITEM NO. | DESCRIPTION | PART NO. | QTY |
|---|---|---|---|
| 13 | HEX NUT          1/4-20 UNC | S100-13 | 8 |
| 12 | TRUSS HEAD SCREW   1/4-20 UNC x 1.50 LG | S100-12 | 8 |
| 11 | HEX NUT          3/8-16 UNC | S100-11 | 4 |
| 10 | HEX HEAD BLOT    3/8-16 UNC x 5.00 LG | S100-10 | 1 |
| 9 | HEX HEAD BLOT    3/8-16 UNC x 4.00 LG | S100-9 | 1 |
| 8 | HEX HEAD BLOT    3/8-16 UNC x 3.25 LG | S100-8 | 2 |
| 7 | BRACE | S100-7 | 1 |
| 6 | SPACER | S100-6 | 3 |
| 5 | KICK STAND | S100-5 | 1 |
| 4 | FOOT REST | S100-4 | 1 |
| 3 | FRAME | S100-3 | 1 |
| 2 | HANDLE BAR | S100-2 | 2 |
| 1 | WHEEL | S100-1 | 2 |

ℭ𝔄𝔅 𝔖upport 𝔄ssociates

DRAWING TITLE:
SCOOTER ASSEMBLY

DRAWN BY:                DATE:

SIZE
C

DRAWING NO.
Drawing 10-4

REV

DATE:

SCALE:                SHEET        OF

# chapter

## COMMANDS

| SETTINGS | DRAW | DISPLAY |
|----------|------|---------|
| SNAP (isometric) | ELLIPSE | VIEW |
| ISOPLANE | | ZOOM (dynamic) |

## OVERVIEW

Learning to use AutoCAD's isometric drawing features should be a pleasure at this point. There are very few new commands to learn, and anything you know about manual isometric drawing will translate easily to the computer. In fact, the isometric snap, grid, and cross hairs make isometric drawing considerably easier on a CAD system than on the drafting board. Once you know how to get into the isometric mode and to change from plane to plane, you will be on your way. You will find that many of the commands you have learned previously will continue to work for you.

## TASKS

1. Use the isometric SNAP mode.
2. Use Ctrl-E to toggle between isometric planes.
3. Use COPY in the isometric mode.
4. Draw angular lines in an isometric drawing.
5. Draw isometric circles (ELLIPSE).
6. Draw ellipses in orthographic views.
7. Save zooms with the VIEW command.
8. Use dynamic ZOOM.
9. Do Drawing 11-1 ("Mounting Bracket").
10. Do Drawing 11-2 ("Radio").
11. Do Drawing 11-3 ("Fixture Assembly").
12. Do Drawing 11-4 ("Flanged Coupling").
13. Do Drawing 11-5 ("Garage Framing").

### TASK 1: Isometric SNAP

*Procedure.*

1. Type or select SNAP.
2. Type "s" or select "style".
3. Type "i" or select "isometric".

*Discussion.* To begin drawing isometrically you need to switch to the isometric snap style. When you do, you will find the grid and cross hairs behaving in ways that may seem odd at first, but you will quickly get used to them.

> Begin a new drawing called "11-1" or "A:11-1".
> Type or select "snap".

    You will see a familiar prompt:

Snap spacing or ON/OFF/Aspect/Rotate/Style <0.25>:

> Type "s" or select "style".

    AutoCAD will prompt for a snap style:

Standard/Isometric <S>:

Standard refers to the orthographic grid and snap you have been using since Chapter 1.

> Type "i" or select "isometric".

    At this point your grid and cross hairs will be reoriented so that they resemble *Figure 11-1*.

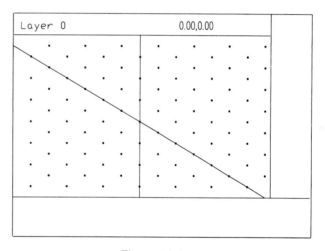

**Figure 11-1**

NOTE: If you have Release 9 or higher, you could also enter the isometric snap style by selecting "Isometric" in the "Drawing Aids" dialogue box.

    This is the isometric grid. Grid points are placed at 30, 90, and 150 degree angles from the horizontal. The cross hairs are initially turned to define the "left" isometric plane. The three "isoplanes" will be discussed in Task 2.

    To get a feeling for how this snap style works, enter the LINE command and draw some boxes, as shown in *Figure 11-2. Make sure that ORTHO is off and SNAP is on, or you will be unable to draw the lines shown.*

### TASK 2: Switching isometric planes

*Procedure.*

1. Press Ctrl-E once to switch to the "top" plane.

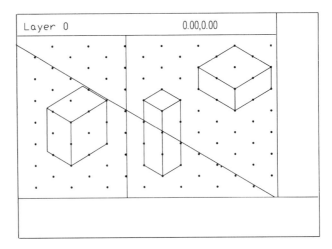

**Figure 11-2**

**2.** Press Ctrl-E again to switch to the "right" plane.

**3.** Press Ctrl-E again to return to the "left" plane.

*Discussion.* If you tried to draw the boxes in Task 1 with ortho on, you will have discovered that it is impossible. Without changing the orientation of the cross hairs you can draw in only one of the three isometric planes. We need to be able to switch planes so that we can leave ortho on for accuracy and speed. There are several ways to do this, but the simplest, quickest, and most convenient is to use Ctrl-E.

Before beginning, take a look at *Figure 11-3*. It shows the three planes of a standard isometric drawing. These planes are usually referred to as top, front, and right. However, AutoCAD's terminology is top, left, and right. We will stick with AutoCAD's labels in this book.

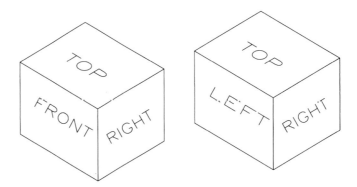

**Figure 11-3**

Now look at *Figure 11-4* and you will see how the isometric cross hairs are oriented to draw in each of the planes.

> Hold down Ctrl and press E to switch from "left" to "top".

    Learn to use Ctrl-E with one hand, probably your left, so that you can keep the other hand on the cursor.

> Press Ctrl-E again to switch from "top" to "right".

> Press Ctrl-E once more to switch back to "left" again.

    If you like, try switching planes using the "Drawing Aids" pull down menu or by entering the "ISOPLANE" command and typing "L", "T", or "R". The problem with the pull down method is that it requires four picks, and the menu

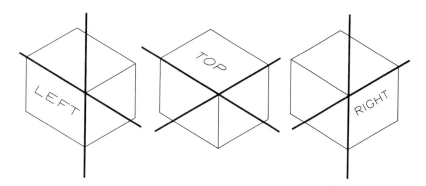

**Figure 11-4**

obstructs your view of the drawing. The problem with ISOPLANE is that you must type it or locate it on the screen menu, and it interrupts the command in progress.

> Now turn ortho on and draw a box outline like the one in *Figure 11-5*.

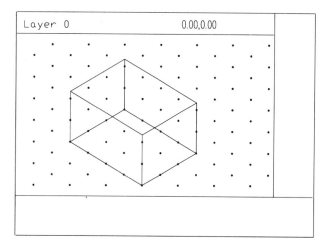

| Layer 0 | 0.00,0.00 |

**Figure 11-5**

Notice that you can switch planes using Ctrl-E without interrupting the LINE command. If you find that you are in the wrong plane to construct a line, simply switch planes. Since every plane allows movement in two of the three directions, you will always be able to move in the direction you want with one switch. However, you may not be able to hit the snap point you want. If you cannot, switch planes again.

### TASK 3: Using COPY and other edit commands

*Discussion.* Many commands work in the isometric planes just as they do in standard orthographic views. In this exercise we will construct an isometric view of a "Bracket," using the LINE, COPY, and ERASE commands. Later we will draw an angled corner and a hole in the bracket using DIST, ELLIPSE, COPY, and TRIM.

> To begin this exercise, clear your screen of boxes and check to see that ortho is on.
> With ortho on, draw the L-shaped surface shown in *Figure 11-6*.

Notice that this is drawn in the "left" isoplane and that it is 1.00 unit wide.

Next, we will copy this object 4.00 units back to the "right" to create the back surface of the bracket.

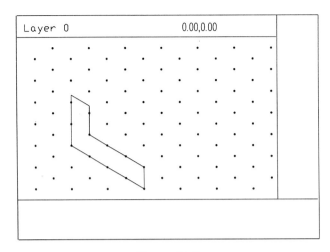

**Figure 11-6**

> Type or select "COPY".

> Use a window or crossing to select all the lines in the L.

> Pick a base point at the inside corner of the L.

At this point it is a good exercise to switch planes and move the object around in each plane. You will see that you can move in two directions in each plane and that in order to move the object back to the right as shown in *Figure 11-7*, you must be in either the top or the right plane.

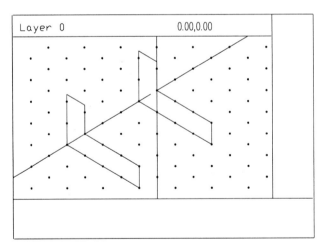

**Figure 11-7**

> Pick a second point of displacement four units back to the right, as shown.

> Enter the LINE command and draw the connecting lines in the right plane, as shown in *Figure 11-8*.

If you wish, you can draw only one of the lines and use the COPY command with the multiple option to create the others.

> Finally, ERASE the two unseen lines on the back surface to produce *Figure 11-9*.

### TASK 4: Drawing nonisometric lines

*Discussion.* The key to drawing angular lines in an isometric view is to understand that dimensions can only be measured along lines that are vertical or horizontal in

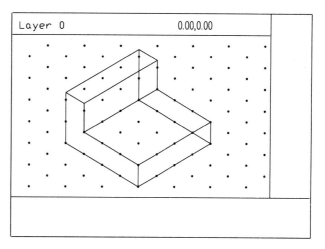

**Figure 11-8**

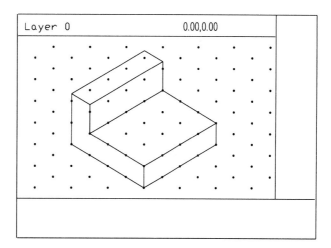

**Figure 11-9**

one of the three planes. This means that in order to draw angular lines you must first locate their end points. In some cases this will necessitate drawing an orthographic view first in order to measure dimensions that are not given to you.

You will encounter this problem in Drawing 11-1. For now, we will simply transfer dimensions from an orthographic front view to alter the bracket you have just drawn.

Take a look at *Figure 11-10*. This is a front view of our bracket after an alteration. The top corners have been cut back. While the .75 and 1.00 lengths can be measured directly in the top and right isoplanes of the bracket, the angular length cannot.

> Use the DIST command to mark points .75 across the top of the bracket and 1.00 down the side. Do this on both sides of the isometric top right of the bracket.
> Turn ortho off and draw lines between the marks.
> COPY the line from the front to the back of the bracket in the left isoplane.
> TRIM away the corners of the bracket.

Nothing to it, right? Your screen should now resemble *Figure 11-11*.

### TASK 5: Drawing isometric circles with ELLIPSE

*Procedure.*

1. Locate the center point.

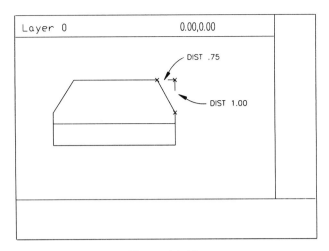

**Figure 11-10**

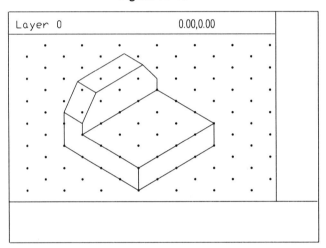

**Figure 11-11**

2.  Type or select ELLIPSE.
3.  Type "I" or select "isocircle".
4.  Pick the center point.
5.  Type or show the radius or diameter.

*Discussion.* The ELLIPSE command can be used to draw true ellipses in orthographic views or circles which appear as ellipses in isometric views. In this task we will use the latter capability to construct a hole in the bracket.

> To begin this task you should have the bracket shown in *Figure 11-11* on your display.

The first thing you will need in order to draw an "isocircle" is a center point. Often it will be necessary to locate this point carefully using DIST or temporary lines. Though you could probably find the circle in this drawing by eye, we will use DIST for practice.

Locate the center point <u>before</u> entering the ELLIPSE command.

> Enter the DIST command and use a midpoint osnap to mark the midpoints of the four sides of the surface where the hole is to be cut, as shown in *Figure 11-12*.

> Type or select ELLIPSE.

AutoCAD will prompt:

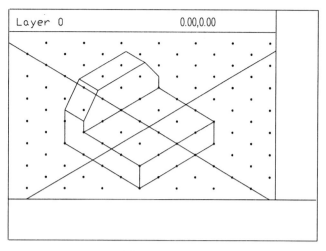

**Figure 11-12**

<Axis endpoint 1>/Center/Isocircle:

Notice that the default option is first on the list this time. This is not the usual order and can cause confusion. The option we want is "Isocircle". We will ignore the others for the time being.
> Type "I" or select "Isocircle".
AutoCAD prompts:

Center of circle:

If you had not previously located the center point you would have to exit the command now and start over.
> Switch into the top isoplane, if you are not already there, and use the midpoint guides to pick the center of the surface, as shown in *Figure 11-13*.

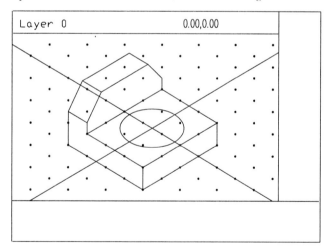

**Figure 11-13**

AutoCAD gives you an isocircle to drag, as in the CIRCLE command, and prompts:

<Circle radius>/Diameter:

A radius specification is the default here, as it is in the CIRCLE command.
> Type a value or pick a point so that your isocircle resembles the one in *Figure 11-13*.

Next, we use the COPY and TRIM commands to create the bottom of the hole.

> Enter the COPY command.
> Select the isocircle by pointing, or "last".
> Pick the center of the isocircle as the base point.

Actually any point could be used as the base point. Another good choice would be the top of the front corner. Then choosing the bottom of the front corner as a second point would give you the exact thickness of the bracket.

> Switch to either the top or left isoplanes if you have not already done so.
> Pick a second point 1.00 unit below the base point.

Your screen should now resemble *Figure 11-14*.

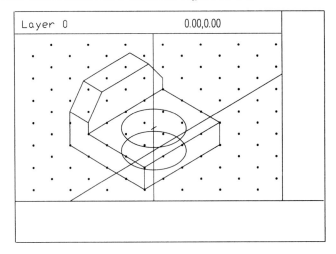

**Figure 11-14**

The last thing we must do is TRIM the hidden portion of the bottom of the hole.

> Type or select TRIM.
> Pick the first isocircle as a cutting edge.
> Press enter to end cutting edge selection.
> Select the hidden section of the lower isocircle.
> Press enter to exit TRIM.

The bracket is now complete and your screen should resemble *Figure 11-15*.

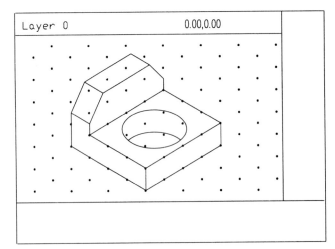

**Figure 11-15**

This completes the present discussion of isometric drawing. You will find more in the drawing suggestions at the end of this chapter.

We will now go on to explore the nonisometric use of the ELLIPSE command and then to show you two new tricks for controlling your display.

### TASK 6: Drawing ellipses in orthographic views

*Procedure.*

1. Type or select "ellipse".
2. Pick one end point of an axis.
3. Pick the second end point.
4. Show the length of the other axis.

*Discussion.* The ELLIPSE command is important for drawing isocircles, but also for drawing true ellipses in orthographic views.

An ellipse is determined by a center point and two mutually perpendicular axes. In AutoCAD, these specifications can be shown in two nearly identical ways, each requiring you to show three points (see *Figure 11-16*). In the default method you will show two end points of an axis and then show half the length of the other axis, from the midpoint of the first axis out. The other method allows you to pick the center point first, then the end point of one axis, followed by half the length of the other.

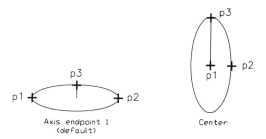

**Figure 11-16**

> In preparation for this exercise, return to the standard snap mode using the following procedure:

1. Type or select "snap".
2. Type "s" or select "style".
3. Type "s" or select "standard".

You will see that your grid is returned to the standard pattern and the cross hairs are horizontal and vertical again. Notice that this does not affect the isometric bracket you have just drawn.

We will briefly explore the ELLIPSE command and draw some standard ellipses.

> Type or select "ellipse".

AutoCAD prompts:

<Axis endpoint 1>/Center:

> Pick an axis endpoint as shown on the ellipse at the lower left of the display in *Figure 11-17*.

AutoCAD prompts for the other endpoint:

Axis endpoint 2:

> Pick a second endpoint as shown.

AutoCAD gives you an ellipse to drag and a rubber band so that you can show the length of the other axis. Only the length of the rubber band is significant; the angle is already determined to be perpendicular to the first axis.

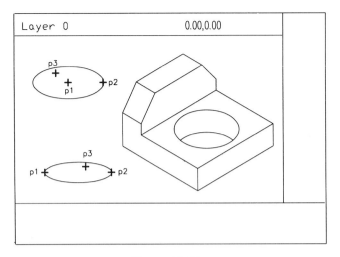

**Figure 11-17**

This is why the rubber band will only fall on the ellipse if it is perpendicular to the first axis.

> Pick a third point as shown.

    The first ellipse is now complete.

Now draw one showing the center point first.

> Reenter the ELLIPSE command.
> At the "<Axis endpoint 1>/Center:" prompt, type "c" or select "center".

    AutoCAD will give you a prompt for a center point:

Center of Ellipse:

> Pick a center point, as shown in *Figure 11-17*.

    Now you will have a rubber band stretching from the center to the end of an axis and the following prompt:

Axis endpoint:

> Pick an endpoint as shown.

    The prompt that follows allows you to show the second axis distance as before, or a rotation around the first axis:

<Other axis distance>/Rotation:

    We will not explore the "rotation" option here; see the *AutoCAD Reference Manual*, Section 4.6, for more information.

> Pick an axis distance as shown.

    Here again the rubber band is significant for distance only. The point you pick will fall on the ellipse only if the rubber band is stretched perpendicular to the first axis.

    Your screen should now resemble *Figure 11-17*.

### TASK 7: Saving and Restoring displays with the VIEW command

*Procedure.*

1. Type or select "VIEW".
2. Type "s" to save or "r" to restore a view.
3. Type a view name.

    *Discussion.* The word "view" in connection with the VIEW command has a special significance in AutoCAD. It refers to any set of display boundaries that have been named and "saved" using the VIEW command. Views that have been saved can be restored rapidly and by direct reference rather than by redefining the location and size of the area to be displayed. This feature can be handy when you know that you will be returning frequently to a certain area of a large drawing. It saves having to zoom out to look at the complete drawing and then zoom back in again on the area you want.

Imagine that we have to do some extensive detail work on the area around the hole in the bracket and also on the top corner. We can define each of these as a view and jump back and forth at will.

> To begin this exercise, you should have the bracket on your screen as shown in *Figure 11-17*.
> Type or select "view".

AutoCAD responds:

?/Delete/Restore/Save/Window:

Notice that there is no default in this prompt. You must specify an option. In this exercise we will use "window" and "restore". The "?" is well known by now. "Delete" erases previously defined views from the drawing database. "Restore" calls out a defined view. "Save" uses the current display window as the view definition. And "window" allows you to define a new view without actually displaying it.

> Type "w" or select "window".

AutoCAD prompts for a view name:

View name to save:

> Type "h" for "hole".

Views are designed for speed, so it is advisable to assign them one-letter or one-number names.

AutoCAD now prompts for corners as usual in a window selection process.
> Pick first and second corners to define a window around the hole in the bracket, as shown in *Figure 11-18*.

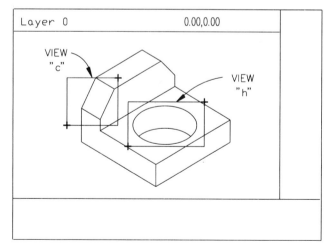

**Figure 11-18**

When this is done, the command sequence is complete. The window you selected is now defined as a view that can be "restored," or called up, using the view name "h".

But first, let's repeat the process once more to define a second view called "c" for corner.

> Repeat the VIEW command.

> Type "w" or select "window".
> Type "c" for the view name.
> Define a window, as shown in *Figure 11-18*.

You have now defined two views. To see the command in action we must "restore" them.

> Repeat the VIEW command.
> Type "r" or select "restore".
  AutoCAD prompts:

View name to restore:

> Type "h" to switch to the view of the hole.
  Your screen should resemble *Figure 11-19*.

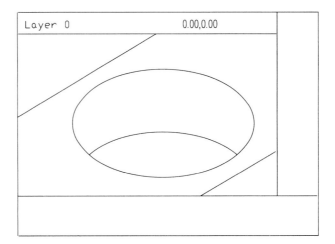

**Figure 11-19**

Now switch to the corner view.

> Repeat the VIEW command.
> Type "r" or select "restore".
> Type "c".
  Your screen should resemble *Figure 11-20*.

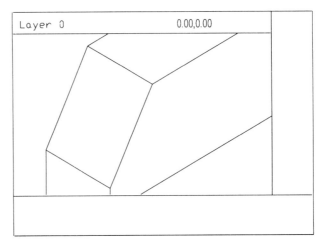

**Figure 11-20**

It would be worthwhile at this point to switch back and forth a few more times. How rapidly can you do it?

### TASK 8: Using Dynamic ZOOM

*Procedure.*

1. Type or select "ZOOM".
2. Type "d" or select "dynamic".
3. Show a pan.
4. Show a zoom.
5. Press enter or the enter button.

*Discussion.* Dynamic ZOOM allows you to choose your display area while looking at the complete drawing area, without having to wait for the drawing to regenerate. In large, slow to regenerate drawings this can be an indispensable timesaver.

> To begin this exercise, your screen should be showing one of the views defined in Task 5. Either will do.
> Enter the ZOOM command.
> Type "d" or select "dynamic".

AutoCAD will immediately switch to a screen that resembles *Figure 11-21*, without the text. In order to see the white view box shown, you will need to move the cursor.

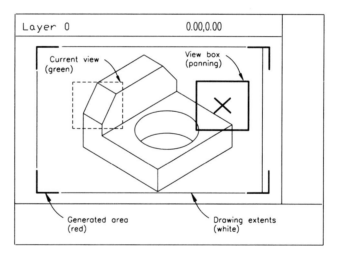

**Figure 11-21**

This screen display can be bewildering. Take a minute to look at the text in the figure to see what each of the boxes is used for. There are four boxes. The most significant is the white view box with the "x" inside. This is the only box you can move and the one you will use to define the area you want to display.

The dotted box (green if you have a color monitor) frames the current view, that is, the area you were looking at before entering dynamic zoom.

The large solid box (white on a black screen or black on a gray one) represents the drawing extents. Extents refer to the actual drawing area currently in use.

The four corner brackets (red on a color monitor) show the boundaries of the area that is currently generated. If you zoom within these boundaries, AutoCAD will merely REDRAW the screen. If you zoom out of bounds, a regeneration will be required, causing considerable delay in a large drawing. AutoCAD will warn you of this by displaying an "hourglass" as shown in *Figure 11-22*.

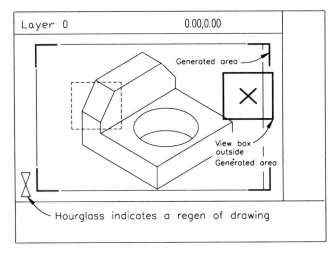

**Figure 11-22**

To use dynamic zoom, you must become accustomed to the two ways in which you can move the view box. When the "x" is showing, you can move the view box anywhere on the screen to frame a new area to display. Let's try it.

> Move the view box around the screen.

Notice that the box remains the same size and that if you go outside the brackets the "hourglass" appears at the lower left of the screen.

> Press the p<u>ick</u> button (not the enter button).

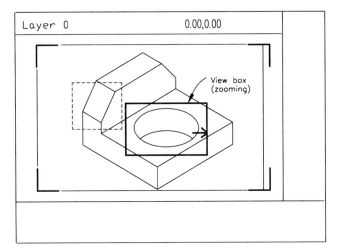

**Figure 11-23**

You should see an arrow at the right of the view box, instead of the x in the center, as shown in *Figure 11-23*. The pick button switches between "panning" and "zooming." In other words, with the x showing you can reposition the box, whereas with the arrow you can change its size.

> Move the cursor to the right and left.

Notice how the box stretches and shrinks in both the horizontal and vertical directions. Unlike the usual ZOOM window, this box is always proportioned to show the actual area that will be displayed.

> Press the pick button again.

This brings back the x so that you can move the box again.

> Press enter, the space bar, or the enter button on your cursor.

This completes the dynamic ZOOM procedure and displays the area you defined with the view box.

Now that you know how to control the size and position of the box, try using dynamic ZOOM to display the area around the hole in the bracket, similar to the area you defined previously as the "h" view. Then use dynamic ZOOM to display the front corner, as in the "c" view.

### TASKS 9, 10, 11, 12 and 13

The five drawings that follow will give you a range of experience in isometric drawing. The bracket drawing is an extension of the previous tasks, the radio drawing uses the "box method" and text on isometric angles, both the fixture and the flanged coupling drawings require you to work off an isometric center line, and the garage drawing is an architectural drawing that introduces a method for using the ARRAY command in the isometric planes.

## DRAWING 11-1: MOUNTING BRACKET

This drawing is a direct extension of the exercise in the chapter. It will give you practice in basic AutoCAD isometrics and in transferring dimensions from orthographic to isometric views.

### *DRAWING SUGGESTIONS*

> When the center point of an isocircle is not on snap, as in this drawing, you will need to create a specifiable point and snap onto it. Draw intersecting lines from the midpoints of the sides so that you can snap to that intersection, or use DIST and draw a point there. Then use a "node" snap.

> Often when you go to select a group of objects to copy, there will be many crossing lines that you do not want to include in the copy. This is an ideal time to use the "remove" option in object selection. First window the objects you want along with those nearby that are unavoidable, and then remove the unwanted objects one by one.

> Frequently you will get unexpected results when you go to TRIM an object in an isometric view. AutoCAD will divide an ellipse into a series of arcs, for example, and only trim a portion. If you do not get the results you want, use the BREAK command to control how the object is broken, and then erase what you do not want.

> There are no isometric options in the ARC command, so semicircles like those at the top and bottom of the slots must be constructed by first drawing isocircles (ellipses) and trimming or erasing unwanted portions.

> Use COPY frequently to avoid duplicating your work. Since it may take a considerable amount of editing to create holes and fillets, do not COPY until edits have been done on the original.

> The row of small arcs that show the curve in the middle of the bracket are multiple copies of the fillet at the corner.

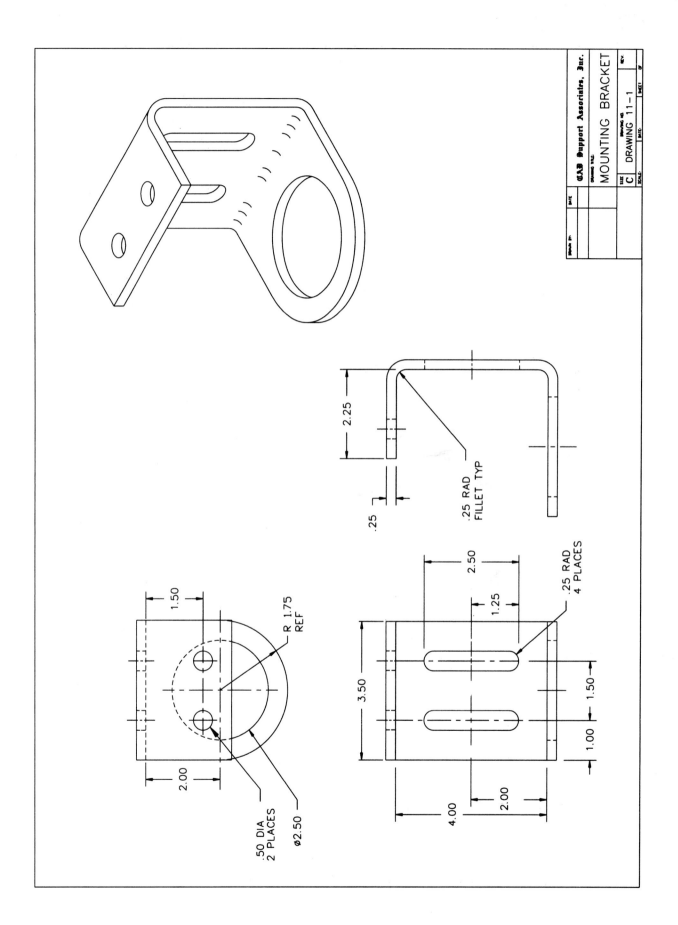

MOUNTING BRACKET

CAD Support Associates, Inc.

DRAWING 11-1

2.25

.25

.25 RAD
FILLET TYP

1.50

R 1.75
REF

2.00

.50 DIA
2 PLACES

Ø2.50

2.50

1.25

.25 RAD
4 PLACES

3.50

1.50

1.00

4.00

2.00

277

## DRAWING 11-2: RADIO

This drawing introduces text and will be greatly simplified by the use of the rectangular ARRAY command. Placing objects on different layers so they can be turned on and off during TRIM, BREAK, and ERASE procedures will make things considerably less messy.

### *DRAWING SUGGESTIONS*

> Use the "box method" to do this drawing. That is, begin with an isometric box according to the overall outside dimensions of the radio. Then go back and cut away the excess as you form the details of the drawing.

> The horizontal "grill" can be done with a rectangular array, since it runs straight on the vertical. Look carefully at the pattern to see where it repeats. Draw one set and then array it. Later you can go back and trim away the dial and speaker areas.

> Draw isocircles over the grill and break away the lines over the speaker. When you are ready to hatch the speaker, draw another trimmed isocircle to define the hatch boundary, create the hatch, and then erase the boundary.

> The knobs are isocircles with copies to show thickness. You can use tangent to tangent osnaps to draw the front to back connecting lines.

> The text is created on two different angles that line up with the left and right isoplanes. We leave it to you to discover the correct angles.

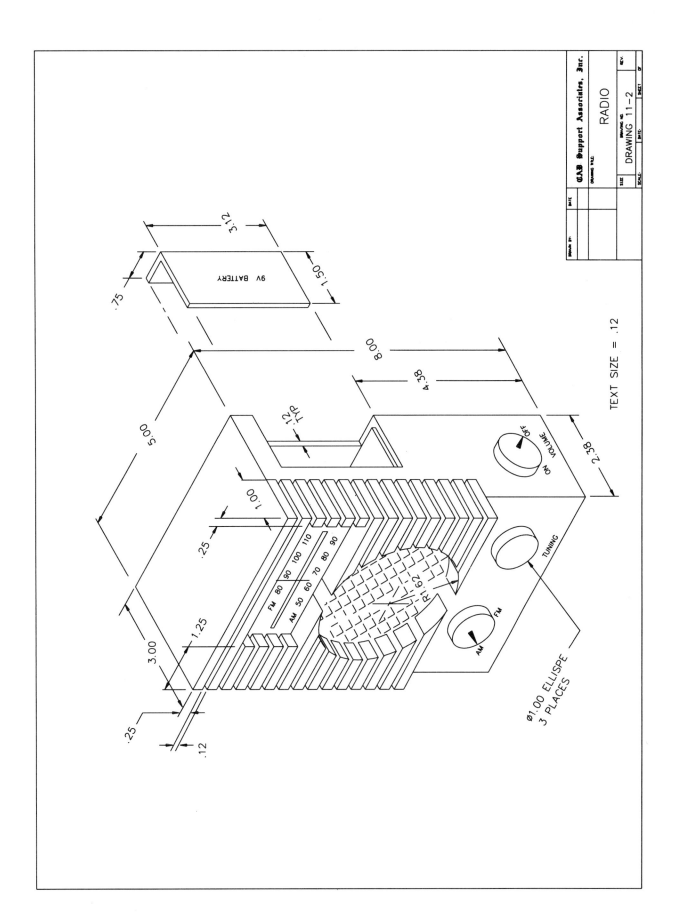

9V BATTERY

3.12

.75

1.50

8.00

5.00

4.38

2.38

.12 TYP

1.00

.25

FM 80 90 100 110

AM 50 60 70 80 90

R1.62

VOLUME
ON OFF

TUNING

AM FM

1.25

3.00

.25

.12

Ø1.00 ELLISPE
3 PLACES

TEXT SIZE = .12

RADIO

DRAWING 11-2

DRAWN BY:
DATE
SIZE
DRAWING NO.
REV
SCALE:
DATE:
SHEET
OF

279

## DRAWING 11-3: FIXTURE ASSEMBLY

This is a difficult drawing. It will take time and patience but will teach you a great deal about isometric drawing in AutoCAD.


### *DRAWING SUGGESTIONS*

> This drawing can be done either by drawing everything in place as you see it, or by drawing the parts and moving them into place along the common centerline that runs through the middle of all the items. If you use the former method, draw the centerline first and use it to locate the center points of isocircles and as base points for other measures.

> As you go, look for pieces of objects that can be copied to form other objects. Avoid duplicating efforts by editing before copying. In particular, where one object covers part of another, be sure to copy it before you trim or erase the covered sections.

> TRIM will not always work as you expect it to in isometric drawings. Use BREAK instead whenever necessary.

> To create the chamferred end of item 4, begin by drawing the 1.00 dia cylinder 3.00 long with no chamfer. Then copy the isocircle at the end forward .125. The smaller isocircle is .875 (7/8), since .0625 (1/16) is cut away from the 1.00 circle all around. Draw this smaller isocircle and TRIM away everything that is hidden. Then draw the slanted chamfer lines using LINE, not CHAMFER. Use the same method for item 5.

> In both the screw and the nut you will need to create hexes around isocircles. Use the dimensions from a standard bolt chart.

> Use three-point arcs to approximate the curves on the screw bolt and the nut. You are after a representation that looks correct. It is impractical and unnecessary to achieve exact measures on these objects in the isometric view.

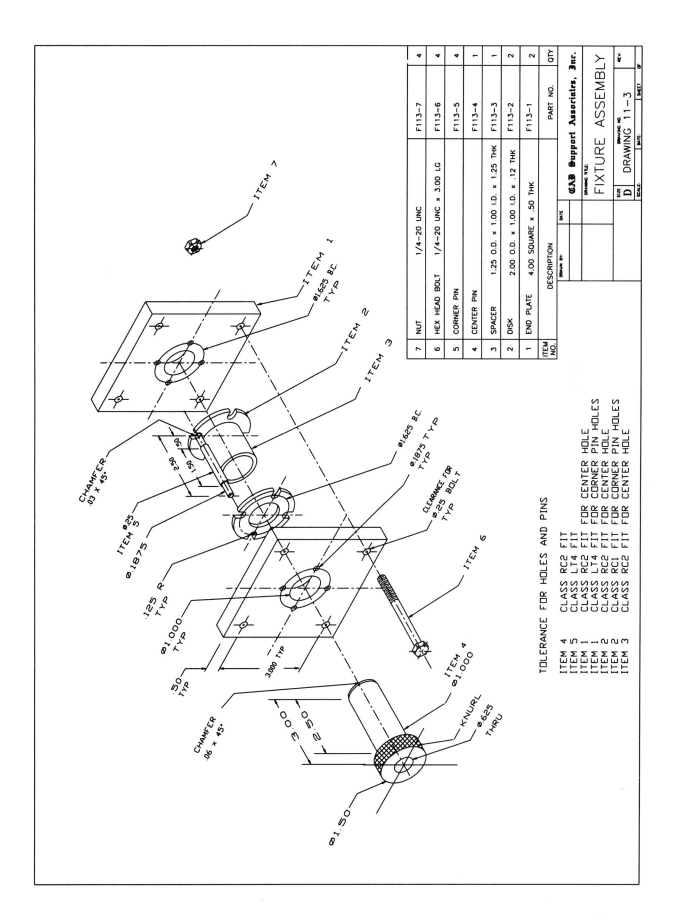

ITEM 7

ITEM 1

Ø1.625 B.C.
TYP

ITEM 2

ITEM 3

CHAMFER
.03 x 45°

ITEM 5

Ø.25
Ø.1875

.125 R
TYP

Ø1.000
TYP

.50
TYP

3.000 TYP

CHAMFER
.06 x 45°

.50
1.50

Ø1.625 B.C.
TYP

Ø.1875 TYP
TYP

CLEARANCE FOR
.25 BOLT
TYP

ITEM 6

ITEM 4
Ø1.000

KNURL

Ø.625
THRU

Ø1.50

3.00
2.50

TOLERANCE FOR HOLES AND PINS

ITEM 4   CLASS RC2 FIT FOR CENTER HOLE
ITEM 5   CLASS LT4 FIT
ITEM 1   CLASS RC2 FIT FOR CORNER PIN HOLES
ITEM 1   CLASS LT4 FIT FOR CENTER HOLE
ITEM 2   CLASS RC2 FIT FOR CORNER PIN HOLES
ITEM 2   CLASS RC1 FIT FOR CENTER HOLE
ITEM 3   CLASS RC2 FIT FOR CORNER PIN HOLES
ITEM 3   CLASS RC2 FIT FOR CENTER HOLE

| ITEM NO. | DESCRIPTION | | PART NO. | QTY |
|---|---|---|---|---|
| 7 | NUT | 1/4–20 UNC | F113–7 | 4 |
| 6 | HEX HEAD BOLT | 1/4–20 UNC x 3.00 LG | F113–6 | 4 |
| 5 | CORNER PIN | | F113–5 | 4 |
| 4 | CENTER PIN | | F113–4 | 1 |
| 3 | SPACER | 1.25 O.D. x 1.00 I.D. x 1.25 THK | F113–3 | 1 |
| 2 | DISK | 2.00 O.D. x 1.00 I.D. x .12 THK | F113–2 | 2 |
| 1 | END PLATE | 4.00 SQUARE x .50 THK | F113–1 | 2 |

CAD Support Associates, Inc.

DRAWN BY:    DATE:

DRAWING TITLE:

FIXTURE ASSEMBLY

SIZE: D    DRAWING NO. DRAWING 11–3    REV.

SCALE:    DATE:    SHEET:    OF:

281

## DRAWING 11-4: FLANGED COUPLING

The isometric view in this three-view drawing must be done working off the centerline. Notice the suggestion on using a polyline to simplify the hatching procedure.


### *DRAWING SUGGESTIONS*

> Draw the major centerline first. Then draw vertical center lines at every point where an isocircle will be drawn. Make sure to draw these lines extra long so that they can be used to trim the isocircles in half. By starting at the back of the object and working forward, you can take dimensions directly from the right side view.

> Draw the isocircles at each centerline and then trim them to represent semicircles.

> Use end point, intersection, and tangent to tangent osnaps to draw horizontal lines.

> Trim away all obstructed lines and parts of isocircles.

> Draw the four slanted lines in the middle as vertical lines first. Then, with ortho off, CHANGE their end points, moving them in .125.

> Remember, MIRROR will not work in the isometric view, although it could be used effectively in the right side view.

NOTE: When you are ready to HATCH, you can simplify the operation by drawing a pline of 0 width around the boundary of the hatched area. Then when AutoCAD asks for the area to be hatched, you need only to select the pline. This is usually considerably easier than breaking out the boundaries.

> If you have made a mistake in measuring along the major centerline, STRETCH can be used to correct it. Make sure that ortho is on and that you are in an isoplane that lets you move the way you want.

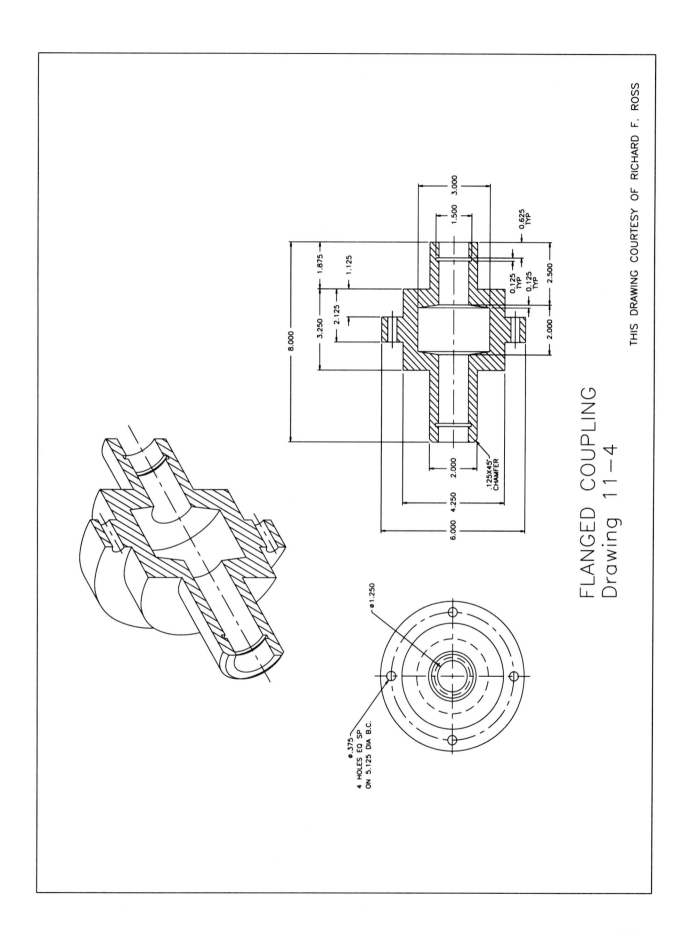

FLANGED COUPLING
Drawing 11-4

THIS DRAWING COURTESY OF RICHARD F. ROSS

283

# DRAWING 11-5: GARAGE FRAMING

This is a fairly complex drawing that will take lots of trimming and careful work. The use of SETVAR to change the "snapang" (snap angle) variable so that you can draw slanted arrays is a major timesaver and can be used frequently in isometric drawing.

## DRAWING SUGGESTIONS

> You will find yourself using COPY, ZOOM, and TRIM a great deal. OFFSET will also work well. This is a good place to use dynamic zoom.

> You may want to create some new layers of different colors if you have a color monitor. Keeping different parts of the construction—walls, rafters, joists—on different layers will allow you to have more control over them and add a lot of clarity to what you see on the screen. Turning layers on and off can considerably simplify trimming operations.

> You can cut down on repetition in this drawing by using arrays on various angles. For example, if the "snapang" variable is set to 150 degrees, the 22' wall in the left isoplane can be created as a rectangular array of studs with 1 row and 17 columns set 16 inches apart. To do so, follow this procedure:

1. Type or select "SETVAR".
2. Type "snapang".
3. Enter a new value so that rectangular arrays will be built on isometric angles (30 or 150).
4. Enter the ARRAY command and create the array. Use negative values where necessary.
5. Trim the opening for the window.

> An alternative to this array method is to set your snap to 16" temporarily and use multiple COPY to create the columns of studs, rafters, and joists.

> The cutaway in the roof that shows the joists and the back door is drawn using the standard nonisometric ELLIPSE command. Then the rafters are trimmed to the ellipse and the ellipse is erased. Do this procedure before you draw the joists and the back wall. Otherwise you will be trimming these as well.

> You can use chamfer to create the chamferred corners on the joists.

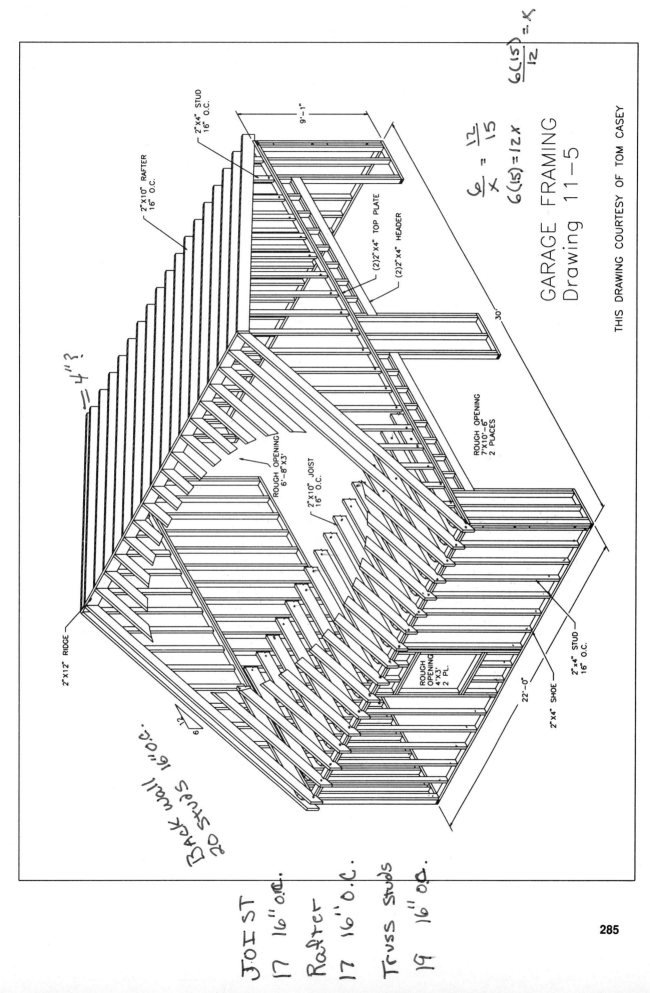

2"X4" STUD
16" O.C.

2"X10" RAFTER
16" O.C.

9'-1"

(2)2"X4" TOP PLATE

(2)2"X4" HEADER

30'

GARAGE FRAMING
Drawing 11–5

$\frac{6}{x} = \frac{12}{15}$

$6(15) = 12x$

$\frac{6(15)}{12} = x$

THIS DRAWING COURTESY OF TOM CASEY

ROUGH OPENING
7'X10'-6"
2 PLACES

ROUGH OPENING
6'-8"X3'

2"X10" JOIST
16" O.C.

= 4"?

2"X12" RIDGE

ROUGH
OPENING
4'X3'
2 PL.

2"X4" STUD
16" O.C.

2"X4" SHOE

22'-0'

$\frac{12}{6}$

BACK WALL
20 STUDS 16" O.C.

JOIST
17 16" o.c.

Rafter
17 16' O.C.

Truss Studs
19 16" oa.

# chapter

## COMMANDS

| UCS | DISPLAY | 3D | SETTINGS |
|-----|---------|-----|----------|
| UCS | VPOINT | RULESURF | UCSICON |
|  | PLAN |  |  |

## OVERVIEW

In this chapter we will focus on "User Coordinate Systems," a major feature which sets Release 10 apart from previous AutoCAD releases. Tasks 1–6 will take you through a complete 3D wire frame modeling exercise using four different coordinate systems that we will define.

You will find that working on isometric drawings has prepared you well for 3D drawing. There will be a similar process of switching from plane to plane, but there are two primary differences. First, you will not be restricted to three isometric planes: you can define a User Coordinate System aligned with any specifiable plane. Second, and most important, the model you draw will have true 3D characteristics. You will be able to view it, edit it, and plot it from any 3D point of view.

## TASKS

1. Create and view a 3D "box".
2. Define and save three "User Coordinate Systems."
3. Use standard edit commands in a UCS.
4. Construct a slot through an angled surface in 3D.
5. Create a 3D fillet using FILLET and RULESURF.
6. Create working drawings with orthographic and 3D views.
7. Create 3D view points.
8. Do drawing 12-1 ("Clamp").
9. Do drawing 12-2 ("Guide Block").
10. Do drawing 12-3 ("Slide Mount").
11. Do drawing 12-4 ("Stair Layout").

## TASK 1: Create and view a 3D box

*Discussion.*    In this task we will create a simple 3D box that we can edit in later tasks to form a more complex object. The 3D tasks you will be performing here are not possible with versions of AutoCAD before Release 10. If you want to see where we are going, look ahead to *Figures 12-25* and *12-26*.

The first time you see the Release 10 screen, you immediately notice the coordinate system icon in the lower left of the screen, as shown in *Figure 12-1*. In Chapter 1 we showed how to turn this icon off and on. For drawing in 3D, you will want it on. If your icon is not visible, follow this procedure to turn it on:

1.    Type or select "ucsicon".
2.    Type or select "on".

The UCS icon is part of the key 3D feature that separates Release 10 from earlier versions of AutoCAD—the ability to define "User Coordinate Systems". These are discussed at length in Task 2. For now, simply observe the icon as you go through the process of creating the box, and be aware that you are currently working in the same coordinate system that you have always used in AutoCAD. It is called the "World Coordinate System," to distinguish it from others you will create yourself.

Currently, the origin of the WCS is at the lower left of your screen. This is the point (0,0,0) when you are thinking 3D, or simply (0,0) when you are in 2D. X coordinates increase to the right horizontally across the screen, and Y coordinates increase vertically up the screen as usual. The Z axis, which we have ignored up until now, currently extends out of the screen towards you and perpendicular to the X and Y axes. This orientation of the three planes is also called a **plan view**. Soon we will switch to a "front, right, top" view.

Let's begin.

> Draw a 2.00 by 4.00 rectangle near the middle of your screen, as shown in *Figure 12-1*.

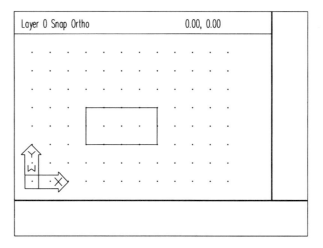

| Layer 0 Snap Ortho | 0.00, 0.00 |

**Figure 12-1**

## Changing views with VPOINT

In order to move immediately into a 3D mode of drawing and thinking, our first step will be to change our viewpoint on this object. There are two commands which will allow you to create 3D points of view, VPOINT and DVIEW. The VPOINT command, which we will use in this chapter, is simpler and best used for setting up basic views during the drawing and editing process. DVIEW, which is discussed at the end of Chapter 13, is more complex and best suited for creating carefully adjusted presentation images.

Although there are five different ways to use VPOINT, we find ourselves using the 3D Viewpoints icon menu more than any of the others. You may never need any of the other methods, and there is no need to get bogged down in understanding them, since the value of the VPOINT command is speed and simplicity. However, since a general understanding of the other methods may be desired, we have included an optional discussion of them at the end of the chapter. For our current purposes, the pull down system is all you will need.

The "Vpoint 3D..." icon menu is shown in *Figure 12-2*. We will use this menu to create a "front, right, top" view.

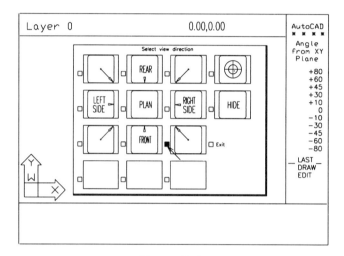

**Figure 12-2**

> Select "Display" from the pull down menu bar.

A pull down menu will appear.

> Select "Vpoint 3D..." from the pull down menu.

The 3D viewpoints icon menu will appear, as shown in *Figure 12-2*.

> Select the lower right-hand square for a "front, right" view.

In the command area you will see a complex prompt:

VPOINT Rotate/<View point> <0.00,0.00,1.00>: R
Enter angle in X-Y plane from X axis <270>: 315
Enter angle from X-Y plane <90>:

Looking at this prompt carefully, you can see what your icon menu selection has accomplished. On the first line, it has entered the VPOINT command and automatically typed an "R" to specify the "Rotate" option. This option establishes a 3D viewpoint by calling for two angles. The first angle, called for in line two of the prompt sequence, takes the object's current orientation as 0 degrees and rotates it a specified angle from the X axis. In our case, the angle of 315 from the X axis, as specified in the second line, gives us our "right, front" viewpoint. It ·may be easier to visualize the rotation if you keep in mind that +315 is the equivalent of –45. When the rotation is complete, the front and back edges of the square will be at –45 degree angles from the horizontal, as shown in *Figure 12-3*.

The second angle, which we will set at +30, "elevates" our viewpoint on the object by moving us up or down out of the X-Y plane. AutoCAD has given you

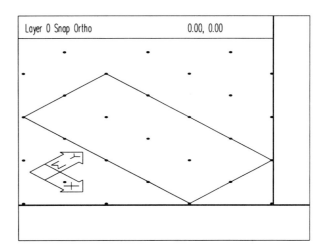

Layer 0 Snap Ortho                                    0.00, 0.00

**Figure 12-3**

cross hairs and a rubber band connected to the last point drawn and is waiting for the second angle specification. You can show the angle value, type a value, or select a value from the screen menu.

The angle you specify will be a Z dimension viewing position. Think of this as a viewing angle above or below the object, or, at ground level, even with it. We will choose to look down at an angle of 30 degrees.

> Type, show, or select (from the screen menu) an angle of +30. The screen menu selection is our preferred method for entering this value.

Your screen should now be redrawn as shown in *Figure 12-3*. Notice how the grid and the coordinate system icon have altered to show our current orientation. These visual aids are extremely helpful in viewing 3D objects on the flat screen and imagining them as if they were positioned in space.

NOTE: At this point you can easily readjust the second angle, the height of your viewing angle, by using the values on the screen menu. First select any of the three lines at the top of the screen menu—"Angle", "From XY", or "Plane"—and then select an angle. For example, to retain the front right rotation but look up at our rectangle from an angle of –60, you could select "Angle" and then "–60". This will create a "worm's eye view" from below the object.

By using the pull down icon menu to set rotation in the X-Y plane and the screen menu to adjust viewing height, you can create a large variety of points of view. You may wish to experiment with these now. In the process, pay attention to the UCS icon. Variations of the icon you may encounter here and later on are shown in *Figure 12-4*. When you are done experimenting, be sure to return to our previous "front, right, top" view (*Figure 12-3*). We will use this view frequently throughout this and the next two chapters.

Whenever you change viewpoints, AutoCAD displays the drawing extents, so that the object fills the screen and is as large as possible. Often you will need to zoom out a bit to get some space to work in. This is easily done using the "Scale(X)" option of the ZOOM command.

> Type or select "zoom".

Do not use the pull down menu, as this system does not allow for the "Scale(X)" option.

AutoCAD prompts:

All/Center/Dynamic/Extents/Left/Previous/Window/<Scale (X)>:

| ICON | DESCRIPTION |
|------|-------------|
| 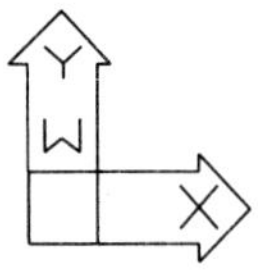 | WCS  (WORLD COORDINATE SYSTEM) "W" appears on "Y" arm |
| 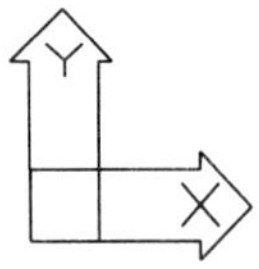 | UCS  (USER COORDINATE SYSTEM) NO "W" appears on "Y" arm |
| 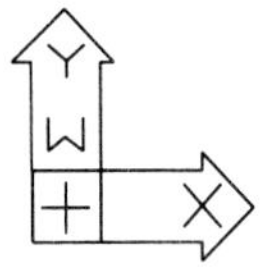 | + appears in box and "W" appears on "Y" arm if the current UCS is the same as the WCS |
| 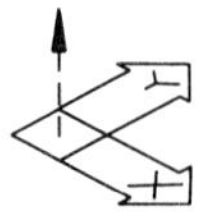 | Box appears at the base of ICON if viewing UCS from above its X–Y plane |
| 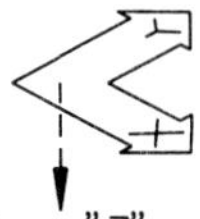 | Box is missing if viewing UCS from below its X–Y plane |
|  | Broken pencil ICON appears if viewing direction is "EDGE ON" or near "EDGE ON" X–Y plane of current UCS |
| 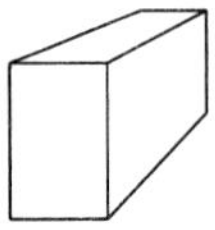 | Isometric box ICON appears if DVIEW perspective is on          (Chapter 13) |

**Figure 12-4**

> In response to the ZOOM prompt, type ".5x".

Don't forget the "x". This tells AutoCAD to adjust and redraw the display so that objects appear half as large as before.

Next, we will create a copy of the rectangle placed 1.25 above it. This brings up a basic 3D problem: AutoCAD interprets all point selections as being in the X-Y plane, so how does one indicate a point or a displacement in the Z direction? There are three possibilities: typed 3D coordinates, X/Y/Z point filters, and object snaps. Object snap requires an object already drawn above or below the X-Y plane, so it will be of no use right now. We will use typed coordinates first, then discuss how point filters could be used as an alternative. Later we will be using object snap as well.

### Entering 3D coordinates

3D coordinates can be entered from the keyboard in the same manner as 2D coordinates. Often this is an impractical way to enter individual points in a drawing. However, within COPY or MOVE it provides a simple method for specifying a displacement in the Z direction perpendicular to the X-Y plane.

> Type or select "COPY".
AutoCAD will prompt for object selection.
> Type "w" to indicate a window selection.
> Window the complete rectangle.
> Press enter, the space bar, or the enter equivalent button on your pointing device to end object selection.
AutoCAD now prompts for the base point of a vector or a displacement value:

<Base point or displacement>/Multiple:

Typically, you would respond to this prompt and the next by showing the two end points of a vector. However, we cannot show a displacement in the Z direction this way. This is important for understanding AutoCAD. coordinate systems. Unless an object snap is used, all points picked on the screen with the pointing device will be interpreted as being in the X-Y plane of the current UCS. Without an entity outside the X-Y plane to use in an object snap, there is no way to point to a displacement in the Z direction.
> For the base point, type "0,0".
We could type "0,0,0", but AutoCAD will always assume that Z is 0 unless we specify otherwise.
AutoCAD now prompts:

Second point of displacement:

> Type "0,0,1.25".
AutoCAD will create a copy of the rectangle 1.25 directly above the original. Your screen should now resemble *Figure 12-5*.

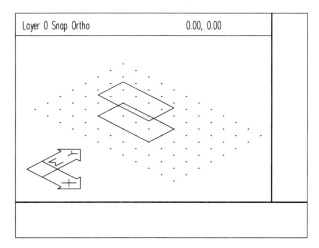

**Figure 12-5**

### X/Y/Z Point Filters

Point filters can be very useful in 3D, although they may seem odd until you get a feel for when to use them. Notice that in the two points we just entered, (0,0,0) and (0,0,1.25), the only thing that changes is the Z value. Notice also that we could specify the same displacement from any point in the X-Y plane, for example, (3,6,0) to

(3,6,1.25). In fact, we don't even need to know what X and Y are as long as we know that they don't change.

That is how an ".XY" point filter would work. We borrow, or "filter," the X and Y values from a point, without pausing to find out what the values actually are, and then specify a new Z value. Other types of filters are possible, of course, such as ".Z" or ".YZ".

You can use a point filter, like an object snap, any time AutoCAD asks for a point. After a point filter is specified, AutoCAD will always prompt with an "of". In our case you are being asked, "you want the X and Y values of what point?" In response, you pick a point, then AutoCAD will ask you to fill in Z. Notice that point filters can be "chained" so that, for example, you can filter the X value from one point and combine it with the filtered Y value from another point.

To use an .XY filter in the COPY command instead of typing coordinates, for example, you would follow this procedure:

1. Enter the COPY command.
2. Select the rectangle.
3. For the displacement base point, pick any point on the screen.
4. At the prompt for a second point, type or select ".xy" (filters are on a submenu of the "Tools" pull down).
5. At the "of" prompt, type "@" or pick the same point again.
6. At the "(need Z):" prompt, type "1.25". The result would be *Figure 12-5*, as before.

## Using Object Snap

We now have two rectangles floating in space. Our next job is to connect the corners to form a wire frame box. This is easily done using "ENDpoint" object snaps. This is a clear example of how object snaps allow us to construct entities not in the X-Y plane of the current coordinate system.

> Type or select OSNAP to turn on a running osnap mode.
AutoCAD prompts:

Object snap modes:

> Type "end" or select "ENDpoint".
The running ENDpoint object snap is now on and will affect all point selection. You will find that object snaps are very useful in 3D drawing and that ENDpoint mode will be used frequently.
Now we need to draw some lines.
> Enter the line command and connect the upper and lower corners of the two rectangles, as shown in *Figure 12-6*. (We have removed the grid for clarity, but you will probably want to leave yours on.)

Before going on, pause a moment to be aware of what you have drawn. Particularly if you have drawn 3D objects with other versions of AutoCAD, using elevation and thickness, you should notice the difference. The box on your screen is a true wire frame model. It is made up of nothing but lines in space. There are no surfaces or extruded entities.

In the next task you will take a much greater step beyond older versions of Auto-CAD, as we begin to define our own coordinate systems that will allow us to perform drawing and editing functions in any plane we choose.

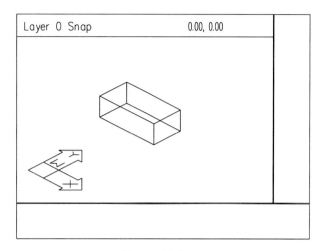

**Figure 12-6**

### TASK 2: Defining and saving User Coordinate Systems

*Procedure.*

1. Type "UCS".
2. Choose an option.
3. Specify a coordinate system.
4. Repeat the UCS command to name and save the new coordinate system.

*Discussion.* In this task you will begin to develop new vocabulary and techniques for working with objects in 3D space. The primary tool will be the UCS command. You will also learn to use the UCSICON command to control the placement of the coordinate system icon.

Until now we have had only one coordinate system to work with. All coordinates and displacements have been defined relative to a single point of origin. In Task 1 we changed our point of view, but the UCS icon changed along with it, so that the orientations of the X, Y, and Z axes relative to the object were retained. With Release 10 you can define new coordinate systems at any point and any angle in space. When you do, you can use the coordinate system icon and the grid to help you visualize the planes you are working in, and all commands and drawing aids will function relative to the new system.

The coordinate system we are currently using is unique. It is called the "World Coordinate System" and is the one we always begin with. The "w" at the base of the coordinate system icon indicates that we are currently working in the world system. A "User Coordinate System" is nothing more than a new point of origin and a new orientation for the X, Y, and Z axes.

We will begin by defining a User Coordinate System in the plane of the top of the box, as shown in *Figure 12-7*.

> Leave the ENDpoint osnap mode on for this exercise.
> Type or select "ucs".
The UCS command gives you the following prompt:

Origin/ZAxis/3point/Entity/View/X/Y/Z/Prev/Restore/Save/Del/?/<World>:

In this chapter we will explore all options except "ZAxis" and "Entity". For further information, see the *AutoCAD Reference Manual*, Section 8.6, and the UCS icon chart, *Figure 12-4*.

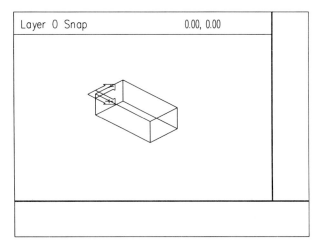

**Figure 12-7**

First we will use "Origin" to create a UCS which is parallel to the WCS.
> Type "O" to specify the origin option.

AutoCAD will prompt for a new origin:

Origin point <0,0,0>:

This option does not change the orientation of the three axes. It simply shifts their intersection to a different point in space. We will use this simple procedure to define a UCS in the plane of the top of the box.
> Use the ENDpoint osnap to select the top front corner of the box, as shown by the location of the icon in *Figure 12-7*.

You will notice that the "w" is gone from the icon. However, the icon has not moved. It is still at the lower left of the screen. It is visually helpful to place it at the origin of the new UCS, as in the figure. In order to do this we need the UCSICON command.
> Type or select "ucsicon".

AutoCAD prompts:

ON/OFF/All/Noorigin/ORigin <ON>:

The first two options allow you to turn the icon on and off. The "All" option affects icons used in multiple view ports, which we will discuss in Chapter 13. "Noorigin" and "ORigin" allow you to specify whether you want to keep the icon in the lower left corner of the screen or place it at the origin of the current UCS.
> Type "or" for the "ORigin" option.

The icon will move to the origin of the new current UCS, as in *Figure 12-7*. With UCSICON set to "ORigin", the icon will shift to the new origin whenever we define a new UCS. The only exception would be if the origin were not on the screen or too close to an edge for the icon to fit. In these cases the icon would be displayed in the lower left corner again.

The "top" UCS we have just defined will make it easy to draw and edit entities that are in the plane of the top of the box and also to perform editing in planes that are parallel to it, such as the bottom. In the next task we will begin drawing and editing using different coordinate systems, and you will see how this works. For now, we will spend a little more time on the UCS command itself. We will define two more User Coordinate Systems, but first, let's save this one so that we can recall it quickly when we need it later on.

> Type or select "ucs".

This time we will use the "Save" option.

> Type "s" or select "Save".

AutoCAD will ask you to name the current UCS so that it can be called out later:

?/Name of UCS:

We will name our UCS "top". It will be the UCS we use to draw and edit in the top plane. This UCS will also make it easy for us to create an orthographic top view later on.

> Type "top".

The top UCS is now saved and can be recalled using the "Restore" option.

NOTE: Strictly speaking, it is not necessary to save every UCS. However, it usually saves time, since it is unlikely that you will have all your work done in any given plane or UCS the first time around. More likely, you will want to move back and forth between major planes of the object as you draw. Be aware also that you can return to the last defined UCS with the "Previous" option.

Next we will define a "front" UCS using the "3point" option of the UCS command.

> Press enter or the space bar to repeat the UCS command.

> Type "3" to specify the "3point" option.

AutoCAD prompts:

Origin point <0,0,0>:

In this option you will show AutoCAD a new origin point, as before, and then a new orientation for the axes as well. Notice that the default origin is the current one. If we retained this origin, we could define a UCS with the same origin and a different axis orientation.

Instead, we will define a new origin at the lower left corner of the front of the box, as shown in *Figure 12-8*.

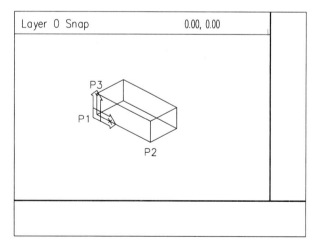

**Figure 12-8**

> With the ENDpoint osnap on, pick point 1, as shown in the figure.

AutoCAD now prompts you to indicate the orientation of the X axis:

Point on positive portion of the X axis <1.00,0.00,–1.25>:

> Pick the right front corner of the box, point 2, as shown.

The osnap ensures that the new X axis will now align with the front of the object. AutoCAD prompts for the Y axis orientation:

Point on positive-Y portion of the UCS X-Y plane <0.00,1.00,–1.25>:

By definition, the Y axis will be perpendicular to the X axis, therefore Auto-CAD needs only a point that shows the plane of the Y axis and its positive direction. Because of this, any point on the positive half of the Y plane will specify the Y axis correctly. We have chosen a point that is on the Y axis itself.

> Pick point 3, as shown.

When this sequence is complete, you will notice that the coordinate system icon has rotated along with the grid and moved to the new origin as well. This UCS will be convenient for drawing and editing in the front plane of the box, or editing in any plane parallel to the front, such as the back.

Now save the "front" UCS.

> Press enter to repeat the UCS command.

> Type "s" to save.

> Type "front" to name the UCS.

Finally, we will use the "Origin" and "Y" axis rotation options together to create a right side UCS.

> Repeat the UCS command.

> Type "o" or select "Origin".

> Pick the lower front corner of the box for the origin, as shown in *Figure 12-9*.

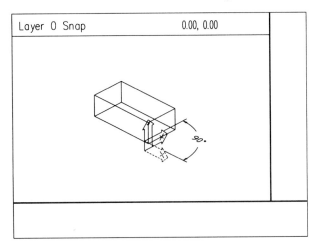

**Figure 12-9**

> Repeat the UCS command.

We will rotate the UCS icon around its Y axis to align it with the right side of the box.

In using any of the rotation options ("X", "Y", and "Z"), the first thing you have to decide is which axis is the axis of rotation. If you look at the current position of the icon and think about how it will look when it aligns with the right side of the box, you will see that the Y axis retains its position and orientation while the X axis turns through 90 degrees (see *Figure 12-9*). In other words, since X rotates around Y, Y is the axis of rotation.

> Type "Y".

Now AutoCAD prompts for a rotation:

Rotation angle around Y axis <0.0>:

It takes some practice to differentiate positive and negative rotation in 3D. If you like, you can use AutoCAD's "right hand" rule, which can be stated as follows: If you are hitchhiking (pointing your thumb) in a positive direction along the axis of rotation, your fingers will curl in the direction of positive rotation for the other axis. In our case, align your right thumb with the positive Y axis, and you will see that your fingers curl in the direction we want the X axis to rotate. Therefore, the rotation of X around Y is positive.

> Type "90".

You should now have the UCS icon aligned with the right side of the box, as shown in *Figure 12-9*. Save this UCS before going on to Task 3.

> Repeat the UCS command.
> Type "s".
> Type "right".

### TASK 3: Using draw and edit commands in a UCS

*Discussion.*    Now the fun begins. Using our three new coordinate systems and one more we will define later, we will give the box a more interesting "slotted wedge" shape. In this task we will cut away a slanted surface on the right side of the box. Since the planes we will be working in are parallel to the front of the box, we will begin by making the "front" UCS current. All our work in this task will be in this UCS.

> Repeat the UCS command.
> Type "r" to specify the "Restore" option.
   AutoCAD will ask for the UCS to restore:

?/Name of UCS to restore:

> Type "front".
   The UCS icon should return to the front plane.

NOTE: In this case we could also have used the "Previous" option.

Before going on, we need to turn off the running ENDpoint osnap.

> Type or select "osnap".
> Press enter at the prompt for object snap modes.
   There will now be no running object snap modes in effect.

Look at *Figure 12-10*. We will draw a line down the middle of the front (line 1) and use it to trim another line coming in at an angle from the right (line 2).

> Type or select "line".
> At the "From point:" prompt, type "mid" or select "MIDpoint".
> Point to the top front edge of the box.
   AutoCAD will snap to the midpoint of the line.
> Make sure that ortho is on (F8).

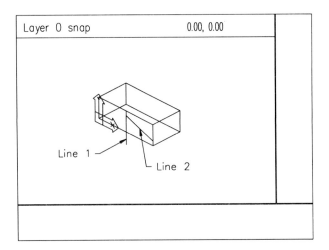

Layer 0 snap                                    0.00, 0.00

Line 1

Line 2

**Figure 12-10**

Notice how ortho works as usual, but relative to the current UCS.
> Pick a second point anywhere below the box.
This line will be trimmed later, so the exact length does not matter.

Next we will draw line 2 on an angle across the front. This line will become one edge of a slanted surface. Your snap setting will need to be at .25 or smaller, and ortho will need to be off. The grid, snap, and coordinate display all work relative to the current UCS, so it is a simple matter to draw in this plane.

> Check your snap setting and change it if necessary.
> Turn ortho off (F8).
> Repeat the LINE command.
> With snap on (F9), pick a point .25 down from the top edge of the box on line 1, as shown in *Figure 12-10*.
> Pick a second point .25 up along the right front edge of the box.

Now trim line 1.

> Type or select "trim".
You will see the following message in the command area:

View is not plan to UCS. Command results may not be obvious.

In the language of Release 10 3D, a view is plan to the current UCS if the X-Y plane is in the plane of the display and its axes are parallel to the sides of the screen. This is the usual 2D view in which the Y axis aligns with the left side of the display and the X axis aligns with the bottom of the display. In previous chapters we always worked in plan view. In this chapter we have not been in plan view since the beginning of Task 1. We will return to plan views at the end when we create orthographic projections of our 3D wire frame model.

With this message, AutoCAD is warning us that boundaries, edges, and intersections may not be obvious as we look at a 3D view of an object. For example, lines which appear to cross may be in different planes.

Having read the warning, we continue.
> Select line 2 as a cutting edge.
> Press enter to end cutting edge selection.
> Point to the lower end of line 1.
Your screen should resemble *Figure 12-11*.

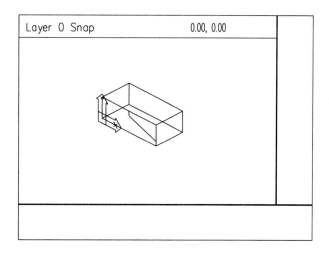

**Figure 12-11**

Now we will copy our two lines to the back of the box. Since we will be moving out of the front plane, we will require the use of ENDpoint object snaps to specify the displacement vector. We will also be using the ENDpoint osnap in the next sequence, so let's turn on the running mode again.

> Type or select "osnap".
> Type "end" or select "ENDpoint".
> Type or select "copy".

If you are using the AutoCAD pull down menu, be sure to select the two lines with a crossing box, since you will be allowed only one selection.

> Pick lines 1 and 2.
> If not using the pull down, press enter to end object selection.
> Use the ENDpoint osnap to pick the lower front corner of the box, point 1 as shown in *Figure 12-12*.

Actually, any of the front corners would do. We need to show a displacement from the front to the back of the box and this could be shown along any of the four edges that run from front to back.

> At the prompt for a second point of displacement, use the ENDpoint osnap to pick the lower back corner of the box, point 2 as shown.

Your screen should now resemble *Figure 12-12*.

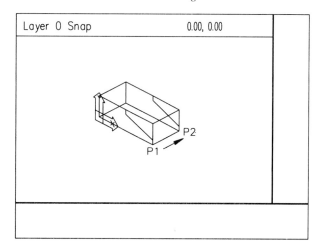

**Figure 12-12**

What remains is to connect the front and back of the surfaces we have just outlined and then trim away the top of the box. We will continue to work in the front UCS
and to use ENDpoint osnaps.

We will use a multiple COPY to copy one of the front-to-back edges in three
places.

> Enter the COPY command.

> Temporarily turn off the end point osnap by typing "non" or selecting "None"
from the "Tools" pull down.

     This is a single point override which will leave the running ENDpoint osnap
in effect. It is convenient when you need to make a selection without an object
snap but want to leave the running osnap on for points that follow.

> Pick any of the front to back edges for copying.

> Type "m" or select "multiple".

> Pick the front end point of the selected edge to serve as a base point of dis-
placement.

> Pick the top end point of line 1 (point 1 in *Figure 12-13*).

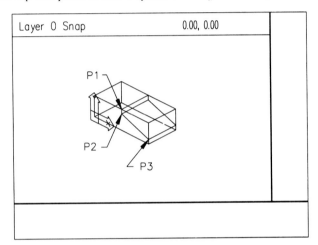

**Figure 12-13**

> Pick the lower end point of line 1 (point 2) as another second point.

> Pick the right end point of line 2 (point 3) as another second point.

> Cancel the COPY command.

Finally, we need to do some trimming.

> Type or select "Osnap" and turn off the running "ENDpoint" mode by pressing
enter or selecting "None" at the prompt.

> Type or select "trim".

> For cutting edges, select lines 1 and 2 and their copies in the back plane (lines 3
and 4 in *Figure 12-14*).

     A quick alternative to selecting these four separate lines is to use a crossing
box to select the whole area. As long as your selection includes the four lines, it
will be effective.

NOTE: Trimming in 3D can be tricky. Remember where you are. Edges which do
not run parallel to the current UCS may not be recognized at all.

> Press enter to end cutting edge selection.

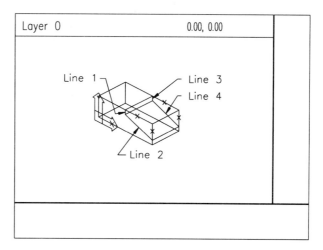

**Figure 12-14**

> One by one, pick the top front and top back edges to the right of the cut, and the right front and right back edges above the cut, as shown by the Xs in *Figure 12-14*.
> Press enter to exit the TRIM command.
> Enter the ERASE command and erase the top edge that is left hanging in space.

Your screen should now resemble *Figure 12-15*.

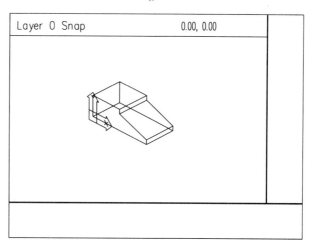

**Figure 12-15**

## TASK 4: Working on an angled surface

*Discussion.* In this task we will take our 3D drawing a step further by constructing a slot through the new slanted surface and the bottom of the object. This will require the creation of a new UCS. In completing this task, you will also use the OFFSET command and continue to develop a feel for working with multiple coordinate systems.

> Type or select "ucs".
> Type "3" for the "3point" option.
> Using an ENDpoint osnap, pick point 1, as shown in *Figure 12-16*.
> Using an ENDpoint osnap, pick point 2, as shown.
> Using an ENDpoint osnap, pick point 3, as shown.

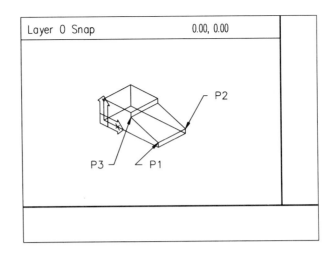

**Figure 12-16**

> Press enter to repeat the UCS command.
> Type "s" for the "Save" option.
> Type "angle" for the name of the UCS.

Now we are ready to work in the plane of the angled surface.

NOTE: From here on, we have moved our UCS icon back to the lower left of the screen for the sake of clarity in our illustrations. You may leave it at its origin on your screen, if you like, or move it by entering the UCSICON command again and typing "no" or selecting "NOorigin".

> If ortho is off, turn it on (F8).
> If you have used a running ENDpoint osnap, turn it off.
     Create line 1 across the angled surface, as shown in *Figure 12-17*, by offsetting the right front edge of the wedge.

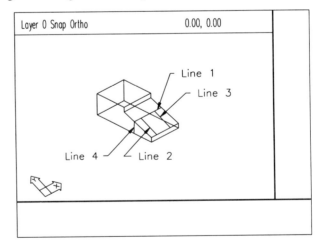

**Figure 12-17**

> Type or select OFFSET.
> Type or show a distance of 1.50.
> Pick the right front edge.
> Point anywhere above and to the left of the edge.

> Draw lines 2 and 3 perpendicular to the first, as shown. They will be over .50 and 1.50 from the current Y axis.

Watch the coordinate display and notice how the coordinates work in this UCS as in any other.

> Turn ortho off.

> Using snap for the top point and a "PERpendicular" osnap (single point override) for the lower point, drop line 4 down to the bottom front edge.

Notice again how osnap modes work for you, especially to locate points that would be difficult to define in the current UCS.

> Create lines 5 and 6, as shown in *Figure 12-18*, by making two copies of line 4, extending down from the ends of lines 2 and 3, as shown.

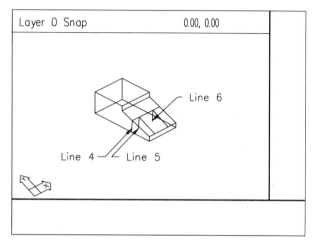

Layer 0 Snap                    0.00, 0.00

Line 6

Line 4 — Line 5

**Figure 12-18**

> ERASE line 4 from the front plane.

> Using ENDpoint osnaps, connect lines 5 and 6 to each other in the plane of the bottom of the object.

> Using ENDpoint and PERpendicular osnaps, connect lines 5 and 6 to the bottom edge of the right side.

> Using ENDpoint osnaps, draw two short vertical lines on the right side, connecting to lines 2 and 3.

> TRIM line 1 and the two lines on the right side across the opening of the slot.

When you are done, your screen should resemble *Figure 12-19*.

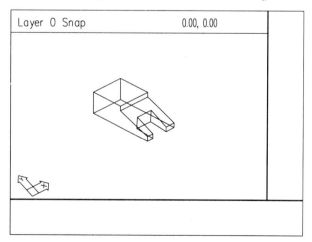

Layer 0 Snap                    0.00, 0.00

**Figure 12-19**

### TASK 5: Using RULESURF to create 3D fillets

*Procedure.*

1. Create fillets in two planes.
2. Type or select RULESURF.
3. Pick a fillet.
4. Pick the corresponding side of the fillet in the other plane.

*Discussion.*    We have two remaining tasks in this chapter. First we will use a new command to create a 3D fillet, and then we will BLOCK our drawing to create orthographic projections.

First, we must fillet the top and bottom corners of the slot drawn in Task 4. This will be done in the usual manner, except that we will need to pay attention to our coordinate systems. We will use the "angle" UCS to fillet the top of the slot and the "top" UCS to fillet the bottom. The "top" UCS can be used this way because the top of the object is parallel to the bottom.

> To begin this task you should be in the "angle" UCS, as in Task 4, and your screen should resemble *Figure 12-19*.
> Type or select "Fillet".
   AutoCAD will remind us that our view is not plan to our UCS and then prompt as usual:

> View is not plan to UCS. Command results may not be obvious.
> Polyline/Radius/<Select two objects>:

> Type "r" to choose the "Radius" option.
> Type ".25" for the radius value.
> Press enter to repeat the FILLET command.
> Pick two lines that meet at one of the upper corners of the slot.
> Press enter to repeat the FILLET command.
> Pick two lines that meet at the other upper corner of the slot.

The upper fillets are done. Before we can do the lower ones, we must change to a UCS which is parallel to the bottom of the object.

> Type or select "UCS".
> Type "r" to choose the "Restore" option.
> Type "top" to restore the top UCS.

We are now ready to fillet the bottom of the slot.

> Type or select "fillet".
> Pick two lines that meet at one of the lower corners of the slot.
> Press enter to repeat the FILLET command.
> Pick two lines that meet at the other lower corner of the slot.
> ERASE the two vertical lines at the corners.
   Your screen should resemble *Figure 12-20*.

Now we will use a new command to connect the upper and lower fillets with 3D surfaces. RULESURF is one of several new commands that create 3D surfaces. These commands create entities called "3D polygon meshes," which are discussed in detail in Chapter 13. This will serve as a quick introduction.

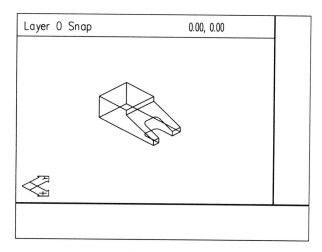

**Figure 12-20**

The RULESURF command allows you to create a 3D surface between two lines or curves in 3D space. Our two curves will be the upper and lower fillets at each of the two corners.

> Type or select "rulesurf".
>     AutoCAD will prompt:

Select first defining curve:

> Pick one of the top fillets, as shown in *Figure 12-21*.

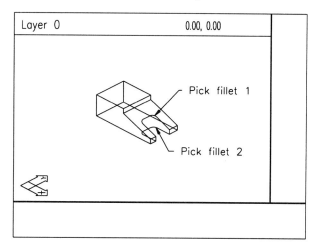

**Figure 12-21**

AutoCAD will prompt for a second curve:

Select second defining curve:

> Pick the corresponding fillet in the bottom plane, with a pick point on the corresponding side, as shown.
>     AutoCAD will draw a set of faces to represent the surface curving around the fillet radius, as shown in *Figure 12-22*.
>     The trick in using RULESURF is to be sure that you show a pick point towards one side of the curve, and that you pick the next curve with a point on

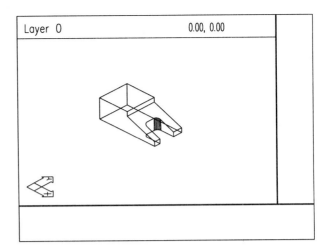

**Figure 12-22**

the corresponding side. Otherwise you will get an hourglass effect, as shown in *Figure 12-23*.

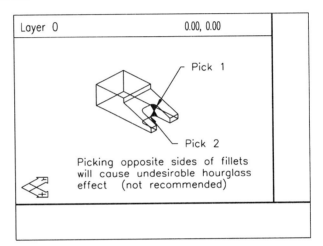

**Figure 12-23**

We will work more with 3D surfaces in the next chapter. To complete this task, repeat the RULESURF command and draw the fillet at the other corner of the groove. When you are done, your screen should resemble *Figure 12-24*.

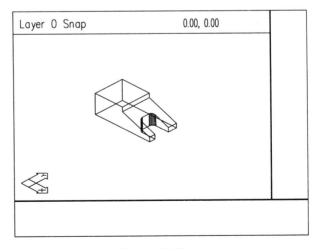

**Figure 12-24**

**TASK 6: Creating orthographic views of a 3D object**

*Procedure.*

1.  Restore the UCS that is parallel to the desired projection.
2.  BLOCK the object.
3.  Use OOPS to return the object to the screen.
4.  Restore the UCS for other projections, and block these in the same manner.
5.  For a 3D view, define a UCS using the "View" option and BLOCK as before.
6.  Clear the screen, return to the WCS plan view, and INSERT blocks in desired locations.
7.  Explode blocks and TRIM or ERASE any unwanted entities.
8.  Add dimensions.

*Discussion.*  The procedure listed above works effectively to produce orthographic projections of an object drawn in 3D. In this task we will use it to create a complete working drawing with three orthographic views and a 3D model.

> To begin this task you should have the completed slotted wedge on your screen, as shown in *Figure 12-24*.

The last UCS in use was "top", so it should still be current. If for any reason you have switched to another UCS, enter the UCS command now and restore the "top" UCS before going on.

In order to create an orthographic projection, all we need to do is define a block with the appropriate UCS in effect. Then when we INSERT this block, it will automatically be drawn plan to whatever coordinate system is current at the time of the insert. Complete this exercise and you will see what we mean.

> With the "top" UCS current, type or select "block".
  AutoCAD prompts:

> Block name (or ?):

It is convenient to use the name of the UCS for the name of the block.
> Type "top" for the name of the block.
  AutoCAD prompts:

> Insertion base point:

Since we have defined our UCS with its origin at a convenient point on the object, we can use the same point for the insertion base point of the blocked view.
> Type "0,0" or pick the origin point of the top UCS.
  This point will be the left front corner of the top of the object.
  AutoCAD prompts:

> Select objects:

> Type "w" and window the complete object. The block will disappear from your screen. We can use OOPS to bring it back.
> Type or select "oops".
  Your screen should resemble *Figure 12-24* again.

We will repeat this procedure to define blocks in the "front" UCS and the "right" UCS.

> Type or select UCS.
> Type "r" for the "Restore" option.
> Type "front" for the name of the UCS to restore.
> Type or select "block".
> Type "front" for the block name.
> Type "0,0" or pick the "front" UCS origin.
> Type "w".
> Window the complete object.
> Type or select "oops".

Repeat this three-step process once again to create a "right" block: restore the UCS, create the block, then execute the OOPS command.

Finally, we need to create one more block, so that we can call out a 3D view of the object for plotting. To do this, we will create a new UCS that is aligned with the current display. When this block is called out, it will appear just as it does now, regardless of what UCS is current at the time.

> Type or select "ucs".
> Type "v" or select "View".
       Notice how the UCS icon changes so that the axes are aligned with the display.
> Create a block of the object in this UCS and call it "view".
       This time, when you are done, do not use OOPS to return the object to the screen.

At this point, all our blocks are ready to create views and projections. In Release 10, *blocks are always inserted plan to the current UCS,* so that it does not really matter which UCS we use. However, in order to keep track of where we are, it is advisable to return to the WCS.

This can be done most efficiently using the PLAN command. PLAN will quickly give us a plan view relative to any coordinate system that is defined in the drawing.

First we need to make the WCS current.

> Type or select "ucs".
> Press enter to specify a return to the World Coordinate System.
       Notice the "w" on the UCS icon.

Now we are ready to execute PLAN.

> Type or select "plan".
       AutoCAD will prompt:

<Current UCS>/UCS/World:

The default will give us a plan view in the current UCS. If we type in the name of a UCS, the display will be redrawn plan to that UCS. If we type a "w", we will return to the original plan view of the WCS.

Since we just made the WCS current, typing "w" or pressing enter would give us the same result.
> Press enter.
       Your screen should be redrawn plan to the WCS.
       You will also notice that the grid is spread out. Even though there is no object presently on the screen, AutoCAD displays the drawing extents whenever it

switches views. What we see now is the drawing area which we have actually used in creating our object, even though the object is not there. We will need more space for our four-view working drawing, so we need to zoom out.

> Type or select "zoom" (or select "Display" from the pull down bar).

> Type "a" or select "All" ("Zoom all" on the pull down menu).

We are now ready to insert our blocks.

> INSERT all four blocks, as shown, to create *Figure 12-25*.

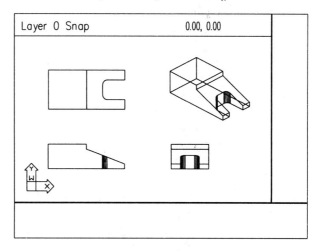

**Figure 12-25**

Notice that the front and right blocks need to be edited slightly.

> EXPLODE the front and right blocks.

> ERASE the lines made by the RULESURF fillets.

You will need to erase two surfaces in each view. In the front view the second is hidden behind the first, so it will appear only after the first is erased and the display is redrawn.

To complete this drawing, you should create the hidden line in the front view and dimension the projections. The results should resemble *Figure 12-26*.

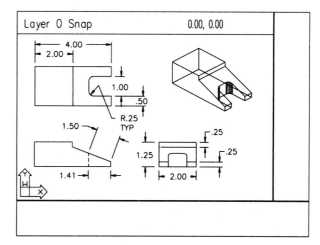

**Figure 12-26**

## TASK 7: Other methods of using VPOINT (optional)

*Discussion.* This discussion of other methods of using VPOINT is intended as a reference. The information presented here is not necessary to completing the drawings in this chapter, and no specific exercise is intended. However, if you are interested in gaining a complete understanding of the VPOINT command and its options, try creating the views described and outlined in the charts and figures. But remember, all you really need is the "Vpoint 3D" pull down menu for creating standard views, and later the DVIEW command for fine tuning and creating special effects.

### Entering 3D coordinates of a viewpoint

From the "Rotate/<View point>" prompt of the VPOINT command, the default method is to type in 3D coordinates. When you first enter the VPOINT command from the WCS plan view, the default viewpoint is given as (0,0,1). This means that you are currently viewing the object from a point somewhere along the positive Z axis. You are at 0 in the X and Y directions and at +1 in the Z direction. In other words, you are directly above the X-Y plane looking straight down, a plan view. Think of the X coordinate as controlling right-left orientation, the Y coordinate as controlling back-front, and the Z coordinate as controlling up-down.

By changing the X coordinate to 1 (right), leaving Y at 0 (neither front nor back), and Z at 1 (above), you could create a viewpoint above and to the right of the object (1,0,1). Similarly, (1,–1,1) would move you to the right (X=1), back you up a bit (Y=–1) so that you are in front of the object, and raise your point of view (Z=1) so that you are above the object looking down. This common (1,–1,1) viewpoint is the same as the "right, front, top" viewpoint used throughout this chapter, but previously we have defined it using the pull down icon menu.

We will explore other methods of specifying viewpoints in a moment, but first, look at the following chart. It summarizes the effects of the X, Y, and Z coordinates and gives you coordinates for some standard views. You should have a good understanding of why each view appears as it does.

| X Right-Left | Y Back-Front | Z Up-Down | View Description |
|:---:|:---:|:---:|:---|
| 0 | 0 | 1 | Plan |
| 0 | 0 | –1 | "Worm's eye" |
| 1 | 0 | 0 | Right side |
| –1 | 0 | 0 | Left side |
| 0 | 1 | 0 | Back |
| 0 | –1 | 0 | Front |
| 1 | 1 | 1 | Right, Back, Top |
| 1 | –1 | 1 | Right, Front, Top |
| | etc. | etc. | |

We suggest that you try some of these viewpoints and experiment with others not listed. Your goal should be to get a feel for how different coordinate combinations move your point of view in relation to objects on the screen.

### Rotation

The other option shown in the prompt is "Rotation". This is the option that is used by the Release 10 pull down icon menu, as described earlier in this chapter. Rotation can also be adjusted by typing "r" or selecting "Rotation" at the "Rotate/<View point>" prompt. Then AutoCAD will prompt for two angles. The first is an angle in the X-Y plane. It is measured from the X axis, with 0 being straight out to the right, as usual. In Task 1, we set this by picking one of the nine boxes on the icon menu.

The second angle goes up or down from the X-Y plane, with 0 being ground level. Thus an angle of 90 degrees from the X-Y plane would define the plan view.

The following chart will give you the rotation versions of some of the same major views shown on the pull down menu and the previous chart.

| From X | From X-Y | View Description |
|---|---|---|
| 0 | 0 | Right |
| 0 | 90 | Plan |
| 90 | 0 | Back |
| 180 | 0 | Left |
| 270 | 0 | Front |
| 45 | 30 | Back, Right, Top |
| –45 (or +315) | 30 | Front, Right, Top |
| 45 | –30 | Back, Right, Bottom |
| etc. | etc. | |

## The "VPOINT 3D" pull down

If you are working with Release 9 or higher, you have a pull down available that allows you to choose named views from an icon menu. In Release 9 the pull down uses an automated system of entering 3D coordinates, while in Release 10 the system uses the two angles of rotation as described earlier instead.

When you pick any of the views other than "Plan", you will be given a list of options on the screen menu that vary the viewing angle, giving you degrees of height in relation to the object. "0" will put you at ground level. Anything above that will have a positive viewing angle, anything below that a negative angle.

The pull down is the method we recommend.

## The compass and axes system

If you enter the VPOINT command and then press enter in response to the "Rotate/<View point>" prompt, you will see a display that resembles *Figure 12-27.*

The triple axes represent the orientation of the object. When you move your cursor, you will see these rotating. Some users may find this visualization easier to comprehend because it represents the object itself rather than your point of view in relation to the object. However, this effect is now much more clearly realized in Release 10's DVIEW command, discussed in Chapter 13.

The other part of the display is a rather unusual representation of a globe. The horizontal and vertical axes show the X and Y dimensions as you would expect, and the circles show the Z dimension. This actually shows a globe transformed into a cone and then flattened. The "north pole" of the globe has become a point at the center of the compass, while the "south pole" has been widened into a circle at the outside of the compass. In between is another circle representing the "equator," or ground 0 region.

This simply means that anywhere inside the first circle will give you a top-down view; outside the first circle will give you a bottom-up view. Anywhere on the middle circle will give you a ground-level view.

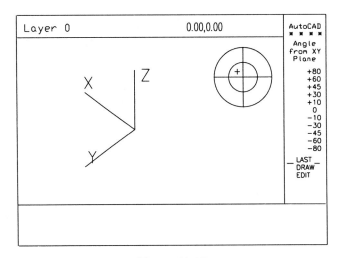

**Figure 12-27**

Notice the blip that moves as you move your cursor. This represents your point of view in the coordinate system.

*Figure 12-28* gives you a good summary of the compass points and how they relate to standard views. Try them out if you like.

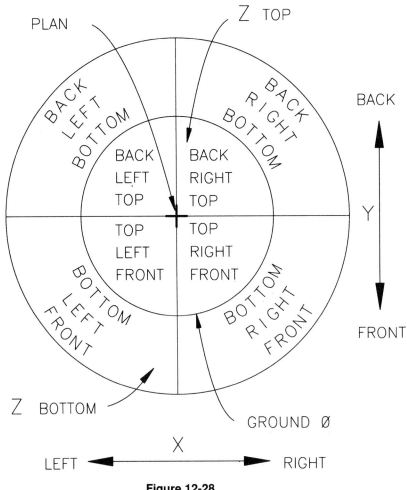

**Figure 12-28**

## TASKS 8, 9, 10, and 11

The drawings that follow are all 3D wire frame models that use the techniques and procedures introduced in this chapter. Drawing 12-1 also introduces the technique of 3D dimensioning. Drawings 12-2 and 12-3 are four-view working drawings like the one you completed in Task 6. Drawing 12-4 is a 3D architectural detail. Your primary objective in completing these drawings should be to gain facility with User Coordinate Systems and 3D space.

## DRAWING 12-1: CLAMP

This drawing is similar to the one you did in the chapter. Two major differences are that it is drawn from a different viewpoint and that it is dimensioned in the 3D view rather than in orthographic projections. This will give you additional practice in defining and using User Coordinate Systems. Your drawing should include dimensions, border, and title block.

### DRAWING SUGGESTIONS

> We drew the outline of the clamp in a horizontal position and then worked from a front, left, top point of view.

> Begin in WCS plan view drawing the "horseshoe" shaped outline of the clamp. This will include fillets on the inside and outside of the clamp. The more you can do in plan view before copying to the top plane, the less duplicate editing you will need to do later.

> When the outline is drawn, switch to a front left view.

> COPY the clamp outline up 1.50 using typed coordinates or an .XY filter.

> Define User Coordinate Systems as needed, and save them whenever you are ready to switch to another UCS. You will need to use them in your dimensioning.

> The angled face and the slots can be drawn just as in the chapter.

> Use RULESURF to draw the fillet surfaces.

> The only trick to dimensioning a 3D object is that you will need to restore the appropriate UCS for each set of dimensions. Think about how you want the text to appear. If text is to be aligned with the top of the clamp (i.e., the 5.75 overall length), you will need to draw that dimension in a "top" UCS; if it is to align with the front of the object (the 17 degree angle and the 1.50 height), draw it in a "front" UCS, and so forth.

> Define a UCS with the "View" option in order to add the border and the title block.

### SETTING SURFTAB1

Notice that there are 16 lines defining the RULESURF fillets in this drawing, compared to 6 in the chapter. This is controlled by the setting of the variable Surftab1, which is discussed in Chapter 14. For now, simply change it by entering the SETVAR command, typing "Surftab1" for the name of the variable, and entering "16" for the new value. Or, you can select "Surftab1" from the 3D construction pull down and then type in the new value.

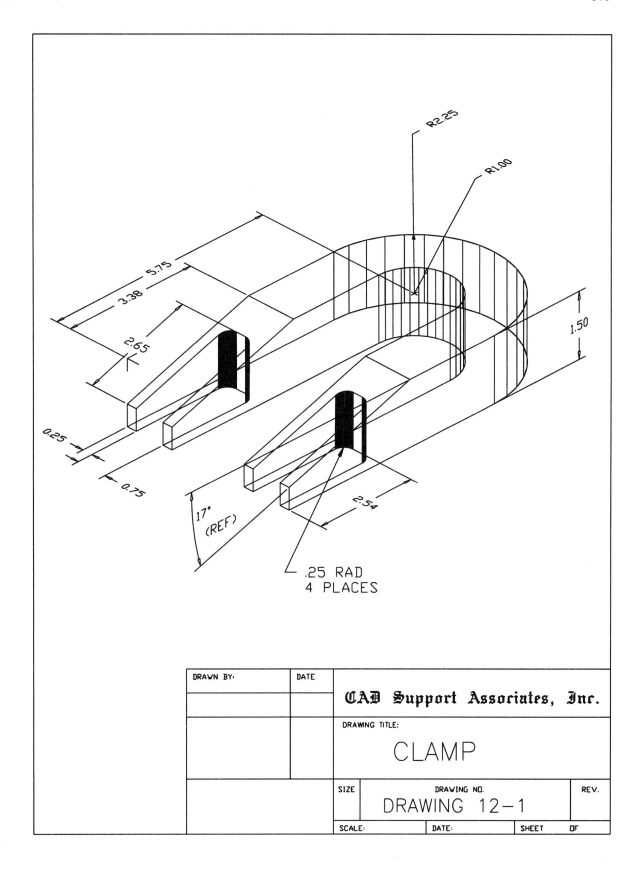

R2.25
R1.00
5.75
3.38
2.65
1.50
0.25
0.75
17°
(REF)
2.54
.25 RAD
4 PLACES

DRAWN BY:
DATE

CAD Support Associates, Inc.

DRAWING TITLE:

CLAMP

SIZE
DRAWING NO.
REV.
DRAWING 12-1

SCALE:
DATE:
SHEET
OF

## DRAWING 12-2: GUIDE BLOCK

In this drawing you will be working from dimensioned views to create a wire frame model. This brings up some new questions. Which view should you start with? How do you translate the views into the 3D image? A good general rule is this: draw the top or bottom in the X-Y plane of the WCS, otherwise you will have trouble using the VPOINT command.

### *DRAWING SUGGESTIONS*

> In this drawing it is tempting to draw the right side in WCS plan view first, because that is where most of the detail is. If you do this, however, you will have difficulty creating all the views as shown. Instead, we suggest that you keep the bottom of the object in the WCS X-Y plane and work up from there, as has been the practice throughout this chapter. The reason for this is that the VPOINT command works relative to the WCS. Therefore, front-back, left-right, and top-bottom orientations will make sense only if the top and bottom are drawn plan to the WCS.

> Draw the 12.50 by 8.00 rectangle shown in the top view, and then copy it up 4.38 to form the top of the guide's base.

> Change over to the same front, right, top 3D viewpoint we used in the chapter.

> Connect the four corners to create a block outline of the base of the object.

> Now you can define a new UCS on the right side and do most of your work in that coordinate system, since that is where the detail is. Once you have defined the right side UCS, you may want to go into its plan view to draw the right side outline, including the arc and circle of the guide. Then come back to the 3D view to copy back to the left side.

NOTE: You can save some time switching viewpoints by using the save and restore options of the VIEW command. When a view is saved, it includes the 3D orientation along with the zoom factor that was current at the time of the save. Also, ZOOM previous can be used to restore a previous 3D point of view. It will not, however, restore a UCS.

> Use RULESURF with Surftab1 set to 16 to fill in surfaces between the arcs and circles.

> When the 3D object is complete, define a UCS and block for each of the four views shown. Insert the blocks in WCS plan along with a border and title block, then explode, dimension, and hatch to create the completed drawing.

> Remember, you can make hatching easier by outlining the hatch boundary with a 0 width polyline.

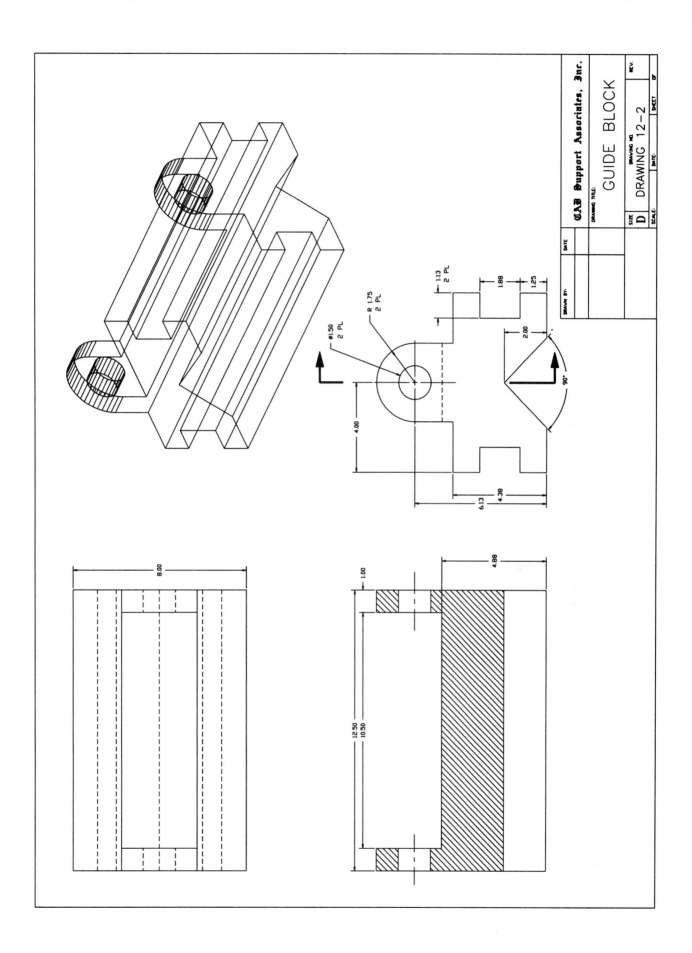

∅1.50
2 PL

R 1.75
2 PL

1.13
2 PL

1.88

1.25

2.00

90°

4.00

6.13

4.38

8.00

1.00

4.88

12.50
10.50

## DRAWING 12-3: SLIDE MOUNT

This drawing continues to use the same views, coordinate systems, and techniques as the previous drawings, but it has more detail and is a bit trickier.

### DRAWING SUGGESTIONS

> Draw the "H" shaped outline of the top view in WCS plan.
> Copy up in the Z direction.
> Connect the corners to create a 3D shape.
> Define a right side view, and create the slot and holes.
> Copy back to the left side, connect the corners, and trim inside the slot.
> Return to WCS (bottom plane).
> Use RULESURF between circles to create mounting holes.
> Draw filleted cutout and countersunk holes. Each countersunk hole will require three circles, two small and one larger.
> Use RULESURF to create inner surfaces of countersunk holes.
> When the 3D view is complete, define views and blocks. Insert blocks in WCS plan view along with a border and title block. Explode, dimension, and trim as necessary to complete the drawing.

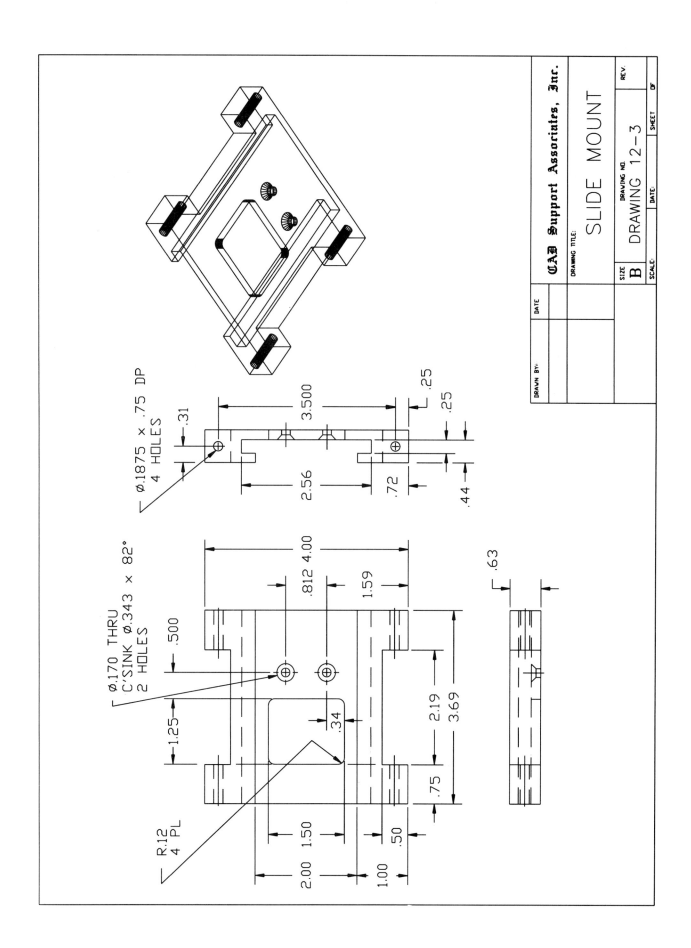

Ø.1875 × .75 DP
4 HOLES

Ø.170 THRU
C'SINK Ø.343 × 82°
2 HOLES

R.12
4 PL

3.500
.31
2.56
.72
.25
.25
.44

4.00
.812
1.59
.500
1.25
2.00   1.50
1.00   .50
.34
2.19
3.69
.75

.63

CAD Support Associates, Inc.

DRAWING TITLE:
SLIDE MOUNT

DRAWING NO.
DRAWING 12-3

SIZE
B

REV.

SCALE:        DATE:

SHEET    OF

DRAWN BY:

DATE

## DRAWING 12-4: STAIR LAYOUT

This wire frame architectural detail will give you a chance to use architectural units and limits in 3D. It will require the use of a variety of edit commands.

### *DRAWING SUGGESTIONS*

> In the WCS plan view, begin with a 2″ x 12′ rectangle that will become the bottom of a floor joist. This will keep the bottom floor in the plan view, consistent with our practice in this chapter.

> COPY the rectangle up 8″ and connect lines to form the complete joist.

> ARRAY 16″ on center to form the first floor.

> COPY all joists up 9′-6″ to form the second floor.

> Create the stairwell opening in the second floor with double headers at each end.

> Add the 3/4″ subfloor to the first floor.

> The outline of the stair stringers can be constructed in a number of ways. One possibility is as follows: draw a guideline down from the front of the left double header and then another over 10′-10″ to locate the end of the run; from the right end of the run draw one 7 1/2″ riser and one 9 1/2″ tread, beginning from the top surface of the subflooring; use a multiple copy and ENDpoint osnaps to create the other steps; when you get to the top, you will find you need to TRIM the top tread slightly to bring it flush with the header.

> We leave it to you to construct the back line of the stringer. It needs to be parallel with the stringer line and down 1′ from the top tread, as shown.

> Your final drawing should include the 3D view, the top view, the dimensioned front view, a title block, and a border.

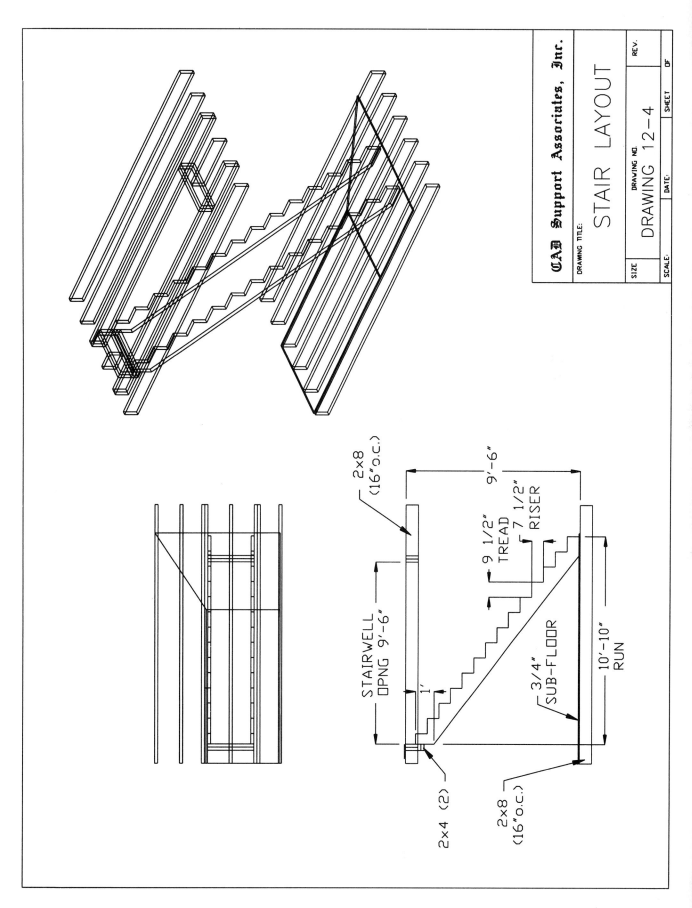

2×8
(16"o.c.)

STAIRWELL
OPNG 9'-6"

2×4 (2)

2×8
(16"o.c.)

9'-6"

9 1/2"
TREAD

7 1/2"
RISER

3/4"
SUB-FLOOR

10'-10"
RUN

1'

CAD Support Associates, Inc.

DRAWING TITLE:
STAIR LAYOUT

DRAWING NO.
DRAWING 12-4

REV.

SIZE

SCALE:

DATE:

SHEET

OF

# chapter

## COMMANDS

| 3D | DISPLAY | Variables |
|---|---|---|
| 3DMESH | VPORTS | Surftab1 |
| RULESURF | REDRAWALL | Surftab2 |
| TABSURF | REGENALL | |
| REVSURF | DVIEW | AutoLISP Functions |
| EDGESURF | HIDE | BOX |
| | | DOME |
| | | PYRAMID |

## OVERVIEW

In this chapter we will continue to explore Release 10 3D drawing features. Our focus will be on entities which have been specifically added for 3D drawing, and on two new display commands, VPORTS and DVIEW. Five commands will be introduced that create "polygon meshes" to represent surfaces based on existing wire frame geometry. VPORTS (or VIEWPORTS) will allow the creation of multiple view ports so that an object may be viewed from several points of view simultaneously. DVIEW will provide a dynamic alternative to the VPOINT command for viewing objects in 3D, and for creating perspective and cutaway views.

## TASKS

1. Use VPORTS to create multiple view ports.
2. Use TABSURF, RULESURF, EDGESURF, and REVSURF to create surfaces from previously drawn boundaries.
3. Create a simple 3D mesh.
4. Draw 3D objects with AutoCAD-supplied AutoLISP functions.
5. Use the DVIEW command to create 3D views with perspective and cutaway effects.
6. Use HIDE to remove hidden lines.
7. Do Drawing 13-1 ("REVSURF Designs").
8. Do Drawing 13-2 ("Tire and Rim").
9. Do Drawing 13-3 ("Globe").
10. Do Drawing 13-4 ("Nozzle").

### TASK 1: Using multiple view ports

*Procedure.*

1. Type or select "VPORTS".
2. Enter number of view ports desired.
3. Enter orientation of view ports.
4. Define views in each view port.

*Discussion.*     A major feature introduced with Release 10 is the ability to view an object from several different points of view simultaneously as you work on it. The VPORTS, or VIEWPORTS, command is easy to use and can save you from having to jump back and forth between different views of an object. View ports can be used in 2D to place several zoom magnifications on the screen at once, as shown in Chapter 3. More important, view ports can be used to place several 3D viewpoints on the screen at once. This can be a significant aid. If you do not continually view an object from different points of view, it is easy to create entities that appear correct in the current view, but that are clearly incorrect from other points of view.

In this task we will divide your screen in half and define two views, so that you can visualize an object in plan view and a 3D view at the same time. As you work, remember that this is only a display command. You cannot plot multiple view ports to create multiple-view working drawings.

> Begin a new drawing called "13-1" or "A:13-1".
> Type or select "vports", or pick "Display" and then "Set Viewports..." from the pull down.
    AutoCAD will prompt:

Save/Restore/Delete/Join/SIngle/?/2/<3>/4:

The first three options allow you to save, restore, and delete view port configurations. "Join" allows you to reduce the number of windows so that you move from, say, four windows to three. "SIngle" is the option that returns you to a single window. "?" will get you a list of previously saved view port configurations. The numbers 2, 3, and 4 will establish the number of different view ports you want to put on the screen.

The pull down menu system has an icon menu that will show you all the different ways in which the screen display may be split for multiple view ports. To use it, select "Display" and then "Set Viewports...". This will call out an icon menu like the one shown in *Figure 13-1*. It begins on the upper left with a single window, then two windows split vertically, two split horizontally, and so forth.

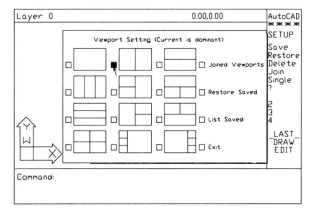

**Figure 13-1**

Any of these could also be specified by typing and following the sequence of command prompts.

If you are typing, the default is three windows with a full pane on the right and a horizontal split on the left. For our purposes we will create a simple two-way vertical split, the second box on the icon menu.

> Type "2" or select the second box on the icon menu.

If you type the number, AutoCAD will prompt for the direction of the split:

Horizontal/&lt;Vertical&gt;:

> Press enter to accept the default vertical split.

Your screen will be regenerated to resemble *Figure 13-2*.

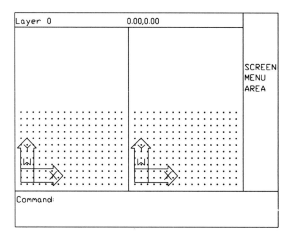

**Figure 13-2**

You will notice that the grid is rather small and confined to the lower part of each window. The shape of the view ports necessitates this reduction in drawing area. You can enlarge details as usual using the ZOOM command. Zooming and panning in one view port will have no effect on other view ports. However, you can have only one UCS in effect at any time, so a change in the coordinate system in one view port will be reflected in all view ports.

If you move your pointing device back and forth between the windows, you will see an arrow when you are on the left and the cross hairs when you are on the right. This indicates that the right window is currently active. Drawing and editing can be done only in the active window. To work in another window, you need to make it current by picking it with your pointing device. Often this can be done while a command is in progress.

> Move the cursor into the left window and press the pick button on your pointing device.

The cross hairs will now appear in the left view port, and you will see the arrow when you move into the right view port.

> Move the cursor back to the right and press the pick button again.

This will make the right window active again.

There is no value in having two view ports if each is showing the same thing, so our next job will be to change the viewpoint in one of the windows. We will leave the window on the left in plan view and switch the right window to a 3D view. For consistency, we will use the familiar "front, right, top" view used in the last chapter.

> Select "Display" and then "Viewpoint 3D" from the pull down.

> Select the lower right box for a front right view.
> Type or select a viewing angle of 30 degrees up from ground zero.

NOTE: As an alternative, type or select "vpoint" and then "1,–1,1". This will give you a similar view.

Your screen should now be redrawn with a right, front, top view in the right view port as shown in *Figure 13-3*. To complete this task, we will draw an arc and a line to be used in the next task.

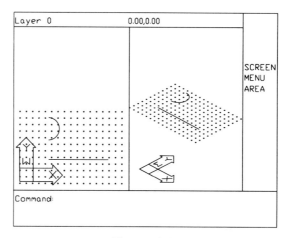

**Figure 13-3**

Once you have defined view ports, any drawing or editing done in the active view port will appear in all the view ports. As you draw, watch what happens in both view ports.

> Draw an arc and a line below it as shown in *Figure 13-3*. Exact sizes and locations are not important.

The entities may be drawn in either view port. You might want to draw the arc in the current view port, then switch to the other to draw the line.

Now we will go on to define some 3D surfaces using the arc and line you have just drawn.

### TASK 2: Using TABSURF, RULESURF, EDGESURF, and REVSURF

*Procedure.*

1. Draw a wire frame outline of the surface.
2. If necessary, set Surftab1 and Surftab2.
3. If necessary, outline surface boundaries with PLINE or 3DPOLY.
4. Enter a 3D polygon mesh command.
5. Use existing geometry to define the surface.
6. If necessary, edit with PEDIT.

*Discussion.* In Chapter 12, we produced wire frame models. These consisted of lines and arcs to represent the boundaries and edges of objects in space. The only time we created a surface was when we used the RULESURF command to construct 3D fillets. In this task we will create surfaces using RULESURF, TABSURF, EDGESURF, and REVSURF.

Surface modeling commands and techniques are used to represent the surfaces between edges that would exist if the object were in the real world. When surface model drawings are complete, they are typically processed by rendering software, such as AutoSHADE, to create realistic light and shadow images. The addition of surfaces to previously drawn wire frame models may necessitate dividing a single surface into several geometric regions that AutoCAD commands can handle.

Release 10 includes a number of commands that make the creation of some types of surfaces very easy. These commands create "3D polygon meshes" or "3D objects", all of which are included on the "3D Construction" icon menu illustrated in *Figure 13-4*. Polygon meshes are made up of 3D faces (see Chapter 14) and are defined by a matrix of vertices. They can be treated as single entities and edited with the PEDIT command, or exploded into individual 3D faces.

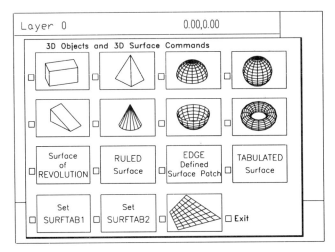

**Figure 13-4**

The 3D polygon mesh commands are powerful. However, they can be quite tricky, as we will show in the next chapter. For now, the objects you draw will have completely defined surfaces, but we will not focus on specific surface qualities and problems until Chapter 14.

> To begin this task, you should have two view ports on your screen, with an arc and a line, as shown previously in *Figure 13-3*.

## TABSURF

The first surface we will draw is called a "tabulated surface." In order to use the TAB-SURF command, you need a line or curve to define the shape of the surface and a vector to show its size and direction. The result is a surface which is generated by repeating the shape of the original curve at every point along the path specified by the vector.

> Type or select "tabsurf", or select "Tabulated Surface" from the 3D icon menu (under "Draw", "3D Construction...").
AutoCAD will prompt:

Select path curve:

The path curve is the line or curve that will determine the shape of the surface. In our case it will be the arc.
> Pick the arc.

AutoCAD will prompt for a vector:

Select direction vector:

We will use the line. Notice that the vector does not need to be connected to the path curve. Its location is not significant, only its direction and length.

There is an oddity here to watch out for as you pick the vector. If you pick a point near the left end of the line, AutoCAD will interpret the vector as extending from left to right. Accordingly, the surface will be drawn to the right. By the same token, if your point is near the right end of the line, the surface will be drawn to the left. Most of the time you will avoid confusion by picking a point on the side of the vector nearest the curve itself.

> Pick a point on the left side of the line.

Your screen will be redrawn to resemble *Figure 13-5*.

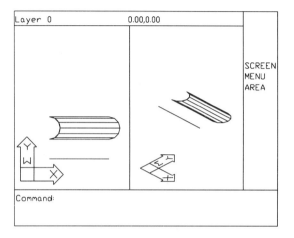

**Figure 13-5**

Notice that this is a flat surface. This may be not be clear in the plan view, but is apparent in the 3D view.

Tabulated surfaces can be fully 3D, depending on the path and vector chosen to define them. In this case we have an arc and a vector which are both entirely in the X-Y plane, so the resulting surface is also in that plane.

You will also notice that the surface is defined by six lines that run parallel to the vector. If you zoom up on either end of the surface, you will also see that the arc is only approximated by the end points of these six lines. This is not like the polygons AutoCAD often uses to approximate arcs and circles in order to speed regeneration times. This is the actual current definition of this surface. In order to achieve a more accurate approximation, we need to change the setting of a variable called "Surftab1" and draw the object again.

You will find Surftab1 and Surftab2 conveniently located at the bottom of the 3D construction icon menu (select "Draw" and then "3D Construction..." from the pull down bar). We will discuss Surftab2 later.

Now let's undo the tabulated surface so that we can draw it again with a new Surftab1 setting.

> Type "U" and then execute a REDRAW.

Notice that only the current view port is redrawn. In order to redraw all view ports simultaneously, you could enter a new command called REDRAWALL. There is also a REGENALL command for regenerating all view ports.

> Select "Draw" and then "3D construction..." from the pull down menu.

Alternatively, type "Setvar" and then "Surftab1".
You should now see the following in the command area:

'setvar Variable name or ?: surftab1
New value for SURFTAB1 <6>:

The first line has entered the "setvar" command (the apostrophe makes the command transparent) and the name of the variable we want to set. The second line asks for the new setting and shows us that the current setting is six. This explains the six lines in the tabulated surface. When we change the setting, we will get a different number of lines and degree of accuracy.
> Type "12".

If you are using the pull down system, the 3D construction icon menu will automatically return to the screen after you set Surftab1. AutoCAD assumes that you will want to select a surface command after setting the variable.
> Type "tabsurf" or select "Tabulated Surface" from the icon menu.
> Pick the arc for the path curve.
> Pick the line for the direction vector.

Your screen should now resemble *Figure 13-6*.

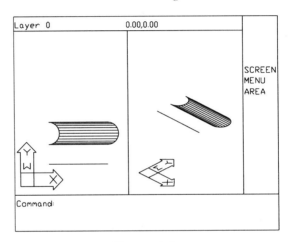

**Figure 13-6**

## RULESURF

TABSURF is useful in defining surfaces that are the same on both ends, assuming you have one end and a vector. Often, however, you have no vector, or you have a surface that is to be drawn between two different paths. In these cases you will need the RULESURF command.

For example, what if we needed to define a surface between the line and the arc? Let's try it.

> Type "U" to undo the last tabulated surface, then execute a REDRAW or REDRAWALL.

It is not absolutely necessary to do the REDRAW, but it makes it easier to pick the arc.
> Type or select "rulesurf", or select "Ruled Surface" from the 3D construction icon menu.

You are familiar with this command sequence from Chapter 12. The first prompt is:

Select first defining curve:

> Pick the arc, using a point near the bottom.

Remember that you must pick points on corresponding sides of the two defining curves in order to avoid an "hourglass" effect.

AutoCAD prompts:

Select second defining curve:

> Pick the line, using a point near the left end.

Your screen should resemble *Figure 13-7*.

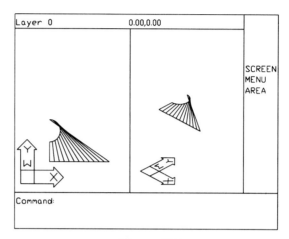

**Figure 13-7**

Again, notice that this surface is within the X-Y plane. Ruled surfaces may be drawn just as easily between curves which are not coplanar. For purposes of demonstration, we have elected to keep our curves in the same plane so that they can be easily drawn.

If you look closely, you will also notice that this ruled surface is drawn with 12 lines, the result of our Surftab1 setting.

Some other typical examples of ruled surfaces are shown on the chart, *Figure 13-13*, at the end of this task.

## EDGESURF

TABSURF creates surfaces that are the same at both ends and move along a straight line vector. RULESURF draws surfaces between any two boundaries. There is a third command, EDGESURF, which draws surfaces that are bounded by four curves. Edge defined surfaces have a lot of geometric flexibility. The only restriction is that they must be bounded on all four sides. That is, they must have four edges that touch.

In order to create an EDGESURF, we need to undo our last ruled surface and add two more edges.

> Type "U" and execute a REDRAW or REDRAWALL.
> Add a line and an arc to your screen, as shown in *Figure 13-8*.

Remember, you can draw in either view port.

> Type or select "edgesurf", or select "Edge Defined Surface Patch" from the icon menu.

AutoCAD will prompt for the four edges of the surface, one at a time:

Select edge 1:

> Pick the smaller arc.

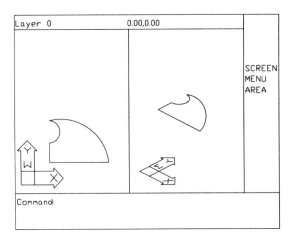

**Figure 13-8**

AutoCAD prompts:

> Select edge 2:

> Pick the larger arc.
>    AutoCAD prompts:

> Select edge 3:

> Pick the longer line.
>    AutoCAD prompts:

> Select edge 4:

> Pick the smaller line.
>    Your screen should now resemble *Figure 13-9*.

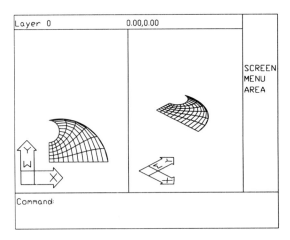

**Figure 13-9**

There is something new to be aware of here. With TABSURF and RULESURF, surfaces were defined by lines moving in only one direction. With EDGESURF, you have lines going two ways to create a web or mesh effect. You will notice that there are 12 lines going one way and 6 going the other, as shown in the figure. This brings us to the variable "Surftab2". If we change its setting to 12 also, we will see 12 lines in each direction.

Try it.

> Type "U" to undo the EDGESURF command.
> Execute a REDRAW or REDRAWALL.
> Set Surftab2 to 12 using the pull down, the screen menu, or the keyboard (SET-VAR command).
> Enter the EDGESURF command and draw a new surface inside the four edges on your screen.

The result should resemble *Figure 13-10*.

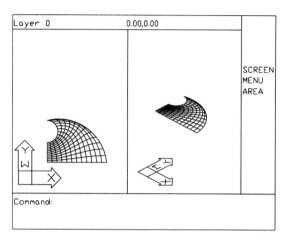

**Figure 13-10**

### REVSURF

We have one more surface command to explore, and this one is in some ways the most impressive of all. REVSURF creates surfaces by spinning a curve through a given angle around an axis of revolution. Just as tabulated surfaces are always spread across a straight path, surfaces of revolution always follow a circular path, though they need not complete the circle.

> In preparation for this exercise, undo the EDGESURF and REDRAW (or REDRAWALL) your screen so that it resembles *Figure 13-8* again.

We will create two surfaces of revolution. The first will be a complete 360 degree surface using the smaller arc and the smaller line for definition. The second will be a 270 degree surface using the larger arc and the larger line.

> Type or select "revsurf", or select "Surface of Revolution" from the "3D Construction..." icon menu.

AutoCAD needs a curve path and an axis of revolution to define the surface. The first prompt is:

> Select path curve:

> Pick the smaller arc.

AutoCAD prompts:

> Select axis of revolution:

> Pick the smaller line.

AutoCAD now needs to know whether you want the surface to begin at the curve itself or somewhere else around the circle of revolution:

Start angle <0>:

The default is to start at the curve.
> Press enter to begin the surface at the curve itself.
   AutoCAD prompts:

Included angle (+=ccw, -=cw) <Full circle>:

Entering a positive or negative degree measure will cause the surface to be drawn around an arc rather than a full circle. The default will give us a complete circle.
> Press enter.
   Your screen should be drawn to resemble *Figure 13-11.*

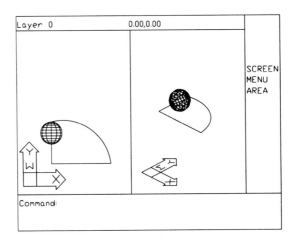

**Figure 13-11**

If you look closely, you will see that this globe has 12 lines in each direction. REVSURF, like EDGESURF, uses both Surftab1 and Surftab2. Also notice that this command gives us a way to create spheres. If the curve path is a true semicircle and the axis is along the diameter of the semicircle, then the result will be a sphere. You will also notice that there is a sphere shown at the top of the 3D construction pull down. This provides another way to create a sphere which we will explore in Task 4.

   Now we will create a larger surface that does not start at 0 degrees and does not include a full circle.

> Press enter to repeat the REVSURF command.
> Pick the larger arc for the curve path.
> Pick the left end of the longer line for the axis of revolution.
   If you pick the right end, the positive and negative angles will be reversed in the two steps following.
> Type "90" for the start angle.
   This will cause the surface to begin 90 degrees up from the X-Y plane.
> Type "–270" for the included angle.
   This will cause the surface to revolve 270 degrees clockwise around the axis. The result should resemble *Figure 13-12.* You may have to use PAN in one or both view ports to position the objects on the screen as we have shown them.

   Next, we will be drawing a simple 3D mesh and then going on to explore "3D objects" and the DVIEW command. Take a look at the polygon mesh examples in *Figure 13-13* before proceeding.

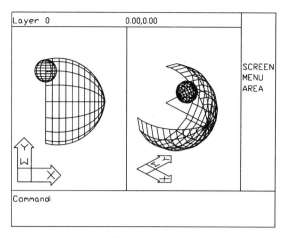

**Figure 13-12**

| POLYGON MESH COMMANDS | | | |
|---|---|---|---|
| COMMAND | BEFORE | SETVAR SETTINGS | AFTER |
| TABSURF | | SURFTAB1 = 6 | |
| RULESURF | | SURFTAB = 12 | |
| | | SURFTAB1 = 6 | |
| | | SURFTAB1 = 6 | |
| | | SURFTAB1 = 6 | |
| EDGESURF | | SURFTAB1 = 6<br>SURFTAB2 = 8 | |
| | | SURFTAB1 = 6<br>SURFTAB2 = 8 | |
| | | SURFTAB1 = 6<br>SURFTAB2 = 8 | |
| | | SURFTAB1 = 12<br>SURFTAB2 = 10 | |
| REVSURF | | SURFTAB1 = 16<br>SURFTAB2 = 8 | |

**Figure 13-13**

### TASK 3: Creating a simple 3D mesh using the pull down

*Procedure.*

1. Select "Draw" and then "3D Construction" from the pull down.
2. Select the 3D mesh at the lower right.
3. Outline a rectangle with four points.
4. Enter the number of vertices in the "M" direction.
5. Enter the number of vertices in the "N" direction.

*Discussion.*    The 3DMESH command allows you to create 3D polygon meshes "manually," vertex by vertex. Because of the time involved, the complete command is best used as a programmer's tool. However, the pull down menu has a very simple version of the 3DMESH command that we will demonstrate here. Those interested in the full command sequence should see the *AutoCAD Reference Manual*, Section 4.9.1, and the *AutoCAD Release 10 Tutorial*, Pages 127–32.

The pull down version of the 3DMESH command is the angled mesh at the lower right of the "3D Construction..." icon menu. It allows you to create simple rectangular 3D meshes in one plane. We will use this method to create a mesh in the current X-Y plane with four vertices in each direction.

> Use a window selection in the ERASE command to clear all objects from your screen.
> Select "Draw" and then "3D Construction" from the pull down.
> Pick the 3DMESH icon from the bottom of the "3D Construction" icon menu.
   AutoCAD will give you the following message:

    Please wait... Loading 3D objects.

We will be drawing 3D objects in the next task. The objects at the top of the 3D construction icon menu, along with this simple 3D mesh at the bottom, are all created through AutoLISP programs contained in a file called "3D.lsp". Whenever you use any of them for the first time in a drawing session, the file will need to be loaded. Otherwise, they work very much like AutoCAD commands.

Once the file has been loaded, AutoCAD will begin the prompt sequence for the mesh:

    First corner:

We will be prompted for four corners to define the outer boundaries of the mesh, and then for two numbers to specify the number of vertices.
> Make the left (plan) view port active, and pick a corner, as shown in *Figure 13-14*. AutoCAD will prompt for another corner:

    Second corner:

> Pick a second corner, moving around the perimeter of the mesh you are defining. Exact dimensions are not significant for this exercise.
> Pick third and fourth corners, as shown.

When you have picked four corners, your mesh should be outlined and one side highlighted. AutoCAD is asking for the number of vertices to be defined in the "M" direction:

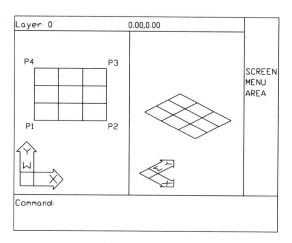

**Figure 13-14**

Mesh M size:

The highlighted side shows the "M" direction. This is equivalent to the Surftab1 setting. The highlighted side will be divided equally by the number of vertices we specify.

> Type "4".

AutoCAD highlights a side perpendicular to the first, and prompts:

Mesh N size:

Like Surftab2, the "N" specification will determine the number of vertices in this direction.

> Type "4" again.

Your screen will be redrawn to resemble *Figure 13-14*.

In the next task we will create three 3D objects from the 3D construction pull down and place them on top of the 3D mesh you just drew.

### TASK 4: Constructing "3D Objects"

*Procedure.*

1. Select an object from the icon menu.
2. Follow the prompts.

*Discussion.* In Release 9, five 3D objects were included on a "3D Objects" pull down. They were drawn using AutoLISP routines which act just like commands. In Release 10, the number has been expanded to eight objects, all shown at the top of the "3D Construction.." menu. Like the 3D meshes explored in Task 2, 3D objects can be treated as single entities or EXPLODEd and edited as collections of 3D faces (see Chapter 14). Each of the objects has its own set of prompts, depending on its geometry. We will place three of the objects in the rectangular spaces of the mesh created in Task 3 and then use the whole collection to demonstrate the DVIEW command.

> To begin this task, you should have the mesh from Task 3 on your screen, as shown in *Figure 13-14*.

We will begin with a box, the object in the upper left corner of the icon menu.

> Pick "Draw" and then "3D construction..." to activate the 3D construction pull down. (Alternatively, you can type "box" at the keyboard).

> Pick the "box" (upper left corner).

AutoCAD will first load a file called "3D.lsp", which contains the routines for creating 3D objects, and then prompt as follows:

Corner of box:

NOTE: While "sphere", "cone", "torus", etc. appear to work just like commands, they are actually AutoLISP functions. Therefore, they will not work if AutoLISP is not loaded with appropriate memory allocation. If you have a problem, see your instructor or the *AutoCAD Installation and Performance Guide*, Section 4.4.

> Pick a point near a corner of the back left section of the mesh, as shown by point 1 in *Figure 13-15*.

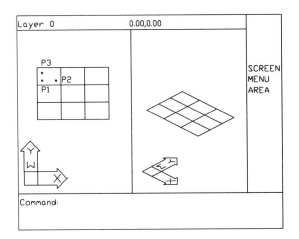

**Figure 13-15**

AutoCAD prompts:

Length:

The length will be drawn in the positive X direction of your current UCS, regardless of the direction you actually point. You will have the opportunity to rotate the box around the Z axis later.

> Pick a point to show the X direction length of the box (point 2). Exact size and location are not important for this exercise.

AutoCAD prompts:

Cube/<Width>:

If you respond with a "c" for "cube", AutoCAD will know that you want all edges to be the same size as the "length" just defined. Otherwise you will need to show a width and then a height.

> Pick a point to show the Y direction "width" of the box (point 3).

AutoCAD prompts:

Height:

You can show the height in any direction, but AutoCAD will draw the height in positive Z.
> Pick a point in any direction to specify a height similar to that shown in *Figure 13-16*.

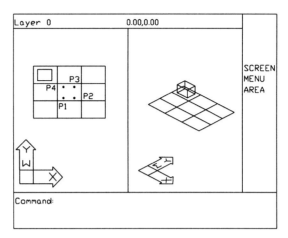

**Figure 13-16**

Now AutoCAD gives you the opportunity to rotate the box around the Z axis:

Rotation angle about Z axis:

Move your cursor back and forth and observe the dragged box showing you the effect of rotation. Then return to the original position, which we will retain.
> Type "0" for no rotation, or show a rotation angle of 0 degrees.
Your screen should resemble *Figure 13-16*.

Now we will place a "pyramid" in the middle of the mesh. This will require the use of an .XY filter to locate the top of the pyramid.

> Type or select "Pyramid", or pick the pyramid from the 3D construction icon menu (the second object in the top row).
AutoCAD will prompt for three or four base points and then ask us to define the top of the pyramid. The first prompt is:

First base point:

> Pick a point, as shown by point 1 in *Figure 13-16*.
AutoCAD prompts:

Second base point:

Unlike the "box" function, this routine will draw base lines as you show them, and there will be no opportunity to rotate the pyramid at the end. For our purposes, we will keep the rectangular base aligned with the mesh.
> Pick a second base point, like point 2 in the figure.
AutoCAD prompts:

Third base point:

> Pick a point similar to point 3.
AutoCAD prompts:

Tetrahedron/<Fourth base point>:

If you type "t" for "tetrahedron", AutoCAD will construct a triangular base from the three points already shown and proceed to prompt for the definition of the top of the pyramid. When you want a quadrilateral base, pick a fourth point.
> Pick a fourth point, like point 4 in the figure.
AutoCAD now prompts:

Ridge/Top/<Apex point>:

"Ridge" and "Top" allow you to create two- and four-point tops on your pyramid. We will draw a classic one-point apex.
We need to pick a point in the Z direction, above the X-Y plane of the base. We cannot use an object snap, so we will use an .XY filter. If you haven't tried filters yet, here is your chance.
> Type ".XY".
AutoCAD responds to the point filter with:

of

As discussed previously, AutoCAD is saying "you want the X and Y coordinates of what point?"
> Pick a point at or near the center of the pyramid base. For the purposes of this exercise, it is not necessary to pick the exact center.
AutoCAD has two out of three of the coordinates it needs. Now it asks for the third:

(need Z):

> Type "2".
Your screen should resemble *Figure 13-17*.

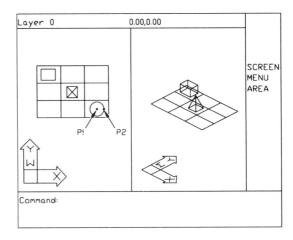

**Figure 13-17**

We will draw one more 3D object and then go on to explore the DVIEW command. Continuing across the top of the icon menu, the next object is called a "dome".

Watch closely as it is drawn, and you will see how the DOME function uses an automated version of the REVSURF command.

> Type or select "dome" or pick the dome from the icon menu.
AutoCAD prompts:

Center of dome:

Domes, dishes, and spheres all follow the same basic prompt sequence. The only difference is which part of a total sphere will be drawn.
> Pick a point near the center of the front right section of the mesh, as shown in *Figure 13-17*.
AutoCAD prompts:

Diameter/<Radius>:

Just as in the CIRCLE command, you can define spheres, domes, and dishes with a radius or a diameter.
> Show a radius that will keep the dome neatly inside the mesh, as shown in the figure.
AutoCAD now needs to know how accurate a representation you want. This is equivalent to setting Surftab1 and Surftab2 for this entity:

Number of longitudinal segments <16>:

> Press enter to accept the default of 16 segments.
AutoCAD prompts again:

Number of latitudinal segments <8>:

Notice the difference in the default settings. Before you press enter to accept the default, be ready to watch the routine in action. If your computer is not too fast you will clearly see what happens. AutoCAD will rotate the UCS 90 degrees around the X axis and construct a temporary axis of rotation through the center point. Then it will draw a 90 degree arc that touches the axis at the top. It uses the arc and the axis to create a 360 degree REVSURF. Finally, it will erase the axis, leaving the completed dome.
> Press enter to accept the default of 8 segments and watch closely...
When the DOME function has done its work, your screen should resemble *Figure 13-18*.

Our current work with 3D objects is complete. In the next task we will take the collection of objects on your screen and view them in a number of different ways, using the DVIEW command.

### TASK 5: Creating 3D views with DVIEW

*Procedure.*

1. Type or select "DVIEW".
2. Select objects to view.

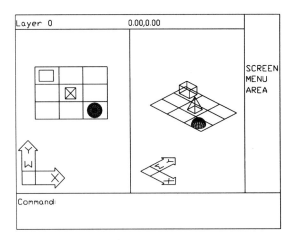

**Figure 13-18**

3. Specify a DVIEW option.
4. Specify a view.
5. Specify another option or exit the command.
6. Use VIEW to save 3D views.

*Discussion.* For most drawing purposes, using the 3D Vpoint icon menu (VPOINT command) is adequate and efficient for visualizing 3D views of objects. However, the DVIEW ("Dynamic View") command introduced in Release 10 has several capabilities that do not exist in VPOINT. DVIEW allows you to "drag" the object or portions of it as you define the view. In addition, it has the capability of creating perspective views and allows you to "clip" the object at specified planes to create "cutaway" effects or to temporarily remove objects.

Within the DVIEW command there are also options to zoom, pan, and rotate ("Twist") to achieve the exact display you want, and to remove hidden lines to better visualize the view you are creating. As a general rule, DVIEW is best used when your drawing is complete and you want to create a plot or display that shows it to best advantage. Perspective views, for example, are strictly for presentation. Many draw and edit commands will not even work in a perspective view.

In this task we will test many of the DVIEW options on the mesh and collection of objects you have just completed. But first, let's return to a single view port so that we can see the DVIEW symbols and procedures on the full screen.

> To begin this task, you should have a plan view and a 3D view of the objects, as shown in *Figure 13-18*.
> Make the 3D view active (right view port).
> Type or select "VPORTS", or select "Display" and then "Set Viewports..." from the pull down menu.

NOTE: In many drawing situations you will want to save a view port configuration before abandoning it. This is easily done by typing "s" or selecting "save" and then giving the configuration a name. The position and number of windows is saved along with the UCS and viewpoint information. Saving view ports does not save the current condition of the objects on the screen; editing and newly drawn objects will be included when you restore the saved view port configuration. It is not necessary to save your view port configuration in this exercise.

> Type "si" or select "single". On the icon menu, pick the single, undivided window.

Your screen will be regenerated as a single window with a 3D view, as shown in *Figure 13-19*. Now we will adjust this view with the DVIEW command.

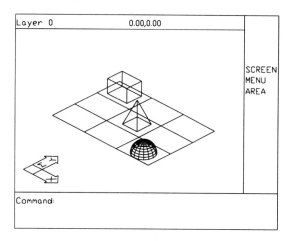

**Figure 13-19**

> Type or select "dview". Do not use the pull down system at this point, because it provides a very limited range of options.
AutoCAD prompts for object selection:

Select objects:

One of the advantages of DVIEW is that it lets you adjust your view of objects in 3D space dynamically. In order to do this effectively, however, the number of objects on the screen may need to be limited. If you have ever tried to "drag" a complex object across the screen, you will be familiar with the problem. The object is drawn and redrawn so slowly as you move your pointing device that the dragging process becomes too cumbersome to be useful. In the DVIEW command, you select a portion of your drawing to serve as a "preview image" for the process of dynamic view adjustment. The rest of the drawing is temporarily invisible and ignored. When you have defined the view you want by manipulating the preview image, exit DVIEW and the complete drawing will be restored in the newly defined view.
For our purposes, we will select the mesh and the box. These will give us a clear 3D image that is easily dragged.

NOTE: AutoCAD provides an alternative to this selection process. If you press enter at the "Select objects:" prompt, DVIEW will show a simple wire frame house for your preview image. If you want, you can even create your own default image. (See the *AutoCAD Reference Manual*, Section 6.6.2.2.) For most purposes, however, you will want to see at least a portion of your own drawing.

> Pick the box and the mesh.
> Press enter to end object selection.
The pyramid and the dome will vanish, and AutoCAD will prompt for a DVIEW option:

CAmera/TArget/Distance/POints/PAn/Zoom/TWist/CLip/Hide/Off/Undo/<eXit>:

These options vary considerably in their effect and ease of use. We will begin with "Zoom" because it is simple to use and will introduce you to DVIEW's "slider bar" symbols.

### "Zoom" and "Pan"

> Type "z" or select "Zoom".

AutoCAD places a "slider bar" at the top of the screen, as shown in *Figure 13-20*, and prompts:

Adjust zoom scale factor <1>:

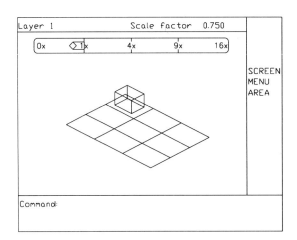

**Figure 13-20**

The slider bar consists of a scale with numbered divisions (0X,1X,4X,9X,16X), a diamond-shaped "cursor" that is controlled by your pointing device, and two rubber bands that connect you to a short line that marks the current value of the setting you are adjusting. In the "Zoom" option, the current value is always "1X". If you move the cursor to the right, objects on the screen will be enlarged by the factors shown on the scale; if you move to the left, they will be reduced by fractional factors.

A good practice in learning to use slider bars is to begin each adjustment by moving the diamond back to the "current" position (diamond directly over the short line). With one exception, to be discussed in a moment, this will make the image on your screen appear as it did before you entered the option. This way you will always start from where you left off and understand more clearly what is happening as you move the cursor.

Try it.

> Move the cursor so that the diamond is on the short vertical line at the "1X".

The preview image will appear as it did before you entered the zoom option, except that any colors will be gone.

> Now stretch the rubber bands to the right and left and watch the image expand and shrink.

Notice that it doesn't take much movement to produce a significant change. Also, pay close attention to the coordinate display. It will show you your zoom scale factor to three decimal places.

> Pick a zoom factor less than 1, say around .750.

Your image will be reduced by the scale factor shown, and AutoCAD will return to the DVIEW options prompt:

CAmera/TArget/Distance/POints/PAn/Zoom/TWist/CLip/Hide/Off/Undo/<eXit>:

If your image is not positioned near the middle of your screen, you may want to try out the "PAn" option. It is easy to use. First specify a base point. Then you can drag objects around the screen in any direction.

### "Camera" and "Target"

Next we will change our view of the image using the "CAmera" option. "Camera" and "Target" refer to two aspects of a point of view relative to a 3D object. ("Distance" is a third we will discuss shortly.)

The photographic metaphor was originally introduced in AutoSHADE, the Autodesk software package used in creating the effect of light and shadow on modeled surfaces. When you sight through an actual camera, what you see is dependent on the location of the camera and the direction its lens is pointed. In the metaphor, "Camera" refers to the placement of your point of view (the camera) in space, and "Target" refers to the point at which the camera is aimed. In the DVIEW command you can change views by moving the camera location, by aiming it in another direction, or both.

Setting the "Camera" placement is very similar to using the rotation option of the VPOINT command (the option used on the 3D Vpoint icon menu). If you recall, in using "VPOINT Rotate" you first define an angle of rotation within the X-Y plane and then a viewing angle above or below the plane. With "Dview Camera" the order is reversed. First you will move your camera up or down from the X-Y plane, then you will rotate its placement right or left around the target. You will use slider bars for the two settings, and you will see the image on your screen changing as you adjust your angles.

> Type "ca" or select "Camera".

You will see a vertical slider bar along the right side of the screen, as shown in *Figure 13-21*. Notice that the scale is in degrees from -90 to +90 and that the current position is between 0 and 45.

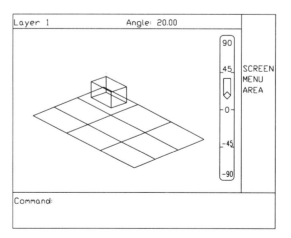

**Figure 13-21**

> Move the cursor so that the diamond is at the current position.

Your coordinate display should be reading very close to 30 degrees. Recall that this is the position we defined when we selected +30 degrees in the VPOINT command.

> Move the cursor up and down slowly and observe the effect.

As the camera moves up and down, the preview image appears to tip forward and back. It may be difficult to visualize what is happening as you pass below 0 degrees. As you pass zero, the front of the object begins to tip away from you so that you are looking up from underneath.

> Observe the coordinate display and pick a new viewing angle of about +15 degrees.

As soon as you pick the first setting, AutoCAD shows you a horizontal slider bar and waits for you to define an angle of rotation in the X-Y plane.

Notice how the preview image has shifted due to AutoCAD's interpretation of the position of your pointing device.

> Move the cursor so that the diamond is at the "current" position.

This should be close to –45. Do you remember why? This is the angle that was defined first in the VPOINT command. It is the equivalent of a 315 degree positive rotation that defined our front right view.

Take a moment to look at the horizontal slider and think about what it means. Imagine an object sitting at the intersection of the X and Y axes, and keep in mind AutoCAD's polar coordinate system. If you move directly out to the right and look in along the X axis, the object is being viewed from 0 degrees, so 0 is a direct right view. If you move all the way around to the negative X side, you are at 180 or –180 and you are getting a full "left" view. If you back up along the Y axis, you are at –90, getting a front view. If you move forward, you will pass the object and look back from +90 degrees, a back view. All of this works exactly the same in the DVIEW command as it does in VPOINT Rotate.

> Now move the cursor to the right and left and observe the effects on the preview image.

Look at right, front, left, and back views. Notice that the two extremes of the slider, 180 and –180, give you the same left view.

A direct "right" view will work well in a perspective view of our objects, so we will move to an angle of 0 degrees.

> Type "0" or pick a rotation of 0.00 degrees.

Your screen should be redrawn to resemble *Figure 13-22*.

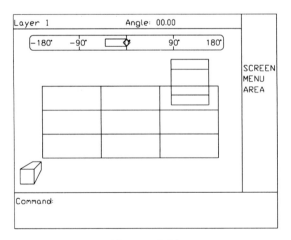

**Figure 13-22**

We will not use the "TArget" option in this exercise. The process is exactly the same. Vertical and horizontal slider bars are used to define viewing angle and rotation. The difference is that the camera location does not change. Instead, we change the direction in which the camera is aimed. It is like "panning" with a movie camera. The camera pans up and down with the first slider bar, left and right with the second. You will notice that the image on the screen shifts more radically than in the "Camera" option and that it is easy to "pan" away from the image so that it flies off the screen entirely.

### "Distance" and Perspective

Another aspect of any camera-to-target relationship is the distance between the two. So far we have been able to ignore this, because AutoCAD chooses a default distance based on the viewpoint defined before we entered DVIEW. This relationship can be defined explicitly using the "Distance" option. You must be aware, however, that choosing the "Distance" option also turns on perspective viewing. If you want to enlarge an image without going into perspective, use the "Zoom" option.

Our next step here will be to create a perspective view using "Distance".

> Type "d" or select "Distance".

The distance option is the exception to the rule about current settings. That is, the first time you enter the distance option and move your cursor to the "current" setting, you will not see the preview image the way it appeared before you entered the option. Instead, it will appear so large that you will see only part of the image. After you have set the distance once, however, you will be able to use the "1X" setting in the same way you did with "Zoom". For your first setting you will need to move the diamond all the way over to "16X". Then we will enter "distance" again and see that the slider works as usual.

> Move the cursor to "16X" and press the pick button.

Your screen will resemble *Figure 13-23*. Notice the perspective effect and the perspective icon that replaces the UCS icon.

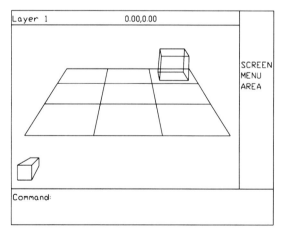

**Figure 13-23**

> Type "d" or select "Distance" again.
> Move the cursor to the "1X" position. Observe that this now represents the current image, as shown in *Figure 13-23*.

> Move the cursor back and forth and watch the image move along the lines of perspective.

You can take it all the way to the vanishing point by moving to the right, or move directly over the mesh by moving to the left.

> Pick "1X" or something slightly larger or smaller, as you like.

NOTE: If you enter the "Zoom" option while in a perspective view, you will see AutoCAD prompt for a "Lens length" rather than a zoom factor. In perspective, "DVIEW Zoom" operates like changing lenses on a camera to enlarge or reduce the field of vision. This is consistent with the photographic metaphor. However, the effect is what you would expect in any zooming operation.

Now let's exit the DVIEW command for a moment and see the complete effect of what we have done so far.

> Press enter to exit DVIEW.

Your screen will be redrawn with a perspective view including the dome and the pyramid, so that it resembles *Figure 13-24*.

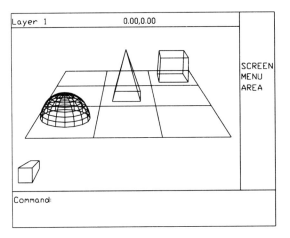

**Figure 13-24**

### Saving 3D views with VIEW

Once you are in perspective, you will find that your drawing capabilities are severely limited. Many commands will not work at all. Perspective is a presentation feature, not an editing or drawing feature. If you wish to do more drawing and editing, you will need to leave the perspective view and go back to the usual parallel projection. However, by using the VIEW command you can save all the view adjustment work you have done so that you can come back to it at any time without going through DVIEW again. When you do, any editing done in the meantime will be included. Let's try it.

> Type or select "view".

AutoCAD prompts:

?/Delete/Restore/Save/Window:

> Type "s" or select "Save".

AutoCAD prompts:

View name:

> Type "p" for "perspective".

The current perspective view, including the camera angle, view point, and distance, is now saved and can be restored at any time. We will restore it later in this exercise.

## Clipping planes

Next we will enter the DVIEW command once again to learn one last feature. By using a "clipping" plane, we will temporarily remove part of the drawing to create a cutaway effect. We will be working with the dome, so we will select it as part of our preview image instead of the box.

> Type or select "dview". Again, do not use the pull down because of the limited range of options.
> At the "Select objects:" prompt, pick the dome and the mesh.
> Type "cl" or select "clip".
    This option allows you to create cutaway effects by temporarily removing everything in front of or behind a specified plane.
    AutoCAD prompts:

Back/Front/<Off>:

A "back" plane will remove everything behind it; a "front" plane will remove everything in front of it. We will use a front clipping plane to open up the dome and show its internal structure.
> Type "f" or select "front".
    AutoCAD places a horizontal slider bar at the top of the screen.
> Move the cursor all the way to the right.
    This places the clipping plane completely behind the mesh and box, so that the entire image is clipped.
> Move the cursor slowly to the left.
    Watch the image gradually appear as the clipping plane covers up less and less. You will observe significant change with even a small movement, so you may want to try using the arrow keys. Keep moving to the left until the whole image is visible.
> Now move the cursor back to the right until you have an open dome similar to the one in *Figure 13-25*.
> Press enter to exit the DVIEW command.
    Your screen will be redrawn with the pyramid and the box included.

NOTE: To avoid confusion, AutoCAD switches to the WCS whenever you enter DVIEW. DVIEW proceeds with the WCS in effect and then returns you to your UCS when you exit the command. We have been working in the WCS in this chapter anyway, so this has not been noticeable.

Clipped images, like perspective views, can be saved using the VIEW command. Before going on, save the current clipped view.

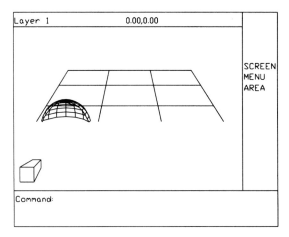

**Figure 13-25**

> Type or select "view".
> Type "s" or select "Save".
> Type "c" for "clipped view".

Now restore the perspective view to see that it is still available.

> Type or select "view".
> Type "r" or select "restore".
> Type "p" for the perspective view previously saved.

Finally, repeat the process once more to restore the clipped view, which you will need for the next task.

### TASK 6: HIDEing unseen lines

*Procedure.*

1. Create the view you want, using VPOINT, DVIEW, or VIEW.
2. Type or select HIDE.
3. Wait...

*Discussion.* The HIDE command is easy to execute. However, it can take a very long time in large drawings, and it may take a lot of work to create a drawing that hides the way you want it to. This is a primary objective of surface modeling. When you've got everything right, HIDE will temporarily remove all lines and objects that would in fact be obstructed in the current view, resulting in a more realistic representation of the object in space.

> To carry out this simple exercise, you should have the clipped view of the dome, pyramid, box, and mesh on your screen.
> Type or select "hide".
    AutoCAD gives you a message that says:

Regenerating drawing.
Removing hidden lines: 25

As you watch, the number of hidden lines being removed changes. In this case it will continue increasing by twenty-fives until you get up to about 275. This is a simple drawing, yet notice how long the process takes. With 3D polygon meshes in particular, you can easily create drawings that will take hours to hide.

When AutoCAD has done all the hidden line removal, it will draw the new image. This also proceeds slowly. When the HIDE process is complete, your screen should resemble *Figure 13-26*. Notice that clipping plane boundary lines at the front of the image have been added by the HIDE command.

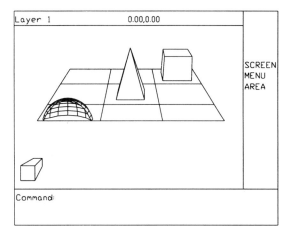

**Figure 13-26**

We will have a lot more to say about the HIDE command in the next chapter, when we do surface modeling. For now, we will finish with these few important points about hidden line removal:

1. Hidden line removal can be done at the time of a PLOT or PRPLOT. However, due to the time involved and the difficulty of getting a hidden view just right, it is usually better to experiment on the screen first, then plot when you know you will get the image you want.

2. Whenever the screen is regenerated, hidden lines are returned to the screen.

3. The image created through hidden line removal is <u>not</u> retained in BLOCKing, WBLOCKing, or saving VIEWs. On the other hand, clipping, perspective, and hidden line removal can all be captured in slides (the MSLIDE and VSLIDE commands, Chapter 9). Since these images are designed for presentation, saving them as slides is a viable option.

4. There is a "Hide" option within the DVIEW command that allows you to hide your preview image. This can help in visualizing the 3D object and as a preview of the HIDE command itself. Hidden lines are only removed temporarily. They will return as soon as you exit DVIEW.

5. In order to understand and anticipate how an object will hide, it is important to know how the HIDE command interprets various entities. This will be a major topic of Chapter 14.

Before going on, it is extremely important that you turn off perspective and clipping. With perspective on, you will be unable to execute most drawing functions. Try zooming, for example, and you will get a standard message:

This command may not be invoked in a perspective view

Clipping planes are somewhat less inhibiting, but remain in effect even as you change views. This can yield some pretty strange results.

Both effects may be turned off by reentering the DVIEW command. The "Off" option of the first subprompt will turn perspective off, while "CLip" has its own "Off" suboption. In either case, you can speed up the process by pressing enter at the "Select objects:" prompt and ignoring AutoCAD's default preview image.

In many cases, however, there are quicker methods. For example, you will usually leave a perspective view in order to work in another 3D view or a plan view. You can go directly into these by entering the VPOINT or PLAN commands and specifying a new view.

This will turn perspective off but not clipping planes. When you switch views using VPOINT or PLAN, clipping planes will remain in effect. However, if you have saved any views, you can restore them using the VIEW command. This will remove clipping planes. The brief exercise that follows will demonstrate these procedures.

> You should have the clipped and hidden image on your screen, as shown in *Figure 13-26.*
> Type or select "vpoint" or pick "Viewpoint 3D..." from the "Display" pull down menu.
> Create our standard "front, right, top" view.

Perspective will be turned off, but notice how the clipping plane is still in effect, as shown in *Figure 13-27.*

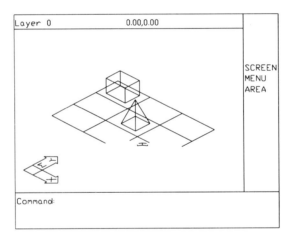

**Figure 13-27**

> Type or select "view" and restore the "p" view.

You will now have the perspective view with no clipping planes, as shown previously in *Figure 13-24.*
> Use VPOINT once more to create a "front, right, top" view.

There will no longer be a clipping plane or perspective view.

In summary, you can use VIEW or DVIEW to remove clipping planes and perspective, VPOINT or PLAN to remove perspective only.

## TASKS 7, 8, 9, and 10

You are currently at an intermediate stage between wire frame modeling and surface modeling. The commands introduced in this chapter create surface entities, but we have not yet dealt with some of the complexities of applying surfaces to wire frames already drawn. The drawings that follow will include many surfaces, but they are not intended as complete surface models. There is a rather wide range of difficulty. *Drawing 13-1* is a simple exercise in recognizing and creating surfaces of revolution. *Drawings 13-2* and *13-3* are more difficult and make use of 3D objects and polygon meshes. *Drawing 13-4* is a very challenging 3D drawing requiring careful use of the UCS command and several polygon mesh commands.

## DRAWING 13-1: REVSURF DESIGNS

The REVSURF command is fascinating and powerful. As you get familiar with it, you may find yourself identifying objects in the world that can be conceived as surfaces of revolution. To encourage this process, we have provided this page of 12 REVSURF objects and designs.

   To complete the exercise, you will need only the PLINE and REVSURF commands. In the first six designs we have shown the path curves and axes of rotation used to create the design. In the other six you will be on your own.

   Exact shapes and dimensions are not important in this exercise. Imagination is. When you have completed our designs, we encourage you to invent a number of your own.

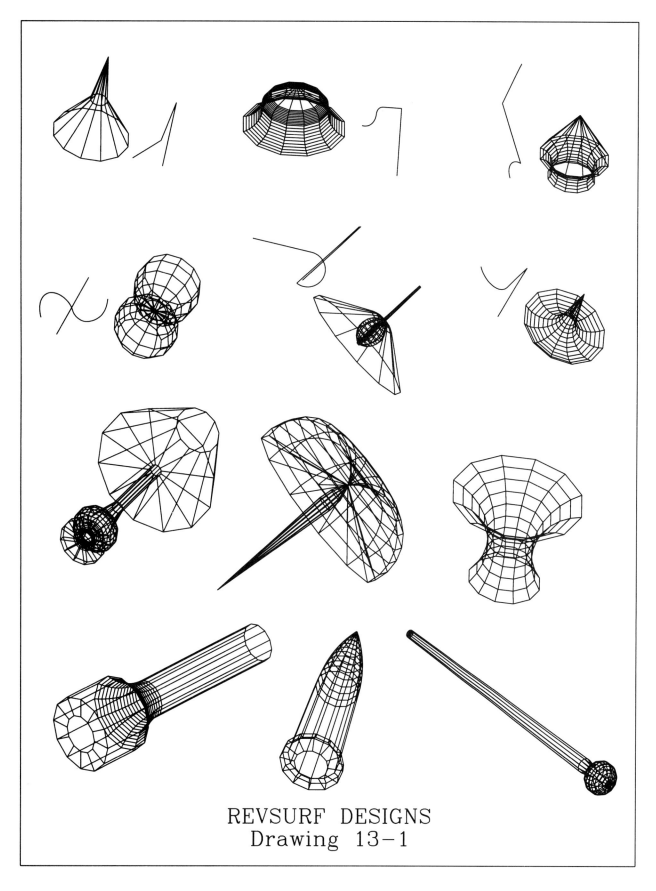

REVSURF DESIGNS
Drawing 13−1

## DRAWING 13-2: TIRE AND RIM

This drawing makes use of two of the "3D objects". The tire can be drawn as a torus, and the rim is made up of two cones with a circular plate between. You may find it useful to work with a three view port configuration as described following.

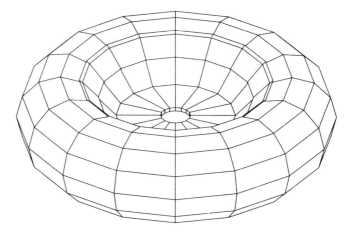

### DRAWING SUGGESTIONS

> You can make good use of three view ports in this drawing by putting a plan view and a ground-level front view in two smaller view ports on the left of the screen and the 3D view in a larger view port on the right. These correspond to the three views shown here.

> You will have to move around the object with the UCS command to draw all the pieces. You can use the "View" option of the UCS command to align a UCS with any view port once you have defined a view within that view port. This essentially turns that view into a plan view in the new UCS, which is often what you want.

> There are some tricks to drawing the circular plate with the hole in the middle so that it hides the way we have shown it in the reference drawing. We will be dealing with this type of problem at length in Chapter 14. For now, draw both the larger and smaller circles as donuts with inner and outer diameters equal (2.00 for the small donut, 8.00 for the large donut). If you use circles, your drawing will not hide properly.

> The vertical lines between the two smaller donuts that form the inside of the hole in the plate, as well as the radial lines around the center hole, are ruled surfaces (RULESURF command). In order to select the smaller donuts as path curves for both surfaces, you will have to put whichever surface you draw first on a separate layer and turn it off temporarily while you draw the other ruled surface. This is a common problem. 3D meshes obstruct object selection and therefore create a demand for careful layering.

> Remember to set Surftab1 to control the number of faces in your ruled surfaces. If you want them to line up with the faces in the cones and torus, set Surftab1 and the number of longitudinal segments in the 3D objects to the same number (16).

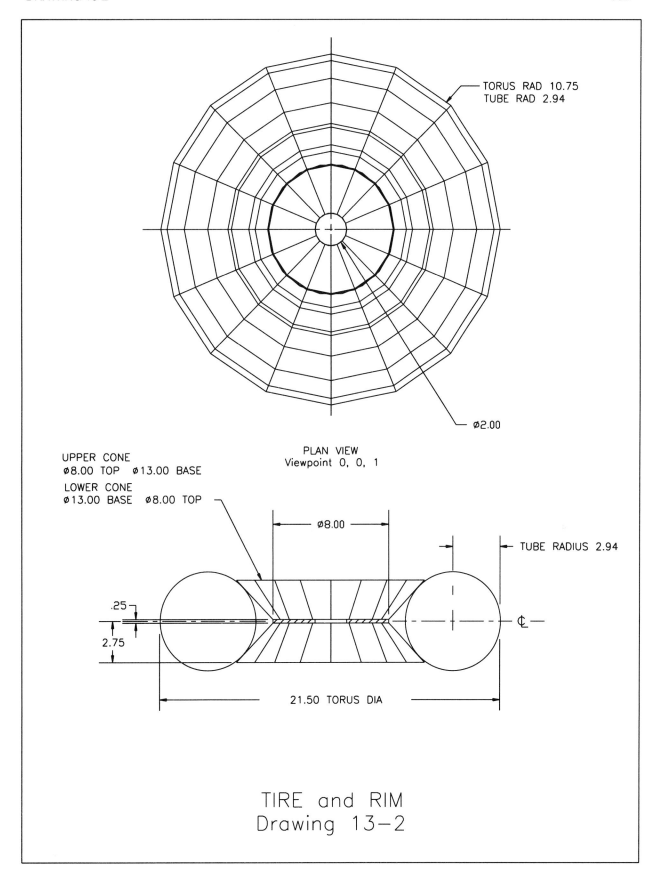

TORUS RAD 10.75
TUBE RAD 2.94

Ø2.00

PLAN VIEW
Viewpoint 0, 0, 1

UPPER CONE
Ø8.00 TOP   Ø13.00 BASE

LOWER CONE
Ø13.00 BASE   Ø8.00 TOP

Ø8.00

TUBE RADIUS 2.94

.25

2.75

Ȼ

21.50 TORUS DIA

TIRE and RIM
Drawing 13-2

## DRAWING 13-3: GLOBE

This drawing uses several of the 3D mesh commands. Some of the 3D construction is a little tricky, but you may be pleasantly surprised. Follow the suggestions and you will find that this one is easier than it looks.

### DRAWING SUGGESTIONS

> Use a three view port configuration with top and front views on the left and a 3D view on the right.

> Begin with the base circles, drawing in the plan (top) view, then MOVE the circles into place along the Z axis.

> MOVE the small inner circle up 12.25 to locate the top of the shaft. Draw the center line from the center of this circle to the top center of the base. Then COPY this line on itself and ROTATE the line and circle 23.5 degrees around the midpoint of the line to position the center of the shaft.

> OFFSET the shaft center line .125. Later, you will TRIM a 4.00 diameter circle to this line. Then using the centerline of the shaft as the axis of rotation for a REVSURF will leave a hole in the middle of the globe for the shaft.

> Draw the 4.00, 4.75, and 5.38 circles and TRIM them to the vertical, 23.5 degree, and 46 degree lines as shown.

> With your UCS parallel to the front view, COPY the 4.75 and 5.38 circles +.25 and −.25 in the Z direction to form the two sides of the globe support. ERASE the original circles.

> TABSURF the shaft.

> RULESURF the base circles. There will be three ruled surfaces to complete the base.

> REVSURF the top of the base, using a single line from a quadrant to the center for a path curve and the vertical centerline for the axis.

> RULESURF the globe support. This will require four ruled surfaces.

> REVSURF the globe.

> Freeze all nonsurface lines before HIDEing.

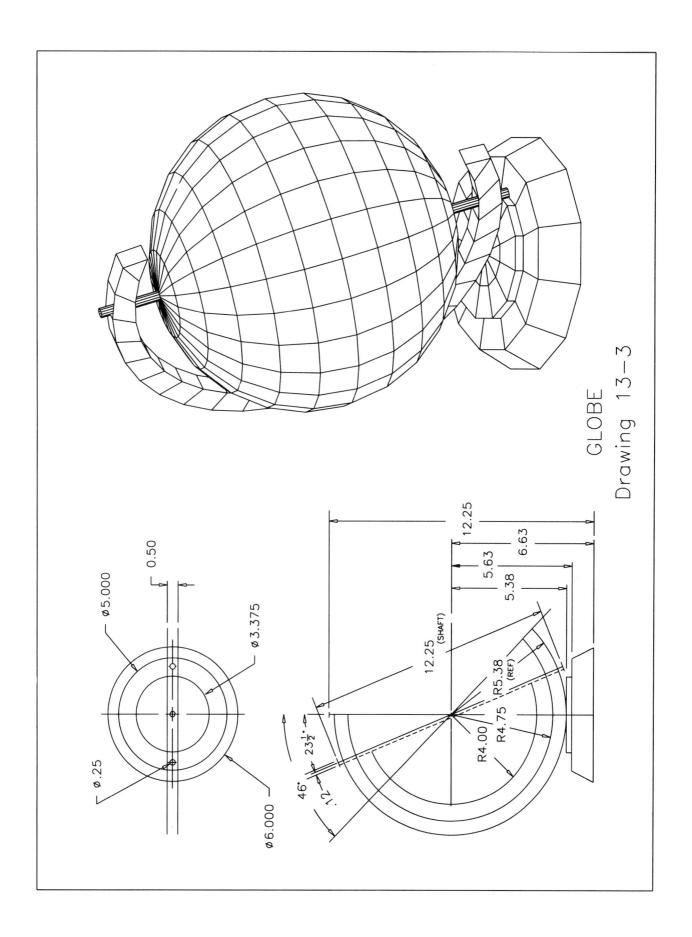

GLOBE
Drawing 13-3

ø5.000

0.50

ø3.375

ø.25

ø6.000

12.25

12.25
(SHAFT)

5.63

6.63

5.38

R5.38
(REF)

R4.00

R4.75

46°

23½°

1.2

## DRAWING 13-4: NOZZLE

This is a tough drawing that will give you a real 3D workout. You will need to define numerous UCSs as you go. Your goal should be to create the two views A and B. Dimensioning is not part of the exercise. Once again, the dimensioned figure is not a complete wire frame, but a guide to show you the abstract relationships necessary to complete the surface model.

### *DRAWING SUGGESTIONS*

> We began in a front, right, top view. This puts the main centerline of the nozzle in the X-Y plane of the WCS, while the circles that show the outlines of the nozzle will be perpendicular to it. When we were done, we rotated the objects slightly to show them more clearly.

> Make ample use of COPY and OFFSET in drawing the circles and centerlines of the nozzle, the hexes and circles of the knob, and the polyline curve path of the nozzle.

> The circle and centerline after the 45 degree angle can be constructed using a COPY and ROTATE of the circle and centerline just in front of the angle. This must be done in a UCS parallel to the WCS.

> The curve in the nozzle is a –45 degree REVSURF around the centerline 1.00 to the right of the turn.

> The two darkened lines show the path curves used with REVSURF to draw the nozzle and the knob. Construct lines first and then go over them with PLINE or 3DPOLY. 3DPOLY is similar to PLINE, but it uses 3D points instead of 2D points and has no option to draw arcs. In general, 3D polylines are more flexible and can be drawn at times when the current UCS would not allow the construction of a 2D polyline.

> The centerline through the knob (along the arrow) runs perpendicular to the polyline outline of the nozzle. Use a PERpendicular osnap to construct the centerline, and then define UCSs in relation to the centerline to construct the knob.

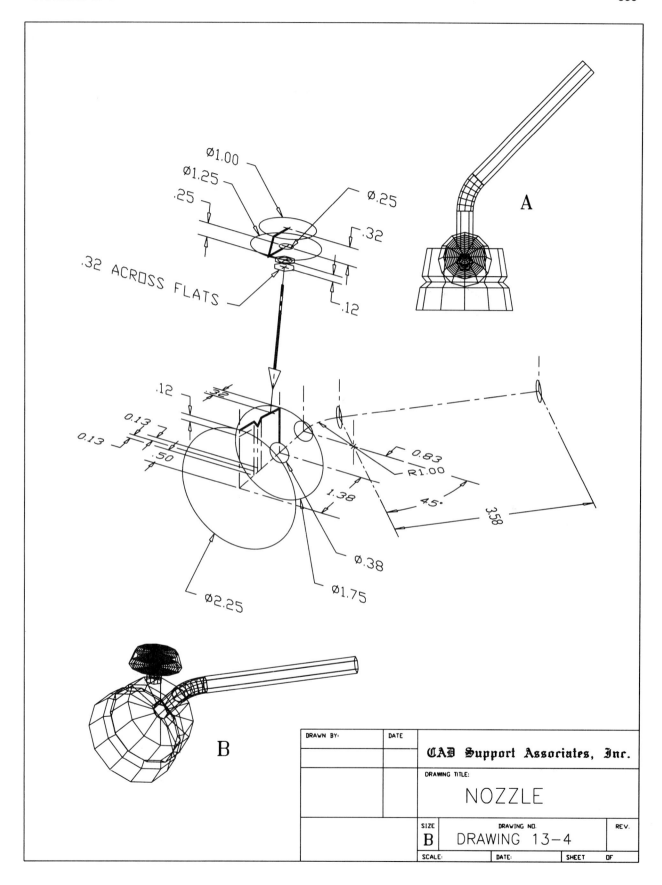

Ø1.00
Ø1.25
.25
Ø.25
.32
.32 ACROSS FLATS
.12

A

.12
0.13
0.13
.50
0.83
R1.00
1.38
45°
3.58
Ø.38
Ø1.75
Ø2.25

B

| DRAWN BY: | DATE | **CAD Support Associates, Inc.** | | |
|---|---|---|---|---|
| | | DRAWING TITLE: NOZZLE | | |
| | | SIZE **B** | DRAWING NO. DRAWING 13-4 | REV. |
| | | SCALE: | DATE: | SHEET OF |

# chapter 14

## COMMANDS

| 3D | DISPLAY | Variables |
|----|---------|-----------|
| 3DFACE | HIDE | SPLFRAME |
|  |  | SURFTYPE |
|  | EDIT | SPLINETYPE |
|  | CHPROP |  |
|  | PEDIT |  |

## OVERVIEW

In this chapter we will explore Release 10 surface modeling techniques. We will introduce you to a number of typical problems encountered in constructing surface models and show you some solutions. You will create surfaces using 3D mesh commands from the previous chapter, along with the 3DFACE command. PEDIT will be used to edit polygon meshes so that they fit neatly into the geometry of a wire frame model. Along the way, we will be dealing with the HIDE command frequently in order to reach an understanding of how AutoCAD interprets surfaces in 3D. Also included are optional exercises on curve and surface approximation using the PEDIT command.

## TASKS

1. Create an open cylinder using PLINE and CHPROP.
2. Use PLINE and RULESURF to create a flat surface surrounding an opening.
3. Edit polygon mesh vertices with PEDIT.
4. Use 3DFACE to create surfaces with straight edges.
5. Manipulate layers to control the HIDE command.
6. Draw 3D faces with invisible edges.
7. Create spline curves using PEDIT.
8. Create approximated surfaces using PEDIT.
9. Do Drawing 14-1 ("Bushing Mount").
10. Do Drawing 14-2 ("Link Mount").
11. Do Drawing 14-3 ("3D Assembly").
12. Do Drawing 14-4 ("Picnic Table").

### TASK 1: Creating extruded entities with CHPROP

*Procedure.*

1. Draw entities in one plane.
2. Type or select "CHPROP".
3. Select objects.
4. Press enter to end object selection.
5. Type "t" or select "thickness".
6. Type a thickness value.

*Discussion.*     The results obtained with 3D meshes and 3D objects (as you worked with in Chapter 13) can be fascinating and impressive. But what happens when you need a surface which does not conform to the geometry of these commands? Frequently you will find yourself spending hours trying to solve what appear to be simple problems. In this chapter we will try to anticipate some of the problems and begin to develop your surface modeling technique.

Fitting surfaces is time-consuming. It takes experimentation combined with an understanding of how AutoCAD interprets objects, particularly within the HIDE command. Such common drafting problems as representing a circular hole cut through a metal plate (see *Figure 14-1*) can be surprisingly tricky. In this chapter we will demonstrate one solution to this particular problem. Much of what you learn in the process can be generalized to other surface modeling problems.

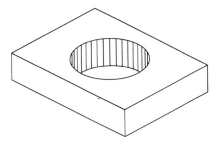

**Figure 14-1**

The operational definition of a surface in Release 10 is an object that is recognized by the HIDE command as opaque, so that it hides objects behind it. Surfaces may be created in several ways. To begin with, certain objects, notably circles, are interpreted by the HIDE command as opaque. In effect they generate a surface within their boundaries. Then there are the 3D faces and entities, such as 3D meshes and 3D objects, that are collections of 3D faces. Finally, other objects which behave like surfaces can be created through the process of "extrusion," or adding "thickness" to a 2D entity. All of these methods will come into play in the surface modeling problem presented in this chapter.

We will be creating an object like the one in *Figure 14-1*, a fully surfaced plate with a hole cut through the middle. Ultimately, you will probably follow a procedure of drawing a wire frame model first and then adding surfaces to it. Here, for simplicity of presentation, we will construct surfaces as we go.

We will begin by creating two extruded objects, a common circle and a polyline circle. These will demonstrate some important issues about surface modeling.

> Begin a new drawing called "14-1" or "A:14-1".

> Use the VPORTS command or "Set Viewports" from the "Display" pull down menu to create a two-view configuration, as shown in *Figure 14-2*. This is the same configuration used in the last chapter, with a plan view in the left view port and a "front, right, top" in the right view port.

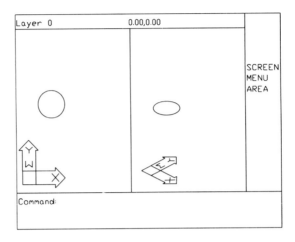

**Figure 14-2**

> Draw a 2.00 radius circle at the left side of your view port as shown in the figure.

We will "extrude" the circle so that it becomes a cylinder in the 3D view. An extruded object is a simple 2D object that has been drawn out perpendicular to the X-Y plane to give it thickness in the Z dimension. Extruded points become lines, lines become planes, circles become cylinders, etc.

Objects are extruded by giving them "thickness." To do this we will use the CHPROP ("change properties") command. CHPROP is a Release 10 variation of the CHANGE command. It provides only the property change options, thereby eliminating the step of asking for a change point.

> Type or select "chprop", or select "Modify" and then "Properties" from the pull down.

AutoCAD prompts for object selection in the familiar manner.

> Pick the circle in either view.

AutoCAD prompts:

Change what property (Color/LAyer/LType/Thickness) ?

Notice the options. The "LAyer" option is probably the most frequently used. It allows you to change the layer of all selected objects. We will use the "Thickness" option now and "LAyer" in Task 4.

> Type "t" or select "Thickness".

AutoCAD prompts:

New thickness <0.00>:

All objects initially have 0 thickness. You can set thickness before drawing an entity by using the ELEV command. However, this command is due to be eliminated in the next major AutoCAD release, so we do not recommend developing the habit of using it. If you are interested in ELEV, see the *AutoCAD Reference Manual*, Section 7.11.

> Type ".75" to extrude the circle 0.75 above the X-Y plane.
Your screen will be redrawn to resemble *Figure 14-3*.

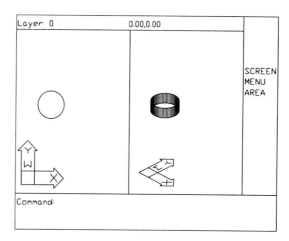

**Figure 14-3**

Next, we will HIDE the cylinder to see what surfaces are present.

> Be sure that the right view port, the 3D view, is active before proceeding. HIDE only works in one view port at a time.
> Type or select "hide".

In a moment your screen will resemble *Figure 14-4*.

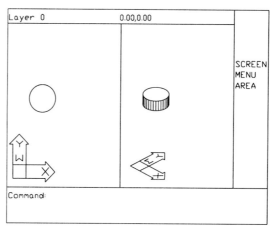

**Figure 14-4**

You might have expected the circle to be interpreted as an open hole, but the image with hidden lines removed makes it clear that this is not so. There is a top on the cylinder. HIDE sees a circle as opaque. An extruded circle has a top and a bottom. How, then, can we solve the common problem of drawing a cylindrical opening, as in a hole, a slot, or a tube? Two solutions which come to mind are to draw the circle as two semicircular arcs, or to draw it as a donut with equal inner and outer diameters. Either of these will work to create an open cylinder when extruded. However, they will bring up other problems when we try to draw the surface of a rectangular plate around them. A more complete solution is to draw a polyline circle, a circle formed of two zero width semicircular arcs drawn in the PLINE command.

NOTE: Autodesk provides an AutoLISP routine called "SLOT" (on the AutoCAD Release 10 bonus disk) which addresses this same problem. However, not everyone will have it loaded, and those who use it will still have to solve all of the problems we explore here.

We will draw the polyline circle to the right of the previous circle. Be sure to draw the figure just as it is shown. The way in which you construct the circle will be very important later on.

> Make the plan view active, and observe *Figure 14-5*.

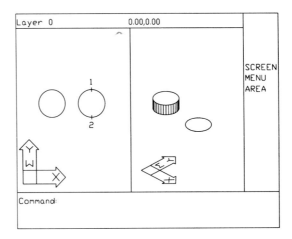

**Figure 14-5**

> Enter the PLINE command and pick a first point at the top quadrant of the circle, as shown in the figure.
AutoCAD will respond:

> Current line-width is 0.00
> Arc/Close/Halfwidth/Length/Undo/Width/<Endpoint of line>:

> Type "a" or select "arc".
AutoCAD will show an arc and a chord. The prompt asks for an end point, or a method of arc specification:

Angle/Center/Close/Direction/Halfwidth/Line/Radius/Second pt/Undo/Width/<Endpoint of arc>:

> Pick a point directly below the first point, at the opposite quadrant, point 2 in the figure.
In effect you are using the chord to show a 2.00 diameter of the circle from top to bottom.

NOTE: If you have been doing any work in this drawing with the PLINE command, you may find that your arc is not drawn in the same direction as ours. This is because PLINE remembers the direction of your last polyline and draws arcs tangent to it. You can use the "Direction" option and show a line to the left (180 degrees) to fix this.

> Now, pick point 1 again to complete the pline circle.
The polyline circle is complete. Next we will give it a thickness.

> Type or select "chprop", or select "Modify" and then "Properties" from the pull down.

AutoCAD prompts for object selection.

> Pick the polyline circle.

Notice that it is a single entity. This will be important when we draw the flat surface around it in Task 2.

AutoCAD prompts for a new thickness.

> Type "1".

The polyline circle will be extruded, as shown in *Figure 14-6*.

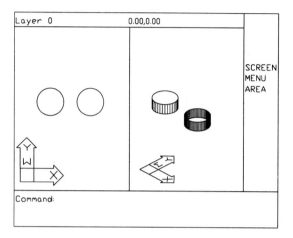

**Figure 14-6**

Now, let's hide the cylinders again.

> Make the right view port active.
> Type or select "hide".

In a moment your right view port will be redrawn as in *Figure 14-7*. The extruded polyline circle has no top and no bottom. The difference between the two cylinders is clearly significant.

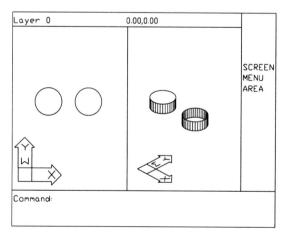

**Figure 14-7**

NOTE: It may have occurred to you that the open cylinder could be drawn using RULESURF or TABSURF with polyline circles instead of an extrusion. This is certainly true, and it has the advantage of allowing you to control the number of faces used to represent the surface. With an extrusion, we do not have this control. An example of how this capacity can be used will be shown later (see *Figure 14-17*, version B).

In the next task we will be continuing to work with the open polyline cylinder. Before going on, erase the closed cylinder on the left, and move the open cylinder to the middle of your view port, as in *Figure 14-8*.

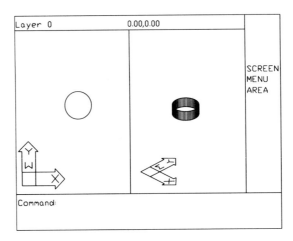

**Figure 14-8**

## TASK 2: Creating a surface around a hole

*Procedure.*

1. Draw a polyline circle.
2. Draw a polyline entity starting at a corresponding point and moving in the same direction.
3. Use RULESURF to create a mesh between the circle and the outer figure.
4. Use PEDIT to edit mesh corners.

*Discussion.*   In this task we will continue the construction of a surface model plate with a hole in the center. The current problem is how to draw a surface between a circle and a rectangle. As we will see in Task 3, a 3D face is the usual way to draw a rectangular surface. However, there is no way to cut a hole in the middle of a 3D face. Instead, we need to create the circle and the rectangle as curve paths that can be selected in the RULESURF command. A polyline rectangle and circle will work well as long as we follow the same order in defining the two, and if we use PEDIT to adjust the corners of the ruled surface between them, as we will do in Task 4.

> To begin this task you should have the extruded polyline circle on your screen, as shown in *Figure 14-8*.

In drawing the polyline rectangle, be sure to follow the order and instructions given here. We will be drawing a 3.00 by 4.00 polyline rectangle centered on the cylinder. Exact size is not critical, but the way in which points are entered is.

> Enter the PLINE command.
> For the first point, pick a point directly above the first point you used in defining your circle, as shown in *Figure 14-9*. (For a 3.00 width rectangle, start 1.50 up from the center of the cylinder.)

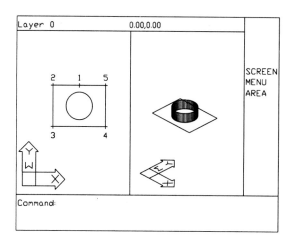

**Figure 14-9**

> Continue entering points moving around the rectangle *in the same direction in which you defined your circle.*

If you have not been using the PLINE command in this drawing before beginning these tasks, the direction will be counterclockwise, as shown.

It is critical that the order of definition of the polyline circle and the polyline rectangle match. RULESURF will draw lines around the two curves according to how they were originally defined. If the two are not defined in the same direction and starting from corresponding points, you can get some bizarre and undesirable results, as illustrated in *Figure 14-10*. We call these things "3D polygon messes." (The main reason we did not use an extruded donut in Task 1, by the way, is that it is more difficult to predict how AutoCAD will choose a starting point for drawing the mesh around a donut.)

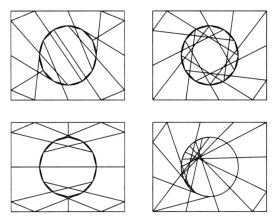

**Figure 14-10**

> When you get to the last line segment, pick point 1 again.

Here's another bit of fussiness. If you completed the pline circle by using "CLose" rather than pointing, you must "Close" the rectangle as well. Otherwise RULESURF will see one as closed and the other as open and give you a message that says:

Cannot mix closed and open paths

It will work either way as long as you are consistent. If you "closed" the polyline circle, then you must "close" the rectangle. If you pick the last point of the circle, then pick the last point of the rectangle as well.

With a polyline circle and a polyline rectangle drawn in a corresponding manner, you are now ready to draw a well-organized ruled surface.

> Using the 3D construction pull down menu or the SETVAR command, set Surftab1 to 12.
> Type or select "rulesurf", or pick "Ruled Surface" from the 3D construction pull down.
> Pick the polyline circle as the first curve path.

AutoCAD will highlight the entire cylinder. Fortunately, however, it will use the base of the cylinder for the ruled surface, because it lies in the current X-Y plane.

> Pick the polyline rectangle as the second curve path.

Your screen should be redrawn to resemble *Figure 14-11*. You will notice that the corners are cut off by the approximation of the RULESURF command. In the next task we will fix these using PEDIT.

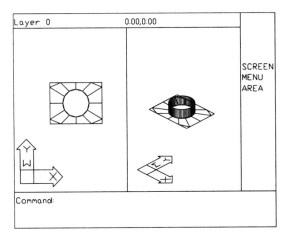

**Figure 14-11**

## TASK 3: Editing 3D polygon meshes with PEDIT

*Procedure.*

1.  Enter the PEDIT command.
2.  Point to a 3D polygon mesh.
3.  Type "e" or select "Ed Vrtx".
4.  Move the "x" to the vertex you want to edit.
5.  Type "m" or select "move".
6.  Specify a new location.
7.  Go on to edit another vertex or exit the command.

*Discussion.* There are many instances in which you will be able to create a surface that approximates the shape you want, but that misses at some critical points. The ruled surface in *Figure 14-11* is a typical example. The solution is to move a few vertices using the PEDIT command.

> Type or select "pedit", or select "Edit Polylines" from the pull down menu under "Modify".

AutoCAD will prompt:

Select polyline:

Although they are not polylines, polygon meshes can be edited with the PEDIT command. Selecting a polygon mesh will lead to a different subprompt from the one you see when you select a polyline.

> Point to the ruled surface created in the last task, or type "l" for last.

AutoCAD does not highlight the mesh, but you know that it has recognized your selection when you see the following prompt:

Edit vertex/Smooth surface/Desmooth/Mclose/Nopen/Undo/eXit<X>:

We will not explore all of these options here. See the *AutoCAD Reference Manual*, Section 5.4.1.3 for further information.

> Type "e" or select "Ed Vrtx" (AutoCAD's screen menu abbreviation of "Edit Vertex").

As soon as this option is selected, AutoCAD will place a light-colored "X" on the vertex that was drawn first. What we will be doing is moving the X to one of the vertices nearest a corner and then moving the vertex itself so that it exactly fits in the corner.

The prompt names the vertex we are on with an ordered pair and gives us six different ways to move the X:

Vertex (0,0).
Next/Previous/Left/Right/Up/Down/Move/REgen/eXit <N>:

There is logic to the directions and the numbering system. However, it is not the logic of the English language. Left may very well mean right and up may appear to be down. You could learn AutoCAD's numbering system and then stop to figure out which direction is which, but it is much quicker to experiment. On a small surface like this one, you can hold down the enter key to specify a series of "Next" responses and watch the "X" skate along the vertices until it reaches one you want to edit. If you need to change directions, try one of the directional options. For example, try typing "u" to move up. If that doesn't get you going in the direction you want, try "d" instead.

> Move the X to one of the corners. Experiment as needed. Stop when you reach one of the four vertices that is nearest a corner.

> Type "m" or select "Move".

AutoCAD puts the cross hairs on the screen and prompts as follows:

Enter new location:

> Carefully point to the corner of the rectangle. Use a snap point or an object snap to make sure that you pick it precisely.

AutoCAD will move the vertex as specified and return the "Edit vertex" prompt:

Vertex (0,0).
Next/Previous/Left/Right/Up/Down/Move/REgen/eXit <N>:

You should now be able to continue around the rectangle by pressing enter repeatedly.

> Move the X to each of the three vertices nearest the other corners and move these in the same manner.

When you are done, your screen should resemble *Figure 14-12.*

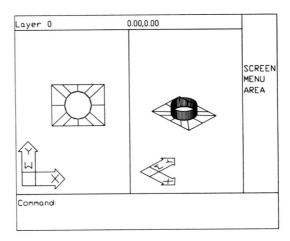

**Figure 14-12**

> Cancel the PEDIT command, or press enter twice to exit.

Next, we need to copy the edited polygon mesh to the upper surface of the plate.

> Enter the COPY command.
> Select the ruled surface surrounding the hole.
> Use typed coordinates or an .XY filter to indicate a displacement of 0.75 in the Z direction.

Now let's use the HIDE command again to see what we have accomplished so far.

> Make sure the right view port is active, then type or select "hide" and wait.

The result should resemble *Figure 14-13.* This is an image of two plates with an open cylinder connecting them. We need to put faces on the vertical edges of the plate to create the effect of a single solid plate. In the next task we will use the 3DFACE command to draw the four vertical surfaces.

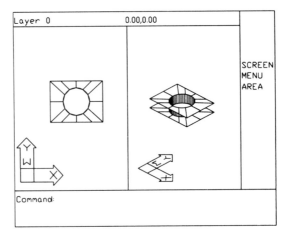

**Figure 14-13**

### TASK 4: Creating surfaces with 3DFACE

*Procedure.*

1. Type or select "3DFACE".
2. Pick three or four points going around the face.
3. Continue defining edges, or press enter to exit the command.

*Discussion.* 3DFACE creates flat triangular and quadrilateral surfaces. Four rectangular 3D faces will work effectively for the sides of the plate. Notice, however, that we could not fit the top and bottom with 3D faces because of the circular openings in the middle.

3D faces are built by entering points in groups of three or four to define the outlines of triangles or quadrilaterals, similar to objects formed by the SOLID command. The surface of a 3D face is invisible, but it is recognized by the HIDE command. Edges can be visible or invisible as desired. To define an invisible edge, type "i" before entering the first point of the edge. You can even define "phantom" 3D faces in which no edges are visible. For a complete discussion of invisible edges in 3D faces, see Task 7 following.

In this task, all edges will be visible. We need only point to the four corners of a side where we want to add a 3D face. But first, we will move upper and lower 3D meshes to another layer so they do not interfere with object snap.

> NOTE: Layering is critical in surface modeling. Surfaces quickly complicate a drawing so that object selection and object snap become difficult or impossible. Also, you may want to be able to turn layers off or freeze them to achieve the results you want from the HIDE command, as discussed in Task 5 following. You may want a number of layers specifically defined for faces and surfaces. For now, we will use the "hatch" layer. If you are using the prototype we created in Chapter 4, this layer is already defined in your drawing.

> Type or select "chprop", or select "Modify" and then "Properties" from the pull down.

AutoCAD prompts for object selection.

> In the right view port, point to both the upper and lower ruled surfaces.
> Press enter to end object selection.

AutoCAD prompts:

Change what property (Color/LAyer/LType/Thickness) ?

> Type "la" or select "layer".

AutoCAD asks for a layer name:

New layer <0>:

> Type "hatch", or the name of a layer defined in your drawing, other than the current layer.
> Press enter again to exit the command.

If you are using our layers, your polygon meshes will now be blue, the color of the "hatch" layer.

> Now turn off the hatch layer.

If you want to use the pull down, select "Settings" and "Modify layer". Picking the "On" box next to "hatch" will cause the check to disappear, meaning that layer "hatch" is off.

If you don't wish to use the pull down, follow this procedure:

1. Type or select "layer".
2. Type or select "off".
3. Type "hatch".
4. Press enter to exit the command.

The upper and lower ruled surfaces should now be gone from your screen. With these surfaces out of the way, we are ready to draw 3D faces.

> Execute a REGEN in order to return hidden lines to the right view port.

This will be necessary so that the back corners are visible.

> First, turn on a running end point osnap.

The procedure is:

1. Type or select "osnap".
2. Type "end" or select "ENDpoint".

> Type or select "3dface".

Note that there is no 3DFACE command on the pull down menu. However, there is a 3DFACE submenu in the screen menu system, which we will use extensively in Task 7. To reach it, select "3D" from the AutoCAD root menu, then "3DFACE" from the 3D submenu.

AutoCAD will prompt:

First point:

> Be sure that the right view port is active before going on.
> Using the running end point osnap, pick a corner of the front face of the plate, as shown in *Figure 14-14*.

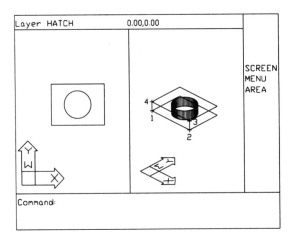

**Figure 14-14**

AutoCAD prompts:

Second point:

> Pick a second point, moving around the face, as shown.

It is important to pick points in order around the face, otherwise you will get a bow tie or hourglass effect. Be aware that the correct order for 3D faces is different from the SOLID command. Otherwise the two command sequences are similar.

AutoCAD prompts:

Third point:

> Pick a third point, continuing around the face.
AutoCAD prompts:

Fourth point:

NOTE: If you pressed enter now, AutoCAD would draw the outline of a triangular face, using the three points already given.

> Pick the fourth point of the face.

AutoCAD draws the fourth edge of the face automatically when four points have been given.

AutoCAD will continue to prompt for third and fourth points so that you could draw a series of surfaces to cover an area with more than four sides. Keep in mind, however, that drawing faces in series is only a convenience. When you are done, you will have a collection of individual three- and four-sided faces.
> Press enter to exit the 3DFACE command.

There is now a surface on the front of the plate. We will draw the other three faces in the same manner and then HIDE the object to show the effect of the new surfaces.

> Press enter to repeat the 3DFACE command.
> Pick the four corners of the right front side of the plate to create a second 3D face.
> Press enter to exit the 3DFACE command.
> Draw 3D faces on the other two vertical sides of the plate in the same manner.
When you are done, your screen should resemble *Figure 14-15.*

## TASK 5: Using layers to control the HIDE command

*Discussion.* You have now drawn a complete surface model of a plate with a hole in the middle. Currently it looks just like a wire frame model you might have drawn in Chapter 12, but when you execute HIDE the difference will be clear.

> Be sure the right window is active, and execute the HIDE command.
The results should look like *Figure 14-16.*

*Notice that the 3D meshes have been recognized by the HIDE command, even though they are on a layer which is turned off.* This is important. If you want layers to

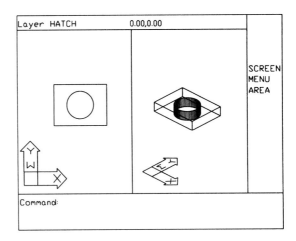

**Figure 14-15**

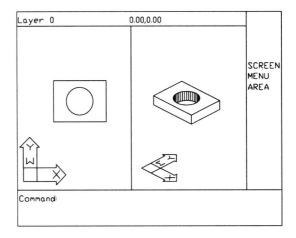

**Figure 14-16**

be ignored by the HIDE command, "freeze" them. Frozen layers remain in the drawing database but are ignored by all commands, including HIDE and PLOT. It is just as if the objects on the frozen layer were gone, but we can call them back at any time by "thawing" the layer. Layers that are "off", on the other hand, are fully present in the process of hidden line removal. Objects on these layers will hide objects behind them, even though they are not currently visible on the screen. This can be very useful in creating images like *Figure 14-16*, which hides properly but is not cluttered by the lines of a polygon mesh.

> NOTE: Watch out for the HIDE command. Release 10 3D drawings become complex very quickly, and the result is that removing hidden lines, whether in the HIDE command or in a plot, can take a <u>very</u> long time. The object we are drawing here will hide in less than a minute, but you can easily create drawings that could take hours to hide.

Two other versions of the object we might like to see are shown in *Figure 14-17*. Version A is simply the current object with the "hatch" layer turned on and hidden lines removed. In version B, the sides of the plate and the inner cylinder were drawn with RULESURF instead of 3DFACE and extrusion. Notice how the faces of the top surface line up with those of the sides and the RULESURF cylinder. The key is keeping Surftab1 set to the same number and using the same polyline rectangles to create the side and top surfaces, and the same polyline circles to create the top and the hole. We

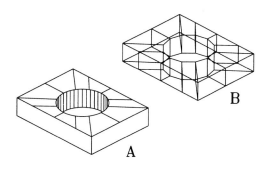

**Figure 14-17**

recommend creating version B as an exercise. It will involve replacing your 3D faces and extruded cylinder with ruled surfaces. You will need to move some vertices of the outer surface to bring them into the corners.

Take time to appreciate what you have done. It may appear simple, but the surface modeling process is full of traps and pitfalls, and there is a great deal of subtlety involved in creating a well-organized model.

NOTE: Remember that in these exercises we have drawn our model with surfaces in mind from the beginning. In actual practice, you may be more likely to draw a complete wire frame and then add surfaces. This should cause you no trouble at this point. It will entail additional layering to separate the wire frame from the surfaces and going over some of the line boundaries with polylines in order to create curve paths for the 3D mesh commands.

### TASK 6: Invisible edges and 3D faces

*Procedure.*

1.  Type or select "3DFACE".
2.  Pick three or four points going around the face.
3.  To draw an invisible edge, type "i" before picking the first point of that edge.
4.  Continue defining edges, or press enter to exit the command.
5.  Use the variable "Splframe" in the SETVAR command or "ShowEdge" and "HideEdge" on the 3DFACE screen menu to turn invisible edges on and off.

*Discussion.*    There are some tricks in the use of the 3DFACE command that we did not have to deal with in the last exercise. We will focus on them here. We will be drawing a number of 3D faces of various shapes using visible and invisible edges. Keep in mind that all 3D faces are combinations of triangles and quadrilaterals, and that invisible edges cannot be selected for editing unless they are made visible by changing the setting of the "Splframe" system variable, as discussed following.

We will begin by drawing 3D faces to cover the surface of an octagon.

> To begin this task, clear your screen of all objects. You can do this by erasing, or if you think you might want to continue experimenting with the surface model plate, BLOCK or WBLOCK it.
> We will not have a need for two views in this exercise, so make the plan view (left view port) current and then switch to a single view port configuration.
> Draw an octagon near the center of your screen, as shown in *Figure 14-18*. This is done with the POLYGON command introduced in Chapter 9. Exact dimensions are not important. For reference, the procedure is as follows:

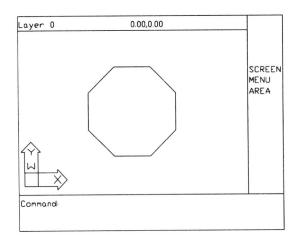

**Figure 14-18**

1. Type or select "polygon".
2. Type "8" for the number of sides.
3. Type "c" or select "circumscribed".
4. Show a radius.

Although this exercise will be done in 2D, you should now be fully aware of the surface characteristics of entities you draw. Objects drawn with the POLYGON command are polylines of 0 width. They are simple linear boundaries or outlines of the type used in constructing wire frame models. They have no surface characteristics and will not form tops or bottoms when extruded.

If we want to cover an octagonal area with a surface, we need to use 3D faces. Since 3D faces are essentially quadrilateral or triangular, we will have to use a series of faces with some common edges. So, the first thing we need to do is visualize the octagon as a set of three- and four-sided objects. A little thought will show that the arrangement of two trapezoids and one rectangle in *Figure 14-19* is as efficient as we can get. However, we will not want the two horizontal lines across the middle showing, so we will make them invisible.

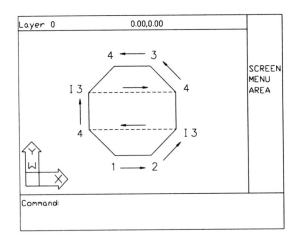

**Figure 14-19**

> Before going on, it will be very helpful to set to another layer so that the octagon and the 3D face edges will appear in different colors.
> Select "3D" and then "3DFACE" from the screen menu.

It is rare that we specifically recommend the screen menu, but in this case it makes a good deal of sense. There is no 3DFACE command on the pull down, and the screen menu contains some useful options that are cumbersome to enter from the keyboard.

AutoCAD will respond with a 3DFACE submenu and the following prompt in the command area:

First point:

It takes practice and careful planning to efficiently draw 3D faces in series, especially when some of the edges will be invisible. Following the order shown in *Figure 14-19* will give you a feel for what works best. Later you can experiment on your own.

> Pick point 1, as shown.

> Pick point 2, as shown.

One of the trickiest aspects of drawing invisible edges is remembering when to indicate that an edge is to be invisible. The rule is simple: Type "i" or select "Invisible" <u>before</u> picking the first point of the invisible edge. This requires looking ahead. Often you will find that you have just picked a point to complete a visible edge without considering that it is also the first point of the next invisible edge.

> Type "i" or select "Invisible".

AutoCAD has no specific response. It has registered your "invisible" but is still waiting for point specification.

> Pick point 3, as shown.

NOTE: This exercise assumes that the variable "Splframe" is initially set to "0" in your drawing. If invisible edges appear on your screen, it probably means that the setting of this variable has been changed. Use SETVAR to change it back to 0 before continuing.

> Pick point 4, as shown.

Notice that no edge is drawn between points 3 and 4, but that there is an edge drawn automatically between points 4 and 1.

AutoCAD prompts again:

Third point:

We have now completed the first of our three quadrilateral shapes. The second will be a rectangle with two invisible edges, the first of which we have already drawn. You can complete the rectangle with new points 3 and 4. Looking ahead, you will also see that the new point 3 is the first point of another invisible edge along the top of the rectangle.

> Type "i" or select "Invisible".

> Pick the second point 3, as shown.

> Pick the second point 4, as shown.

We have now completed two out of the three quadrilaterals. The third is just a mirror image of the first. We have already drawn its one invisible edge. All that is left is to complete its third and fourth points.

> Pick the third point 3, as shown.

> Pick the third point 4, as shown.

Invisible edges are useful, but they can be tricky. Fortunately, AutoCAD provides a way to make invisible edges visible. This is done with the system variable "Splframe". By default it is set to 0, making invisible edges invisible. If you change it to 1, the invisible edges you have drawn will be visible on your screen. If you are using the AutoCAD standard menu (ACAD.mnx), the quickest way to do this is by selecting "ShowEdge" from the 3DFACE screen submenu and then regenerating the drawing. Try it.

> If the 3DFACE screen menu is not showing, select "AutoCAD" at the top of the screen to return to the root menu, then select "3D", then "3DFACE".

NOTE: If your menu system does not have "ShowEdge" and "HideEdge", use the SETVAR command. Type "setvar", then type "splframe", then "1".

> From the 3DFACE submenu, select "ShowEdge".
AutoCAD will show the following message in the command area:

Invisible edges will be SHOWN following the next regeneration.

> Type or select "regen".
Your screen will be regenerated with invisible edges showing.

Now, hide the invisible edges again.

> Select "HideEdge".
> Type or select "regen".

To complete this exercise, try drawing the objects in *Figure 14-20* and then covering them with 3D faces. Covering these shapes with 3D faces will give you a good feel for the tricks involved in drawing faces with invisible edges. When you are done, show the invisible edges and check to see that they are where you intended. Then turn them off again.

NOTE: Sometimes it may be convenient to hide all edges of a 3D face. These "phantom" faces can be very tricky, since they are lost in all editing procedures, including MOVE, COPY, SCALE, ARRAY, and BLOCK. Therefore, remember to *turn invisible edges on before editing objects with phantom faces.*

## TASK 7: Approximated curves (optional)

*Discussion.* Within the PEDIT command there are some very impressive design features which we introduce in this task and the next as optional exercises. These techniques will not be needed in the drawings that follow, but your knowledge of Auto-CAD will be incomplete without them. The techniques of curve and surface approximation are most useful when you have a curved object in mind but have not yet derived exact specifications for it. You may be able to draw an outline and specify some key points, but beyond that, what you conceive may be as vague as a "smooth curve" that follows the basic shape of your outline. AutoCAD provides mathematical algorithms which can translate outlines into curves. This can be accomplished with 2D and 3D polylines and with 3D meshes. In this task we will demonstrate approximation and curving methods with polylines. In Task 8 we will work with surface approximation.

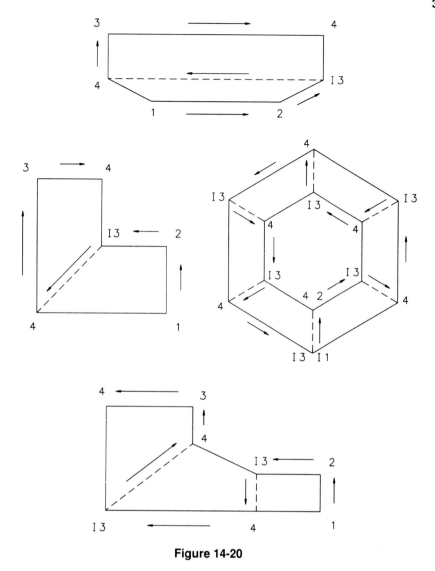

**Figure 14-20**

> To begin this task, clear your screen of all objects left from Task 6.
> Using PLINE, draw an object like the ones in *Figure 14-21* and copy it two times, as shown. Exact sizes and locations are not critical.

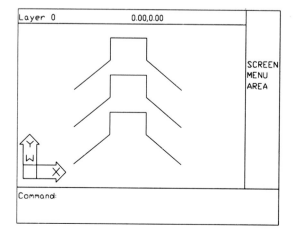

**Figure 14-21**

The first method we will use is called curve fitting. It is handled through the "Fit curve" option of the PEDIT command. Basically, it replaces all straight segments of a polyline with pairs of arc segments. The resulting curve passes through all existing vertices, and new vertices are created to join the arcs.

> Type or select "pedit", or pick "Modify" and "Edit polylines" from the pull down.

AutoCAD prompts for object selection.

> Pick the top object.

AutoCAD prompts for more polylines.

> Press enter to end object selection.

You will see the familiar PEDIT subprompt:

Close/Join/Width/Edit vertex/Fit curve/Spline curve/Decurve/Undo/eXit <X>:

> Type "f" or select "Fit".

Your screen should be redrawn to resemble *Figure 14-22*.

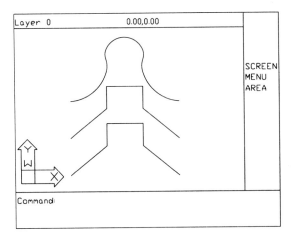

**Figure 14-22**

This is a simple fit. If you were designing an object using this feature, you could refine the curve by adding vertices or by specifying different tangent directions at vertices using the "Edit vertex" option.

Notice that you can return the polyline back to its previous state by using the "Decurve" option.

Now we will curve the second object on your screen using the "Spline" option. Spline curves follow the shape of their straight line "frames," but they do not necessarily pass through all vertices. Instead they pass through the first and last points, and tend toward the ones between according to either quadratic or cubic formulas.

We will alter the second object using the default quadratic style.

> Exit the PEDIT command.
> Press enter to repeat PEDIT.
> Pick the second object.
> Press enter to end object selection.
> Type "s" or select "Spline".

Your screen should resemble *Figure 14-23*.

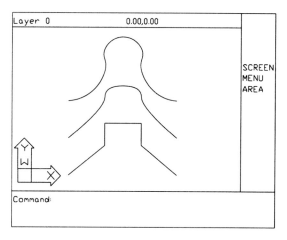

**Figure 14-23**

To create a cubic spline, you will need to change the setting of a variable called "Splinetype". This can be done from the keyboard, using the SETVAR command, or from the screen, using a combination of pull down and screen menu selections. This screen and pull down menu combination is worth exploring, so we recommend it for this exercise.

> Select "Modify" and then "Edit Polylines" from the pull down menu.

This will bring up the select objects prompt.

> Pick the third, uncurved, object.

> Press enter to end object selection.

Notice that when you complete your object selection, AutoCAD calls up a screen menu with the PEDIT options listed. At the bottom there is a selection called "Polyvars". This will allow you to change a number of variables critical to the process of curve and surface approximation.

> Select "Polyvars" from the screen menu.

This selection brings up a new screen and also an icon menu, as shown in *Figure 14-24*.

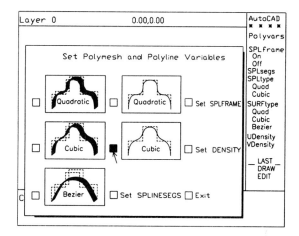

**Figure 14-24**

Take a look at the icon menu. It shows examples of all the approximation methods we will be using in the remainder of this chapter. There are polylines curved in quadratic and cubic forms on the right, and meshes curved in quadratic, cubic, and bezier forms on the left.

> Pick the "Cubic" form from the icon menu, the second spline style, as shown by the arrow in the figure.

The icon menu will disappear. A look at the command area will show you that SETVAR has been called transparently. "Splinetype" has been changed from 5 to 6, and the PEDIT options prompt has been returned. You are now ready to give the selected polyline a cubic spline shape.

> Type "s".

Your screen will be redrawn as shown in *Figure 14-25*.

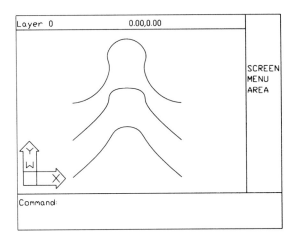

**Figure 14-25**

We will explore one last feature before we move on. AutoCAD saves the "frame" of the polyline (the shape of the polyline before the spline curve approximation is performed). It may be valuable to see both the frame and the curved form at the same time. This can be done by setting the variable "Splframe" to 1. You will recall from Task 6 that Splframe also controls the visibility of invisible 3D faces.

At this point the "Polyvars" screen submenu should still be displayed. If so, this will be the most efficient way to set the variable. If not, you can type in "setvar", "splframe", and then "1".

> Assuming the "Polyvars" submenu is still on your screen, select "SPLframe".
> Select "On".

The variable has been reset, but a regeneration is needed before spline frames will be visible.

> Type or select "regen".

Your screen should resemble *Figure 14-26*. Notice that there is no frame for the "fit" curve. Frames for fit curves are not saved.

> Before going on, turn your frames off by changing Splframe back to 0. Select "Splframe" and then "Off" from the "Polyvars" screen menu. This will be very important for the next exercise.

NOTE: The degree of accuracy of curve approximation can be varied by changing the setting of the variable "Splinesegs". This variable controls the number of segments a polyline will be considered to have in the calculations of the spline formulae.

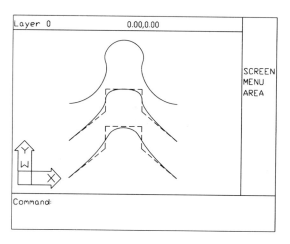

**Figure 14-26**

## TASK 8: Approximated surfaces (optional)

*Discussion.* 3D meshes can be curved in a manner similar to the polylines you have just drawn. There are three styles, controlled by the variable "Surftype" (not to be confused with Surftab1 and Surftab2). Surftype is analogous to Splinetype and can be set to 5 for a quadratic approximation, 6 for cubic, and 8 for bezier. These settings can be made from the same icon menu or screen menu as Splinetype.

In this exercise, we will create a simple rectangular 3D mesh in one plane, move two of its vertices to give it three dimensions, and then use the "Smooth" option of the PEDIT command to create approximated surfaces.

> To begin this task, clear all objects from your screen.

We will use the 3D construction icon menu to create a simple 3D mesh, as we did in Chapter 13.

> Pick "Draw" and then "3D Construction..." from the pull down.
> Pick the 3D mesh at the lower right of the icon menu.
> Pick four points to create a 3.00 by 4.00 rectangle near the center of your screen, as shown in *Figure 14-27*.

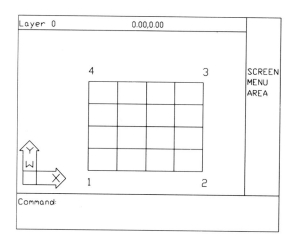

**Figure 14-27**

> Type "5" for the M size.

> Type "5" for the N size.

The mesh will be drawn with five vertices in each direction. Later we will copy it twice so that we can produce three different types of smooth surfaces, but first we need to move some vertices up and down in the Z direction to give it three-dimensionality. This can be done in the PEDIT command, using .XY filters.

Also, we need to switch to a 3D viewpoint to see the effect of our edits.

> Create a front right top view, as shown in *Figure 14-28*. This is the same 3D view we have used frequently since Chapter 12.

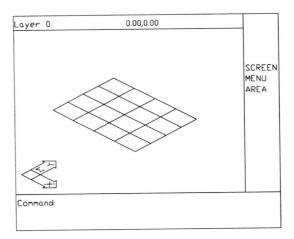

**Figure 14-28**

> Type or select "pedit", or pick "Modify" and then "Edit Polylines" from the pull down.

> At the "Select objects" prompt, pick the 3D mesh.

> Press enter to end object selection.

> Type "e" or select "Ed Vrtx".

This procedure will work just as it did in the last chapter, except that now we will be moving vertices up or down out of the X-Y plane. The vertices we will move will be at opposite corners, so the one where the "x" marker is now will do to start.

> Type "m" or select "Move".

AutoCAD prompts:

Enter new location:

> Type or select ".xy".

AutoCAD prompts:

of

We are going to move the vertex straight up into the Z dimension, so we want the same X and Y coordinates with a new Z. We can pick the vertex itself to show X and Y, or we can type "@", indicating the current position.

> Type "@" or pick the current vertex.

AutoCAD responds:

(need Z):

> Type "2".

This will move the corner vertex up 2.00, as shown in *Figure 14-29*.

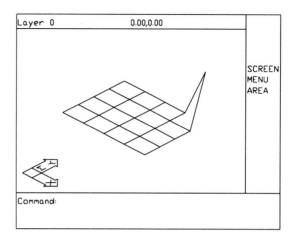

**Figure 14-29**

Now we will move the opposite corner down –3.00.

> Move the vertex "x" marker to the opposite corner by holding down the enter key.
> Type "m" or select "Move".
> Type or select ".xy".
> Type "@".
> Type "–3".

We are now ready to create a quadratic-style smoothed surface from our 3D mesh.

> Type "s" or select "Smooth".
Your screen will be redrawn to resemble *Figure 14-30*.

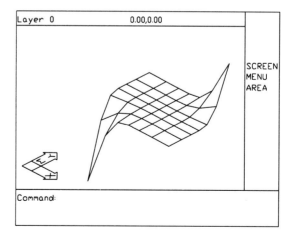

**Figure 14-30**

NOTE: If Splframe is set to 1, your screen will show no change. Because of the complexity of meshes, AutoCAD does not show a curved surface and its "frame" at the same time. With Splframe set to 0, you will see the smoothed version, with the variable set to 1, you will see the original polygon mesh with vertices moved.

At this point you should have no trouble continuing the exercise on your own to create cubic and bezier surfaces, as shown in *Figure 14-31*. Make two copies of the mesh, and use the screen and icon menus to reset the "Surftype" variable to 6 (cubic) or 8 (bezier). If you want to use the "Polyvars" screen menu to change the type of surface, remember to select "Surftype" first and then "Cubic" or "Bezier". Each time you reset the variable, smooth one of the surfaces.

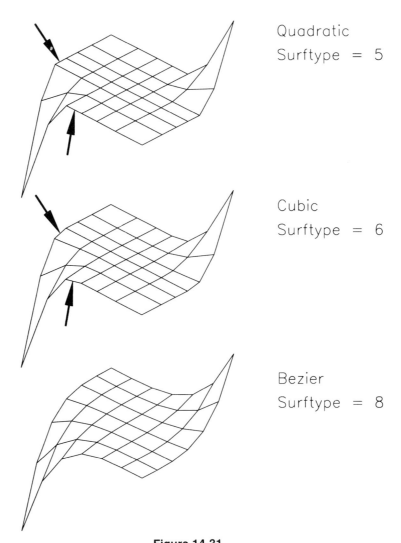

Quadratic
Surftype = 5

Cubic
Surftype = 6

Bezier
Surftype = 8

**Figure 14-31**

NOTE: The differences between cubic and quadratic surfaces in this object will be slight. In fact, you may have to look hard to see them. We have indicated them with arrows for your convenience. In order to show a more dramatic difference, you would need to create a more dramatic 3D figure by moving more vertices up or down. If you have the time, be our guest. Also consider changing the density of surface approximation through the variables "Surfu" and "Surfv". More information is given in the *AutoCAD Reference Manual*, Section 5.4.1.3, and the *AutoCAD Release 10 Tutorial*, pages 144–50.

### TASKS 9, 10, 11, and 12

The drawings in this chapter all involve surface modeling. In general, you will be drawing a wire frame model, or the outline of one, and then adding surfaces in the form of 3D faces or polygon meshes. Take your time and don't be surprised by glitches, problems, and commands that don't behave as you anticipate. Surface modeling is tricky and a good deal of trial and error is to be expected.

## D R A W I N G   1 4 - 1 :   B U S H I N G   M O U N T

This drawing makes use of many of the techniques introduced in the chapter. Notice how you can use the MIRROR command in 3D to avoid repeating the work involved in defining and editing ruled surfaces.


### DRAWING SUGGESTIONS

> It is very important to make extensive and well-planned use of layering whenever you do surface modeling. You will be placing polylines on top of lines and polygon meshes on top of polylines. In order to control all this, you will need to be able to turn layers off in order to select objects that are obstructed. Also, you will want to selectively freeze or turn layers off in order to achieve effects with the HIDE command. We suggest separate layers for the wire frame, the 3D faces, the 3D polygon meshes, and the polylines that are needed to define some polygon mesh boundaries.

> Draw the wire frame as shown, defining whatever UCSs you find necessary along the way.

> The circles shown in the wire frame of the bushing are not a complete wire frame model, but they show what you need to do to define the outline of the bushing. We suggest drawing the circles on the layer with the other wire frame entities and using them as a guide to draw a polyline that can be used as a path curve in REVSURF.

> Carefully draw polylines surrounding the holes and rectangles in the mount using the principles discussed in the chapter. RULESURF to create surfaces and then PEDIT the corners. Notice that the lower surfaces should extend to the midline of the bottom of the mount.

> When you have drawn and edited the ruled surfaces on the right side, you can use MIRROR with a mirror line along the midline of the bottom of the mount to create all the ruled surfaces on the left side.

NOTE: This drawing is intended as an exercise in surface modeling. The finished product should look like reference "A" before HIDE and "B" after. The dimensions on the wire frame are difficult and are not necessarily part of the exercise.

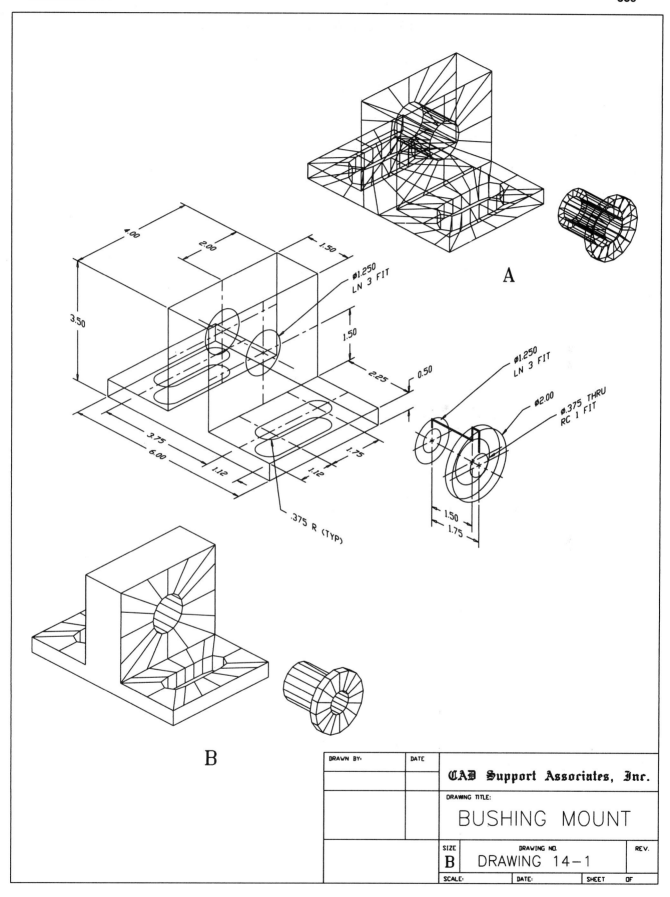

Ø1.250
LN 3 FIT

4.00

2.00

1.50

3.50

1.50

2.25

0.50

3.75

6.00

1.12

1.75

1.12

.375 R (TYP)

A

Ø1.250
LN 3 FIT

Ø2.00

Ø.375 THRU
RC 1 FIT

1.50

1.75

B

| DRAWN BY: | DATE | **CAD Support Associates, Inc.** | | |
|---|---|---|---|---|
| | | DRAWING TITLE: | | |
| | | BUSHING MOUNT | | |
| | | SIZE **B** | DRAWING NO. DRAWING 14-1 | REV. |
| | | SCALE: | DATE: | SHEET OF |

# DRAWING 14-2: LINK MOUNT

This drawing demonstrates the problem of drawing surfaces on objects that have several holes. There is no surface command that will allow you to fill in a single surface around multiple holes. Therefore, you will need to divide the geometry and draw four separate ruled surfaces, as shown.

## *DRAWING SUGGESTIONS*

> Using three view ports—plan, front, and a 3D view—start in the X-Y plane of the WCS and work up to create the wire frame of the complete object. This can all be done on one layer.

> The circular plate in the center of the mount can be drawn as a circle with .38 thickness. This has the advantage of creating top and bottom surfaces.

> Once the wire frame is complete, block top, front, and right views so that you can easily create the orthographic projections later on. Doing this before any of the surfaces are added will save you from having to erase them when you insert the blocks.

> Draw polylines over the wire frame wherever needed in order to create ruled surfaces. Be sure to match starting points and directions for the inner and outer boundaries. This will take some careful use of the PLINE arc options. If you get stuck, try drawing a three-point PLINE arc using end point osnaps for the start and end of the arc and a nearest osnap for the second point.

> You can use MIRROR effectively to mirror ruled surfaces. Draw a single ruled surface, PEDIT corners, then MIRROR twice to create the other three surface areas.

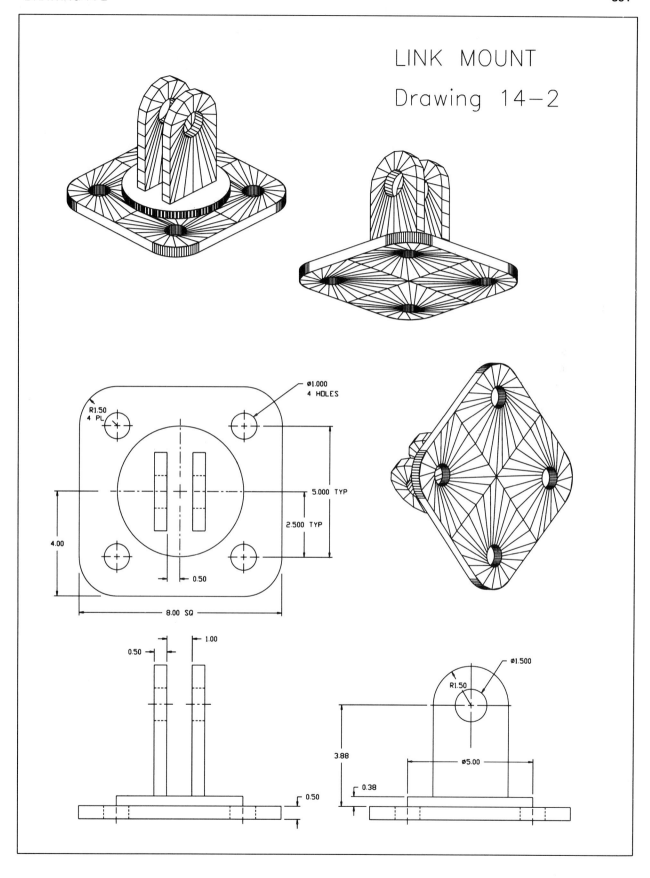

LINK MOUNT

Drawing 14-2

Ø1.000
4 HOLES

R1.50
4 PL

5.000 TYP

2.500 TYP

4.00

0.50

8.00 SQ

0.50

1.00

0.50

1.500

R1.50

3.88

Ø5.00

0.38

0.50

## DRAWING 14-3: 3D ASSEMBLY

There is some careful work to be done in creating all the surfaces shown on this 3D object. You will find use here for many varieties of surface creation—thickness, 3D meshes (RULESURF), and 3D faces. Efficient use of MIRROR and layering will help you to cut down on the time involved.

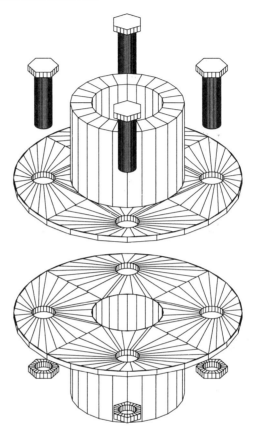

## *DRAWING SUGGESTIONS*

> Use at least two view ports, for a plan view and a 3D view.

> First draw the wire frame of the upper half, beginning in the WCS X-Y plane and using COPY and MOVE to position all of the circles up along the Z axis according to the dimensions shown in the orthographic side view. Later you can use MIRROR to create much of the bottom half with very little duplication of effort. Be sure to add surfaces before mirroring to the bottom half.

> You can use the centerlines along with intersection and nearest osnaps to help draw the polyline boundaries around the bolt holes. Also make full use of the PLINE arc options, including "Direction", to get your arcs going the way you want.

> Create and PEDIT a ruled surface around one of the holes on the upper and lower sides of the circular surface, and then use MIRROR twice to create surfaces around the other three holes.

> Thickness can be used to create the cylindrical surfaces of the bolts and the sides of the hexes. 3D faces with one invisible edge across the middle can be used for the tops of the hexes.

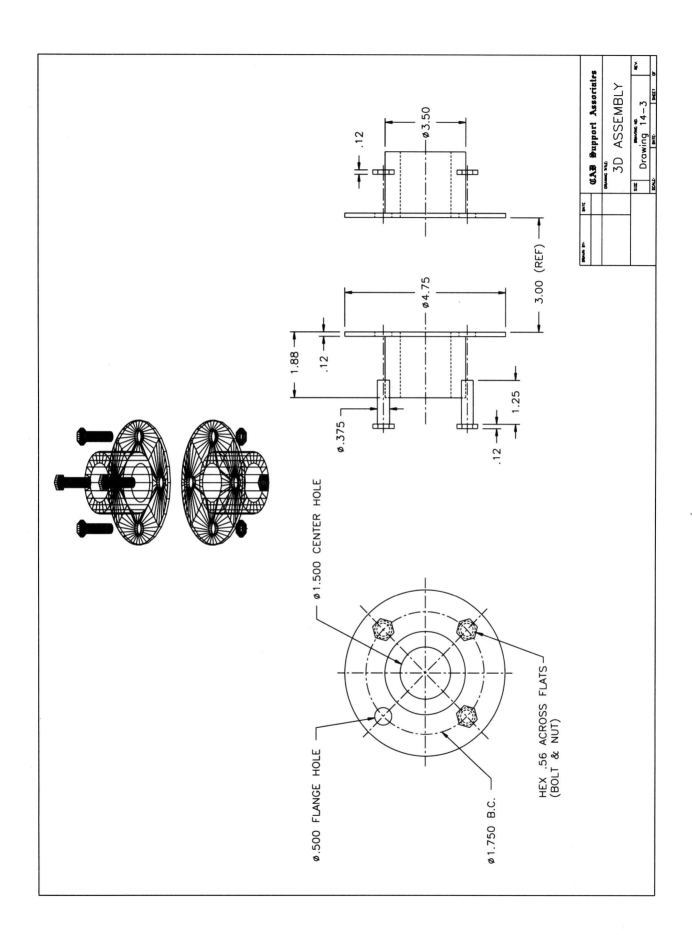

Ø3.50

.12

3.00 (REF)

Ø4.75

1.88

.12

Ø.375

1.25

.12

Ø1.500 CENTER HOLE

Ø.500 FLANGE HOLE

Ø1.750 B.C.

HEX .56 ACROSS FLATS
(BOLT & NUT)

CAD Support Associates

3D ASSEMBLY

Drawing 14-3

## DRAWING 14-4: PICNIC TABLE

This is a tricky drawing that must be done carefully. It requires efficient use of the UCS command along with a number of edit commands. In order to create an image that hides as shown in the reference, you must cover all surfaces with 3D faces.

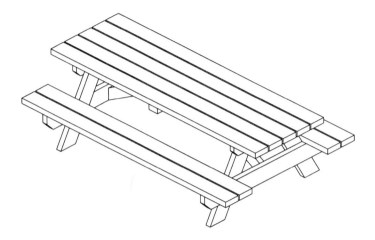

## *DRAWING SUGGESTIONS*

> Use a three view port configuration, with top (plan) and front views on the left and a 3D view on the right. Be sure to keep an eye on all view ports as you go, since it is quite likely that you will create some lines that look correct in one view but not in others.

> Use a separate layer for 3D faces, and add the faces as you go. This will save you from retracing your steps. Notice that the faces on the chamfered braces are drawn with one invisible line across the middle. This is the same as one of the examples in the chapter (*Figure 14-20*).

> We recommend you start with the top of the table and work down. Placing the legs directly behind the chamfered braces can be tricky. One way to do this is to draw the legs even with the side of the table first (in a UCS with its X-Y plane flush with a side of the table), and then MOVE them back 1'-2".

> Save the angled braces for last. Once the leg braces are drawn, you can locate the angled braces by drawing a line from the midpoint of the small brace in the middle of the table top to the midpoint of the bottom of a leg brace. Then OFFSET this line 1" each way to create the two lower edges of one angled brace.

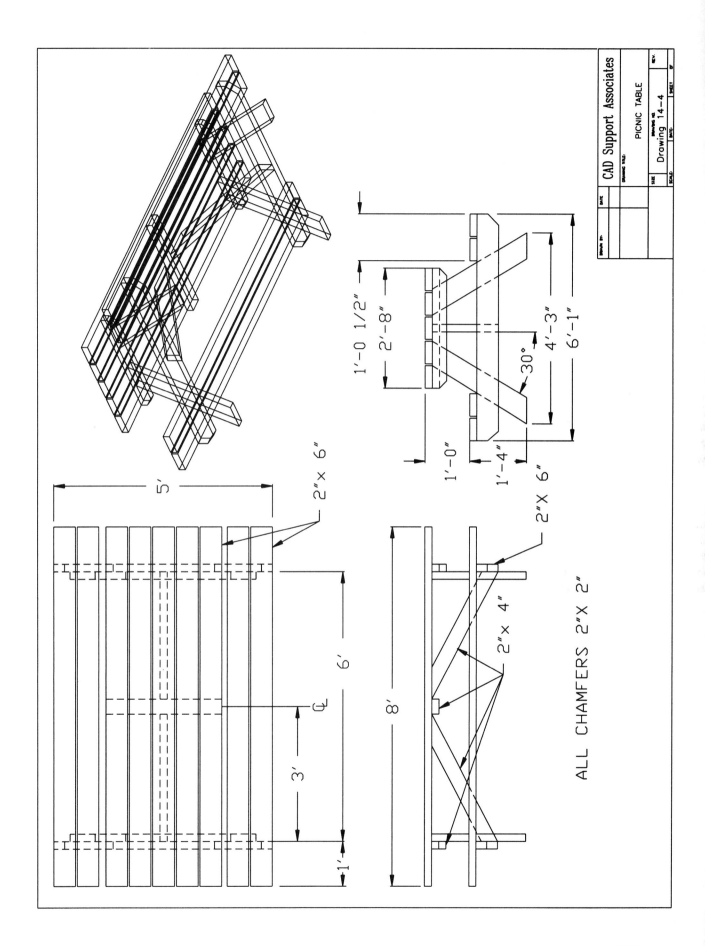

ALL CHAMFERS 2"X 2"

5'

2"× 6"

6'

3'

1'

8'

2"× 4"

2"X 6"

1'-0 1/2"

2'-8"

30°

4'-3"

6'-1"

1'-0"

1'-4"

2"X 6"

CAD Support Associates

DRAWING TITLE: PICNIC TABLE

DRAWING NO. Drawing 14—4

REV.

SIZE

SCALE: DATE: SHEET

DRAWN BY: DATE

# appendix

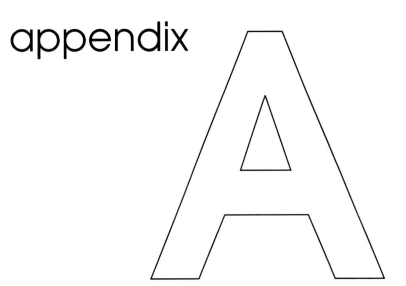

# Plotting Your Drawings

You can plot drawings on a pen plotter or a printer. In order for either to work, the plotting device must be correctly connected to your computer and AutoCAD must be configured to use it. For information on configuring AutoCAD, see the *AutoCAD Reference Manual*, Appendix D, and the *AutoCAD Installation and Performance Guide*, Chapters 3, 7, and 8.

Exactly what happens when you plot a drawing will depend, to some extent, on your hardware configuration. At the most general level, the procedure is as follows:

1. From the Main Menu: Select 3 for a plot, or 4 for a printer plot. Then type the name of the drawing.

   From the drawing editor: Type or select "PLOT" for a plot, or "PRPLOT" for a printer plot. The current drawing will be used.

2. Specify the portion of the drawing you wish to plot.

3. Indicate whether you wish to change any of the plotting parameters. If so:

   a. Change pen specifications (plotters only).

   b. Change basic plot specifications.

4. Position paper and prepare plotting device.

5. Press enter to begin plotting.

6. Press Ctrl-C if you wish to abort.

7. When all information has been sent to the plotting device, AutoCAD will return to the Main Menu or the drawing editor, depending on where you started.

## Printer Plotting

As an example, suppose we have just completed Drawing 1-1 and want to plot it on a printer plotter.

> At the "Command:" prompt, type or select "PRPLOT".
AutoCAD will ask us to specify the area to plot:

What to plot - Display, Extents, Limits, View, Window <L>

"Display" refers to the area currently shown on the monitor. "Extents" refers to the area that actually contains drawn objects. "Limits" are set with the LIMITS command, as discussed in Chapter 3. A "View" is defined using the VIEW command, as discussed in Chapter 11. A "Window" is selected by showing two corners, as discussed in Chapter 2.
> Press enter to plot the limits of Drawing 1-1.

AutoCAD switches to the text screen, shows a list of basic plot specifications, and asks if we want to change anything. This list will look something like the following:

Plot will NOT be written to a selected file
Sizes are in Inches
Plot origin is at (0.00,0.00)
Plotting area is 7.99 wide by 11.00 high (MAX size)
Plot is NOT rotated 90 degrees
Hidden lines will NOT be removed
Plot will be scaled to fit available area

Do you want to change anything? <N>

These options are discussed following. We will proceed first on the assumption that you do not want to change anything.
> Press enter to retain all basic plot specifications.

AutoCAD will tell you how much of your paper size will actually be used by the plot and then pause while you prepare your printer:

Effective plotting area: 7.99 wide by 5.99 high
Position paper in printer.
Press RETURN to continue:

> Press enter (RETURN).
> If you wish to terminate the plotting process, press Ctrl-C.

After sending all the plot information to your printer, AutoCAD will return to the drawing editor. Press F1 to return to the graphics screen.

## Basic Plotting Specifications

If you answer "y" or "yes" to the question "Do you want to change anything?", you will be given the opportunity to change each of the basic plot specifications. Following is a list of what changes can be made.

*Plot to a file.*    Allows you to send all plotting information to a file instead of to a plotting device. This is a useful feature only if you have software to plot directly from a file to a plotter. This is often used in large companies for "batch" processing of drawing files.

*Size units.*    Allows you to select standard (inches) or metric (millimeters) format.

*Plot origin.*    Moves the point on the paper at which the plot originates. For example, to move the origin in one inch and up two inches, type "1,2". Moving the origin reduces the portion of the paper the plotter or printer will use. This will be reflected in the plotting area.

*Plotting area.*    The default size will be set as part of the configuration procedure. You can select a different size by typing numbers, as you would in the LIMITS command (i.e. "8.5,11" for an A size sheet). Or, you can type a sheet size, such as "A". Exact values for each sheet size will depend on your plotting device.

*Plot Rotation.*    This allows you to plot vertically or horizontally on your paper. That is, on an A size sheet you can plot with the 11 inch side going across instead of up and down.

*Hidden lines.*    In plotting a 3D drawing, you can remove hidden lines as part of the plotting process.

*Plot scale.*    This allows you to specify the scale of the drawing. You can type a scale relation in the form <plotted units> = <drawing units> or scale the plot to fit the plotting area. For example, if you type "1=1", then an area specified as an inch in your drawing will appear an inch long on the plot. If you plot to fit, AutoCAD will use as much of the area as possible.

## Plotting with a Pen Plotter

Plotting with a plotter is exactly like printer plotting except that there are two additional basic specifications and a table of pen settings. The additional specifications also relate to pens and are as follows:

*Pen width.*    When the pen width is correctly specified, AutoCAD knows how many passes it should take to fill in a solid area (drawn with SOLID, TRACE, or PLINE, Chapter 9).

*Area fill adjustment.*    Allows a finer adjustment to accommodate the width of the pen. The outline of a filled area will be moved in one-half of the pen's width so that the outer measurement of the drawn line is accurate. Ordinarily this degree of precision is not necessary.

Now, as an example, suppose we have just completed Drawing 1-1 and want to plot it on a plotter instead of a printer.

> At the "Command:" prompt type or select "PLOT".
    AutoCAD will again ask us to specify the area to plot:

What to plot - Display, Extents, Limits, View, Window <L>

> Press enter to plot the limits of Drawing 1-1.
    The list of basic specifications is the same, except for the addition of pen width and area adjustment.

Plot will NOT be written to a selected file
Sizes are in Inches
Plot origin is at (0.00,0.00)
Plotting area is 7.99 wide by 11.00 high (MAX size)
Plot is NOT rotated 90 degrees
Pen width is 0.010
Area fill will NOT be adjusted for pen width
Hidden lines will NOT be removed
Plot will be scaled to fit available area

Do you want to change anything? <N>

If you do not want to change anything, the procedure will be the same as before from this point. If you answer "y" or "yes", however, you will be given information on the current pen settings and an opportunity to change them before going on to make changes in the basic plot specifications.

> Type "y".

You will see a screen that resembles the following:

| Entity Color | Pen No. | Line Type | Pen Speed | Entity Color | Pen No. | Line Type | Pen Speed |
|---|---|---|---|---|---|---|---|
| 1(red) | 1 | 0 | 24 | 9 | 1 | 0 | 24 |
| 2(yellow) | 1 | 0 | 24 | 10 | 1 | 0 | 24 |
| 3(green) | 1 | 0 | 24 | 11 | 1 | 0 | 24 |
| 4(cyan) | 1 | 0 | 24 | 12 | 1 | 0 | 24 |
| 5(blue) | 1 | 0 | 24 | 13 | 1 | 0 | 24 |
| 6(magenta) | 1 | 0 | 24 | 14 | 1 | 0 | 24 |
| 7(white) | 1 | 0 | 24 | 15 | 1 | 0 | 24 |
| 8 | 1 | 0 | 24 | | | | |

```
Line types      0 = continuous line
                1 = ...................
                2 = . . . . . . . . .
                3 = ------------------
                4 = - - - - - - - - - -
                5 = -- -- -- -- -- -
                6 = --- --- --- --- ---
                7 = -- - -- - -- - -- -
                8 = __ --__ --__ --__ --__ -
```

Do you want to change any of these parameters? <N>

> Type "y" to indicate that you do want to make a change.

AutoCAD prompts:

Enter values, blank=Next value, Cn=Color n, S=Show current values, X=Exit

| Entity Color | Pen No. | Line Type | Pen Speed | |
|---|---|---|---|---|
| 1(red) | 1 | 0 | 24 | Pen number <1>: |

Notice the options. If you enter a new value, it will be shown in the appropriate column and the prompt at the right will switch to the next item.

> For example, type "2".

The prompt will switch to:

| Entity Color | Pen No. | Line Type | Pen Speed | |
|---|---|---|---|---|
| 1(red) | 2 | 0 | 24 | Line type <0>: |

As indicated by the options, you can go to the next item without changing the current one by pressing enter or typing a space (blank).

> Press enter.

The information will stay the same, but the prompt at the right will change to:

Pen Speed <24>:

If you wanted to change the color in the first column to yellow, you would type "c2".

After making a number of changes you might want to see the whole chart again. To do this, you would type "s".

Finally, when you are through making changes, type "x" to exit. This will take you out of the pen specification prompts and back to the basic plot specifications, beginning with:

Write plot to a file? <N>

From here the procedure will be much the same as in printer plotting.

# appendix

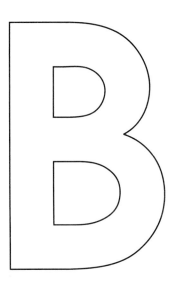

# Release 10
# Pull Down Menus and
# Primary Screen Menu
# Hierarchy

On the next two pages you will find charts to help you find your way around in the AutoCAD standard menu systems. The first shows you what is available in the pull down menus, and the second shows you where to find commands and subcommands in the screen system.

# AutoCAD® Release 10
## (Primary Screen Menu Hierarchy)

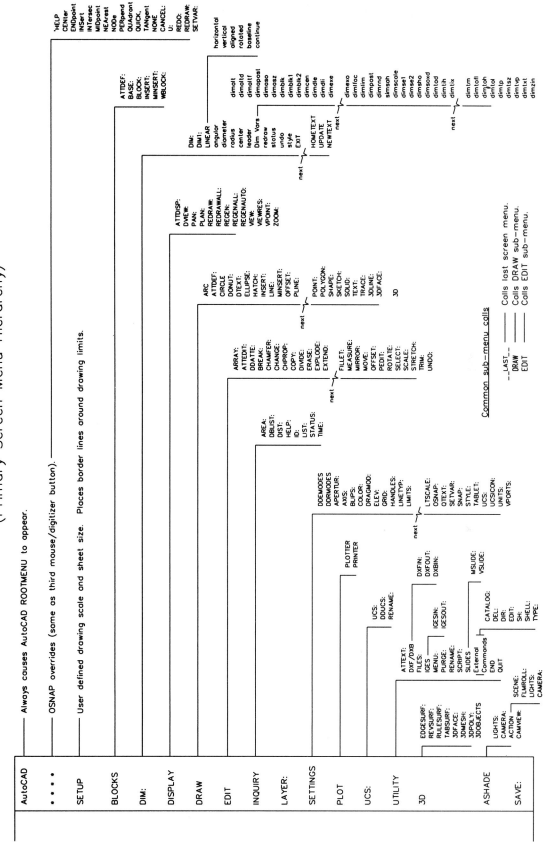

Reprinted from the AutoCAD Reference Manual for AutoCAD Release 10
with permission from Autodesk, Inc. Copyright 1989

# AutoCAD® Release 10
## (Menu Bar and Pull-Down Menus)

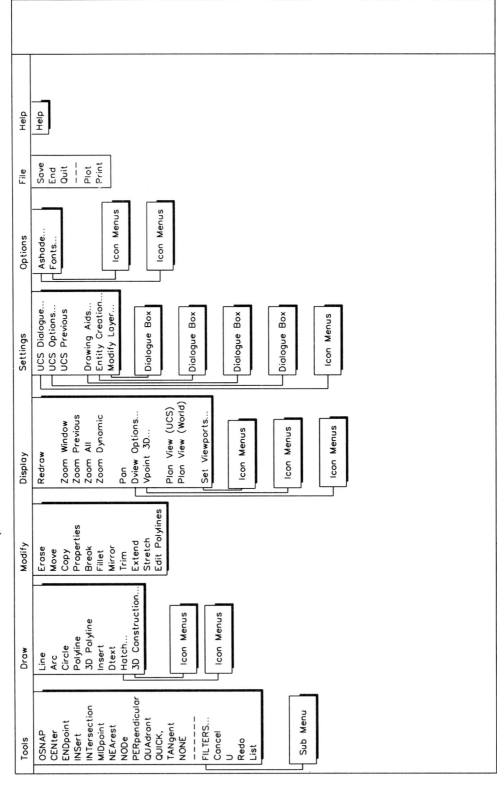

Reprinted from the AutoCAD Reference Manual for AutoCAD Release 10
with permission from Autodesk, Inc. Copyright 1989

# appendix

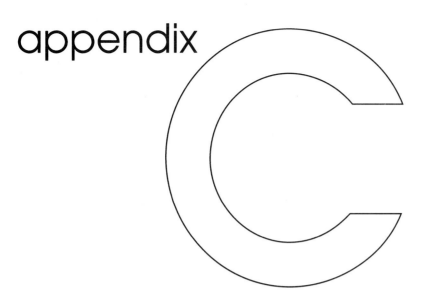

# Menus, Macros, and AutoLISP

There are three areas you will need to study to gain a complete knowledge of how menu systems are created. Two of these, the organization of a menu file and the language of macros, are easy to learn. The third, AutoLISP, is a programming language that is relatively accessible if you know other programming languages, and probably out of reach if you do not.

The following discussion assumes a basic knowledge of MS-DOS, at least regarding file names and extensions.

### What is an AutoCAD Menu?

Most likely, every time you have begun a drawing in AutoCAD you have used either the AutoCAD standard menu or some other menu that is available on your system. This menu is what makes it possible for you to select commands off the screen or tablet. Without a menu, you are limited to typing commands.

Menu files have a standard format that AutoCAD can read, and standard extensions so that AutoCAD can recognize them. The extensions include .mnx files and .mnu files. Files with the .mnx extension are the actual executable files that AutoCAD uses. They are written in machine language and compiled from files that have the same name, but a .mnu extension. The .mnu files can be created in a word processing program or text editor and are easy to read and understand once you know the syntax.

For example, the AutoCAD standard menu is contained in a file called ACAD.mnx. This file is loaded when you begin a new drawing using the ACAD.dwg prototype or any other prototype drawing that was created using ACAD.mnx. But there is also an ASCII version of ACAD.mnx called ACAD.mnu. ACAD.mnx was created by compiling ACAD.mnu into machine code. The importance of ACAD.mnu is that you can look at it with a word processor and revise it if you wish. Then you can compile it again with your changes included.

Once you know the language, you can create your own menu that is completely separate from the ACAD file. You would create the file in any word processor or text editor with an ASCII format and give it a name with a .mnu extension. Then when you wanted to load it into a drawing you would follow this procedure:

1.  At the "Command:" prompt, type "menu".
2.  Type your menu's name with no extension.
3.  Wait... AutoCAD will first create the .mnx file and then load it. (Once the .mnx file is created, it will not have to be recompiled the next time you load it).

## What does a menu look like?

If you go into whatever word processor or text editor you have available on your system and load the file ACAD.mnu (it will be located in the same MS-DOS subdirectory as ACAD.exe), you will see the lines shown on the left of the menu chart following. This is the original Release 10 version of ACAD.mnu; any other version of AutoCAD will be slightly different.

Menu files are quite large and this is only a small portion. The complete menu file will be close to 50 pages long. The best way to learn about menus is to obtain a hard copy from your instructor or print one out yourself and study it, using the chart, the list of characters at the end of this appendix, and the *AutoCAD Reference Manual*, Appendix B.4.

## How is a menu organized?

Take a look at a representative section from ACAD.mnu:

```
        .
        .
        .
***SCREEN
**S
[AutoCAD]^C^C$S=S $P4=P4A
[* * * *]$S=OSNAPB
[SETUP]^C^C(load "setup") $S=UNITS
        .
        .
        .
```

If you look closely at the words in brackets at the left of the third, fourth, and fifth lines, you will recognize the top of the familiar main menu of the ACAD.mnu screen menu system.

Using this example, we can make the following general points about organization:

1.  The menu is organized into lines. Each line is associated with a single item on a screen menu, an item on a pull down menu, or a box on a tablet menu. The only exceptions to this are those lines in the menu which begin with asterisks and serve organizational purposes.
2.  Section headers begin with asterisks. These lines serve only organizational purposes.
    -   "three-star headers" such as "***SCREEN" identify major sections, including the button functions, the pull down menus, the screen menu, and the four tablet areas.
    -   "two-star headers" such as "**S" identify individual menus and submenus.
    -   Menus and submenus are called using the format $S=S (notice that the asterisks are dropped in the call). The pull down equivalent is $Pn=Pnx, where "Pn" identifies the pull down area and "Pnx" identifies a particular submenu. Similarly, icon menus are called using $i=name.
3.  Words written in brackets, such as [AutoCAD], are labels. They do not perform functions but are simply written on the screen as identifiers.

| Menu Line | Function |
|---|---|
| ***BUTTONS | Section Header |
| ; | enter button |
| $p1=* | "Tools" pull down |
| ^c^c | cancel |
| ^B | snap on/off |
| ^O | ortho on/off |
| ^G | grid on/off |
| ^D | coordinate on/off |
| ^E | isoplane on/off |
| ^T | tablet on/off |
| ***AUX1 | Section Header |
| ; | (This section is a |
| $p1=* | repeat of the last. |
| ^C^C | It is available for |
| ^B | programming an |
| ^O | auxiliary function |
| ^G | box, a device that |
| ^D | has function buttons |
| ^E | but no pick button.) |
| ^T | |
| ***POP1 | Section Header |
| [Tools] | Pull down label |
| [OSNAP]^C^C$p1= $p1=* OSNAP \ | † OSNAP command |
| CENter | center osnap |
| ENDpoint | endpoint osnap |
| INSert | insert osnap |
| [INTersection]INT | intersec osnap |
| MIDpoint | midpoint osnap |
| NEArest | nearest osnap |
| NODe | node osnap |
| [PERpendicular]PER | perpend osnap |
| QUAdrant | quadrant osnap |
| [QUICK,]QUICK,^Z$p=* | quick osnap |
| TANgent | tangent osnap |
| NONE | none |
| [~--] | blank line |
| [FILTERS... ]$p1=filters $p1=* | submenu call |
| [Cancel]^C^C | cancel |
| [U]^C^CU | cancel and undo |
| [Redo]^C^CREDO | cancel and redo |
| [List]^C^CLIST | LIST command |
| **filters | filters submenu |
| [Filters] | submenu label |
| .X | x point filter |
| .Y | y point filter |

† This line is typical of menu items that include a series of functions. There is the label [OSNAP], then a double cancel (^C^C), then "Tools" is pulled down again so that osnap modes can be picked ($p1= $p1=*), then the OSNAP command is entered (OSNAP), and then there is a pause for mode input (\).

### What is a "macro"?

Macros are available in numerous software packages and always have the function of storing lengthy and frequently used sequences of keystrokes in a reduced "shorthand" form. Most of AutoCAD's menu system depends on macros. In order to understand and create macros in this system, there are a few items of syntax that you need to know.

Let's look at a very simple item from the LINE command submenu of the screen menu system. It looks like this:

[LINE]^C^CLINE;

**[LINE]**   You will see brackets in items on the screen menu or the pull down system but never in the tablet area. These entries simply write text to the screen to identify the function that the line is to perform. This is the way all text is written to the screen for the screen and pull down menus.

**^C^C**   This appears frequently. The "^" character is read by AutoCAD as the equivalent of the Ctrl key on your keyboard. So what you see here is the menu equivalent of typing Ctrl-C twice. This is to ensure that any command in process is cancelled before another one is entered.

**LINE**   This is the LINE command. Commands on the menu are typed exactly as they would be on the keyboard.

**;**   The semicolon is the macro symbol for pressing enter. A blank space has the same meaning in the middle of a line, but ; must be used at the end of a line and where there are multiple presses of enter in sequence.

Taken as a whole, then, this line does four things:

1.  [LINE] writes the word "LINE" to the screen menu.
2.  ^C^C cancels any command in progress.
3.  LINE types "LINE" on the command line.
4.  ; enters the command.

The list of macro characters at the end of this appendix should now be useful to you.

## What is AutoLISP?

AutoLISP is a programming language based on LISP. LISP is a "list processing" language. All LISP statements are enclosed in parentheses. LISP statements may be nested as deeply as needed. To maintain the proper structure of nesting, every left parenthesis must be balanced by a right.

A simple AutoLISP statement is as follows:

(setq a 3)

"Setq" is used for variable assignment. This statement sets the variable "a" equal to 3.

A slightly more complex statement showing nesting is:

(setq a (+ b c))

This statement sets the variable "a" equal to the sum of the values of variables "b" and "c". For information on AutoLISP see the *AutoLISP Programmer's Reference*.

## How is a tablet configured?

AutoCAD reads the tablet sections of a menu file in a particular way that must correspond to the configuration of the physical tablet overlay that is attached to the digitizer. In ACAD.mnu there are four tablet areas, each with its own section. Each line corresponds to a box on the overlay, and boxes are read from left to right, top to bottom, area by area. This means that there must be a way to tell AutoCAD how many rows and columns are contained in each tablet area. This is done using the TABLET command and the following procedure (the tablet overlay must be securely in place on your digitizer before you begin):

1. Type or select "TABLET".
2. Type or select "CFG" (configure).
3. Enter the number of tablet areas on your overlay.
4. Type "y" to indicate that you want to realign the tablet menu areas.
5. In response to AutoCAD's prompts, point to the upper left, lower left, and lower right corners of each tablet menu area. Be sure that you do this in the same order as the tablets are named in the .mnu file.
6. After the outline of each area is specified, also specify the number of columns and rows in that area.

For additional information on tablets, see the *AutoCAD Reference Manual*, Section 12.4 and Appendix A.2.4.

AutoCAD Macro Characters

(in order of appearance in ACAD.mnu)

| | |
|---|---|
| *** | Major section header. |
| ; | Same as pressing enter while typing. |
| $ | Begins any screen or pull down menu call. |
| $p1=* | Pulls down the menu called for pull down area 1. |
| ^ | Ctrl |
| ^C | Ctrl-C |
| ^C^C | Double cancel. Cancels any command, ensures a return to the "Command:" prompt before a new command is issued. |
| ***POPn | Identifies one of the 10 possible pull down menu areas. |
| [  ] | Brackets enclose text to be written directly to the screen or pull down menu area. Eight characters are printed on the screen menu. Pull down menu size varies. |
| $p1= | A menu call without a named menu calls the last menu. |
| \ | Pause for user input. Allows for keyboard entry, point selection, and object selection. Terminated by press of enter or pick button. |
| ~ | Begins a pull down menu label that is "greyed out." May be used to indicate a function not presently in use. |
| [--] | Writes a blank line on a pull down menu. |
| ' | Transparent command modifier. |
| ** | Submenu header. |
| *^C^C | Immediately following a label, this set of characters will cause the menu item to repeat. |
| space | A single blank space in the middle of a line is treated as a press of the enter key. |
| $i=name | Calls an icon menu. |
| $i=* | Displays an icon menu. |
| si | Specifies single object selection mode. Chapter 2, ARM, Section 2.9. |
| auto | Specifies automatic selection. Chapter 2, ARM, Section 2.9. |
| (()) | Parentheses are used to enclose AutoLISP routines. |
| + | Used at the end of a line to indicate that the menu item continues on the next line. |

# appendix

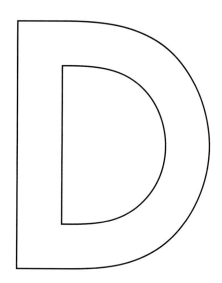

# AutoCAD Commands
# Not Covered
# In The Text

In order to make this text clear, concise, and useful we have had to set some priorities about what to include. The following is a glossary of commands we have not discussed. Some are obsolete or seldom used, while some are very useful but only for a limited range of applications.

All commands that are marked with an apostrophe (') can be used transparently. That is, they can be executed while other commands are in process.

**BLIPMODE:**   When set to "off", blips are not shown.

**COLOR:**   Establishes color of subsequently drawn entities. Responses include a color name or number, "By block", and "By layer". By layer is the default setting, so that entities are colored according to the layer on which they are drawn.

**'DDEMODES:**   When "on", makes a dialogue box available for setting current layer, color, linetype, elevation, and thickness (Release 9 or higher).

**'DDLMODES:**   When "on", makes a dialogue box available for defining properties of individual layers (Release 9 or higher).

**'DDRMODES:**   When "on", makes a dialogue box available for setting snap, grid, and axis (Release 9 or higher).

**DDUCS:**   Displays a dialogue box for defining, saving, and selecting User Coordinate Systems.

**DELAY:**   Used in script files to pause for a specified period of time.

**DIVIDE:**   Draws marker points at evenly spaced intervals along an object, dividing it into a specified number of parts. These points can be used as "nodes" for object snap.

**DRAGMODE:**   When set to "A", allows dragging to occur automatically, without request, whenever possible. When "on", allows dragging by request only. When "off", inhibits all dragging.

*DXBIN:*   Inserts a "DXB" format, binary coded file into a drawing.

*DXFIN:*   Loads a "DXF" format, drawing interchange file into a drawing. DXF files are standard ASCII text files that can be easily processed by other programs.

*DXFOUT:*   Creates a drawing file in "DXF" format.

*FILES:*   Allows access to the "File utility" menu from within the drawing editor.

*FILMROLL:*   Writes a file for use with AutoShade.

*'GRAPHSCR:*   Switches to the graphics screen. Used in script files in conjunction with TEXTSCR to switch between text and graphics.

*HANDLES:*   Assigns a unique identification number to every entity in a drawing.

*IGESIN:*   Loads an IGES, Initial Graphics Exchange Format, drawing file.

*IGESOUT:*   Writes a drawing file in IGES format.

*LOAD:*   Loads a file of shapes to be used by the SHAPE command.

*MEASURE:*   Draws marker points at specified intervals along an object. These points can be used as "nodes" for object snap.

*QTEXT:*   When "on", allows text to be written without displaying actual characters on the screen. Instead, the text area is outlined for faster regeneration. When desired, turn QTEXT "off" and perform a REGEN to replace outlined areas with actual text.

*REDEFINE:*   Restores the definition of built-in AutoCAD commands that have been temporarily deleted using UNDEFINE.

*REGENAUTO:*   When "off", inhibits automatic regenerations that occur as the result of certain commands.

*RENAME:*   Allows user to change the names of layers, linetypes, blocks, views, and text styles.

*'RESUME:*   Used in script files to resume execution of a script that has been interrupted.

*RSCRIPT:*   Used in script files to repeat the script. Allows for continuous running of slide show presentations.

*SCRIPT:*   Loads and executes a script file.

*SELECT:*   Allows object selection to occur before entering other commands. Options are the same as those in most edit commands.

*SH:*   Allows access to MS-DOS/PC-DOS commands while running AutoCAD. Requires less memory than SHELL.

*SHAPE:*   Draws shapes that have been defined in the drawing database using the LOAD command.

*SHELL:*   Allows access to operating system and utility programs while running Auto-CAD. Available memory may restrict what programs can be run. Requires more memory than SH.

*'TEXTSCR:*   Switches to the text screen. Used in script files in conjunction with GRAPHSCR to switch between text and graphics.

*3DPOLY:*   Creates a polyline from 3D points. Constructs straight line segments only; there are no arc options.

*TIME:*  Displays current time and date, time and date current drawing was created, time and date of last update, time of current session in drawing editor, and elapsed time. Elapsed time is a timer function. To begin timing, it must first be set to "on".

*UNDEFINE:*  Temporarily deletes the definition of a built-in AutoCAD command. This allows the command name to be used for an alternate function defined in an AutoLISP program. See REDEFINE.

*UNDO:*  Undoes multiple commands. UNDO is similar to "U", but it contains options to define a series of commands as a "group" that can be undone at once.

*VIEWRES:*  Controls the precision with which arcs and circles are displayed prior to regeneration. The higher the resolution, the longer it takes to display objects. Resolution is based on the number of sides displayed in a "circle".

# index